Breaking Barriers
Teaching Handbook

Written and developed by
Ruth Atkinson, Louise Pennington, Romey Tacon and
Dr Tony Wing

OXFORD

OXFORD
UNIVERSITY PRESS

Great Clarendon Street, Oxford, OX2 6DP, United Kingdom

Oxford University Press is a department of the University of Oxford.
It furthers the University's objective of excellence in research, scholarship,
and education by publishing worldwide. Oxford is a registered trade mark
of Oxford University Press in the UK and in certain other countries.

ISBN 978-0-19-835413-0

10 9 8 7 6 5 4 3 2

Typeset by Phoenix Photosetting, Chatham, Kent

Paper used in the production of this book is a natural,
recyclable product made from wood grown in sustainable forests.
The manufacturing process conforms to the environmental regulations
of the country of origin.

Printed in China by Leo Paper Products Ltd

Acknowledgements

Written and developed by Ruth Atkinson, Louise Pennington, Romey Tacon
and Dr Tony Wing

Cover photograph by Suzy Prior

Technical artwork by Phoenix Photosetting

Photographs:

pp.6, 7, 96, 110, 112, 130, 133, 136, 138, 139, 150, 159, 185, 186, 204,
207, 219, 230, 232, 242: Chris King; pp.17, 24, 31, 33, 35, 48, 53, 55, 65,
68, 84, 121, 124, 127, 147, 167, 211, 213, 215, 218, 246, 247, 256: Jonty
Tacon; pp.18, 20, 22, 26, 28, 37, 39, 41, 42, 45, 47, 51, 56, 58, 60, 100,
162, 171, 193, 223: Damian Richardson; p.72: Elif Demiroz/Shutterstock;
p.75: mrfiza/Shutterstock; p.77: Olga Tolmacheva/Shutterstock; p.80: Poly
Liss/Shutterstock; p.81: Romey Tacon; p.88: AlexMax/iStockphoto; p.92:
Rtimages/Getty Images; p.105: kosam/Shutterstock; p.115: Stacey Newman/
Shutterstock; p.118: FernandoMadeira /Shutterstock; p.180: Suzy Prior;
p.189: Brian A Jackson /Shutterstock; p.197: LP7/iStockphoto; p.201: Aqnus
Febriyant /Shutterstock; p.237: Kovaleva_Ka/Shutterstock; p.251: Lostry7/
Shutterstock; p.255: Opachevsky Irina/Shutterstock; p.260: greg801/
iStockphoto.

With special thanks to SS Aidan & Oswald R.C. Primary School, Oldham;
St. Alban's Catholic Primary School, Cheshire; Pegasus Primary School,
Oxfordshire

The authors and publisher would like to thank all schools and individuals
who have helped to trial and review Numicon resources.

www.oxfordprimary.co.uk

About Numicon

Numicon is a distinctive multi-sensory approach to children's
mathematical learning that emphasizes three key aspects of
doing mathematics: communicating mathematically, exploring
relationships, and generalizing.

Numicon was founded in the daily experience of intelligent children
having real difficulty with maths, the frequent underestimation of
the complexity of the ideas that young children are asked to face
when doing maths and recognition of the importance of maths to
them and to society as a whole.

Numicon aims to facilitate children's understanding and enjoyment
of maths by using structured imagery that plays to children's strong
sense of pattern. This is done through research-based, multi-sensory
teaching activities.

Numicon takes into account the complexity of abstract number ideas
and seeks to foster the self-belief necessary to achieve in the face of
challenge or difficulty.

Through the combination of communicating mathematically
(being active, talking and illustrating), exploring relationships
and generalizing, children are given the support to structure their
experiences: a vital skill for both their mathematical and their overall
development.

A multi-sensory approach, particularly one that makes use of
structured imagery, provides learners with the opportunity to play to
their strengths, thereby releasing their potential to enjoy, understand
and achieve in maths. By watching and listening to what children do
and say, this enjoyment in achievement is also shared by teachers
and parents.

Numicon strives to support teachers' subject knowledge and
pedagogy by providing teaching materials, Professional Development
and on-going support that will help develop a better understanding
of how to encourage all learners in the vital early stages of their own
mathematical journey.

Contents

Getting started

Welcome to the *Breaking Barriers Teaching Handbook*.

In this handbook, you will find:

- Suggestions to help teachers ensure the basic ideas of number are accessible to children experiencing difficulty. There is also guidance on how to address the underlying difficulties that may hinder children's learning. It is strongly recommended that teachers read through the Teaching Guide chapters prior to starting to teach the activities. There is no linear narrative to the Teaching Guide and, as a result, the different sections can be accessed whenever necessary to help you with your teaching.

- A recommended teaching progression for the activity groups.

- An overview of the Counting, Pattern and Algebra, Numbers and the Number System and Calculating activity groups.

- 50 activity groups arranged into the above strands.

Before you start teaching, we recommend you take some time to familiarize yourself with the *Breaking Barriers Assessment and Photocopy Masters* and the Breaking Barriers apparatus pack.

Breaking Barriers Assessment and Photocopy Masters

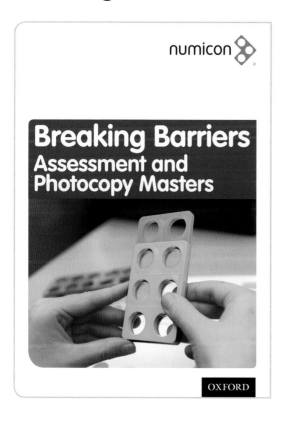

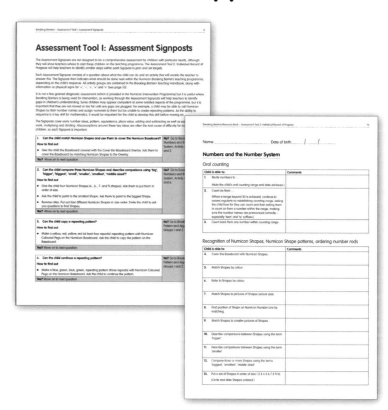

The *Breaking Barriers Assessment and Photocopy Masters* book contains all the photocopiable resources required for teaching the Breaking Barriers activities, along with a comprehensive assessment section.

This book contains **Assessment Signposts**, which are used to identify where children should start in the Breaking Barriers teaching programme. There is an **Individual Record of Progress** with steps linked to every activity group and arranged into strands to reflect the structure of the *Breaking Barriers Teaching Handbook*, so that teachers can clearly track children's progress.

The **Child Profile** will enable teachers to build an idea of an individual child's strengths and weaknesses in order to aid planning and ongoing assessment of a child's needs and abilities.

The **Photocopy Masters** provide resources to photocopy and cut out for use with the activities.

What's in the Breaking Barriers apparatus pack?

The following list of apparatus supports the *Numicon Breaking Barriers Teaching Handbook*. These resources should be used in conjunction with the activities described in the activity groups.

Apparatus pack contents

Numicon Shapes – box of 80
Extra Numicon 10-shapes – bag of 10
Extra Numicon 1-shapes – bag of 20
Numicon Coloured Pegs – bag of 80
Numicon Baseboard
Numicon Baseboard Number Bond Overlays
Numicon Baseboard Picture Overlays
Numicon Feely Bag
Numicon 10s Number Line
Numicon Spinner
Numicon 0–100 Numeral Cards
Numicon 0–100 cm Number Line – set of 3
Numicon Large Format Table-top Number Line
Numicon 0–31 Number Line – set of 3
Numicon Dice – set of 4

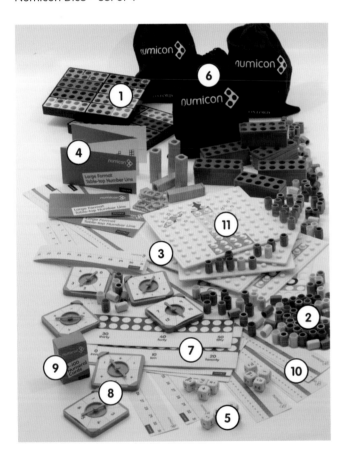

Numicon Shapes

These offer a tactile and visual illustration of number ideas. The Shapes are also a key feature of the *Numicon Software for the Interactive Whiteboard*. However, the Software is not a substitute for children actually handling the Shapes themselves.

Numicon Coloured Pegs

These red, blue, yellow and green Pegs are useful for making patterns and arrangements.

Numicon Baseboard

The square Baseboard has 100 raised studs to hold Numicon Shapes and Pegs.

Numicon Large Format Table-top Number Line

This goes from 0 to 21 with numerals, number words and Numicon Shapes. It crosses the tens boundary twice, thus providing a visual image of how the number system is constructed. It shows an increase of '1 more' which helps children to really visualize the pattern in number, which is not obvious in all (teen) number names. It can be folded in four to show just sections of the number range, e.g. 0–4 or 0–10.

Numicon Dice

A set of four 22 mm dice, featuring Numicon Shape patterns alongside the numerals: two 0–5 Dice, one 5–10 Dice and one +/– Dice.

Numicon Feely Bag

By feeling for Numicon Shapes in the Feely Bag, children simultaneously visualize the properties of the Shapes, helping them to develop their mental and tactile imagery of number.

Numicon 10s Number Line

This number line shows Numicon 10-shapes laid horizontally end to end and marked with multiples of 10 from 0 to 100. It helps children to develop a 'feel' for the cardinal value of numbers to 100 and connect this to place value.

Numicon Spinner

The Numicon Spinner can be used in many activities as an alternative to dice. Different overlays (provided as photocopy masters) can be placed on the spinner to generate a variety of instructions for children to follow, including: numerals, Numicon Shape patterns, and symbols of arithmetic notation. The spinner also features on the *Numicon Software for the Interactive Whiteboard*.

Numicon 0–100 Numeral Cards

The pack of 0–100 Numeral Cards may be used in activities to generate numbers for children to work with.

Numicon 0–100 cm Number Line

The points on this number line are 1 cm apart and are labelled from 0 to 100. The number line is divided into tens sections, distinguished alternately in red and blue. It can also be used with number rods, as an alternative to the 1–100 cm Number Rod Track.

Numicon Baseboard Picture Overlays 11

Double-sided, these fit on Numicon Baseboards and show images, e.g. an aeroplane composed of Numicon Shapes. Some are grey to help children focus on the pattern of the Shapes rather than the colour.

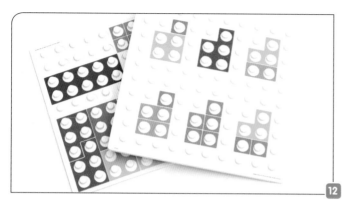

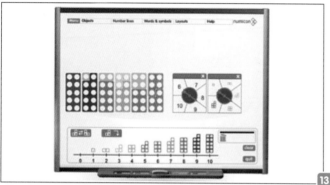

Numicon Baseboard Number Bond Overlays

Double-sided, these fit on Numicon Baseboards. Some are grey to help children focus on the pattern of the Shapes rather than the colour.

Numicon 0–31 Number Line

This shows the numerals 0–31, spaced so that children can place a counter on each numeral in independent counting activities, helping them to generalize the idea that the last number in their count tells them 'how many'.

Available separately
Numicon Software for the Interactive Whiteboard

This rich interactive tool includes: number lines featuring the Numicon Shapes, the Numicon Pan Balance, shapes, coins, Numicon Spinners and much more.

Individual sets of Numicon Shapes 1–10

They are especially useful for introducing coins, helping children to link each coin with its value in pounds or pence. They can also be used in conjunction with the *Numicon Software for the Interactive Whiteboard* to help teachers assess children's individual responses.

Numicon Large Foam Shapes

Giant foam Numicon Shapes that can be used outdoors.

Numicon Grey Shapes

Numicon Shapes 1–10 in grey, available in a box of 80.

Numicon Post Box

A card 'post box' through which items can be posted.

Numicon 1–100 cm Number Rod Track

Designed to take number rods, the tens sections click together into a metre-long track. This resource is useful for supporting children in their measurement work.

Numicon Pan Balance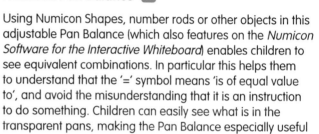

Using Numicon Shapes, number rods or other objects in this adjustable Pan Balance (which also features on the *Numicon Software for the Interactive Whiteboard*) enables children to see equivalent combinations. In particular this helps them to understand that the '=' symbol means 'is of equal value to', and avoid the misunderstanding that it is an instruction to do something. Children can easily see what is in the transparent pans, making the Pan Balance especially useful for comparing quantities as part of measurement work.

Numicon Display Number Line

A central component of number-rich classrooms, the Numicon Display Number Line provides a visual reference for children connecting Numicon Shapes, numerals and number words with the number line.

Numicon 0–41 Number Rod Number Line

Another central component of number-rich classrooms, the Numicon 0–41 Number Rod Number Line provides a visual reference for children connecting number rods, numerals and number words with the number line.

Number rods

A box of number rods contains multiple sets of ten coloured rods, 1 cm square in cross section. The shortest is 1 cm in length, the longest 10 cm. Being centimetre-scaled, they can be placed along the Numicon 0–100 cm Number Line. These offer another structured illustration for number and for many activities they can be used as a further check that children's understanding of number and calculation is secure.

Numicon Number Rod Trays 1–10 and 20

This set comprises a Number Rod Tray for each number up to 10, plus one for 20. They are useful for building up patterns and for number fact work with the number rods.

Other equipment

Some activities use apparatus found in most classrooms, e.g. sorting equipment and interlocking cubes, measures equipment. Other items such as modelling dough or string are useful to have to hand. Opportunities to use these are highlighted in the 'Have ready' sections of individual activities, and in the 'Connecting activities – Measures' section of certain activity groups.

Using the activity groups

> The first page of each activity group is clearly coloured according to the **strand** it appears in (Counting – green, Pattern and Algebra – red, Numbers and the Number System – yellow, Calculating – dark blue). The title and the numbering of the activity group allow you to easily identify the content of the activity group and how far through the strand you are.

> The **key mathematical ideas** highlight the important ideas children will be meeting within each activity group.

> The **Communicating** section gives information on the classroom **imagery** that will benefit learning, and the key **words and terms** to use with children.

> The **educational context** gives a clear outline of the content covered in the activity group, for example: how it builds on children's prior learning; how it connects with other activity groups; the foundation it establishes for children's future learning.

> Each activity group has a suggested **context** to help children identify with the topic and contextualize their learning.

> The **aims** signal key objectives for the activity group.

Key Mathematical Ideas: Pattern   **Pattern and Algebra**

Odd and even

7

Educational context

Children might already be using the terms 'odd' and 'even' when describing Numicon Shapes, because the odd Numicon Shapes are obvious. However, it is still important for them to work through the activities in this group to help them to **generalize ideas about odd and even numbers**. These ideas lay an important foundation for much of their later learning, when they look for **patterns in multiplication tables** (leading to work on factors and prime numbers and recognizing divisibility). The first two activities focus on understanding the term 'odd', connecting odd and even to Numicon Shapes and numerals. In Activity 3, children's attention is drawn to the alternating pattern of odd and even Shapes and their connected numbers, and the regular alternating pattern of odd and even numbers.

The activities for children moving on quickly provide opportunities to make some further generalizations about odd and even numbers – firstly, through exploring odd and even numbers with number rods (children will need to be confidently naming odd and even numbers, referring to number rods by number names and labelling them with numerals, before they do this activity) and, secondly, by experimenting and looking for patterns in totals when adding odd and even Numicon Shapes.

In all the activities, children should be encouraged to organize their work systematically, helping them to realize that this makes it easier to spot patterns.

Aims

- To use the terms 'odd' and 'even' when referring to numbers and totals
- To name odd and even numbers to 10
- To begin to explore what happens when odd and even numbers are added together
- To look for patterns and notice that an odd number always follows an even number (or an even number always follows an odd number) when counting whole numbers in ones

Communicating

Imagery
Numicon Display Number Line, Numicon 0–41 Number Rod Number Line (if available); display of objects that are in pairs, objects arranged in odd and even Numicon Shape patterns

Equipment
See the individual 'have ready' for each activity; various items for the activities in the 'Extending the activities' section

Words and terms for instruction (supported with signs and symbols)
put in order, build, group, arrange, find, feel, check, sort, look carefully, label, separate, match

Mathematical words and terms (supported with signs and symbols)
pairs, partners, odd one, odd Shapes, even Shapes, odd numbers, even numbers, odd, even, set, sort, in between, match, every other, next, before, always, because

Assessment

Individual Record of Progress: Pattern and Algebra 41, 42, 120, 121

Putting the activities into context

Talk about things that go together in pairs, e.g. shoes, socks and gloves, and explain that if we have only one of a pair we call it 'an odd shoe', 'an odd sock', 'an odd glove', and so on. Discuss working in pairs, establishing that this means there will be two children working together. Discuss working or walking with a partner, establishing that this means there will be two children working or walking together.

Link to Number, Pattern and Calculating 1

Pattern and Algebra 3

> The relevant steps on the **Individual Record of Progress** are signposted for continual tracking of children's progress.

> Most activity groups contain a **link** to the associated activity groups in the Numicon core teaching programme for reference.

Each activity group includes several **activities**, each titled to show the specific learning points addressed by the activity. Many activities also include **smaller steps** for children who need more support, and **further practice** activities that should be repeated until children are fluent and secure in their understanding.

The activities

Activity 1: Exploring odd and even with pairs of small-world people (or children)

Have ready: Numicon Shapes, ten small-world people

Step 1

Explain to children that often people walk or dance in pairs. Discuss occasions when children work or walk in pairs at school, e.g. on school outings, for some mathematics activities and in PE or dance lessons.

Step 2

Show five small-world people (or work with five children if the group size allows). Children arrange the small-world people into a Numicon 5-pattern to check how many there are, and find the matching 5-shape. Discuss and agree not every person has a partner: there is an odd one (see Fig. 1).

Step 3

Show ten small-world people (or children). Children arrange the people into a 10-pattern and find the matching 10-shape. Discuss and agree that every play person has a partner; there is not an odd one.

Step 4

Continue for each number of small-world people from ten down to one. Each time, find the matching Numicon Shape and agree whether all the small-world people have partners or whether there is an odd one.

Smaller steps

- Work first on the idea of an odd one using three different coloured pairs of socks and a seventh sock of a different colour. Work with children to put the pairs of socks together and discuss that there is an odd one. This can be repeated with gloves, cutlery where there are pairs of knives and forks and an odd fork, or cups and saucers where there is an odd saucer.

Further practice

- Children take a handful of objects, from a basket of ten mixed objects, and find out whether they can be made into pairs or not by arranging them into Numicon Shape patterns. They check by finding the Numicon Shape to match the pattern.

Activity 2: Connecting odd and even Numicon Shapes with odd and even numbers

---

The **Have ready** section at the start of each activity provides a list of the equipment that is used to help support children's learning.

Activities are broken down into **step-by-step** instructions.

7

Step 5

Explain that the numbers matched to odd Shapes are called 'odd numbers' and those matched to even Shapes are called 'even numbers'.

Smaller steps

- For some children it may be helpful to do this activity first with the Numicon Large Foam Shapes (if available).

Further practice

- Working in pairs, children take turns to take a Numicon Shape from a Numicon Feely Bag and decide whether it is odd or even. Together they compile a set of odd Shapes and a set of even Shapes; they then label the Shapes with numeral cards.
- Working in pairs, children shuffle numeral cards 1–10 (from photocopy master 11) and place them face down on the tabletop. One child turns over a card and says whether it is odd or even. The second child finds the matching Numicon Shape to check.

Activity 3: Noticing the alternating pattern of odd and even numbers

Have ready: Numicon Shapes

Step 1

Ask children to put a set of Numicon Shapes 1–10 in order.

Step 2

Ask children to look carefully and say what they notice: e.g. an odd number always follows an even number and an even number always follows an odd number.

Smaller steps

- Work with Numicon Large Foam Shapes (if available) so that children can 'walk the pattern' of odd and even. Put the Large Foam Shapes in order and look carefully at the repeated sequence of odd and even. Children step along the ordered Shapes saying the pattern 'odd', 'even', 'odd', 'even' etc. as they step from Shape to Shape.

Further practice

- Working in pairs, one child puts a Shape into a Numicon Feely Bag without the other child seeing. The second child feels the Shape and says whether it is odd or even, and reveals the Shape. Together they find the two Shapes that the Shape is 'in between' and decide whether they are odd or even.
- Give children opportunities to practise building repeating patterns with odd Shapes or even Shapes.
- Give children repeating patterns or sequences of odd or even numerals to build with Numicon Shapes.

Extending the activities

Connecting activities

- Children cover the Numicon Baseboard with odd or even Shapes – decide whether children should cover the board just with odd Shapes or just with even Shapes and note which they find easier to use and why. Look for children who become systematic using the patterns of number facts to help and those who are able to adjust Shapes to make them fit.
- Children create and label repeating patterns with odd or even Shapes, e.g. Fig. 4. They may like to record their patterns in colour on a paper Baseboard (printed from photocopy master 3) and label them with numerals.

The **Extending the activities** section contains essential **connecting activities**, including those for relevant **measures** work, and suggested activities for **children moving on quickly**.

Numbers in activities are used for illustration purposes and the activity should be repeated often with a range of numbers to encourage fluency.

Simple **illustrations** provide additional support throughout the activity group.

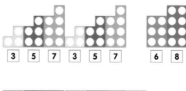

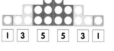

Planning – overview of the activity groups

50 activity groups are organized into four strands, each of which addresses a specific aspect of the mathematics curriculum, identified by the name of the strand and the colour of the header: Counting (green), Pattern and Algebra (red), Numbers and the Number System (yellow) and Calculating (blue).

Each strand is designed to build children's understanding cumulatively in that aspect of mathematics. The activity groups are numbered to show progression within each strand.

Counting

Activity Group Title	
Counting	1

Pattern and Algebra

Activity Group Title		Key Mathematical Ideas
Simple repeating patterns	1	Pattern
Pattern, direction and orientation	2	Pattern, Direction
More complex repeating patterns	3	Pattern
Similarities and differences – sorting	4	Mathematical thinking and reasoning
Labelling repeating patterns with numerals	5	Pattern
Equivalence – amounts and measures	6	Equivalence, Mathematical thinking and reasoning
Odd and even	7	Pattern
Reasoning about numbers	8	Mathematical thinking and reasoning
Introducing the '<' and '>' symbols – comparing amounts and measures	9	Mathematical thinking and reasoning
Introducing the '=' symbol	10	Equivalence, Adding, Mathematical thinking and reasoning

Numbers and the Number System

Activity Group Title		Key Mathematical Ideas
Exploring Numicon Shapes and Baseboard	1	Pattern, Shape
Matching Numicon Shapes	2	Pattern, Shape, Mathematical thinking and reasoning
Making comparisons to understand bigger	3	Order, Comparison, Mathematical thinking and reasoning
Making comparisons to understand smaller	4	Order, Comparison, Mathematical thinking and reasoning
Matching Numicon Shapes to pictures of the Shapes	5	Pattern, Order, Shape
Making comparisons using the language of comparison	6	Order, Comparison
Learning to order Numicon Shapes	7	Order, Comparison
Securing ordering of Numicon Shapes	8	Order, Comparison
Beginning to learn Numicon Shape patterns	9	Pattern, Shape
Giving the Numicon Shapes their number names	10	Counting
Labelling Numicon Shapes with numerals	11	Order
Seeing how many without counting from Numicon Shape patterns	12	Counting, Place value, Grouping, Mathematical thinking and reasoning
Building and naming teen numbers	13	Pattern, Ordering, Place value, Mathematical thinking and reasoning
Teen numbers – notation	14	Pattern, Ordering, Place value, Mathematical thinking and reasoning
Comparing and ordering to 20	15	Counting, Order, Place value, Equivalence, Mathematical thinking and reasoning
Counting by grouping in tens	16	Counting, Place value, Pattern

Numbers and the Number System continued

Activity Group Title		Key Mathematical Ideas
Exploring number lines and counting in steps of 10	17	Counting, Pattern, Order, Mathematical thinking and reasoning
Structure of 2-digit numbers	18	Counting, Pattern, Order, Place value, Equivalence, Mathematical thinking and reasoning
Structure of 2-digit numbers – notation	19	Counting, Pattern, Order, Place value, Equivalence, Mathematical thinking and reasoning
Comparing and ordering higher numbers	20	Counting, Pattern, Order, Place value, Equivalence, Mathematical thinking and communicating
Counting in steps of 2 and 5	21	Counting, Pattern, Order, Mathematical thinking and reasoning

Calculating

Activity Group Title		Key Mathematical Ideas
Practical adding – starting with the total	1	Adding, Mathematical thinking and reasoning
Practical adding – combining to find how many altogether	2	Adding, Mathematical thinking and reasoning
Practical adding – adding more	3	Adding, Mathematical thinking and reasoning
Practical subtracting – take away	4	Subtracting, Mathematical thinking and reasoning
Practical subtracting – decrease	5	Subtracting, Mathematical thinking and reasoning
Practical subtracting – difference	6	Subtracting, Mathematical thinking and reasoning
Practical subtracting – comparing numbers to say how many more to equal	7	Subtracting, Mathematical thinking and reasoning
Introducing the '+' symbol	8	Adding, Mathematical thinking and reasoning
Introducing the '–' symbol	9	Subtracting, Mathematical thinking and reasoning
Adding and subtracting 1	10	Adding, Subtracting, Mathematical thinking and reasoning
Money – coin equivalence	11	Equivalence, Adding, Subtracting
Further ideas for developing fluency – adding and subtracting with each number to 10	12	Adding, Subtracting, Mathematical thinking and reasoning
Fractions – part–whole relationships	13	Equivalence, Fractions, Mathematical thinking and reasoning
Practical multiplying	14	Sequence, Pattern, Adding, Multiplying
Introducing the '×' symbol	15	Sequence, Pattern, Repeated adding, Multiplying, Mathematical thinking and reasoning
Practical dividing	16	Pattern, Sequence, Multiplying, Grouping, Mathematical thinking and reasoning
Introducing the '÷' symbol	17	Pattern, Sequence, Multiplying, Dividing, Mathematical thinking and reasoning
Fractions – Exploring halves and quarters of wholes	18	Equivalence, Part-whole relationships, Fractions, Division, Mathematical thinking and reasoning

Planning – teaching progression

The Breaking Barriers teaching progression gives the recommended order for teaching the activity groups. Teaching the activity groups in this order has been recommended because achieving understanding of the ideas in one section or strand is dependent on understanding the ideas in another.

The teaching progression is designed to be followed sequentially. However, the first activity groups on Counting, Pattern and Algebra and Numbers and the Number System are ongoing and introduce activities that should run continuously with the rest of the programme. Children enjoy repeating the activities independently and this gives them useful practice. The remaining activity groups can be followed in order, although many of them will need to be repeated often until children's understanding is secure.

Within each activity group, a range of activities is provided. Though it is intended that the majority of children will achieve mastery of these activities eventually, it may be that for some children the activities remain out of reach. Some may progress to work at the level of their age-peers very quickly; the 'for children moving on quickly' activities provided in most activity groups may be suitable for them. There are also relevant links to the Numicon Teaching Resource Handbooks (aimed at whole-class teaching) in most activity groups.

Children who take longer to assimilate the ideas in the basic activities will benefit from following the 'Smaller steps' suggested. For children who have previously worked with Numicon we suggest that teachers establish the child's starting point by using the Assessment Signposts (included in the Assessment Tools section of the *Breaking Barriers Assessment and Photocopy Masters* book). Children with no experience of working with Numicon will need to start with the first activities and progress at their own pace.

Three strands of foundation activities to work in parallel

Pattern and Algebra	Counting	Numbers and the Number System
1 Simple repeating patterns	Counting Activity Group	1 Exploring Numicon Shapes and Baseboard
2 Pattern, direction and orientation		2 Matching Numicon Shapes
3 More complex repeating patterns		3 Making comparisons to understand bigger
		4 Making comparisons to understand smaller
		5 Matching Numicon Shapes and pictures
		6 Making comparisons using the language of comparison

Strand and Activity Group Number		Activity Group Title
Pattern and Algebra	4	Similarities and differences – sorting
Numbers and the Number System	7	Learning to order the Numicon Shapes
Numbers and the Number System	8	Securing ordering of Numicon Shapes
Numbers and the Number System	9	Beginning to learn Numicon Shape patterns
Numbers and the Number System	10	Giving the Numicon Shapes their number names
Numbers and the Number System	11	Labelling Numicon Shapes with numerals
Pattern and Algebra	5	Connecting repeating patterns with numbers
Numbers and the Number System	12	Seeing how many from Numicon Shape patterns
Pattern and Algebra	6	Equivalence – amounts and measures
Pattern and Algebra	7	Odd and even
Pattern and Algebra	8	Reasoning about numbers
Calculating	1	Practical adding – starting with the total
Calculating	2	Practical adding – combining to find how many altogether
Calculating	3	Practical adding – adding more
Calculating	4	Practical subtracting – take away
Calculating	5	Practical subtracting – decrease
Calculating	6	Subtracting – comparing numbers to find the difference
Calculating	7	Practical subtracting – comparing numbers to say how many more to equal
Numbers and the Number System	13	Building and naming teen numbers
Numbers and the Number System	14	Teen numbers – notation
Calculating	8	Introducing the '+' symbol
Pattern and Algebra	9	Introducing the '<' and '>' symbols – comparing amounts and measures

Strand and Activity Group Number		Activity Group Title
Pattern and Algebra	10	Introducing the '=' symbol
Numbers and the Number System	15	Comparing and ordering to 20
Calculating	9	Introducing the '–' symbol
Calculating	10	Adding and subtracting one
Calculating	11	Money – coin equivalence
Calculating	12	Further ideas for developing fluency – adding and subtracting within 10
Numbers and the Number System	16	Finding how many by grouping in tens
Numbers and the Number System	17	Exploring number lines and counting in steps of 10
Numbers and the Number System	18	Structure of 2-digit numbers
Numbers and the Number System	19	Structure of 2-digit numbers – notation
Numbers and the Number System	20	Comparing and ordering 2-digit numbers
Numbers and the Number System	21	Counting in steps of 2 and 5
Calculating	13	Fractions – parts and wholes
Calculating	14	Practical multiplying
Calculating	15	Introducing the 'x' symbol
Calculating	16	Practical dividing
Calculating	17	Introducing the '÷' symbol
Calculating	18	Halves and quarters of wholes

Teaching guide

Breaking Barriers introduction

Doing mathematics: Thinking and communicating mathematically

Mathematics is an activity – something we do – not a collection of facts and ideas that we must just try to remember. Certainly, we do remember things as we learn more and more mathematics (and it often helps us greatly if we do), but learning all our multiplication tables off pat won't help us at all if we can't also work out *when* to multiply and *when* to divide.

Learning to do mathematics involves learning to think mathematically; that is how mathematics is done – by thinking. Children learn to think mathematically by joining in with the mathematical thinking we introduce them to, as we engage in various activities and situations with them. We introduce them to our own mathematical thinking through our mathematical communicating as we work with them.

Children 'internalize' the mathematical communicating that they develop with us as they work, and that internalized communicating becomes their own mathematical thinking. We learned to do mathematics in the same way as children ourselves, by internalizing the mathematical communicating of adults and experts around us. We still do, as we learn even more.

All our mathematical communicating and thinking, both with ourselves and with others, involves much more than simply using language (words and symbols). Mathematical

thinking and communicating also depend upon and involve a great deal of action and imagery, as well as the special mathematical words and symbols that we use. Action, imagery and conversation are all vital.

Looking for patterns and generalizing

Another aspect of doing mathematics that makes it such a distinctive activity is that mathematics is about looking for patterns in situations, generalizing, and then using our generalizations to help us in new situations.

The thinking and communicating that we do in mathematics is therefore full of generalizations. Mathematical success depends upon our being able to generalize and then use our generalizations in a wide variety of situations. Recognizing which situations connect with which generalizations is what will tell us, e.g. *when* to multiply and when to divide.

As an early instance of generalizing, think about the number sentence:

$$3 + 4 = 7$$

It is a generalization: three of anything and four of anything will always make seven things altogether, whatever they are. So, whenever we meet a new situation in which three of something and four of something are added together, provided we have made this generalization earlier we will know in advance that there are going to be seven things altogether; no counting is required.

Later on we will generalize that it doesn't make any difference which way round we add two numbers together, their total will always be the same, so we also know,

$$3 + 4 = 4 + 3 = 7$$

This is how doing mathematics progresses; we are always looking for the next generalizations and their usefulness.

Children with special educational needs live in the same world as the rest of us

Children who, for whatever reason, find learning to do mathematics, that is, learning how to think and communicate mathematically, harder than most, are not somehow later 'excused' from having to face the mathematical challenges of everyday life that we all face. Time keeping, finance and personal organization are aspects of life that affect us all. Children's future chances of adult independence depend crucially upon how far they can learn to do the mathematics necessary to modern life.

Nor is there a 'special' simplified kind of mathematics on offer for those who find the subject difficult. We cannot advise some children to 'just stick to the easy numbers' because all numbers are difficult ideas that took the human race many thousands of years to dream up. Anyone trying to learn mathematics faces the same communicative challenges, and the same requirement to generalize, as everyone else.

Thus children who consistently find learning mathematics harder than most, and children who are struggling even temporarily (such as those not speaking their first language in school, or those who have been away for a long period) will progress more slowly than their contemporaries. Inevitably this means they will learn less than their classmates, and teachers have the tricky task of deciding how to reduce their curriculum whilst disadvantaging them as little as possible.

Individual children require that teachers make individual decisions, but as a general rule there are some areas of mathematics which are essential for any child or adult to be secure with, to get by in the wider world.

Teaching the essentials

The mathematical activities offered here are restricted to those regarded as essential, and these activities are often introduced within key contexts of everyday life: measuring, in particular time and money, and personal organization.

The focus is on counting, adding, subtracting, multiplying, dividing and introductions to fractions as essentials since these all crop up so regularly in everyday life. The contexts are chosen to help children connect their work in mathematics directly to their everyday experiences; they are engaged in the essential mathematics that they can see will be of use to them.

Communicating and generalizing are essentials

Each individual child's difficulties are different and teachers need to be aware of them. However, all children face the same basic and essential challenges of learning to communicate (and thus, think) mathematically, and of generalizing, to the fullest extent that they can.

Therefore, all activities require children to be active (almost always with physical materials and visual imagery) and to communicate as richly and effectively as possible. Additionally, the materials and imagery used are invariably structured, or require children to structure them, so that patterns and regularities are as evident as possible.

Generalizing depends upon noticing regularities; as we do mathematics we make sure regularity is emphasized in every situation and we constantly ask children to show us and talk about the regularities and patterns that they see.

Summarizing

Working with children who are finding mathematics difficult requires us to do three things: be very clear about each individual child's particular difficulties and work to minimize these (see the 'Barriers to joining in with mathematics' section on page 30); prioritize – decide what content is essential, and what can be left; concentrate on the two key essential aspects of children's mathematical work – their generalizing and their communicating.

Hopefully you and your children will thoroughly enjoy working productively with these activities as well!

Key mathematical ideas for Breaking Barriers

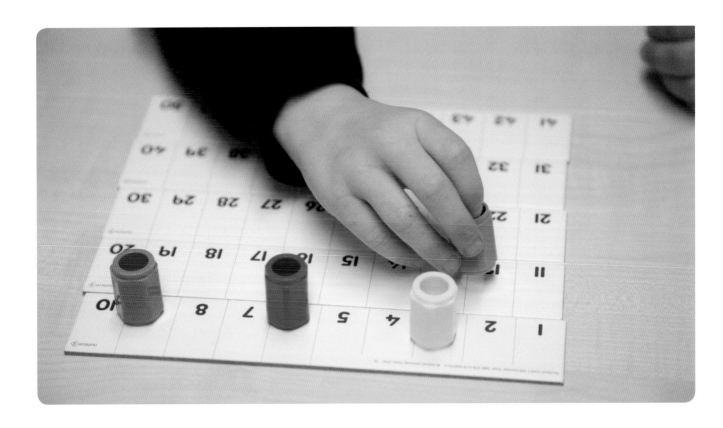

Thinking and communicating mathematically – two sides of the same coin

Thinking and communicating are two sides of the same coin; we communicate in the ways that we think, and think in the ways that we communicate. Our thinking is, in effect, our communicating with ourselves.

Children learn how to think mathematically by joining in with how we think mathematically. We show children how we think mathematically by doing our own mathematical thinking 'out loud', that is, we show children how we think mathematically in the ways that we communicate with them mathematically, as we work together.

Children who experience difficulties doing mathematics therefore have problems communicating mathematically even when they have not been categorized as having 'Speech, Language and Communication Needs' (SLCN). Many more general speech, language and communication difficulties often underlie a high proportion of Special Educational Needs and Disabilities (SEND).

Because of the close relationship between communicating and thinking, children who also have SLCN will often require additional support in developing their mathematical thinking in the form of:

- especially careful verbal and/or practical modelling of mathematical communicating by the teacher

- scaffolding of a child's thinking in relation to a particular mathematical task, e.g. through provision of a visual framework of the sequence of activities needed to solve a particular mathematical task, that is a 'task board'

- supportive correction of erroneous or unhelpful communicating, ensuring that a child is not left feeling that their approach was completely 'wrong'.

Thinking and communicating in mathematics always involves much more than just words and symbols. Whenever we think and communicate mathematically there are usually actions involved, and gestures and visual imagery are certainly involved at all times. Even when we are thinking or communicating about just pure numbers, e.g. we say that their 'size' is important, as is their 'order'. We also say some numbers are 'bigger' or 'higher' than others, and that some come 'before' or 'after' others. All of this spatial imagery is often explicitly visualized with the help of a number 'line'.

Numicon emphasizes visual imagery constantly; mathematics is essentially a study of relationships, and relationships are usually very well described visually.

As well as involving much more than words and symbols, mathematical thinking and communicating are also distinctive in several other important ways:

(i) Reasoning mathematically crucially depends upon making and using generalizations. All children learning mathematics need to learn both to generalize and to use generalizations in their reasoning. Generalizing correctly will allow us to make situations predictable. Making situations predictable is exactly what we use mathematics for and why it is found to be such a powerful subject. Teachers should encourage children's generalizing by taking every opportunity to ask, 'Do you think this will always happen?' and 'What if those numbers were different?' and so on.

As an example, an important early generalization that children need to make is noticing that, in our sequence of counting numbers, each next number describes an amount exactly 'one bigger' than the previous number (this is sometimes called the 'successor relation' between numbers). Later on, children will use this generalization to reason that if 3 + 3 = 6, then 3 + 4 = 7 (sometimes this is called working out a 'near-double').

Of course, reasoning about near-doubles like this involves much more than just knowing that each next number is one bigger than the previous number. It involves another essential mathematical idea called equivalence as well. However, unless children have already made that first generalization about how our number sequence grows, deriving new number facts from ones they already know will be very difficult. Actually the numbers '3', '4', '6' and '7' are themselves all generalizations; when we do arithmetic we use them to mean '3 of anything', '4 of anything' and so on.

The near-double example also illustrates how much more effective we are at doing mathematics if we use our reasoning, than if we just try to remember everything blindly. If children were to try to remember every single number fact as if it were an isolated fact by itself, they would have an enormously difficult memory task to accomplish. Whereas if they can reason about connections between number facts their thinking becomes so much more fluent and effective as they exploit number relationships of many kinds.

Triadic relations between numbers, e.g. 3, 4 and 7 are especially important to children as they put them together in important 'part–whole' relationships that establish 3 and 4 as related 'parts' of a 'whole' 7. Such a triad enables children to swiftly connect:

$$3 + 4 = 7$$
$$4 + 3 = 7$$
$$7 - 4 = 3$$
$$7 - 3 = 4$$

Such part–whole relations are particularly well illustrated with 'trios' of Numicon Shapes and of number rods.

To encourage children's generalizing it is important to look for patterns in all situations, because 'seeing a pattern' is itself an important kind of generalizing. It also helps to appeal to as many of children's senses as possible when we want them to notice a pattern. For instance, noticing the 'successor relation' between whole numbers (see above) is strongly supported visually and kinaesthetically by using both sequences of Numicon Shapes and 'staircases' of number rods.

(ii) It is also essential for children to approach situations systematically when doing mathematics. Being systematic is a key aspect of effective reasoning and often provides a secure foundation for generalizing. Working with Numicon offers many opportunities for children to work systematically. It is important to encourage children to resist an impulse to make wild or quick guesses when doing mathematics, and to develop the patience to explore what could happen fully, and in detail, before reaching conclusions. This means allowing children sufficient time to be systematic, in practice, and not giving them the impression that those who are quick are somehow more successful, or that there is only one answer that the teacher is looking for.

(iii) The final key element in thinking mathematically involves being able to connect a world of abstract mathematical generalizations with practical and particular situations in an everyday world. In effect, this involves children learning not only how to do some mathematics, but also when that mathematics is appropriate. Simply remembering all the number facts there are will not be of any use to children if they cannot also work out when to subtract, add, multiply and divide.

Numicon sets the mathematics we want children to learn within everyday situations, in order to help them connect abstract mathematics (generalizations) with their everyday lives. Very often this will involve introducing children's number work within contexts of measuring, especially involving time and money. Learning to reason logically and systematically will also help children in their everyday personal organization and thus help them develop increasing independence in their lives.

It should always be remembered that mathematical thinking and communicating continues to be important throughout children's learning, as well as being an integral part of their mathematical experience. Young children do not yet reason logically in the ways that most adults are able to do. Their gradual progress towards adult logical thinking and communicating depends very much on the reasoning they do and learn with us. We cannot expect young children, and some older children with particular cognitive difficulties, or with social, emotional, or mental health needs, to think like adults immediately. However, it will always help to discuss any child's thinking with them and to help them reflect upon their reasoning within it.

Pattern

Since doing mathematics is essentially about generalizing, and reasoning with generalizations, being able to spot patterns and regularities, and communicate with and about them, is essential to success in mathematics for everyone. Noticing regularities and patterns in situations is actually how we generalize.

Human beings are usually very good at noticing patterns; we all first learned to speak and communicate through noticing patterns in the noises, gestures and sounds made around us. Our technology, our culture, our scientific and medical achievements and so on, have all developed on the basis of noticing patterns and using them to make our world more predictable and controllable.

Some children however, for various individual reasons, are not so good at noticing patterns generally, and so Numicon emphasizes patterns in as many different activities and media as possible. Doing number work only with numerals on paper would conceal many patterns that are important to understanding relationships between numbers. Using Numicon Shapes from the beginning emphasizes such relationships both visually and kinaesthetically. Number rods that increase regularly in length also offer visual and tactile relationships that parallel the patterns of relationships we want children to recognize between numbers. Other kinds of arrays and number lines (illustrating regular order) are also exploited whenever possible.

Patterns and regularities of one kind or another are the basis of all mathematics, the basis of its generalizations, from the earliest regularities of our number system through to the most advanced research being undertaken at universities today. It is essential to encourage children to look for patterns in every situation, and to constantly encourage them with questions such as, 'Will that always work?'

Order and direction

Children will notice from their earliest attempts at counting that the order in which they say number words is important, although initially they will not know why. Later, as they begin to use number words to count things, they will learn that the order in which they use number words remains essential, although the order in which they count the actual objects is not; the order in which we count off the objects in a collection is irrelevant to their total number. Thus the idea of 'order' is crucial to children's number work from the very beginning, yet in different ways. Children who have difficulties with sequencing more generally will also find much in their early number work taxing for this reason alone.

Later on, as children become more proficient at counting things, they will need to notice the 'successor relation', that is, that each 'next' number refers to an amount 'one more' than the previous one. This relationship of a regularly increasing step size between whole numbers contributes much to children's developing number sense and is a vital early generalization to make if children are later to calculate effectively.

Numicon Shapes and number rods are designed to emphasize the successor relation clearly, both visually and kinaesthetically, since number words and numerals by themselves do not.

As children learn to work with, name and order larger numbers they will need to generalize again as they learn our place-value code for naming an increasing sequence of numbers. Learning our system of ordered number names will again be vital for children's effective calculating later on.

Later still, as children learn to add and subtract, multiply and divide, they will learn that the order in which we add numbers doesn't matter, but the order in which we subtract them does. Similarly, it matters which way around we divide numbers but not the order in which we multiply them.

Later, as fractions are introduced, children will gradually learn that although fractions are ordered in size, there is no successor relation between them. Individual fractions do not have 'successors'; there is no 'next' fraction that comes immediately after any fraction we choose. This may be children's first introduction to ideas about infinitely small things, and here again the fundamental idea of 'order' is significantly involved.

Finally, it is important to remember that underlying any ordering of things that are different lies a 'direction' in which that order unfolds or progresses; without a given direction it is impossible to interpret what moving 'forwards' and 'backwards' might mean, and also 'before', 'after' and 'next'. And Piaget was very clear that an essential flexibility in thinking involves 'reversibility', that is, being able to both 'do' and 'undo' actions. This has very important implications for children understanding how adding and subtracting relate to each other (and multiplying and dividing), and for making sense of the passage of time.

It is important that when children are working to order any collection of things (Numicon Shapes, lengths, numbers, containers) they are also asked to reverse the order, that is, go 'backwards'. Counting on *and back* is what will give children the flexibility with number order that they will need if they are to calculate effectively.

Counting

Counting is not simple, and to make matters even more difficult for them, children are usually taught how to count long before they have any idea of what counting is for, practically. Put another way, children are commonly taught how to count before they understand what it is that counting achieves. This makes the early stages of counting, for most children, simply a mysterious social ritual without any clear practical point.

Children are vitally concerned with physical quantities of many kinds however, from the moment they are born; a sense of 'enough', 'more', 'no more' and so on are very significant physical experiences from day one. Children are usually taught counting in their early years as a purely social accomplishment and not as something that helps them solve practical problems with quantities. It therefore generally takes a surprising amount of time before most children begin to connect their growing understanding of physical quantities with counting, and appreciate that a counting procedure they have learned enables them to specify with number words a kind of amount, the size of a collection of objects or an 'amount' of units.

Children with speech and language or motor or physical difficulties are also likely to find counting activities particularly challenging because of difficulties they experience in learning and retaining verbal sequences, producing speech, or coordinating the fine and gross motor sequencing required for manual counting (that is, articulating number names in lockstep with their manual counting or touching of objects). For children with motor coordination or other physical difficulties it is often essential to consider the size and the spacing of objects used in counting activities.

There are three extremely complex demands placed upon all children learning to count: producing a uniquely ordered (and potentially infinite) set of number names; using this sequence in lockstep with an acknowledging of each individual item being counted, one-by-one and once only; and then an announcement that the last number name used specifies 'how many' objects there are in a collection (or units in an amount).

Firstly, children can be helped in the remembering and generating of our sequence of whole number names by continual references to visual number lines, and by simply 'just counting' verbally, regularly. By chanting number names in order, backwards and forwards, and starting and finishing in different places children will realize that after 'twelve' (12), some patterns emerge in the order and sounds of whole number names that can aid memorizing significantly. A consequent generalizing of our place-value system with numerals (see page 25) will finally help children achieve mastery of the ways we conventionally produce an infinite, uniquely ordered set of 'counting number' names in our civilization today.

Similarly, there are regular sound patterns to be noticed in counting out loud, on and back, with simple fractions. These can be very helpfully reinforced and supported by concurrently showing visual fraction number lines as children rehearse their oral counting.

It cannot be assumed, however, that because a child is able to count verbally and accurately from one to a hundred, from zero to five in halves, and appears to understand thousands, hundreds, tens and units, that there is no longer any necessity for them to practise counting on and back, say between 2987 and 3005, or between $3\frac{1}{4}$ and $5\frac{1}{2}$. Many children need to practise these types of counts both with whole numbers and with fractions frequently.

Secondly, one-to-one correspondence relationships lie at the heart of children understanding the ways we use number words to specify the sizes of collections as 'numbers of' objects. Children need much experience both in establishing the one-to-one relationship between number words and objects counted as we count, and (more informally) in comparing sets of objects with each other by one-to-one correspondence.

Quite often children will spontaneously compare two sets of objects by one-to-one correspondence in a sharing situation: 'one for me, one for you' and so on. Situations like this can easily be set up for children, but all opportunities for comparing sets of objects in this way should be taken, both to encourage children in making such comparisons and to connect a concentrated focus on the sizes of collections with the process of counting. (Remember, most children learn to count as a social accomplishment, not for any practical reason, and it takes them a while to work out what counting is for, practically.) Compare sets of objects one-to-one with each other, and count them too.

Finally, children will gradually put such experiences together and learn that if we count two different sets of objects and end on the same number word each time, then we will say in our mathematical communicating that these two sets each have the same 'number of objects' in them, that is we could put the objects in each of the sets into one-to-one correspondence with each other. In such experiences, children will gradually learn how the counting process arrives at what we call the 'number of objects' in a collection. This realization usually takes a surprisingly long time to arrive for most children, and for children with many kinds of additional physical, verbal, or memory difficulties, it can be expected to take longer still.

We can also help children understand that counting is related to establishing the 'sizes' of collections by associating their counting activities with Numicon Shapes and with number rods, especially also in association with number lines. Literally 'seeing' how numbers 'grow' visually as we count along a number line with Numicon Shapes (and/or with number rods) helps children to recognize that the further along the sequence of number names we count, the 'bigger' the collection described. Importantly, both with Numicon Shapes and with number rods, seeing how numbers 'grow' regularly, visually and physically also illustrates the precise and key 'successor relation' very clearly (see 'Order and direction' on page 22).

As important as counting is, however, learning *not* to count is equally important and even more difficult for many children, yet 'not-counting' is an essential key to effective calculating as children progress.

Not-counting

In a very important sense, calculating is 'not-counting'. We could, if we had enough time, try to solve any whole-number arithmetic problem with some kind of laborious counting routine. We could solve 13 375 ÷ 37 by carefully counting out and sharing 13 375 beans into 37 different equal groups, then counting out how many beans ended up in each group, and finally counting the remainder. But it would be crazy to do that today because (a) there are much quicker ways to calculate a result and (b) with such numbers of beans there would be endless opportunities along the way to lose count and to make mistakes and so on, often without even noticing that we had gone astray.

Some people believed for a long time, however, that counting is the foundation of children's ability to calculate. There has been much research during the last 50 years showing that if you leave children to their own devices (and give them piles of beans) they will slowly invent their own counting methods for solving arithmetic problems (see, e.g. Fuson, 1992). What is not usually stated in such research, though, is why it might be thought good educational practice to leave children to their own devices, with only piles of beans (or cubes, or counters), in order to work out answers simply by counting beans so laboriously.

Actually, effective and fluent calculating involves working with numbers, not with beans, and the challenge for children in learning to calculate effectively is how to work with numbers, and not with numbers of counters.

But the 'numbers' that we work with in calculating are abstract mathematical objects that children have to re-invent for themselves in their own thinking and communicating, if they are ever to calculate effectively. The numbers we call '3' and '5' and so on are abstract objects. Helping children to work with such abstract objects instead of spending their time counting piles of beans is usually the most difficult

and central challenge for teachers of young children, and especially for those who teach children with additional needs.

There are two key aspects to helping children work with numbers, and not with scattered collections of beans: firstly, noticing how we communicate about 'numbers', and secondly, offering children whole, or 'complete' physical objects to calculate with, rather than long-winded one-by-one counting procedures.

Firstly, teachers need to recognize that there is a grammar change in our communicating when we shift from talking about 'numbers of (things)' to talking about just 'numbers': we actually shift from using number words as adjectives, to using them as nouns. We shift from talking about 'three pencils' (adjective) to just 'three' (noun). On some level, almost all children detect this grammatical lurch, but very few will ever ask about it; for many it just becomes an inexpressible and uncomfortable mystery.

Be sensitive. Recognize that this is a difficult and yet key step for children, and introduce our new way of using number words as nouns as a kind of 'shorthand'. Teach children that when we say just 'three' or write just '3', we actually mean '3 of anything' – a generalization.

Secondly, turn collections of loose physical things into whole physical objects; help children to think of 'numbers-of-things' not as several individual things to be counted, but as whole collections. We do this with Numicon Shapes and number rods in our approach; for example, presenting children with whole visual Numicon Shape patterns and whole number rod lengths[1] that can be comprehended as 'whole amounts'. This helps children to think of 'numbers' as whole objects and importantly, with Numicon Shapes and number rods, as objects they can physically get hold of.

1   Importantly these number rod lengths are ungraduated, emphasizing their 'wholeness'.

Very significantly too, Numicon Shapes and number rods are not each just 'whole' collections. As objects they are also physically related to each other in ways that parallel abstract 'number' relationships are. The 'successor', 'part–whole', and equivalence number relationships that are so important to understanding how abstract 'numbers' relate to each other are evident as well in these physical objects both visually and kinaesthetically.

Later on, children will find that calculating with these whole physical objects gives meaning to the calculating they are asked to do with abstract 'number objects'. Adding, subtracting, multiplying and dividing can all be done physically by comparing and combining Numicon Shapes and number rods – no counting required. Thus calculating with numbers as objects makes both visual and tactile sense.

Two early activities in particular are essential for children following the not-counting approach: 'finding how many without counting' (Numbers and the Number System 12) and 'making the Numicon Shape patterns' (Numbers and the Number System 9). In the first, children learn how to see the 'number in' (the size of) a collection in one insight, by recognizing whole visual patterns. In the second, they recognize that any collection of discrete physical objects can be made into these particular patterns – a vital generalization.

Naming whole numbers – our 'place-value' and verbal systems

We deal with 'numbers' (including calculating) by writing and saying their names. Since the number naming system we use today has taken thousands of years to evolve, it is not surprising that it can take some time for any child to master it; it is especially difficult for many children who have more general learning and/or language difficulties. Also, unfortunately for children trying to learn our number names, in our society we use two parallel systems for referring to whole numbers that in some ways conflict; we use a system of written numerals, and a different system of words, to read, write and say our numbers.

Individually, these two systems are often quite difficult for children to understand. The fact that the systems also conflict with each other makes learning them both, at the same time, an especially confusing task. As ever, it is the irregularities and inconsistencies in our naming of numbers that make life difficult for children. Therefore, whenever we can, exploiting what patterns there are in our sequence of number names is vital for all. Regularly practising counting on and back verbally helps children to remember important patterns in the sounds of the names.

The way we write numerals to name numbers up to '30' and the way we say number names using words up to 'thirty' are significantly different. It is these particular number names and numerals that children meet most often first of all in their learning. The most frequent conflicts arise in relation to number names up to 'twenty' which children commonly focus on after they have learned number names to 'ten'. (Up to 'ten' there is no discernible pattern at all either in the sounds of the words, or in the appearances of numerals.)
An additional difficulty is that several English words for

quite different numbers are phonologically very similar, e.g. 'thirteen' and 'thirty'.

Thinking first about our ways of using numerals to name numbers, our forebears developed a system for generating symbolic number names that not only allows us to make up new number names ad infinitum, but tells us instantly whereabouts in the series any particular number belongs. For instance, when we read '273' we know that it is the name of the whole number that immediately follows '272', and is one hundred before '373'. It is not necessary for us to remember every individual numeral number name and its place in the order (which would be impossible anyway since there are infinitely many of them). We need only to understand the system that generates patterns in our number names.

There are actually two essential ideas underlying our system of using numerals for naming numbers. The first is grouping, and in this respect the number we call 'ten' (in numerals, '10') is the most important number in our naming system. When we count collections of anything, every time we have counted ten of something, we group and call that whole group one of something else. So ten 'ones' are called one group of 'ten'; ten 'tens' are called one group of a 'hundred', ten 'hundreds' are called one group of a 'thousand' and so on.

The second essential idea is place value. The number of 'ones' (or units) in any count has its own place when recording an amount with numerals, the number of 'tens' has its place, the number of 'hundreds' its own place, and so on. This is how each place in a numeral number name comes to have its own special value, and if there are, say, no groups of 'ten' in a number name then we use a zero (0) to keep that 'tens-place' empty.

In relation to children's grouping activities, when they move on to 'find how many' objects there are in a collection without counting (Numbers and the Number System 12), it is important to encourage them physically to first 'group in Numicon 10-shapes' whenever there are enough objects in the collection to do so. After all the possible grouping in 10-shapes has been done, there will be a final grouping of remaining objects to be done, putting these into the Numicon Shape of whatever number of objects (fewer than ten) are left. The fact that the largest of the Numicon Shapes is the '10-shape' easily encourages an economy in the practice of grouping objects; encourage children to 'make the biggest groups you can, first'. (This is one way of being systematic.)

Unfortunately, some children who experience particular difficulty learning mathematics also have physical organizational difficulties. For such children the physical grouping of collections into tens may pose problems for their ideational (establishing an internal visual/motor representation) and motor execution (executing a motor plan to realize a representation) abilities. Children with such organizational difficulties will benefit from having the grouping into Numicon Shapes process (called 'finding how many without counting') modelled carefully for them, and having extra practice at undertaking such grouping activities independently. Some children, in order to be able to perceive each group of ten as a distinct entity, may also need to be taught specifically to organize sets of objects systematically, e.g. through initially placing their objects into left-to-right or top-to-bottom lines before arranging them into Numicon Shape patterns.

The grouping of objects in order to organize a collection into 'ones' (or units), 'tens' and 'hundreds' and so on so that we can 'find how many without counting' of course involves at the same time giving these very same names to the groups we make. Thus children are actually physically making 'tens' and so on as they do this activity, and the actions involved contribute much to their understanding of what is sometimes called column value (the 'column value' of the '2' in '427' is two tens, that of the '4' is four hundreds and so on).

When it comes to the second big idea of our numeral system, place value, it is important to remember that the principles involved are purely conventional. There is a regular pattern, in that numeral places multiply up by 'ten' in value as we move to the left of a multi-digit number name (or alternatively, divide down by 'ten' in value as we move to the right). However, placing the values in this order, and choosing 'ten' as the multiple, are simply conventions that children have to learn. We all just have to remember conventions, and there's often nothing much to explain; we just all do it that way to enable us to communicate with each other.

Number lines have an important role in helping children to understand place value, not only because they visually reinforce the order of our number names, but also because they help children understand what is sometimes called quantity value. The 'quantity value' of the '2' in '427' is twenty, and so on. (Further reinforcement of the 'tens' structure of our number naming system is also afforded by other number lines, that is, the Numicon 10s Number Line itself, but also any number line for larger numbers that uses alternating colours to emphasize tens divisions.)

It is vital that children see the equivalence of 'column value' and 'quantity value', that is, that the two tens (column value) in 427 are equivalent to twenty (that is, their quantity value) and that the four hundreds are equivalent to four hundred. Seeing this equivalence will be of enormous importance to children as they learn to calculate with 'numbers'.

The Numicon Display Number Line is an essential visual image that helps children to 'see', for instance, how the number we call twenty (as a quantity value) comprises two 10-shapes (in column value) and is twenty (quantity value) spaces along the line from zero. Similarly, the number we call 'sixteen' comprises one 'ten' and six 'ones', but is also sixteen spaces along from zero.

It cannot be assumed that where a child seems to be able to use our numeral system for labelling numbers effectively, they also understand our parallel verbal system for naming numbers. Although those of us who are well used to both systems find numerals and number words readily exchangeable with each other, to children who are meeting these parallel systems for the first time the two systems' differences often present unhelpful conflicts.

For instance, the words 'ten', 'eleven' and 'twelve' do not signal anything significant happening as we count beyond nine, whereas the symbolic numeral code '10', '11' and '12' signals a shift to grouping in tens. In English, these three spoken number words therefore verbally conceal a crucial introduction to grouping in tens and place value that is evident in the written symbolic code.

It is possible with some children to bridge between the arbitrary nature of the words 'ten', 'eleven' and 'twelve', and their symbolic numeral versions '10', '11' and '12', by using British Sign Language (BSL) and Makaton® signs for these numbers, alongside Numicon images. For instance, the manual sign for eleven in Makaton® consists of the signs for 'ten + one' combined in sequence. This shares a key visual and kinaesthetic link with the BSL sign for eleven (the index finger of the one from the Makaton® eleven (ten + one) sign is the index finger that taps the thumb in the BSL sign for eleven). Alongside this, the Numicon 10-shape and 1-shape arranged together to represent 11 help to explain that when we want to say 'ten-one' (with Makaton® sign ten + one) in everyday English, we say the word 'eleven' (with BSL sign for eleven).

There's no relief either when we reach the number 'thir-teen' verbally; 'thir' is a corruption of 'three' and 'teen' is a corruption of 'ten'. Likewise, the stems of the words 'twenty', 'thirty', and 'fifty', that is 'twen-', 'thir-', 'fif-', are corruptions that obscure the 'two-', 'three-', 'five-' meanings reflected in the numerals of their symbolic representations. Unhelpfully also, for the whole range of 'teen' number names the spoken word order used is the reverse of the corresponding numeral order, e.g. we say, 'eight-teen' (with the eight first) but write '18' (with the ten first).

Also, as noted earlier, the phonological similarity between many of the words used to name numbers is confusing. For instance, 'fourteen' is phonologically different from 'forty' by only one sound (/n/) and the difficulty is compounded since the nasal sound is very difficult to perceive in a noisy classroom.

Finally, there are also conflicts between the names and the symbolic numeral codes for bigger numbers, e.g. 'two hundred and three' and the symbolic code '203'. Children will (sensibly) often write '2003' instead of '203' because '200 and 3' is the how we actually say it.

Many children with difficulties in learning mathematics often become very understandably exasperated with the complexities of how we communicate about 'numbers' in their early years. Such frustration can easily impact negatively on their self-esteem, confidence and self-image as learners of mathematics.

Equivalence

Equivalence is an extremely important kind of relationship that affects mathematical thinking and communicating powerfully. For instance, anyone not realizing that there is an equivalence between common fractions, decimal fractions, percentages, proportions and ratios will find learning these different ways of communicating about the same things very hard to comprehend. Being able to use '$\frac{1}{4}$' and '0·25' and '25%' and '1:4' as equivalent expressions, however, establishes very important connections between what look superficially like completely different things.

It is always useful to remember that equivalent means 'looks different, but is worth the same'. The conventional mathematical symbol for an equivalence relationship is '=', as used in the expression '$\frac{1}{4}$ = 25%'.

Children learning to think and communicate mathematically will find their way forward effectively blocked if they cannot treat several important mathematical objects and actions as equivalent. Probably one of the hardest things for children to distinguish in learning any new way of communicating is 'which things that seem different are actually equivalent, and which things that seem different really are different?' For instance, it will help children enormously to establish both that:

$$2 + 5 = 5 + 2$$

and that:

$$17 \neq 71$$

Similarly, children will be effectively blocked if they cannot use the expressions 'two tens' and 'twenty' as equivalent (see column value and quantity value on page 26), or if they mistakenly use '5 – 2' and '2 – 5' as if they were the same expression. Sorting out what is equivalent, and what is not, is crucial to all progress.

Teachers need to be very alert to situations in which it is important for children to establish an equivalence. The physical (weight) equivalence between combinations of Numicon Shapes, or between combinations of number rods, allows us in practice to use a common balance to illustrate how various arithmetic actions are equivalent to something else. In this way we can introduce, e.g. the fact that:

$$3 + 4 = 7$$

by showing physically and visually how '3' and '4' together balance (or are equivalent to) '7' and so on.

Later on, even children who find learning to do mathematics very difficult will find themselves in an everyday world in which ratios are important relationships, and in this they will find it just as important as anyone else to recognize equivalences as well. Not just that '$\frac{1}{2}$' is equivalent to '$\frac{2}{4}$' and '$\frac{3}{6}$' and so on, but that common fractions, decimals, percentages and proportions are all equivalent ways of communicating about ratios.

Introducing some language of common fractions within a broader approach to 'multiplicative thinking' (that includes multiplying and dividing as well) will take children further into common, and important, everyday ways of communicating about ratio relationships.

Adding

Adding has two aspects: amounts being added together, and instances of 'something *more* being added' (that is, an increase). Generally, in introducing children to adding, we need to introduce both aspects using appropriate language. Two key words are 'together' and 'more'. Adding up prices while shopping is adding 'together', while discussing how much a child has grown involves 'more'. It is important always to work with both aspects, and to constantly relate children's work with imagery and materials to real-world situations.

Children with difficulties learning mathematics may find it difficult to master different language (and actions) simultaneously when quite subtle differences of meaning and context both result in 'adding'. For these children it may be necessary to teach the meaning of 'together' (with associated actions of combining) and, when this has been mastered, to teach the meaning of 'more' (with associated actions of adding more objects to a collection).

It is usually necessary to introduce the language of adding while handling actual amounts within practical contexts, and later as children become used to describing such amounts with numbers, move to the adding of numbers themselves (that is, pure calculating) using the language of adding that has by now been developed practically.

Subtracting

Subtracting is appropriate in four different types of situation, which is one of the reasons why many children find understanding (and doing) subtracting much more difficult than adding. First there are 'take away' situations in which there is loss of some kind (e.g. when biscuits are eaten, or items are given away). The second type of situation is 'decrease', in which something is less (e.g. when the cost of an item is reduced in a sale). The third is 'difference', where

there is a difference between amounts to be judged (e.g. in finding the difference in the heights of two children). Fourthly we have 'add on' situations, in which subtracting is used to check how far away some target is (e.g. how long it is to lunch time, or in counting out change to a customer in a shop).

All four situations need to be experienced and described by children, using language appropriate in each context. Also, because some children with difficulties in learning mathematics may find it difficult to master different language (and actions) with similar or equivalent results simultaneously, it may be helpful to introduce each context – with its appropriate language – separately, and allow children gradually to connect all these various experiences together under the umbrella term 'subtracting'.

It is usually necessary to introduce the language of subtracting while handling actual amounts within practical contexts, and later as children become used to describing such amounts with numbers, move to the subtracting of numbers themselves (that is, calculating) using the language of subtracting that has by now been developed practically.

The inverse relationship between adding and subtracting

As children become more competent at both adding and subtracting it is usually possible to relate these operations to each other as an example of 'doing' and 'undoing'. We can

'undo' some adding by subtracting, and similarly we can 'undo' some subtracting by adding. Eventually, some children can be encouraged to use this relationship as a device to check for themselves whether a calculation has been done correctly.

There is also an important connection between adding and subtracting facts that, strangely enough, also connects with work on fractions; it involves children's appreciation of 'part–whole' relationships. These relationships turn out to be very important to the understanding and confident recall of number facts.

There is some evidence that, as many children do more and more adding and subtracting, they gradually begin to associate numbers together in threes, for example 7, 4 and 3, or 9, 5 and 4. These 'triads' (as they are sometimes called) very efficiently connect numbers together in 'part–whole' relationships, for example '7' functions as a 'whole' of which '3' and '4' are complementary parts (as are 5 and 2). The value of these associations is that they make remembering number facts and their inverses much, much easier; for instance associating 9, 5 and 4 together in this way helps recall of:

$$5 + 4 = 9$$
$$4 + 5 = 9$$
$$9 - 5 = 4$$
$$9 - 4 = 5$$

Part–whole relationships are again important as children begin to work on fractions.

Multiplicative thinking: multiplying, dividing and fractions

In everyday life – and in basic mathematics – relationships between amounts are generally handled in two quite different ways: additively and multiplicatively. Almost everyone, including children with particular difficulties in learning mathematics, finds multiplicative thinking much harder to engage with, and succeed in, than additive thinking. For all children however, the progression to multiplicative thinking is crucial if they are to be able to function relatively independently in everyday life.

Essentially, additive thinking is about relations of 'more' and 'less' (or 'fewer') between amounts, whereas multiplicative thinking is about relationships of scale and ratio between amounts, or by how many 'times' one amount is bigger (or smaller) than another. As an illustration, it can be helpful to imagine two different ways of comparing two number rods with each other. A dark green rod (often valued as '6') is the length of a pink rod (valued as '4') *more* than the length of a red rod (valued as '2'); we could write this additive relationship as '2 + 4 = 6'. Alternatively, we can say that a dark green rod is *three times* as long as a red rod, and write this kind of multiplicative relationship as '6 = 3 × 2'.

The Breaking Barriers activities concentrate on early introductions to multiplying, dividing and fractions as these are children's first steps towards developing their multiplicative thinking.

Throughout this introductory work on multiplicative thinking, children's focus should be on *actions* with amounts, Numicon Shapes, number rods and imagery, and on the accompanying appropriate language; formal symbolism is much less important at this introductory stage than are actions and language involving realistic amounts.

Multiplying

The key word for children to focus upon when introducing multiplying is 'times', and children's key experience – within as many contexts as possible – is that of repetition. The key *idea* we want them to work towards eventually is that of 'scale' or 'ratio', but scales (ratios) are always described as one amount being a number of *times* bigger (or smaller) than another. In these early activities we focus initially upon the experience of something being repeated time and time again, in a range of contexts, as the essential introductory work.

Dividing

In order to connect work on dividing with work on multiplying from the beginning, a key experience for children is working out 'how many *times*' one amount 'goes into' another. This is a kind of 'inverse' multiplication, and indeed multiplying and dividing have an inverse relationship to each other, that is, we can 'undo' some multiplying by dividing, and *vice versa*.

Later on, children will connect the experience of 'sharing' with dividing, and this can be introduced in a context such as sharing a number of sweets – if the sharer can 'go round' each person in the group (that is, those receiving sweets) three *times* then everyone will each have three sweets, and the whole collection will have been divided (shared) between however many people are in the group.

Fractions

The word 'fraction' comes from the same root as the word 'fracture', and both words are used in connection with breaking (up) something that is whole. Consequently, we approach the introduction of fractions first with work on the experience of everyday 'wholes' as a preparation for then discussing what 'part of a whole' might mean.

Part–whole relations are now discussed again with children (see 'The inverse relationship between adding and subtracting', on page 28), only this time with a view to exploring different kinds of part–whole relations. This investigating leads to a focus upon *equal* parts of a whole, which introduces this key idea underlying fractions.

Later on, children will be able gradually to connect work with fractions with dividing, and dividing with multiplying, thus beginning to put together the various aspects of 'multiplicative thinking' they have been introduced to.

As with adding and subtracting, it is necessary to introduce the language of multiplying, dividing and fractions while handling actual amounts within practical contexts, and only later, as children become used to describing amounts with numbers and fraction notation, move to the multiplying and dividing of numbers themselves and to using the language of fractions with symbols.

Barriers to joining in with mathematics

Difficulties with numerosity – understanding 'how many'

There is some evidence that human beings generally, and many animals, are born with a capacity to notice a difference between sets of one, or two, or three objects (see, e.g. Dehaene, 2011). This is a very minimal perceptual capability that may play a role in helping children begin to know what we are talking about when we speak of the 'number of' objects in very small collections. However, the crucial thing to remember is that it is our communicating with children about numbers that will develop their capacity to communicate and think about the sizes of collections, and more precisely about 'numbers of things', in the ways that we do today. The use of words such as 'two' and 'pair' are very useful if we are to discuss and share our individual perceptions of 'two' objects with each other.

Extremely rarely, a child may have a developmental neural incapacity (or injury) that affects this very primitive perceptual function, but such a disability could be readily diagnosed since this specific capacity is detectable both in animals and in infants only a few days old. It is safe to assume that children finding number work difficult do not lack this capacity, unless it has been specifically diagnosed; a child lacking such a basic capacity would be unlikely to be able to make sense of anything at all to do with numbers, and such children are extremely rare.

Children's early difficulties with 'numerosity' are much more likely to be due to the fact that, initially, children are introduced to counting procedures before they have any idea of what counting achieves, that is, at the time they begin learning to count they do not know that following our counting procedures correctly allows us to describe 'how many' objects there are in a collection, or put another way, the collection's 'numerosity'.

Even for typically developing children it takes a surprisingly long time, perhaps three or four years into primary school (see Nunes and Bryant, 2009), before they connect their growing understanding of quantities with their counting activity.

So children learn how to count, long before they learn what counting does. Children of any ability can learn that when they are asked, 'How many?' in relation to a collection of objects, they are being invited to count things. They may even then know *how* to count the objects correctly and emphasize the last number word they use, yet they still may not realize what this has achieved. When children at such a stage are asked, 'So, how many are there?' after counting a collection, they are likely simply to go through the same counting procedure again, apparently not realizing that the last number word they used is the answer to the question.

Children who have additional difficulties in mastering and coordinating the complex physical and verbal procedures of simply how to count, are likely to take a great deal longer than other children before they are able to connect what they know about quantities (and their relationships) with the elaborate rituals of counting procedures, and then begin to learn what counting achieves.

So until any child learns what counting does, they are trying to learn quite complex rituals that they cannot see the point of. This would be extremely difficult for anyone, let alone for those with additional educational needs. We try children's

patience considerably every day that we ask them to learn to count while they have no idea why. This unavoidable difficulty for them should be clearly understood by teachers, and children's long trials at this stage well rewarded and respected.

Importantly, using Numicon Shapes helps children of all ages to talk about both quantities and collections using words such as 'bigger', 'smaller', 'more' and 'less' (or fewer) and to discuss 'how many' without counting.

Because almost all human beings, including the vast majority of children with additional educational needs, are relatively good at organizing what they see perceptually, the system of patterns used in Numicon Shapes allows almost all children to talk about and compare 'how many' by relating patterns to each other, rather than being distracted by lengthy, laborious and obscure counting procedures that on many occasions are so laborious they make children forget why they began counting in the first place.

Of course learning how to count is an essential activity for children, and it is the combination of developing counting procedures with discussions and comparisons of Numicon visual patterns that allows children a richer (and organized) visual support system for their communicating and thinking about 'numbers of things'.

In practice, it is often difficult to stop children spontaneously counting the holes in Numicon Shapes. 'Counting the holes' provides an important connection between children's developing counting proficiency and their discussion and comparisons of Numicon visual patterns. Through such integrated activities, children begin to work out for themselves two key ways of answering the question 'how many?' One is by counting, the other is by 'seeing (and naming) a pattern'. In these two connected ways children are gradually helped to communicate, and to think, about the 'numerosity' of collections.

Difficulties using words – grammar and sense making

We use words continuously as we do mathematics, both as we think mathematically, that is, communicate with ourselves, and as we work mathematically with others. Consequently, any child who has difficulty using language more generally will face significant further difficulties when learning to do mathematics.

Some words in particular are both crucial in early number work and also notoriously difficult for many children with more general language difficulties. We talk about and compare the cardinal values of whole numbers in terms of, e.g. their 'size' yet sometimes in terms of their 'height'; we say some numbers are 'bigger' than others, and at other times we may speak of 'higher' numbers.

This can be especially confusing when you realize that in English we use the same word 'number' to refer to both abstract number ideas and to written numerals. Which is the biggest 'number' in the sequence below, would you say?

$$1\ 2\ 3\ 4\ \mathbf{5}\ 6\ 7$$

It is thus very important for teachers to be conscious of what children are actually looking at and physically holding when using number words (and/or numerals) during discussions about number ideas. This is why regular use of Numicon Shapes, number rods and number lines helps to illustrate our mathematical thinking and communicating about numbers. Children can't see 'ideas', but they can see physical patterns and the lengths of rods and distances along a number line; they can also touch and feel Numicon Shapes and number rods and take physical steps along a number line. Generally speaking, numerals by themselves don't help children see many number relationships at all.

Alternative or augmentative communication systems, such as Makaton® which use signs and symbols alongside speech, can also be very helpful with children who have specific SLCN, and/or physical and sensory needs, as well as with children who have wider cognitive difficulties. Numicon Shapes, number lines and number rods, combined with signs, symbols and spoken words, can offer powerful communicative options for children with more severe learning difficulties.

It is important to remember also that we do something very odd for children when we switch from using number words as adjectives (as in 'three people', 'two cats', and so on) to using those same words as nouns as in 'three and five make eight' (see section on Not-counting in Key mathematical ideas, page 24). When we begin using number words as nouns, we start talking about 'numbers' as if they are real things and we talk about comparing and connecting them

with each other actually as if they were physical objects, e.g. we say such things as 'ten' is 'bigger' than 'six'.

The active use of physical objects and imagery is what supports children's verbal use of key words in their communicating and thinking about 'numbers' as if they were objects. In particular, the use of nouns, adjectives, comparatives and superlatives as 'numbers' are compared and connected and can be reflected physically in relationships between the physical objects children are handling as they (and we) speak. Thus 'number' relationships can begin to make a physical sense to children whose language difficulties continually create significant barriers to their learning.

Big (bigger, biggest), small (smaller, smallest), more (most), few (fewer), less (least), before, after, next, and so on are all crucial words in our discussions and thinking about numbers and their relationships, and we aim to make these descriptions and relationships visibly and kinaesthetically tangible. For instance, by using Numicon Shapes, number rods and so on we can help children to see and feel the 'successor relation' (see Order and direction in Key mathematical ideas, page 22) as they discuss statements such as 'the number after six is one bigger than six' and 'as we count forwards along the number line the numbers get bigger'.

Since context is crucial to the effective use of any words, the physical Numicon Shapes, number rods, number lines and so on that we use in a teaching situation can offer a clear, locally shared context in which to learn to use key words in discussions of numbers and their relationships.

In particular, many words that are crucial in number work are relative terms (because we are always relating numbers to each other). Children with language difficulties often find these words more difficult to use than absolute terms. For instance, the word 'banana', an absolute term, always refers to a yellow, sometimes squishy, long, slightly bent fruit, whether the banana is in a fruit basket or on a supermarket shelf. However, the words 'big', 'bigger', 'biggest', 'small', 'smaller', 'more', 'more than', 'less', 'after', and so on all depend very much upon given contexts for their varying interpretations.

It pays always to make contexts clear to children: '10' is the 'biggest' number if our context is the numbers 1 to 10, but not in the context of numbers to 100 (in which case it is quite 'small'); '10' is always 'bigger' than '5' however. A '10 year old' is a 'big' person if you're '5', which might make us think of '10' as a 'big' number in relation to age; similarly, '10' is a 'big' number of goals to score in a soccer match.

Children with language, hearing, attention and concentration difficulties also often find it difficult to distinguish between similar sounding words that are used in quite subtly different ways. The common stem and different suffixes involved in the use of 'big', 'bigger' and 'biggest' therefore need to be used in shared contexts that are both clear and systematically varied. Both mathematical and everyday contexts are essential.

It is also often problematic for many children that even the root forms of adjectives, e.g. the words 'big' and 'small', are relative; a 'big' pencil is much 'smaller' than a 'small' car. Context influences the use of even such basic relative words profoundly, and needs careful and explicit attention when working with children for whom language is already

unusually difficult. In fact, for some children who have language difficulties, even using pairs of opposites may be confusing. It is sometimes simpler for a child to learn the use of one word, e.g. 'big' in contrast to 'not big', and then to learn its opposite, that is, 'small' in contrast to 'not small', as separate exercises before trying to use both words within the same context.

The word 'more' is sometimes used instead of 'bigger' when comparing numbers, e.g. '6 is 2 more than 4', or sometimes just '6 is more than 4'. This latter expression could suggest that the speaker is thinking of collections of objects rather than abstract 'numbers'. In fact, such word use can usually be taken as a signal that the speaker has not yet progressed to thinking of 'numbers' as objects, as opposed to thinking of numbers of objects (see Sfard, 2008).

The expression '6 is 2 more than 4' can be nicely linked either to sequences of Numicon Shapes or of number rods or to a number line, in which cases it can be made more explicit either by pointing to holes (or steps) in the relevant three Shapes or rods, or by moving hops along a line and saying '6 is 2 more steps further than 4'. Of course there are problems relating use of the word 'more' in school mathematics lessons to its more common uses at home; in school, children are usually expected to use 'less' (or 'fewer') as the opposite of 'more', yet at home the opposite of 'more' is usually 'no more'. The expression, 'He's got more than me' usually signals another kind of problem entirely.

In relation to number lines and sequences such as Numicon Shapes or number rods in order, it may be that the expression '6 comes after 5' will be used to relate two numbers. Notice that the very important idea of direction in relation to numbers is being used in such expressions. This ties in closely with an essential fact about whole numbers, that they are ordered (see Order and direction in Key mathematical ideas, page 22). Notions of 'order' and 'sequence' (and hence 'direction') are tied in closely to the

ways we speak about time (since time has a 'direction') and so our uses of the words 'before' and 'after' may be sometimes confusingly connected by children with other home-based expressions such as, 'You can go out after lunch' and 'You can do that before bedtime'. Discussion of a 'time-line' with children may help.

Overall, the key to using words successfully in number work with children is to make sure that key words and their uses are fully illustrated physically and visually, within clearly identified contexts and consistent use of key words and terms. It is visual and kinaesthetic experience alongside verbal efforts that will make children's mathematical communicating, and hence their mathematical thinking, progress.

Difficulties using words – hearing, speaking and sense making

Many children with speech and language difficulties have problems distinguishing sounds that make key differences to the identities of words, e.g. distinguishing between and saying the words 'fourteen' and 'forty'. Of course many young children confuse the sound-endings of words for 'teen' numbers with those for tens numbers and then quickly learn the difference, but for children with various kinds of speech and language difficulty the confusions may often be more varied and more numerous, and also less easily correctable. Some children also have difficulties with sound structures (or the phonology of a language), which will mean that significant suffixes, e.g. '-er' and '-est', are insufficiently distinguished or recognized.

Children with such difficulties not only have trouble picking out how significantly different words are used but they will also have trouble remembering their differences. This will result in children developing what are sometimes called 'fuzzy' conceptions of terms used critically in mathematics, such as comparatives, superlatives and number names. There are important connections between what we hear and consequently what we say, and then consequently again, what we say to ourselves as we think. Speech and hearing difficulties considerably affect how we are able to develop our thinking.

It may be impossible for some children to be precise enough about sound differences between e.g. the words, 'big', 'bigger' and 'biggest' which will make it extremely difficult for them to critically pick out the different uses of these words.

The numbers we call 'four', 'five' and 'six' are situated quite closely together along a number line. Their names are each expressed as one syllable and all begin with quite similar unvoiced fricative sounds /f/ or /s/ when pronounced. Additionally, 'five' and 'six' both end with the fricatives /v/ and /s/. Children with speech and hearing difficulties will often struggle to distinguish between, and therefore remember, these names.

As noted above, if children are literally unable to distinguish between 'teen' number word endings and tens number word endings, e.g. between 'fifteen' and 'fifty', many verbal conversations will make no sense at all to them, especially if there is much counting on and back expected in a classroom. How can some numbers appear twice in our number sequence? And why, where they do?

The importance of visual and kinaesthetic communicative support for children with general speech and language difficulties cannot be overestimated. Children at risk of developing 'fuzzy' conceptions of numbers and their relationships need lots of visual and tactile opportunities to support their communicating and thinking about these things.

Whilst a child with language difficulties may easily confuse 'four', 'five' and 'six' because, to them, they sound very similar, Numicon Shapes and number rods relating to these numbers are visually and kinaesthetically quite different. Similarly, when Numicon Shapes or number rods are arranged to represent, e.g. the numbers 'four', 'fourteen' and 'forty' children are able to see that there are clear and important differences in the structures of these numbers, even though the phonological difference between their number names seems to them minimal.

Once again, alternative or augmentative communication systems, such as Makaton®, which use signs and symbols alongside speech, can also be a very helpful addition to visual and kinaesthetic support when communicating with children who have specific SLCN and/or physical and sensory needs.

Difficulties with attention control and listening

Learning to do mathematics, as with any other area of learning, necessarily involves children being able to focus and attend to salient aspects of a situation or activity for productive periods of time, and also upon them being able to 'hear' and read any communicating from others that is relevant. Being able to focus their attention effectively, and to listen and look carefully, are essential to children's productive engagement in mathematical activity with experts and others.

There is some evidence that a child's achievement of attention control and listening ability typically follows a series of developmental stages, but of course there are many reasons why any particular child does not develop in a typical way. Many children struggling with mathematics may not be able to listen carefully enough or to control their attention adequately.

Typical developmental stages are often based upon those identified in Cooper, Moodley and Reynell (1978), and these are often adapted for use by local authorities.[2] They are interpreted as follows:

- Level 1 (0–1 Year): Extreme distractibility. Attention easily shifts from one object, person or event to another. Any new event, such as someone walking by, will immediately distract. Attention is involuntary and 'captured' by stimuli.

- Level 2 (1–2 Years): Single-channelled attention. Can concentrate on a concrete task of their own choosing. Cannot tolerate (ignores) verbal or visual intervention from an adult. May appear obstinate or wilful, but in fact needs to ignore extraneous stimuli in order to concentrate on the task in hand. Attention still involuntary.

- Level 3 (2–3 Years): Still single-channelled. Cannot attend to competing auditory and visual stimuli from different sources, e.g. listening to an adult's direction while playing. But, with an adult's help, can shift full attention to the speaker, and then back to the play.

- Level 4 (3–4 Years): Still alternates full attention between speaker and task in hand. Now does this spontaneously, without the adult needing explicitly to focus and re-focus that attention.

- Level 5 (4–5 Years): Attention is now two-channelled. The child understands verbal instructions related to a task without interrupting the activity to look at the speaker. Concentration span may still be short, but group instruction is possible. Moving from broad to selective pickup of information. Able to focus on a single aspect of a complex situation.

- Level 6 (5–6 Years): The final stage. Auditory, visual and manipulatory channels are fully integrated. Attention is well established and maintained. Gradually able to shut out unwanted, irrelevant information and concentrate only on essential aspects of a task.

Many children experiencing difficulty learning mathematics may be at an earlier stage of attention control and listening development than their chronological age would indicate. They may therefore find it very difficult to sustain attention to a particular task and to listen to a peer or adult at the same time.

Children who have attention and listening difficulties also often find tasks that involve looking and doing easier than those that require continual focused listening, e.g. a pure conversation. The teaching approach we advocate with Numicon materials emphasizes learning through action and learning by seeing and encourages great attention to 'doing'.

2   See, e.g. the following advice from Nottinghamshire Inclusion Support Service at http://www.nottinghamcity.gov.uk/esn/index.aspx?articleid=19500

Importantly, while directing their own activity with physical materials children have continual opportunities to self-correct, which encourages a sense of personal autonomy as well as significantly reducing a need for extraneous and often distracting intervention from others.

Since children are learning to join in with mathematics that others already know how to do, however, there must of necessity be communication with teachers, or peers, as work and activity develop. Those children whose attention level is single-channelled will not be able to engage in a particular task while at the same time listening to verbal contributions from others. Therefore when verbal communicating seems necessary, you may need to ask children to stop and put all materials down before making any visual, verbal, or active contributions of your own. Once you have made your contribution, children can then return to their own action with the materials.

Memory difficulties

What we tend to think of as 'memory' in our daily lives is actually long-term memory.

Memory can be thought of, in simple terms, as a three-stage process: sensory memory (the information we take in through our senses), short-term memory (including working memory) and long-term memory (Atkinson and Shiffrin, 1968). In order for successful learning to take place, information has to move from the sensory or the short-term memory to the long-term memory. This can be a complex process for many children. It can be helpful to consider children's various memory difficulties in school using these three broad categories.

Sensory memory is a very brief recall of a sensory experience, such as what has just been seen or heard. Our short-term memory capability, sometimes described as a combination of 'auditory-verbal working memory' and 'visuospatial-sketchpad working memory', relates to our thinking about immediate tasks. Our long-term memory can be separated into 'semantic', 'visual-spatial', 'procedural (motor)' and 'episodic' memories and relates to our storage and recall of various types of information over longer periods.[3] We are not always consciously aware of what is stored in our long-term memory, but memories here can be called upon by the working memory and used when needed.

The term 'working memory' describes the temporary ability we have to hold and manipulate information in our mind. Working memory is crucial for many elements of mathematics and consists of four strands: phonological loop, visuospatial-sketchpad, central executive and episodic buffer (see Baddeley's revised Working Memory Model cited in Henry 2011).

- The phonological loop is the part of working memory that deals with spoken and written material. It can be used to hold speech for a short period of time and to remember, e.g. a phone number. It consists of two parts:
  - Phonological store: linked to speech perception. This holds information in spoken words for 1–2 seconds.
  - Articulatory control process: linked to the production of speech. This is used to rehearse and then store verbal information from the phonological store (our 'inner voice').

- Visuospatial-sketchpad (VSS): holds and processes visual and spatial (and possibly kinaesthetic) information for short periods of time. The VSS is used for tasks such as navigation.

- Central executive: drives the whole system. It controls all the elements of working memory by focusing and switching attention flexibly between the different elements, as and when necessary. It also deals with cognitive tasks such as mental arithmetic and problem solving (see below).

- Episodic buffer: the newest addition to Baddeley's model of working memory (1974) which was revised in 2000. The episodic buffer makes sense of new experiences by communicating with the long-term memory and linking current experiences to long-term knowledge, thus combining information into a coherent whole. The episodic buffer also acts as a 'back up' and transfer store because it works as a link between short- and long-term memory.

Working memory is often thought of as a 'workspace' that we can use to store important information in the course of our mental activities. For instance, mental arithmetic is a day-to-day activity that requires the use of working memory. Here we are required to hold information (usually numbers that may have been given to us orally) in our mind, recall any associated known facts, hold these temporarily, select calculation methods and then perform the calculation without the use of pen and paper. With a weak working memory we would not be able to carry out this kind of complex mental activity successfully (Gathercole and Alloway, 2007).

Working memory capabilities can vary vastly from person to person. For instance, in a typical class of 7–8 year olds, three could be expected to have working memory capabilities of an average 4 year old and a further three would have working memory capabilities in line with 11 year olds. Children with poor working memory do not catch up with their peers. However, their working memory is able to

---

3 Greater detail on 'working memory' can be found in Henry (2011), http://www.sagepub.com/upm-data/42874_Henry.pdf

increase with age, but at a slower rate than their typically developing peers (Gathercole and Alloway, 2007).

The teaching of early mathematics can too often rely heavily upon the use of verbal explanations and rote verbal counting, which do not play to the usual strengths of young children or struggling mathematicians. Older children who experience difficulties with mathematics are often in a context which relies heavily on auditory-verbal and semantic memory. Approaches that are predominantly verbal in nature can be very demanding for children with language and/ or learning difficulties due to potential weaknesses in these memories. This, coupled with an absence of structured visual and kinaesthetic support, often poses problems for many children as they struggle to make sense of the information presented to them.

Many children with language and/or learning difficulties have relatively stronger visuospatial-sketchpad and procedural (motor) memory capabilities (which address shape, space and actions) than auditory-verbal and semantic memory capabilities (which address mostly sound sequences, word uses and helps us to categorize and group memories). It therefore follows that any learning experience supported by visual and kinaesthetic activities will be more accessible. It is often easier for a child with working memory difficulties to hold structured imagery or kinaesthetic experiences in their visuospatial-sketchpad memories than it is for them to hold the sounds of number names in their auditory-verbal working memories.

Numicon Shapes, number rods and number lines, which offer clear visual structured representations of abstract number objects, allow children to use their visuospatial-sketchpad working memory and their visual-spatial long-term memory to help them process and remember the names and relative magnitudes of numbers and later, addition and subtraction number relationships as well.

Because of this, children are more likely to transfer the information to their long-term memory and be able to successfully retrieve and use this at a later point. Consequently, many children who may have experienced difficulty remembering, e.g. the names, order and cardinal sizes of numbers, and addition and subtraction facts to ten will find that using the Numicon approach makes this much easier.

Visualizing and verbalizing are key to successful use of working memory; this is supported by Numicon when children actively engage in mathematics, using the Numicon resources, and have mathematical conversations. Visualizing should be encouraged throughout children's early exposure to Numicon as this is a key aspect of developing understanding and recall of ideas, particularly with children who experience language and/or learning difficulties. Good practice suggests that language and subject-specific vocabulary is modelled and taught in a structured way; similarly, visualizing may need to be specifically taught. For instance, activities that involve children 'feeling' in the bag for the correct shape will help develop mental imagery. After lots of exposure and opportunities for overlearning, this can be recalled visually at a later stage of development to support mental arithmetic problems.

Difficulties with sequencing

Knowing the order of numbers and the important 'successor relation' between them is of critical importance to children's progress (see 'Order and direction', page 22). However many children with special educational needs and disabilities may have wider difficulties with sequencing that will make it difficult for them to learn even these basic features of whole numbers.

Whilst some children's difficulties with sequencing are often apparent in their use of temporal language (such as misuse of the words 'before' and 'after' in relation to daily activities), their difficulties with sequencing and organization may affect more aspects than temporal language alone, and thus affect their work with mathematical sequences. For instance, if you are not sure what the sequence of your day is, let alone how this sequence is described with temporal words, then learning that '6 comes after 5' may also be challenging.

It is necessary to know the normal sequence of a day's activities, e.g. the relative order of the register, the maths lesson, playtime, snack time, the literacy lesson, lunch time, and so on, in order to be able to map language such as 'we'll have our snack after playtime' to the sequence of the day's activities and, eventually, to learn the conventional use of the word 'after' in this context. It is probable also that learning how to use the word 'after' in sentences such as 'we're having our snack after break' will be related to the different use of 'after' in statements such as '6 is the number that comes after 5' on the number line. In both cases though, a sense of direction is critical.

The visual and kinaesthetic structures of Numicon Shapes, number rods and graduated number lines, showing step-like size increases when placed in order, allow children to see and feel the relative positions of our numbers in sequence and the important 'successor relation'. Instead of a number sequence seeming to be an arbitrary series of sounds (number names) or symbols (numerals), a 'physical logic' for each number's place in the number sequence can be 'seen' and also felt.

With Numicon Shapes, number rods and number line imagery, 'five' is visually and kinaesthetically one more/bigger than 'four' and one fewer/smaller than 'six'. The order of 'four', 'five' and 'six' is illustrated through the relative sizes of the corresponding Numicon Shapes and number rods, and by the numbers of steps along a number line from zero. Both seeing and manipulating Numicon Shapes and number rods into conventional and physical size order help children to develop an understanding of key relationships between abstract numbers and number sequences which are essential both to successful counting and to later calculation.

Difficulties with motoric aspects of counting

For many children, learning the temporal use of words such as 'before' and 'after' is built upon experience and understanding of gross and fine motor (that is, action) sequences such as moving left to right along repeating patterns, and following visual sequences such as visual patterns and pictorial/symbolic visual timetables for a day/week. Crucially, these action experiences all involve pursuing a consistent direction of movement, a kinaesthetic and visual experience of what it means to 'move in a constant direction'.

Therefore for any children who have difficulties in performing the fine, gross and oral movements in time and space that are necessary for motor execution of sequences such as counting objects in order, any associated difficulties with cognitive aspects of sequencing are compounded.

For instance, it is impossible to count a set of objects reliably if you do not have a secure memory of the conventional sequence (order) of numbers. This difficulty is compounded if you also find it difficult to coordinate and synchronize the fine motor skills needed to move your finger from one object to the 'next', with the oral motor skills needed to actually say the numbers in the count (even if only to yourself).

Wherever possible, it helps when children are encouraged to connect their counting activity with number lines so that they can connect the 'size' of the count to the position of the last number in the count on the number line (see Difficulties with numerosity, page 31). However, it is important to remember also that the fine motor skills required to count sets of small objects and to use small number lines is a refinement of gross motor counting. Children with fine motor difficulties need to count using larger motor movements before they learn to localize the motoric aspect of counting in a fine motor count.

A major advantage of a number line, including those with Numicon Shapes and/or number rods marked along them appropriately, is that the 'unit' space, that is, the distance between successive whole numbers, can be consistently varied, practically without limit, in order to permit the use of gross motor skills while counting on and back. Similarly, when counting simple objects, the sizes of the objects, and of the spaces between them, may be varied as necessary in relation to the kinds of motor skills available. Some children may even have to move their whole bodies along a line, while counting.

Attitudes to doing mathematics (anxiety and passivity)

Children's attitudes to doing mathematics, which may result from within-child factors, social, emotional and mental health factors and/or previous experience of teaching and learning mathematics in school, have a significant impact on their progress.

To prevent anxiety developing around doing mathematics, which happily may be less common in younger children than in older children, early intervention in the form of empathic teaching is recommended. The activities we include here will hopefully benefit older children who may already be experiencing anxiety around doing mathematics; most 'maths anxiety' develops not just from being 'wrong' frequently, but from sheer incomprehension about how and why we are wrong.

The use of visual and kinaesthetic experience offers children the opportunity to literally 'get their hands on' these strange abstract things we call 'numbers', move them around physically, and gradually experience increasing control over their properties and relationships.

Even so, whilst developing success in doing mathematics (which these activities aim to facilitate) will obviously be a key factor in overcoming anxiety, some children may yet need sustained additional emotional support as they work, in order to address more deeply ingrained anxiety and to promote a more productive and relaxed engagement with mathematical activities.

Passivity in any learning situation is a great concern, since it will produce little hoped-for learning. Children who have experienced repeated failure will often seek to avoid further pain by a strategy of non-participation. Also, some children with special educational needs may have particularly passive learning styles. The opportunities offered in these activities for simple physical activity, work with patterns and helpful conversation, the chance to be active in an experimental way and also self-correcting, may entice some usually passive children into a physical engagement that will gradually lead to greater involvement more generally.

Doing mathematics in a range of contexts – including functioning in the wider world

Two key contexts – and the relationship between them

Children who find mathematics difficult for whatever reason will not be spared the mathematical demands that everyday life places upon us all. Time-keeping, buying and preparing food, managing money, and not being taken advantage of (so far as this is possible for any of us) are all essential to being able to lead a relatively independent life. The 'everyday world' is one of the contexts within which we all need to be able to do mathematics.

Many activities are practised in different contexts, but mathematics is unusual in that there are two key, and quite different, contexts in which we do mathematics. It is often very difficult for children to connect, or move between them. These used to be called 'pure' mathematics and 'applied' mathematics. The distinction arises because we can either do mathematics in relation to the everyday physical and social universe in which we live (applied mathematics) or we can do it in a world of abstractions and generalizations, just, as it were, 'on paper' and 'in our heads' (pure mathematics).

The context of pure mathematics is a world of relationships between abstract objects, e.g. '3 + 6 = 9', or 'two odd numbers added together will produce an even number'. This abstract world is often felt to be the most difficult world in which to do mathematics, for most people.

The context of applied mathematics is the everyday physical and social world in which we live. This is a world of relationships between physical objects and distances, weights, times, economies, opinion polls and measures of many kinds.

The key connection between these two quite different worlds is that of generalizing; we generalize about the relationships of our everyday world, and then build them as generalizations into our 'pure' world. The abstract world of

pure mathematics is a world populated with generalizations and concerned solely with relationships between them, e.g. '3 + 6 = 9', 'two 2s are 4'.

Most people find they don't want to live in a world of pure abstractions, and many prefer to 'keep their feet on the ground' and 'know where they are'. This means staying within a world of measures, and of people, and of physical objects we can actually touch and feel. Why would anyone want to spend their time in a world of abstractions?

The trouble is, uncomfortable though it may often be, spending a little time in the pure world of abstractions and generalizations can make life in our everyday world much, much easier. We can use the abstractions of our pure world and apply them to new situations in our everyday world.

For instance, it would be very time consuming in our everyday world if, struggling to make some curtains for a new dining room, we had to physically count up armfuls of cloth in order to discover that 3 metres of material for the front window, with another 6 metres for the rear doors would together come to 9 metres that we needed to buy altogether. Suppose that we also then needed to carefully count up individual people in order to discover that if we invite those 6 neighbours from one side to dinner, and the 3 neighbours from the other side too, we would need to plan for 9 visitors altogether to dine and admire our new curtains.

Life is easier if we have previously made the two generalizations that actually '3 of anything' and '6 of anything' will always give you '9 of whatever they are' (which is what the number sentence '3 + 6 = 9' actually means) and also that 'It doesn't matter which way around you add two numbers, their total will always be the same' (so, 3 + 6 = 6 + 3 = 9). No laborious counting up of individual metres of cloth, and then of numbers of individual people, would be required at all.

In our pure mathematical world we deal with relationships between numbers of things in general, and we can then use these generalizations when they apply to particular situations in our everyday world.

It is surprising how often we use abstract numbers in our everyday lives without really thinking that we're doing 'pure mathematics'. Children are expected to learn to 'use numbers' and to 'calculate' from quite early on in their schooling, as if 'numbers' were just everyday things. But actually, 'numbers' such as '3', '6' and '9' are abstract objects from the world of pure mathematics; getting used to using them involves taking a huge step in children's thinking.

The sheer strangeness of suddenly talking about just '3' instead of being precise and specifying '3 apples' or '3 conkers' would be puzzling enough by itself to worry children. However, the fact that no one seems to talk about it, or everyone just behaves as if this transition is the most natural thing in the world, must also tend to make some children think, 'Oh well, it must be only me who's having trouble; I'd better just see if I can work out what they want me to do.' The transition from an everyday world of real things (conkers) to a world of very strange things (such as the generalization just '3') is a massive leap for every child to take. However, if a child is already struggling with the difficulties of inexplicable counting routines and a broader and continuous educational disadvantage too, it must be very easy for them to give up even trying to understand, and to just concentrate on guessing, and blind trial and error. Once a child gives up trying to understand, it is unlikely they ever will.

Yet if we take our pure generalizations a bit further and notice 'part–whole' relations between the trio of numbers 9, 6 and 3, we will find that there are a whole host of other situations in which we won't need to do any laborious counting out of physical things at all, because we will also know in advance that:

$$3 + 6 = 9$$
$$6 + 3 = 9$$
$$9 - 6 = 3$$
$$9 - 3 = 6$$

again, in relation to numbers of anything. That pure world of generalizations is very powerful, potentially saving us an enormous amount of everyday world labour.

The generalizations of our pure mathematical world turn out to be extremely useful much more widely in our everyday world as well. After spending quite a bit of time developing the world of pure mathematics (millennia, in fact), the human race has moved from notches carved into animal bones to being able to build and fly aircraft reliably to anywhere in the everyday world, supply electricity reliably to millions of homes, and to predict global weather patterns, all by using that same constructed world of abstract generalizations and their relationships.

So doing mathematics within the pure and abstract world of generalizations is never easy, and for children with many kinds of special educational needs and disabilities it is, for a great variety of reasons, exceptionally difficult. Yet without at least some capability in the world of abstractions children will grow up unable to use any of the power of those generalizations in their everyday lives. For children who are unable to enter the world of generalized 'pure numbers' at all, their chances of being able to live something approaching a normally independent kind of a life are slim indeed. We need to take each individual child just as far as they can go into the challenging, yet very useful, world of abstractions.

Moving between the everyday world and the world of abstractions

Some children, again for a variety of reasons, may never be able to make generalizations that will take them into the world of mathematical abstractions. Such children are always going to be heavily dependent upon others in managing their everyday lives. Their learning will be punishingly hard and laborious as they try to remember masses of unrelated, individual pieces of information and to learn apparently unconnected routines. It is the relationships between all the various individual things that we learn that make our learning increasingly economical; generalizations are very powerful ways of linking lots of things together into one observation.

Some children seem able to do calculations only within everyday contexts. For instance, some children who feel unable to 'do decimals' would believe that they couldn't solve:

$$7 \cdot 6 - 2 \cdot 75$$

and yet would quite successfully work out:

$$£7 \cdot 60 - £2 \cdot 75$$

Feel the difference. Maybe '7·6' and '2·75' feel like foreign objects to you, whereas '£7·60' and £2·75' feel like more familiar things that you could actually get your hands on. You might also feel you would try to calculate the answers to these two subtractions in entirely different ways. It might even be difficult to connect the two subtractions and to think of calling them 'the same thing'.

Suppose that in some curtain making, you had bought 7·6 metres of material and had already used 2 metres 75 centimetres of it. How much of it would you have left? Does that feel like the same calculation as the one with money, or the one with decimals above?

You might feel that you would always prefer to calculate with concrete objects and materials, such as pounds and pennies, and metres of cloth, rather than to generalize and to calculate with abstract 'decimals'. At a more basic level, many children will also feel that they would much rather work with actual objects they can touch, and move around, than with abstract whole 'numbers' such as '3' and '6', and '9'. Most of us resist moving off into an abstract world of generalizations.

Yet it is often easy for us as teachers who (perhaps) have forgotten that abstract numbers are initially demanding generalizations and now find working with whole numbers quite easy ourselves, to forget exactly what children working at a more basic level may be feeling about these (to us, now) 'simple' objects. However, the first generalizing towards whole numbers such as '3' and '12' and '33' is exceptionally hard. Most of us don't like to be pushed into it; most of us would rather stay with real things we can touch, and work in a familiar everyday world in which we 'know where we stand'.

Yet as noted above, because modern, everyday life will also be very hard for anyone who cannot do even the most basic of calculations with abstract whole numbers, we must try to introduce children who struggle with mathematics to at least a few of those mathematical generalizations that will be useful to them in their everyday lives.

The Breaking Barriers activities are based on everyday contexts that are essential in anyone's everyday life, and offer children physical objects and visual imagery that they can constantly 'get their hands on', and with which they may do their mathematics physically. The aim is for children to begin to make generalizations of their own as they go along and to delight themselves when they do. However, this is a fragile process and cannot be forced.

For instance, it is crucial that children practise counting with a wide range of objects so that they gradually come to generalize that counting works with anything (this is technically known as the 'abstraction principle'). It also helps a great deal if children practise counting with both familiar and unfamiliar objects, and particularly if they begin to count quantities too, e.g. cups of water or coins. This will help them realize that counting works with anything, and also to begin essential work on measures. It would also be helpful to include counting to a beat in music – useful experience as a foundation to work on measuring time. Give children the range of contexts within which they may usefully generalize.

When it comes to connecting Numicon Shape patterns with their counting, it is again important that children work with a whole variety of objects. It is essential that children are allowed to generalize, for themselves, that any objects can be arranged into Numicon Shape patterns in order to 'see' how many there are. Using a wide variety of objects also ensures that children have plenty of stimulating practice as well.

Three further things to remember as you work with children who are struggling:

(i) Progress lies in children moving from particular situations towards making their own generalizations which can then, later, be used by them. Do not introduce children directly to generalizations that someone else has already made. 'Numbers', e.g. '3', '8' and '13' and so on, are all generalizations.

(ii) Recording is the last thing to do. Any kind of written notation that is introduced to children should be used to capture activity already achieved and discussed. For instance, introduce written numerals as a way of recording some successful counting, rather than by trying to explain what they mean. This has sometimes been captured as 'do – talk – record'.

(iii) Allow children to work slowly, at the pace they can accomplish. They are trying to do something that is very hard indeed and every small step forward is a very significant achievement. Any pressure to 'work faster' is likely to be highly counter-productive and will simply add, in most cases, to an already well-developed anxiety. Patience is a virtue – yours as well as theirs.

More specifically – the key essential contexts

Because children who struggle with mathematics will not have time in their schooling to follow the whole curriculum expected of most children, we have to select a reduced set of topics for them to study while in school. We have chosen here to focus specifically upon those areas of everyday life that everyone has to function within if they are to live with a measure of independence. We think of these as time, money, length, mass and capacity.

Personal organization requires competency with time; shopping requires competency with money, mass and capacity; all travelling and home organizing require competency with length and distance; travelling by public transport requires competency with time and money; social situations, such as meeting a friend at a café, also require competency with time and money.

Personal, social, health and citizenship aspects of everyday life will require situation-specific competencies. For instance, healthy eating requires competency with mass, capacity and time; taking a temperature, going to see a doctor and taking medication all require competency with time and other measures.

By concentrating on these everyday contexts, you will be offering children an important variety of contexts from which they may have a chance to generalize to abstract numbers, and also gradually to build an important capacity to function ever more effectively within these key areas of life.

The offered activities may go further than any particular child you are teaching may be able to go, while you are working with them. If you are working with a child who can go further, try some suitable activities from the Numicon *Number, Pattern and Calculating* and *Geometry, Measurement and Statistics Teaching Resource Handbooks* 1, 2 and 3. All children who are struggling with mathematics are individuals,

even though they may be working with you in groups; just try to take each child and each group of children you work with as far as they can go within these essential areas.

Time

Competency with time is important for personal organization, e.g. being in the right place at the right time; knowing what time to get up; having with you all the things you need; for travelling, e.g. knowing what time to catch the bus; social situations, e.g. when you are meeting a friend at a café; staying healthy, e.g. making appointments with the dentist, doctor, hairdresser, and so on.

Although some degree of competency with telling the time can be achieved using a digital clock (and this might be the goal for some children), learning to tell the time with full competency involves:

- using the vocabulary of 'time' effectively, e.g. before, after, and so on

- having a 'feel' for the duration of conventional units of time (second, minute, hour)

- having a 'feel' for time in relation to music, rhythm and so on

- an ability to tell the time, that is, read a clock, use a timer

- an ability to perform calculations using time, e.g. relating cooking instructions such as 'heat for 12 minutes' to the time on a clock.

Numicon Shapes, number rods and number lines can be used to support teaching children to tell the time in the following ways:

- supporting understanding of numerals on a clock face by arranging Numicon Shapes or number rods around the perimeter

- preparing for multiplying: counting in fives and tens around the five minute divisions on a clock face, and relating these intervals to the passage of time

- developing fraction knowledge: learning to use the words 'half' and 'quarter' in relation to periods of time and telling the time

- use of timelines in parallel with number lines.

Money

Competency with money is important for many aspects of independent living, the most obvious of which is shopping. Competency is also necessary for socializing – buying cinema tickets, buying a coffee for a friend; for travelling – paying fares; and, crucially, for avoiding exploitation by knowing how much change should be received, knowing whether utility bills are correct, knowing that wages are correct, and so on. Adults who are innumerate simply have to trust the honesty of those they encounter in all situations where money transactions are involved. Full competency with money involves understanding equivalence, place value, ratios and rates, and an ability to calculate in financial contexts, particularly those involving interest.

At a basic functional level, competency with cash requires:

- an ability to recognize coins

- understanding the relative values of coins, e.g. that a 5p coin is of equivalent value to five 1p coins, that 50p is equivalent to half of £1, and so on

- an ability to calculate successfully using coins

- an ability to use money-specific language, e.g. 'change', 'How much money do you need?' (meaning 'How much cash?'), 'too much/too expensive', 'not enough' and so on.

Numicon Shapes and number rods can be used to help children develop competency with money in various ways:

- making connections between the relative values of the Numicon Shapes (or rods) and relative values of coins by affixing coins to the corresponding Numicon Shapes (or rods)

- when children are using money to shop, provide them with a small 'memory trigger card' that has pictures of coins linked to Numicon Shapes (or rods).

Measures of length, mass and capacity

The ability to measure length, mass and capacity is essential for many aspects of everyday life and is often a requirement for employment. Children need to develop a secure understanding of current standard measures and will generally need many repeated practical activities which give them opportunities to experience and gain a 'feel' for the relative sizes of these standards. A full competency with these measures would involve understanding place value (including decimal notation), equivalence, fractions, ratios, and an ability to calculate in context.

At a functional level, competency with measures requires:

- an ability to use comparative and superlative language associated with measures. In the context of length, long/er/est, short/er/est, narrow/er/est and so on; in the context of mass, heavy/ier/iest and light/er/est; in the context of capacity, full, half full, half empty, empty, and so on

- an understanding (that is, 'feel') of the value of units of mass/weight (kilograms, grams/stones, pounds, ounces), capacity (millilitres, litres/fluid ounces, pints) and length (kilometres, metres, centimetres, millimetres, miles, feet, inches)

- an ability to calculate with and in contexts of mass, length, and capacity measures.

For children who have language difficulties it is often especially useful to link current learning to previous learning. For instance, when children are being taught 'heavier' and 'lighter' a link could be made to 'bigger' and 'smaller' (e.g. 'heavier' is a 'bigger' amount of mass, and 'lighter' a 'smaller' amount). It is always important to activate prior learning at the beginning of any work, to maximize the benefit of this effect. Remind children of previous relevant learning and link all new developments to previous connected activities.

Numicon Shapes, number rods and number lines can be used to help children develop competency with length, mass, and capacity measures in various ways:

- by providing a visual analogy where relative values of different measured amounts are represented with Numicon Shapes, or number rods. For instance, in cooking activities two tablespoons of flour could be linked to the Numicon 2-shape or the 2-rod.

- the mass or capacity of amounts could be measured or compared and represented with Numicon Shapes or number rods to help explain, e.g. that the number of kilograms in 10 kg is bigger than the number of kilograms in 5 kg using the Numicon Shapes and number rod representations of 10 and 5. By analogy, we could say that 10 kg is a heavier (or a bigger) mass and also that it is 'twice as' heavy.

Teaching approaches and organization – general guidance

The Breaking Barriers activities are designed both for children who have Special Educational Needs or Disabilities (SEND) and are likely to require long-term support and for children who, perhaps through circumstance, have fallen significantly behind in their mathematics learning. Both these groups of children are likely to be working in one-to-one or small-group situations. There are no absolute rules about grouping to teach Numicon activities; research on using Numicon in short-term intervention programmes has shown a combination of one-to-one teaching and small-group work, involving two or three children, to be successful, whilst other projects where children have only worked in small groups have also been effective.

In this section you will find information on:

Including all children

The *SEND Code of Practice 2014*, the *Teachers' Standards (2011)* and OFSTED all clearly state that meeting the needs of all learners, including of course those with SEND, is first and foremost the responsibility of the class or subject teacher. It remains generally accepted that what is considered to be good practice for children with additional and complex needs is part of what should be offered through high-quality teaching and is, as such, good practice for all children.

Numicon materials are designed to be used to support high-quality teaching and learning for all children and therefore the use of Numicon in whole-class, group and individual situations should be planned for. The ethos of the classroom needs to promote and support the use of the full suite of Numicon resources and the contribution to learning that multi-sensory activities and resources provide.

Numicon Shapes and number rods can be used to support all levels of learning, including that of the most able children aged 11 and over. It is important that there is no perception within the class that Numicon is used only by children of 'lower ability' or when a learner is 'stuck'; this would potentially make the use of Numicon stigmatizing rather than being a valuable learning tool for all. If one group of children is working with Numicon to develop basic mathematical skills, whenever possible other groups of children should be using, e.g. Numicon Shapes, number rods and other tangible mathematical apparatus to activate prior learning and/or develop more complex mathematics.

These activities can be adapted for use on a computer or interactive whiteboard using the *Numicon Interactive Whiteboard Software*. This may be helpful for pupils who have difficulties with motor control and to provide variety for practice, however it is essential to maintain interaction with others through conversations and communication with children about these activities. Sometimes they may work alone but they should also at times work alongside other children or their teacher.

Wherever possible, children needing additional support should be taught with their peers; where support and intervention are needed, this should be managed and led by the class or subject teacher with any additional adults providing regular and timely feedback regarding the sessions, including progress and issues. Class and subject teachers need to be fully aware of what is happening in an intervention session and should be providing additional opportunities (when the child is in the whole class or larger group setting), to practise and use the skills, language and equipment that are being focused upon away from the main teaching sessions. (This is again a clear message from the *SEND Code of Practice 2014*, the *Teachers' Standards 2011* and OFSTED.)

Similarly, signs and symbols are not only applicable to children with learning difficulties; their use is helpful for all children being introduced to a new mathematical idea, when activating prior knowledge or for linking mathematical ideas together to support generalizing and memory retention. Also, it is important that the teaching of signs for key ideas or processes and the subsequent use of signing applies to the whole class. For children with SEND, the signing will be of immense help in pointing out the important ideas; other children will be able to focus upon the more complex vocabulary, whether or not it is signed.

Please see 'Additional guidance on teaching approaches for specific categories of Special Educational Needs and Disabilities' (page 52) for further suggestions for meeting the needs of some more specific groups of children with identified needs.

Creating a mathematics learning environment for all children

Mathematics is crucial for everyday life and underpins many aspects of our lives. However, the visual profile of mathematics and numbers in learning environments is often low; many children do not see mathematics as being relevant, which can have a potentially negative effect on their attitude to learning the subject. Therefore, in the same way that children should be immersed in a language and literacy rich environment that supports a child's reading and writing development, they need to be immersed in a visually rich mathematics environment which gives children 'opportunities to learn about numbers and how useful they are in daily life'[4] and also supports their learning of mathematics.

Most children notice and take in their surroundings, which makes much of their learning 'opportunistic'. To maximize this, consider these suggestions:

- Highlight and use numerals wherever possible, e.g. label what should be in trays, include numerals in notices to say how many children may work on the computer at one time, add to classroom signs, include in the role-play area. Use signs that incorporate numerals, pictures and words (and perhaps with Makaton® or picture communication systems).

- Ensure everyday objects are visible and attention is drawn to them in context, e.g. clocks, calendars, timetables, calculators.

- Where appropriate to the age and stage of the child's development, provide a mathematics area and/or role-play area that is interactive, contains high-quality equipment, structured and unstructured activities and includes open-ended challenges. This must maximize cross-curricular links and relate to real-life situations wherever possible. A designated mathematics area can stimulate thinking about mathematical ideas, and children can be helped to use it independently.

- Display Numicon number lines and hundred squares at an accessible height for children so that they can refer to them easily while working.

- Ensure there is a relevant display, matched to the child's learning, which includes child work, instructions, key facts and processes, equipment and is interactive in nature. This needs to be referred to often to ensure a child maximizes the opportunity to support their current learning.

- Ensure that independence is fostered in the classroom and resources are stored in easily accessible places for children to access independently.

- Ensure that the ethos of the classroom supports multi-sensory learning and the use of structured resources such as Numicon Shapes and number rods, whatever the age and stage of the children. (The children should be encouraged to keep the classroom tidy.)

- Any numerals included in the display should be in a clear font (or handwriting style) and of a size that is suitable for children with visual impairments. Similarly, care should be taken over the tonal variation between the text and the background. Children quickly accept a display as part of the classroom landscape; it is important to keep displays fresh and interesting whilst maintaining number lines as a constant feature on which children can depend.

- At the same time, be aware and wary of 'visual overload': in the same way that children who have difficulties learning mathematics can be confused through linguistic overload, they can be equally confused by visual overload. Keep displays uncluttered and well-spaced to aid processing of information.

- Some children who have SEND may rarely attend to their visual environment and they may need to be taught how to look at particular aspects of a display and be shown how to use them to support their learning of targeted mathematics.

- It is important to remember that children with autism sometimes find very bright and colourful displays over stimulating and this may cause raised anxiety levels, 'shutting down' and/or challenging behaviour. Some children who are more severely affected may find it easier to work just with the grey Numicon Shapes in an environment with no potentially distracting additions when they are required to concentrate.

Encouraging positive attitudes to learning mathematics

Many children learn best through a multi-sensory approach, using a combination of visual, auditory and kinaesthetic channels. Using Numicon materials generally increases children's confidence; it enables them to make links and explore relationships between mathematical ideas more readily, which in turn supports persistence and a deeper understanding of mathematical ideas.

Children are usually fascinated by the relationships they can see between Numicon Shapes and the combinations they can make with them. Children who have progressed to Key Stage 2 and above, and especially those in mainstream contexts and who have experienced repeated failure with mathematical learning, should be encouraged to use Numicon materials. Children's attitudes to Numicon materials will depend heavily on how its use is introduced. For some older children it may be necessary to refer to activities as 'visual problem solving', or 'discovery challenge', to avoid any association with 'play' or childishness in the classroom which may reinforce a child's negative image of themselves or of mathematics.

The use of Numicon materials and activities to promote active and collaborative learning can assist in providing a stimulating and interesting session for all children where challenge and support involving real-life and abstract situations, (where appropriate for the learners), are enhanced.

---

4   *Number and Calculation: Getting the best Results* Oxford School Improvement. Available to download at www.oxfordprimary.co.uk

The relationships and combinations encountered when using the Numicon materials give children insight into abstract ideas about numbers and arithmetic. Where previously children perhaps had to rely on counting to learn number facts, e.g. 6 + 4 = 10, with Numicon Shapes they can see the fact and know that it is true. This knowledge gives them confidence and enables them to move on from counting into calculating with support. They can also use the patterns of Numicon Shapes to make predictions about number. The visual structure and practical, self-correcting nature of the activities mean that children are likely to be more willing to experiment with ideas whilst their engagement in and enjoyment of the activities will promote their long-term memory of the learning. Because of the practical nature of the materials and children's physical interaction with them, teachers are more likely to recognize where children have a lack of understanding or confusion and can address this in a timely manner and provide effective intervention. Sharing in children's discoveries and praising their efforts will also help to make the experience positive for teachers and children.

Grouping children

The Breaking Barriers activities are designed primarily for long-term support and teaching for children who have SEND and are likely to require more longitudinal support that is matched to the pace of the learner, though they can also be used in intervention programmes. Both these groups of children are likely to be working in one-to-one or in small-group situations.

It is important to note that the individual mathematical difficulties of a child are often specific and unique; this can of course make grouping of learners who require support and intervention difficult. However, there are no absolute rules about grouping to teach Numicon activities.

When Numicon is used in short-term intervention

programmes it has been found that a combination of one-to-one teaching and small-group work involving two or three children is usually most successful.

Whichever way children are grouped, attention must be devoted to developing and maintaining the self-esteem and positive attitude of children who have difficulties learning mathematics. Children will learn at the optimal level only if they feel confident as mathematical learners. To achieve this, we need to consider certain factors.

At Key Stage 2 and above it is recommended that children with mathematical difficulties, whose learning is significantly behind that of their peers, should be taught number work within a small group of children who are working at the same, or very similar, level. This should not preclude their learning with more mathematically able children at other times in the school week – it is important for them to experience the comments and conversations of more mathematically able learners (unless this is detrimental to their self-esteem as mathematical learners).

Where possible, small-group teaching sessions using Numicon materials should take place within the usual mathematics lesson, as one of the adult-supported group activities. The suggested teaching activities in this book link more closely to the early years foundation stage and Key Stage 1 curriculum for mathematics than to Key Stage 2 or higher objectives. However, best practice differentiation entails teaching the same broad mathematical objectives, but at the level determined by the child's needs. For example, if the focus for the whole-class session were 'Counting and ordering numbers to 1000' then children who have SEND may be counting and ordering numbers within their counting range. If this work were undertaken within the whole class (assuming that the learning environment – noise level, behaviour and so on – was conducive to learning) this would likely enhance the children's self-esteem and self-concept as mathematically competent learners.

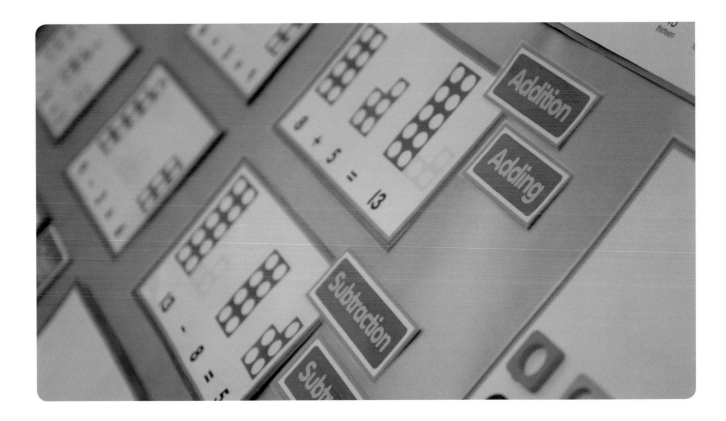

Including and withdrawing special groups

The Numicon teaching programme addresses the number, calculation, geometry, measurement and statistics aspects of the mathematics curriculum 2014. There are specific activity suggestions for shape, space and measures given in the Breaking Barriers activity groups; along with numeracy, understanding and use of measures is an important life skill. It is important also to maintain curriculum balance; children withdrawn to do Numicon number work at a time other than during the daily mathematics lesson must be given the opportunity to experience the parts of the curriculum that they are missing as a result.

On occasion, even though the objectives of the whole-class mathematics lesson relate to number, it is better to withdraw children to undertake Numicon number activities. For example, if the environment of the classroom is noisy or over stimulating and not conducive to the learning needs of children who have SEND. There is considerable evidence that the noise level in the classroom has a significant impact upon the ability of children with SEND to pick out the figure (the sounds of speech) from the ground (the background noise of the classroom), making it very difficult for them to concentrate on the language of instruction. If the level of noise in the classroom makes it difficult for a group of children with SEND to learn, it is probably making it difficult for many other children. Therefore, it is important to control the noise level in the room. Nevertheless, for some children who have SEND, and especially those with autism, the classroom can be over-stimulating, making it difficult for them to focus on the mathematical learning objectives.

Another reason for withdrawing children who have SEND is when the mathematical activities being undertaken by the whole class are so vastly different from the work being done by the small group that it is difficult to link the learning outcomes together. In these cases, children will not be able to link their learning to that of their peers and it may be advantageous to provide a quieter, less distracting environment for all learners if these different activities are taught separately. Careful consideration also needs to be given to how group learning is perceived by all of the children and managed by the teacher to avoid stigmatizing and negative responses to being withdrawn for group work. It is much more conducive to successful learning if all children are aware that successful learning for everyone includes group work that may or may not be facilitated by an adult and that this, for any group of learners, can happen both in and out of the usual learning environment. Attention needs to be given to the aspects of teaching that underline similarity rather than difference. For example, if the group of children with difficulties learning mathematics is the only group using materials or apparatus, there can be a perception that use of materials and learning difficulties are connected. Any association between using Numicon materials and being less able must be avoided. This can be achieved in part by ensuring that the whole class is using structured apparatus in their learning, including Numicon Shapes and number rods. Those conducting intervention programmes report that children benefit where a similar teaching approach is used for the whole class and the withdrawal sessions for one-to-one or small-group teaching, that is, for all to use Numicon materials. Activities can be selected from the Pattern and Algebra strand of the Numicon core teaching activities that will challenge all children.

Planning and structuring teaching sessions with Numicon

It is helpful to check out the Key mathematical ideas behind the chosen teaching activity (see pages 19–29 of this Teaching Guide). Understanding the point of the activity will help you to anticipate the areas of children's likely difficulties and give you the confidence to improvise when they ask questions and respond in ways you had not foreseen. Trying out the activities yourself helps to identify which aspects the children might find difficult; you can then refer to the strategies recommended in this Teaching Guide for overcoming potential barriers to learning. For some children, it may be that an activity requires further modification. The following are examples of modifications that can be planned prior to teaching, or implemented after evaluating a child's response to your initial teaching:

- spending more or less time on certain activities than originally anticipated

- teaching with the recommended signs or using symbols rather than signs (see **Fig 1** on page 55).

- using other visual structures or images, such as number rods, as the primary support for the acquisition of number skills

- using *Numicon Software for the Interactive Whiteboard* so children can 'manipulate' Numicon Shapes and number rods on screen to support their mathematical development from concrete experiences where real things are touched and manipulated to working more with iconic and pictorial representations of real things

- for children with SEND who couldn't actually pick up Numicon Shapes, e.g. those with cerebral palsy, it is helpful for them to touch the Shapes. For example, teachers in a Scope school recommended placing a Numicon shape on a child's hand and then placing their other hand on top, holding both hands together so that the child can sense the Numicon Shape by touch.

It is important to plan the vocabulary and language structures used in the activity carefully, noting the language of instruction, e.g. roll, match, feel, as well as the mathematical language that will be introduced systematically for the activity. Prepare for this to be explained and modelled by an adult, in a way that suits the child's individual needs, always bearing in mind the children's level of language understanding. Often mathematical ideas are more easily understood if signs and/or symbols and reference to Numicon Shapes and Numicon number lines accompany verbal explanations.

The organizational difficulties that many children with SEND experience impact on their mathematical learning. This needs to be borne in mind when planning and organizing small-group work. Some children with SEND persevere, that is, they continue thinking and talking about the previous topic area when the teaching has moved on. To develop children's organization and discourage perseveration, it is useful to use a visual timetable (Bruner, 1966) that represents each part of the group session by a picture or symbol, that is, an alternative augmentative communication system, such as Makaton®.

These timetables can be constructed quickly and simply using IT packages. The symbols used might be for 'finding the same shape' or 'counting forwards to 10' and so on and would clearly remind children about the learning objectives for each part of the session and give the teacher a framework for explaining to children what will be happening in the session.

It is recommended that teaching sessions should last approximately 25 minutes, be well paced and follow a standard structure:

Introduction and activating prior learning

Many children with SEND have listening and attention control difficulties, so it is useful, at the beginning of a small-group session, to do a short listening and attention 'warm up'. This might take the form of a short 'looking and listening'. Alternatively, the warm up could be a familiar and favourite Numicon activity such as putting Numicon Shapes in order or covering a Numicon Baseboard.

Use this element of the session to activate prior learning and remind children about what they did previously and how that links to the focus of today.

Counting activity

Counting is important daily practice for all children working towards acquiring basic number understanding. Advice on counting is given in the Key mathematical ideas, pages 19–29 of this Teaching Guide and ideas for counting activities are explained fully in the Counting activity group. Be mindful of the child's counting range and ability to count one-on-one and provide a range of activities (including real-life situations) where counting forwards, backwards, in steps (not just beginning at 1 or zero) are provided.

Main teaching activity

This will be taken from the activity groups, which should be followed using the suggested order for teaching the activities. Alternatively select activity groups according to specific need. These activities are given a context and contain real-life situations. They are designed to support the child in making links and generalizing from such real-life situations to other situations where the problem may be more abstract in nature.

Check you have sufficient equipment for the size of the group you are working with. The instructions in the 'have ready' section of each activity are sufficient for two children.

Smaller steps/Further practice

Sometimes a child may struggle to access a particular activity or is not yet ready to move on to the next. Support will need to be focused on similar and simplified activities that are linked to the learning outcomes within the activity groups. If a child needs additional opportunities to work on similar tasks, the 'Smaller steps' and 'Further practice' sections found within activity groups, contain suggestions of smaller steps to aid learning and further practice to ensure the child has grasped, understood and is developing fluency with the learning aims of the activity.

Extending the activities

Encourage children to recognize when to use the mathematics they are learning by setting problems in appropriate situations or contexts that are relevant to children's interests and experience.

The 'Connecting activties – Measures' section in some activity groups also provide extension to the main activities.

Reflection

At the end of a session it is important to ask children to explain (through their usual means of communication) what they have done as a way of reinforcing the activity. Remember that for some children with language difficulties what they can express is not always an accurate guide to what they have understood; there may be a discrepancy between the receptive and expressive language skills, and a child may have understood more than they are able to explain. Therefore, encourage children to model and use materials, signs and symbols to aid their reflection. Children could be encouraged to demonstrate their knowledge by manipulating Numicon Shapes or number rods instead of, or in addition to, explaining what they have done in words. Also see the 'Metacognition, self-regulation and asking for help' section below.

Practice and repetition

Mathematical ideas are difficult to learn and use for many children because they are abstract; repetition can contribute to understanding and retention of facts, processes and mathematical ideas. In order to reinforce learning, it is strongly recommended that children have opportunities for repetition and practice several times a week, either during or in addition to their access to small-group work.

- When returning to an activity or topic, recap and activate prior learning for the child and begin with an activity that the child has successfully completed previously. Include here pre- and post-tutoring opportunities for key vocabulary and processes.

- Go over, model and display key signs and symbols that have been previously met and rehearse their use.

- Use familiar equipment and activities first before introducing the new, e.g. begin with Numicon Shapes and then move on to introduce number rods.

- For children with significant memory difficulties, for example, it may be necessary to repeat activities twice a day, e.g. early morning and early afternoon, and also continue to return to learning that the child appears to have mastered previously to ensure it has been remembered and can be recalled. It should not be assumed that a child has understood what has been taught once or even several times. Some children will need to access the same learning objective a significant number of times to be able to make sense of it, remember how to do it and commit this to memory. When children have understood it will become clear, as they will begin to enjoy practising the activities on their own, with success.

Metacognition, self-regulation and asking for help

Metacognition is necessary for problem solving and problem-solving skills are necessary for mathematics. It therefore follows that becoming aware of your own individual strengths and needs, how you learn best, being aware of your thinking and knowing the strategies that work for you

are all key elements for successful learning of mathematics.

'Metacognitive and self-regulation strategies (sometimes known as 'learning-to-learn' strategies) are teaching approaches which make learners think about learning more explicitly. This is usually by teaching children specific strategies to set goals, monitor and evaluate their own learning. Self-regulation refers to managing one's own motivation towards learning as well as the more cognitive aspects of thinking and reasoning. Overall these strategies involve being aware of one's strengths and weaknesses as a learner, such as by developing self-assessment skills, and being able to set and monitor goals. They also include having a repertoire of strategies to choose from or switch to during learning activities.'[5]

The majority of children with SEND can develop some degree of metacognition. However, this is not something that struggling mathematicians pick up by osmosis and learning-to-learn strategies will need to be specifically taught to these children. Encouragingly, evidence suggests that teaching metacognitive and self-regulation strategies tends to be particularly effective with lower-achieving children, as well as with older children who have struggled with their learning in mathematics. Teaching approaches which encourage learners to plan, monitor and evaluate their learning have very high potential, but require careful implementation and explicit teaching. Children will need lots of additional opportunities to see such strategies being modelled by adults involved in their learning and then to be able to use such strategies with support. Provide opportunities to model how the task could go wrong so that key steps for keeping on track can be identified. This will also ensure that children see the worth in learning from mistakes. Children will also need to be taught how to evaluate their work and consider how their approach could be improved upon when they encounter the task in the future. Metacognitive techniques are most effective in small-group scenarios where learners can support each other and make their thinking explicit through discussion or alternative and/or augmented communication methods.

It is important to remind all children that 'I don't know' and 'I've forgotten' are legitimate responses to a question in the first instance. Responding to questions can be facilitated by provision of pictorial (symbol supported) prompt cards for 'I don't know', 'I know', and so on to which a child can point. It is important to stress that there is no stigma in responding, 'I don't know'; the ethos of the classroom or group should be one of acknowledging that 'I don't know' or 'I've forgotten' are good starting points for learning. It is very important that the work challenges the most able children in the group so that they too will respond with, 'I don't know'.

Learning how and when to ask for help is important for successful learning. However, many children need to be taught to recognize when they need help and how to ask for it.

As children move through the key stages of mainstream learning environments, the emphasis may change from being child-centred to becoming progressively more

5 From 'Meta-cognition and self-regulation' from the Education Endowment Fund Teaching and Learning Toolkit: http://educationendowmentfoundation.org.uk/toolkit/meta-cognitive-and-self-regulation-strategies/

curriculum-centred. It is likely, as learning becomes more challenging, that requests for help from children will become more frequent and will become the main way of ensuring support and clarification in the classroom. Again, adults involved in the child's learning will need to model how to ask for help and look for signs that the child requires help and provides scaffolding that encourages and supports the child in asking for help.

Assessment

'There is overwhelming evidence that arithmetical ability is not unitary: it is made up of many components, ranging from knowledge of the counting sequence, to estimation, to solving word problems. Although these components are often correlated, weaknesses can occur in any one of them. Studies have suggested that it is not possible to establish a strict hierarchy of learning in which any one component invariably precedes or follows another. Interventions that focus on the particular components with which an individual child has difficulty are likely to be more effective than those which assume that all pupils' arithmetical difficulties are similar.' (Dowker, 2004: 15–16)

The Child Profile included with the assessment tools in the *Breaking Barriers Assessment and Photocopy Master* book is designed to identify the strengths and needs of individual children in aspects of basic mathematical understanding and also of the within-child factors which affect their access to mathematical teaching and learning and to help teachers record the next steps for those children.

The Assessment Signposts, although not designed to provide a detailed assessment, do help to indicate an appropriate starting point on the Breaking Barriers teaching programme and to identify areas for support and further teaching. Subsequently, all children using Breaking Barriers

should have their learning continuously assessed through observation of their responses to different teaching strategies, and their attainment. This ongoing observation and assessment will help teachers be responsive to children's needs, resulting in continuous modification to the pace of teaching and the teaching strategies employed. Children's progress can be tracked on the Individual Record of Progress which shows the very small steps of the Breaking Barriers teaching programme and which is also helpful for identifying individual targets.

Many children with mathematical learning difficulties will learn better by 'doing' and 'seeing'. Numicon facilitates this by providing representations of number ideas that can be manipulated and visualized, enabling the child to move from the manual manipulation of the physical Numicon Shapes, to internal imaging and the internal manipulation of these mental images, that is, thinking about number. Through this interaction with the materials, children's thinking process, knowledge and understanding can become more 'visible' and hence support ongoing assessment of what they know, understand and are able to do. This also enables timely and effective feedback to be supplied at the right stage of learning and ensures that opportunities to move a child on or address an error or misconception are not missed.

Self-assessment opportunities can also be utilized through the use of Numicon materials. This means that the child becomes more involved and takes more responsibility for their learning. This also links closely to the 'Metacognition, self-regulation and asking for help' section above.

Additional guidance on teaching approaches for specific categories of Special Educational Needs and Disabilities (SEND)

There are particular issues that relate to specific SEND categories. Additional guidance for some of these issues is offered in this section.

In this section you will find information on:

Speech, Language and Communication Needs (SLCN)

Most children who have identified Special Educational Needs and Disabilities (SEND) have some level of SLCN which impact on their ability to do basic mathematics. Understanding the language of mathematics underpins all mathematical thinking and communicating; thus children who have problems with understanding and using words more generally are likely to have significant difficulties in doing mathematics.

However, it is important to profile individual children's language proficiency because although many children with verbal problems may experience difficulties with mathematics, these difficulties '… cannot be used as definite predictors of either the existence or type of mathematical difficulty that a pupil may have' (Dowker, 2004: 10).

Numicon can be successfully used to address the mathematical learning needs of children with SLCN. Some suggested strategies are outlined here:

- Ensure that the mathematical language and language of instruction matches the level of the child's understanding and is accompanied by signs, e.g. the Numicon signs for adding, subtracting, multiplying and dividing (see Fig 1 on page 55).

- Give children time to process what you have said; do not rephrase if a child needs to hear the instruction or question again, just repeat word for word what you initially stated and support the instruction with signing.

- Allow time for children to respond; those with verbal comprehension and word-finding difficulties will take longer to process questions and also their own responses.

- Use visual supports to aid the learning, retention and vocabulary of a mathematics task, e.g. use models and images (including Numicon Shapes), signs and symbols that the child has already had time to become familiar with.

- Introduce new mathematical vocabulary slowly and systematically and support it with signing.

- Teach the use of words and terms systematically, e.g. more, one more than, big, bigger, biggest, small, smaller, smallest. Teach the use of 'big' and 'not big' and 'small' and 'not small' separately; do not try initially to teach the use of opposites together, that is 'big' and 'small'.

- More generally, teach the use of key and new terms one at a time, even if they are related, e.g. to teach the adding language 'more' and 'together', first teach 'together', then teach 'more', and then explain, model and illustrate that 'add' can mean both.

- Use visual images of number size, that is, Numicon Shapes, to support sequential learning such as number lines.

- Use a visual timetable to demarcate the separate components of the day and to develop sequencing skills and language.

- Ensure that each child has plenty of opportunities to show what they know through the use of structured resources such as Numicon, rather than relying solely on describing and explaining verbally.

- Use written or verbal prompts for sentence starters, e.g. 'I took the eight, then added the … ' to reduce verbal demands on an individual with SLCN.

- When necessary, use a visual group-work timetable to distinguish the various mathematical tasks in a mathematical teaching session to inhibit perseveration (getting stuck on the content of a previous task, when another has started).
- Make clear the sound differences between similar sounding numbers, e.g. six, sixteen, sixty, alongside using visual prompts, e.g. signing and Numicon Shapes.
- Encourage self-regulation, metacognition and asking for help (see below).
- See also the suggestions below for teaching mathematics to children with motor and organizational needs and also the strategies suggested for children who have autism or Asperger syndrome. These sections contain additional guidance that may also support children with speech language and communication needs.

Moderate Learning Difficulties (MLD)

A child with Moderate Learning Difficulties (MLD) presents with significant delay in reaching developmental milestones (including learning to speak and express themselves, move independently and develop fine motor skills) and may have much greater difficulty than their peers with basic literacy and numeracy. For example, if a child has fine and gross motor skill difficulties, this affects their ability to engage in a kinaesthetic activity which would help them make sense of their learning.

However, it is important to remember that each child is an individual with their own strengths and needs and therefore support and intervention in mathematics will need to take account of their individual profile. Establishing a profile of need through a multi-agency, person-centred approach is vital in order to put in place comprehensive plans specifically tailored to address these needs.

However, a child with MLD is likely to have additional speech, language and/or other communication needs; therefore, all the above suggestions for children with SLCN are highly likely to apply along with the additional strategies listed here:

- Focus on what the child can do rather than what they cannot do and build on their strengths. Revisit and revise areas of mathematical learning frequently; children with MLD often need significantly more opportunities to revise and overlearn specific aspects of mathematical thinking and communicating.
- Ensure that any written material is clear, uncluttered, is age appropriate and suitable for the child's stage of development.
- Take particular care when selecting visual support, ensuring that the models and images are clear and unambiguous.
- Model thinking out loud and illustrate your communicating with the use of structured resources, e.g. Numicon resources.
- Make the beginning and end of a task or activity clear to avoid ambiguity and define when the task is finished.

- Where appropriate, use visual clues, signs and symbols when presenting tasks, explaining the use of words, and giving instructions.
- See also the suggestions below for teaching mathematics to children who have motor and organizational needs; children with a typical profile for MLD usually have motor and organizational needs alongside SLCN, as stated above.

Severe and profound and multiple learning difficulties

Both the above sets of suggestions are likely to apply to children with severe and profound multiple learning difficulties and, although Numicon materials are designed for sensory motor learning, there is likely to be an even deeper focus on sensory and motor activity for these children. Therefore, consideration will have to be given as to how Numicon Shapes can be explored by children with different levels of learning and motor needs. For example, one child may want to explore the size and shape of a Numicon Shape with his or her tongue; whereas another child may have sufficient manual motor ability to find matching pairs of Numicon Shapes in the Numicon Feely Bag. Also, where appropriate, consider the addition of tactile surfaces to wooden numerals, e.g. sandpaper, felt, bubble wrap, and then add oils such as peppermint or vanilla to maximize on sensory learning opportunities when matching numerals to Numicon Shapes. Use of Numicon Large Foam Shapes might also help children.

An environment where Numicon apparatus is used to label and where a rich sensory curriculum includes Numicon resources is likely to be most helpful for children who are working on the use of basic mathematical words and terms.

For some children with severe and profound difficulties it may be better if mathematics is taught as a component of personal and social life skills. In these cases, consideration needs to be given to the role of Numicon resources within personal and social learning, e.g. when cooking, relate counting spoonfuls of flour to the corresponding Numicon Shape.

Autism and Asperger syndrome

Autism is characterized by difficulty in communicating and forming relationships with other people and in using words, particularly words and terms related to generalizations. Autism is a continuum which means that some children with autism may have mild difficulties with social communication, and words related to generalizing, social relationships and imagination (the triad of impairment) whilst others may have profound difficulties in these areas.

Many children with autism have a relative strength in number in terms of learning sequences, counting and also in calculating and executing processes around calculating. They may have a good memory for number order and number sequences for example, even though numbers are abstract in nature, but they do not generally find abstract concepts across the board (not just in mathematics) easy to grasp.

Add

Multiply

Equals

Divide

Subtract

Alternatively, they may have learning difficulties ranging from mild to profound and multiple. It is very important that all the adults who may influence the children's mathematical learning use consistent strategies, language and resources when supporting them.

Best practice for teaching mathematics to children with autism should consider the National Autistic Society's (NAS) SPELL Approach of: Structure, Positive approaches and expectations, Empathy, Low arousal and Links.[6] 'The SPELL framework can be applied across the autistic spectrum, including for those children with Asperger syndrome. It can prove particularly useful for the teaching of mathematics and provides a context for and is complementary to other approaches, notably TEACCH (Treatment and Education of Autistic and related Communication handicapped Children).'[7] Whilst the SPELL framework is specifically formulated for children with autism, many of its precepts apply to many other children with SEND. Here are some suggestions to help in the teaching of mathematics to children with autism.

Structure

- Use a visual symbol or sign to mark the components of the mathematics session to make the lesson structure clear.

- Ensure the task has a definite finish point and use timers to clearly label how long an activity will last.

- Ensure all planned activities are achievable within the time frame given and also contain elements that are familiar to the child. Explain tasks in small manageable chunks with a clear start and end point.

- Use visual cues (structured resources such as Numicon, pictures and symbols, if appropriate) to support a child's work on an activity.

- Use visual prompts for the stages of mathematical processes, such as counting, adding, and so on, which illustrate what needs to be done, clearly and sequentially (see **Fig 1**).

Positive

- Ensure expectations within the mathematics session are realistic and individual to each child.

- initially, when introducing the child to Numicon, ensure that tasks are achievable whithin the time available, and provide a clear start and finish to the activities to ensure continued motivation and success.

- Where appropriate, identify and use a child's strengths or special interests when planning mathematical activities and be positive about an individual child's strengths in mathematics.

- Make learning in mathematics real and avoid abstract situations or learning scenarios until the child is confident when working in real-life contexts and familiar situations. For example, make use of incidental classroom situations such as sharing out resources within a small group; focus on weights and measures when cooking with a recipe.

- Positive engagement is key to successful learning; mathematical teaching approaches should maximize children's levels of engagement. For example, if a child requires a quiet environment where distraction is low, then ensure that this is provided to enable the child to engage positively in the task.

- Build on natural strengths and interests, e.g. if a child is interested in transport, use trains or buses in problems linked to real-life situations. Where possible, expectations should be positive, that is, high but attainable. Be clear about what the child is learning and what this will help them to do. Be clear about your expectations related to the outcomes of the task, including when the child will know that the task is finished. Provide opportunities, where appropriate, for the child to generalize these skills in real-life situations.

---

6   For more details see: http://www.autism.org.uk/spell
7   For further information see: http://www.autism.org.uk/teacch

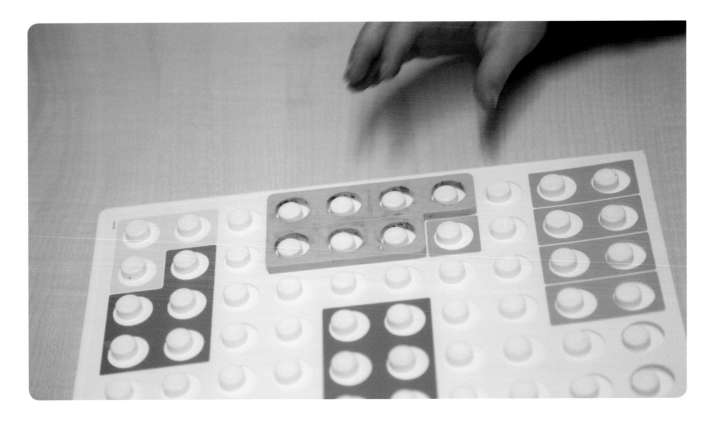

Empathetic

- Offer practical help for difficult areas of mathematics such as problem solving by allowing the child time to talk, think and communicate their thinking through structured resources such as Numicon.

- Ensure actual comprehension has been achieved; understanding may be masked by random repetition of learned phrases or echolalia. Use communication strategies such as visual supports and an alternative augmentative communication system, such as Makaton® to assist this.

- Try to understand the mathematical world from the autistic child's point of view. What is it about mathematics that motivates or interests the child? What is it about number that frightens, preoccupies or distresses the child? If you can, identifying these factors may enable adults to present mathematical tasks and challenges in a way that plays to an individual child's strengths and can be taught in a way that the former factors are emphasized and the latter are alleviated.

Low arousal

- Check the learning environment for potential distractions specific to the individual, e.g. flickering lights, strong smells, noises, bright colours.

- Create a workstation or space with low distraction for work tasks or learning new or complex skills.

- Filter out and remove irrelevant stimuli, e.g. unnecessary illustrations on worksheets.

- Use resources to address individual needs, e.g. ear defenders to block out sounds when working, tangle toys.

- Ensure that mathematical communicating and the tone of voice employed with the child are calm and ordered, to reduce anxiety and support concentration.

- Be mindful of the colours of the Numicon Shapes. Some children with autism may find them too distracting or they may interfere with the child's ability to focus on their size component, which is their most important feature. If this proves to be an issue, consider introducing the grey Numicon Shapes (if available).

Links

- Children with autism typically find it difficult to generalize and to make links between learning situations. They may therefore need considerably more opportunities to practise and overlearn the same mathematical words and terms in different situations and scenarios.

- Activate prior learning, use real-life situations and practical/concrete materials wherever possible to make links between mathematical ideas and processes explicit for children with autism.

- Ensure a consistent approach between home and the educational setting by involving the young person and their family throughout the process of planning and teaching and reviewing mathematical progress. Much of the mathematical thinking and communicating that the child needs to develop may relate to real-life situations and, if possible, the family can support the child in communicating mathematically in appropriate situations outside the learning environment.

- Ensure all involved staff are informed of support strategies and current issues and use naturally occurring situations to reinforce learning in context.

- Share information with other professionals such as speech and language therapists, occupational therapists, educational psychologists and so on.

- Also, see the suggestions on page 53 for teaching mathematics to children who have SLCN.[8]

Specific learning difficulties

Specific Learning Difficulties (SpLDs) affect the way information is learned and processed. They are neurological (rather than psychological), usually run in families and occur independently of intelligence. They can have significant impact on education and learning and on the acquisition of literacy skills. SpLD is an umbrella term used to cover a range of frequently co-occurring difficulties, more commonly: dyslexia, dyspraxia/DCD, dyscalculia, ADD/ADHD and Auditory Processing Disorder.[9]

Other related difficulties could be with visual/perceptual skills, directional confusion, sequencing, word skills and memory. Children with specific learning difficulties may have special difficulties with aspects of mathematics that require many steps or place a heavy load on the short-term memory, e.g. long division or algebra.

Dyscalculia

Children diagnosed with dyscalculia have difficulty doing mathematics. Such children may have difficulty using basic number words, lack an intuitive grasp of numbers, relative numerosity/subitizing and have problems learning number facts and procedures. Early indicators of behaviour associated with dyscalculia are often noticed when children are dealing with sequences and quantities. Learners diagnosed as dyscalculic often have problems with long-term retention of basic facts, are poor at communicating about numbers, and often have difficulties generalizing in everyday situations and in mathematical contexts.

The key to successfully supporting the learning of a child diagnosed with dyscalculia lies in the identification of their individual strengths and needs. This will ensure any support and intervention is correctly targeted. It is often useful to analyse the separate components within a mathematical task, e.g. the vocabulary, basic fact knowledge, use of the words and terms associated with the four operations, memory (see 'Memory difficulties' on page 35 for further information), sequencing ability, generalizing, recording strategies, necessary equipment, spatial awareness, and then to identify which area creates a difficulty for the learner.

The use of Numicon resources for general teaching, and the specific activities in this kit in particular, address all these indicators of dyscalculia, that is, problems with sequencing,

memory, number and patterns. Children who have difficulties in recognizing pattern need to work on copying, continuing and building patterns.

There are a lot of activities designed to support the development of pattern skills in Breaking Barriers. For example, ordering Numicon Shapes, building patterns, organizing items into Numicon Shape patterns.

The use of Numicon resources, therefore, should assist in the teaching of mathematics to children who have received a diagnosis of dyscalculia.

Many of the strategies and considerations outlined in the above sections can be successfully employed to suit the learning needs of a child with dyscalculia. Listed here are some more specific strategies for consideration:

- Access to a familiar, structured and multi-sensory resource, e.g. Numicon apparatus, is useful for illustrating mathematical activity and thinking for the child.

- Use of concrete materials and imagery. Instead of relying solely on printed resources and verbal teaching, children diagnosed with dyscalculia often find it helpful to use concrete materials so that they can have a wider kinaesthetic or hands-on approach to their communicating and thinking. This may include counting blocks, rulers, clock faces, fraction segments or any other materials that you can utilize.

- Praise, rewards and encouragement: many children diagnosed with dyscalculia are embarrassed and frustrated by their difficulties. Offering praise, rewards and encouragement for small steps of achievement can help to motivate them and make them feel proud of their progress.

- As with other specific categories above, children diagnosed with dyscalculia may need to learn the use of particular words or procedures over and over again before they begin to master them.

- Reinforcement: you can reinforce particular aspects of mathematical thinking and communicating by using different approaches to teaching them. Give information verbally, then express it again in written form and also devise practical activities that will richly illustrate the information to the child.

- The use of mathematical vocabulary must be taught explicitly, modelled by others regularly and reinforced daily. Encourage children to utilize any personal strengths in developing their mathematical communicating.

- See also strategies for other SpLD such as dyslexia and motor/organizational skills.

Dyslexia

The British Dyslexia Association (BDA) states that:

- 50–60% of dyslexic children experience difficulties in mathematics.

- About 10% of dyslexic children excel at mathematics.

---

8   The structure of these points is based on the Autism Education Trust website outline of the SPELL technique for general learning, for more information see: www.autism.org.uk/spell

9   SpLDs can also co-occur with difficulties on the autistic spectrum such as Asperger syndrome. (From British Dyslexia Association website www.bdadyslexia.org.uk)

Not surprisingly, difficulties in decoding written words can transfer across into a difficulty in decoding mathematical terms, notation and symbols.

For some dyslexic children, however, difficulty with mathematics may in fact stem from problems with the language surrounding mathematical questions rather than from the use of particular number words, e.g. their dyslexia may cause them to misunderstand the wording of a question.

Therefore those working with dyslexic children must gain an individual child's profile of strengths and needs in relation to mathematical communicating. If a child with dyslexia does indeed have mathematical difficulties, the following points may be useful when planning their support and intervention.

- Mathematics has its own ways of using words, and this can cause significant problems for the dyslexic learner. There is a well documented and well researched link between dyslexia and language difficulties and therefore, as for children with SLCN and dyscalculia, general mathematical terminology needs to be carefully taught and clearly understood before being used in conversation.

- The value of learning the skills of estimation cannot be too strongly stressed for the dyslexic child. As a general rule, individuals with dyslexia tend to have a weakness in the ability to estimate, particularly around time and executing tasks. Use and encourage the use of estimation wherever possible, e.g. when arranging a random set into an ordered set, when agreeing how much work can reasonably be completed in a session.

- Children should be taught and encouraged to get into the habit of checking answers when the calculation is finished, e.g. is the answer possible? is it sensible?

- When using mental arithmetic allow the child to jot down the key number and the appropriate mathematical sign from the question.

- Encourage children to communicate fully, including illustrating with concrete resources such as Numicon apparatus as they talk their way through each step of a problem.

- Rehearse mathematical vocabulary constantly, using multi-sensory/kinaesthetic methods in support.

- The use of colour and opportunities for working in three-dimensional ways can prove helpful for children with dyslexia. For example, the colour of Numicon Shapes can be a helpful memory trigger for dyslexic learners and activities such as 'building towers' with Numicon Shapes enable a child to construct a number in a three-dimensional way.

Motor and organizational needs (including dyspraxia)

Organizational difficulties often underpin other areas of learning difficulty. Some children have specific difficulties with motor organization and below are some suggestions for best practice which could also be used when teaching any child who has language and/or learning difficulties.

- Help the child identify steps needed to begin and complete the task, e.g. ask the child to repeat instructions and, if possible, write down the steps (or write them down yourself, providing pictorial and verbal support, if necessary).

- Give one instruction at a time. After each has been successfully completed, add another instruction.

- Minimize visual distractions. Remove clutter in the direct working environment and on the desk that the child is working at.

- Encourage the child to verbalize what they are doing whilst carrying out the activities. Support this by talking through a process as you are completing it to model the process and thinking for the child.

- Document the length of time a child can focus on one task successfully and structure subsequent tasks so that they can be completed in that length of time. Build on this to extend the length of time that the child can spend on the task.

- Provide opportunities for multi-sensory and tactile experiences when learning mathematical techniques, e.g. use Numicon Shapes or number rods and other Numicon equipment to practically illustrate what happens when adding two or more numbers.

- Rehearse and review what the child has learnt on a regular basis.

- Place mathematical equipment (including Numicon Shapes) on the learning surface in an organized and visually clear manner.

- Teach left to right and top to bottom organization as the primary organizational strategy for all activities, including counting.

- Encourage eye tracking by pointing with your finger (as well as visual pointing) to the start number and pointing as you count, so that children can see where they need to look.

- When counting, ensure that the size and spacing of objects match the child's level of motor and organizational skills to ensure they are able to successfully synchronize the finger checking with the oral sequence of words.

- If necessary, start to teach counting through gross motor organizational activities, that is, counting by walking along numbered carpet tiles or gross motor activities that include the use of the Numicon Large Foam Shapes (if available) so that the use of words and terms such as 'one more' and 'one less (or fewer)' can be introduced by physically moving forwards and backwards. Once this is established, transfer and practise these activities with fine motor movements, e.g. using a finger to count along the Large Format Table-top Number Line.

Children with oral/verbal dyspraxia may be unable to pronounce words clearly, especially the words for numbers that are similar phonologically (such as the 'teen' and 'ty' numbers). Encourage children to 'show what they know' with the Numicon resources and remember that a speech and language therapist should be consulted about how best to support individual children with oral/verbal dyspraxia; the appropriate strategy will depend on the stage the child has reached in their speech therapy.

Sensory needs

Not all children who have sensory needs will have learning difficulties and/or SLCN. For those who do, the above sets of suggestions will be useful. Here are some additional suggestions for children with sensory needs.

Hearing needs

- Children with hearing needs may require extra support in the form of signing (British Sign Language or BSL) either related to signing of the key terms to support the spoken word, or as the main communication strategy.

- Specialist teachers for hearing impairment will need to guide teaching approaches and agree the approach to communication and learning for a profoundly deaf child ('natural aural', or 'total communication', e.g. BSL). This decision will require discussion that involves the child and their parents or carers, as it will have long-term implications for the child's education.

- Maximize communication via visual and kinaesthetic illustration.

- Provide additional opportunities for kinaesthetic activities involving tactile and visual modes in particular.

- Model the use of all new vocabulary and mathematical activities practically with Numicon equipment and/or other tactile and multi-sensory materials.

- Teach and use explicitly the Numicon (or BSL) signs for adding, subtracting, multiplying, dividing and equals and ensure all staff use and reinforce these and other key BSL signs for key mathematical vocabulary or activities.

- Use small-group teaching methods or individual tuition and work at the pace of the child.

- Limit the time children spend having to listen to the teacher, and provide resources such as Numicon apparatus to support the child in their learning.

- Use the full range of materials and imagery in your mathematical communicating, support learning with the writing of key words on the board, and provide notes for reference.

Visual needs

- Children may need more tactile experience with Numicon Shapes (e.g. if they have colour-blindness). Again, the advice of the local authority's sensory needs service should be sought with regard to an individual child's visual needs.

- Encourage the wearing of any glasses when engaging in multi-sensory mathematical tasks.

- Printed Numicon materials may need to be adapted: they may need to be enlarged or have the text to background contrast modified.

- Ensure optimal seating when working in a group. This may apply particularly when a child is using kinaesthetic materials such as Numicon apparatus, to ensure they are involved and included in the group.

- Give careful and detailed verbal feedback to compensate for the difficulty in seeing body language and materials and imagery.

- Back up visual information with verbal instructions or descriptions, e.g. reading out loud what is being written on the board.

- Provide the child with their own copy of information in an accessible font, where appropriate.

- Ensure that Numicon apparatus and other resources are well organized so that the child will have independent access.

- Make sure that there is good lighting in work areas, with no glare. However, where children are photophobic (sensitive to light), they may be more comfortable in a shaded area of the room.

- Give extra time and more tactile resources to aid the successful completion of work.

Specific conditions

Children who have specific conditions, e.g. Down syndrome, fragile X syndrome, cerebral palsy, may well present with aspects of one or more of the special needs described throughout this section.

Numicon resources are recommended by the Down Syndrome Educational Trust because the clear, regular patterns of Numicon Shapes appeal to visual memory, which is often a relative strength in children who have this syndrome.

Numicon, due to its structure and systematic approach, is likely also to be useful for other groups of children who have conditions that result in their having relative strengths in visual memory.

Appendix and bibliography

Appendix: Key mathematical vocabulary with suggested signs and symbols

Key mathematical vocabulary	Sign systems (and adaptation where applicable)	Symbol systems
Number 0-10	Makaton®	Standard English numerals **and** Numicon Shapes
Number 11 and 12 (standard spoken English)	British Sign Language	
Numbers 13-19 (standard spoken English)	British Sign Language (adapted: Makaton® -style hand shapes for 13-19 'flap', at 90 degrees to normal, in British Sign Language style movement for 13-19)	
Numbers 11 to 19 (intermediate step to counting competence: …eight, nine, ten, ten one, ten two, ten three, ten four… etc.)	Makaton® (Adapted: Signed with the ten first)	
Numbers 20 onwards (standard spoken English)	Makaton®	
Big/Small	Makaton®	Widget/Rebus/Boardmaker
Bigger/Smaller	Makaton® (adapted: Replace finger spelling of 'er' with a small additional 'jump' of the hands in the direction of hand travel (outwards for bigger; inwards for smaller)	Widget/Rebus/Boardmaker
Biggest/Smallest	Makaton® (adapted: Replace finger spelling of 'er' with a small additional 'jump' of the hands in the direction of hand travel (outwards for bigger; inwards for smaller)	Widget/Rebus
More/Less	Makaton®	Makaton® (Standard mathematical symbols)
Odd/Even	Makaton®	Makaton®
Add/Subtract	Numicon signs	Standard mathematical symbols
Equals/is equivalent to (is of equal value)	Numicon sign	Standard mathematical symbols
Same ('same' does not mean equal)	Makaton® sign	Rebus/Boardmaker
Whole	(none)	Makaton®
Multiply	Numicon sign, Makaton® sign	Standard mathematical symbols, Rebus, Boardmaker
Divide	Numicon sign, Makaton® sign	Standard mathematical symbols, Rebus, Boardmaker
Fraction	(none)	Standard mathematical symbols, Rebus, Boardmaker

Bibliography

Atkinson, R., Tacon, R., Wing, A. (2004) 'Learning about numbers with patterns' – summary of original classroom-based research project which led to the development of the Numicon Teaching Programme. BEAM Research Paper RES04, BEAM Education, via www.oxfordprimary.co.uk/numicon

Atkinson, R. C. and Shiffrin, R. M. (1968) Human memory: A proposed system and its control processes. In K. W. Spence and J. T. Spence (eds) The Psychology of Learning and Motivation: Advances in Research Theory, pp.89-195. New York: Academic Press

Autism Education Trust Teachers' Guide in Resources section www.autismeducationtrust.org.uk/resources/teachers%20guide.aspx

Boardmaker www.mayer-johnson.com/boardmaker-software

Bone, C., Chapman, C. and Saunders, S. (2006) Visual Images and Models Supported by Signs and Symbols. Brighton: Brighton and Hove City Council.

Bristow, J., Cowley, P. and Daines, B. (1999) Memory and Learning: A practical guide for teachers. London: David Fulton.

British Dyslexia Association (BDA) Dyscalculia, Dyslexia and Maths www.bdadyslexia.org.uk

Bruner, J.S. (1966) Toward a Theory of Instruction. Cambridge, MA: Harvard University Press

Butterworth, B. (2005) 'The development of arithmetic abilities', Journal of Pupil Psychology and Psychiatry 46 (1): 3-18.

Cooper, J., Moodley, M. and Reynell, J. (1978) Helping Language Development: A Developmental Programme for Children with Early Learning Handicaps. London: Edward Arnold

Crick Software www.cricksoft.com

Cumbria County Council Development of Attention Control

Dehaene, S. (2011) The Number Sense. New York: Oxford University Press

Dowker, A. (2004) What Works for Pupils with Mathematical Difficulties? Department for Education and Skills, Research Report 554. London: Department for Education and Skills.

Education Endowment Foundation Teaching and Learning Toolkit, Meta-cognitive and Self-regulation Strategies www.educationendowmentfoundation.org.uk/toolkit/meta-cognitive-and-self-regulation-strategies/

Fuson, K. (1992) Research on whole number addition and subtraction. In D.A. Grows (ed), Handbook of Research on Mathematics Teaching and Learning. New York: Macmillan

Gathercole, S. and Alloway, T. P. (2007) Understanding Working Memory: A Classroom Guide. London: Harcourt Assessment

Grauberg, E. (1998) Elementary Mathematics and Language Difficulties: A book for teachers, therapists and parents. London: Whurr Publishers Ltd.

Haring, N.G., Lovitt, T.C., Eaton, M.D. and Hansen, C.L. (1978) The Fourth R: Research in the classroom. Columbus, OH: Charles E. Merrill Publishing Co.

Henry, L. (2011) The Working Memory Model, chapter 1 of The Development of Working Memory in Children. London: Sage Press www.sagepub.com/upm-data/42874_Henry.pdf

Makaton® National Curriculum Book of Signs; National Curriculum Book of Symbols; Makaton® for Maths Guidelines, all Camberley: Makaton® Vocabulary Development Project.

National Autistic Society (NAS) SPELL at www.autism.org.uk/spell

National Autistic Society (NAS) TEACCH at www.autism.org.uk/teacch

Nottinghamshire Inclusion Support Service www.nottinghamcity.gov.uk/esn/index.aspx?articleid=19500

Nunes, T., Bryant, P., & Watson, A. (2009) Key Understandings in Mathematics Learning. London: Nuffield Foundation

Nunes, T., Bryant, P., Sylva, K. & Barros, R. (2009) Development of Maths Capabilties and Confidence in Primary School. Research Brief DCSF-RB118. London: DCSF

Office for Standards in Education (OFSTED) SEN Code of Practice 2014 and Teachers' Standards 2012

Oxford School Improvement Number and Calculation: Getting the best Results, via www.oxfordprimary.co.uk

Piaget, J. (1952) The Child's Conception of Number. London: Routledge and Kegan Paul

Rinaldi, W. (2005) Language Concepts to Access Learning. Cranleigh, available from the author (18 Dorking Road, Chilworth, Surrey, GU4 8NR)

Rinaldi, W. (2005) Social Use of Language Programme: Infant and Primary School (SULP-IP). Cranleigh: available from the author (18 Dorking Road, Chilworth, Surrey, GU4 8NR).

Sfard, A. (2008) Thinking as Communicating: Human Development, the Growth of Discourses, and Mathematizing. New York: Cambridge University Press

Smith, C., and Hodgson, D. (1998) Communication Link: Dictionary of signs. Beverley: Beverley School

Widget Software www.widgit.com/wws2000prog/index.htm

Counting

Counting

Educational context

This activity group is extensive, with many suggestions for teaching, maintaining and extending children's ability to **recite the count sequence** and to **count collections** accurately. The **activities for counting one-to-one** help to prepare children for the Numbers and the Number System activity groups. The suggestions for **oral counting** and **numeral formation** should continue to be part of children's daily mathematical experiences alongside other activity groups to maintain and extend their counting range. It is important to establish a learning environment that is rich in numbers in order to support and encourage their number understanding. However, be mindful that this may be over-stimulating for some children, who may benefit from personal support of one number line in a calm designated space. Refer to the **Teaching Guide**, page 46, for ideas on creating appropriate learning environments.

The activities cover two important aspects of counting. The first is **reciting the number names in our counting sequence fluently and in the right order** so that children can begin to sense the patterns within our system for naming numbers. Children need to be able to **say number names clearly**, distinguishing between teen number names and corresponding multiples of 10, e.g. thirteen and thirty, and to recognize patterns in the way we name numbers as an essential beginning to understanding place value. This can be challenging for many children, particularly for those who have limited auditory memory. However, with the support of Numicon imagery, children who cannot otherwise remember the count sequence to recall number names may still be able to find numbers on the number line and put numerals in order. Remember always to encourage children to find the last number in the count on a number line.

The second aspect of counting covered by the activities is **learning to count a collection of objects accurately** by **using one number name for each object counted**; so children learn that the size (cardinal value) of the group is given by the last number in the count and that the objects can be counted in any order (order irrelevance principle). They also learn that we count when we need to find out 'how many?'

Work shows with typically developing children that the ability to count up to thirty objects accurately is a reliable indicator of children's readiness to begin to understand **place value**. However, children who have difficulty in remembering the counting sequence but who show understanding of the structure of 2-digit numbers by their ability to build a 2-digit number with structured apparatus, on seeing it written down or hearing its name, have a useful basis for understanding place value.

Children usually have more difficulty with **counting back** than counting forward. The support of number lines is important and it can be helpful to start by asking children for the number that comes before a given number and then to continue to look for the previous number each time.

There are also suggestions for helping children to **recognize and read numerals and to write them**. Writing numerals by forming them correctly is an important skill and children will need practice, but this should not take over children's mathematics time.

Aims

- To learn to recite the number names in order (the count sequence)
- To understand that we count when we need to find out 'how many?'
- To learn strategies for counting collections of objects accurately, saying one number name for each object counted (counting one to one)
- To count on from any number within their counting range
- To count back from any number within their counting range
- To relate counting to the number line and to find numbers on the number line confidently
- To make reasonable estimates of the size of a collection within their counting range

Communicating

Imagery
Numicon Display Number Line, Numicon 0–100 cm Number Line, Numicon 0–31 Number Lines, Numicon Large Format Table-top Number Line, tabletop displays of numbers and number lines, labelling with numbers in the classroom, number displays

Equipment
See the 'have ready' for activities for counting one-to-one.

Words and terms for instruction (supported with signs and symbols)
count, say, point, check, estimate, think, count forwards, count backwards

Mathematical words and terms (supported with signs and symbols)
number names, next, how many?, total, amount, altogether, forwards, backwards

Assessment

Assessing how children's counting is progressing regularly provides insight as to how their understanding of the pattern for naming is progressing. It is recommended that teachers check children's counting range regularly by first asking them how far they can count and then asking them to count on from (and back from) a number within their range. Common sticking points are multiples of ten and multiples of 100. Listen for children's pronunciation of teen numbers and correct sensitively to prevent rehearsal of mispronunciation.

Individual Record of Progress: Numbers and the Number System 1–3, 44–55, 60–64, 81, 82, 94

Putting the activities into context

Establish a number-rich environment in which numbers are used purposefully. Refer to the Numicon website for free display resources and include number lines to support counting, e.g.:

- Use numerals and objects in Numicon Shape patterns to label how many children may work on certain activities from time to time.
- Number storage trays as well as naming them.
- Label storage pots with numerals to show how many pencils, crayons, scissors, etc. should be in each.
- Make sure there are plenty of objects around that feature numerals in everyday situations, such as calendars, clocks, timetables and the register, and refer to them frequently.
- Create displays of objects for children to count.
- Counting stairs and steps – prepare mats showing the numerals and matching Numicon Shapes to label each step on the staircase to support children's counting as they go up and down.

Discuss numbers of personal significance with children, e.g. 'What is your favourite number?', 'How old are you?', 'Does your house have a number?', 'What date is your birthday?' Acknowledge all suggestions but particularly explore those that encourage realization that we count to find out 'how many?': e.g. if they answer 'eight' in response to the question 'How old are you?', establish that this tells us how many birthdays they have had, and how many years they have been alive.

Refer to numbers in use and discuss what they tell us: e.g. refer to the calendar and look at the numbered days of the month; refer to the clock and look at the numbers on the clock face; refer to the labels around the classroom showing how many children can work at one time on a given activity. As you explore these, emphasize the idea that we count to find out 'how many?' When tidying up the classroom, children count to check that the right numbers of pencils, paintbrushes, scissors, etc. are in each labelled storage pot.

Discuss when we need to count things. Younger children may suggest when they count during the school day: e.g. register time, to find out how many children are at school; counting to find out how many children are having a school meal; counting to find out how many pieces of fruit are needed, etc. Older children may suggest counting money, how many objects they have collected, how many goals they have scored in football etc. Discuss children's suggestions and the need to count accurately.

Link to Number, Pattern and Calculating 1

Securing Foundations 1–12, Numbers and the Numbers System activities; Numbers and the Numbers System 1

Counting is one of the four strands in the Breaking Barriers teaching programme. The Counting activities are designed to be used in conjunction with any activity group as required, and with the first four Pattern and Algebra activity groups, and the first four Numbers and the Number System activity groups in particular.

Three strands of foundation activities to work in parallel

Pattern and Algebra	Counting	Numbers and the Number System
Simple repeating patterns	Counting Activity Group	1 Exploring Numicon Shapes and Baseboard
Pattern, direction and orientation		2 Matching Numicon Shapes
More complex repeating patterns		3 Making comparisons I – amounts and measures to understand bigger
		4 Making comparisons II – amounts and measures to understand smaller
		5 Matching Numicon Shapes and pictures
		6 Making comparisons using the language of comparison

The activities

Activities for learning to recite the count sequence (oral counting)

- Look at counting books; read counting stories.
- Sing counting songs and learn counting rhymes.
- Count forwards and backwards in unison – whispering.
- Clapping – children clap once as they say each number name.
- Use percussion – beat once for each number name said.
- Marching – count each step marched.
- Children count in unison to a given number as you point to each child round the group. Move on to children taking turns to say one number name.
- Count aloud while pointing to each number on the Numicon Display Number Line. Initially count forwards from 1.
- Count forwards and backwards, alternately speaking and then whispering number names.
- Count round the group to find how many children there are, or to a given number.
- Ask children to count aloud while one child points to each number on the Numicon Display Number Line.

Activities for counting on (and back from)...

- When children are secure in reciting the count sequence 1–10 they need to learn to count on and back from any number within this range. Put a set of Numicon Shapes 1–10 in order, and point to one of the Shapes for the child to count on from. When children are confident at doing this with the Numicon Shapes, move on to doing the same activity with the Numicon Large Format Table-top Number Line, and then with the 0–10 number line (photocopy master 2) and the Numicon 0–100 cm Number Line.
- Support children to understand what is happening when they are counting backwards by choosing a number on the number line from within their counting range and asking them for the previous number. Continue to look for the previous number each time, eventually moving to reciting the backwards sequence while pointing to each number as it is said.
- Ask children to count aloud while pointing to each number on the number line (forwards or backwards from numbers within children's counting range).
- Select a starting number to count on or back from – vary by turning a numeral card, taking a numeral card from the Numicon Feely Bag, taking a plastic numeral from the Feely Bag.
- Choose a starting number and then ask a child to start counting. When you point to another child, the first child stops and the next child continues the count.
- Children count aloud while one child points to each number on the number line. Start by counting forwards from 1; vary by counting forwards from other numbers and backwards from other numbers.

Smaller steps

- If children have difficulty remembering the count sequence from 1 to 10, it is helpful for teachers to model saying it quickly so children can hold the full sequence in their short-term memory.
- For children who have phonological memory difficulties, and who find it difficult to remember the count sequence, introducing numerals and Numicon Shapes as well as the number names provides them with two visual prompts on which to hang the sounds of the number words.

Activities for recognizing and reading numerals

- As well as displaying the Numicon Display Number Line, set up a counting display to help children to connect each numeral with its Numicon Shape and pattern.
- Play number dominoes, number lotto, number puzzles.
- Children make a little counting book for each number, initially from 1 to 5, extending to 10.
- Hold up numeral cards (from within children's counting range) for children to read and count on from, or back from.
- Using the Numicon Large Format Table-top Number Line, an adult says a number, and the child has to find the numeral.
- Using the Numicon Large Format Table-top Number Line, an adult points to a numeral, and the child says it. Vary using the 0–10 number line (photocopy master 2).
- Sort sets of numeral cards appropriate to children's counting and recognition range.
- Spread out numeral cards face up; an adult says a number and the child points to it.
- Show the child a card; the child calls out the number name. Vary so the child turns cards and says the number names.
- Children spin a Numicon Spinner with numeral overlays (cut from photocopy master 20) and say the number name.
- Put numeral cards or plastic numerals in the Numicon Feely Bag; a child pulls out a card/numeral and says what it is.
- Children read any numerals in the environment – from books, on clocks, telephones, calculators, etc.
- Repeat the above activities with numeral cards 11–20.
- Repeat the above activities where possible with a selection of numeral cards above 20, and refer to the Numicon 0–100 cm Number Line.
- Post numeral cards through the Numicon Post Box to a child who has to say the number name; or an adult says the number name (from a selection of numeral cards previously given to the child) and the child posts the card back to the adult.

Counting

1

Activities for introducing one-to-one matching

- Introduce one-to-one matching through everyday opportunities such as matching one straw to each drink, one biscuit to each plate, etc.
- Use the Counting Frame (photocopy master 4) for children to match one object to each circle. Vary by using different objects, e.g. buttons, play people, balls of modelling dough, and so on.
- Walk the Numicon Display Number Line. Place Numicon Large Foam Shapes 1–10 (if available) in order on the floor. Ask children to stand at the beginning of the row of Shapes (not standing on 1). Ask them to find how many steps they will take to reach the end of the row of Shapes and encourage them to count as they step from Shape to Shape.

Activities for counting objects one to one

Activity 1: Counting up to 10 objects accurately

Have ready: Numicon 0–100 cm Number Line on display, Numicon 0–31 Number Lines, collections of small objects for counting, containers (e.g. small pots, junk lids) that will be unlikely to hold more than ten of the objects, circles of felt or other fabric (these establish the child's field of action, which helps them to organize their work (e.g. **Fig.1**)

Step 1

Children take a container and fill it with objects. They say how many they think there are. Introduce the word 'estimate', explaining that when we estimate we try to make a good guess that we think will be very close to the right number. Ask children how they could check to see if their estimate was correct; agree that they will need to count the objects.

Step 2

As children count their objects, encourage them to develop strategies for accurate counting: e.g. as they say each number name they may rearrange the objects into a row, move each object as they count, and so on.

Step 3

When children have completed their count, share their different strategies.

Step 4

Discuss that the last number they have counted to tells them the total.

Step 5

Explain to children that they now need to find the last number in their count on the 0–31 Number Line. Encourage them to think first about where on the number line they expect to find the number.

Step 6

Children find the number on the 0–31 Number Line (e.g. **Fig. 2**).

Smaller steps

- Provide a counting frame (photocopy master 4) to help children to organize their count lines (e.g. **Fig. 3**).
- Reduce the number of objects to be counted by providing larger objects so fewer will fit in the container.
- Provide a Numicon Large Format Table-top Number Line.

Activity 2: Counting objects accurately by placing them along a number line

Have ready: Numicon 0–100 cm Number Line on display, Numicon Large Format Table-top Number Line, collections of small objects for counting including 1p coins, containers (e.g. small pots, junk lids), that will be unlikely to hold more than ten of the objects, circles of felt or other fabric

1

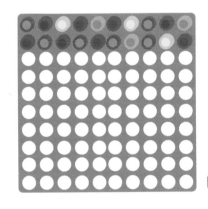

3

+---+---+---+---+---+---+---+---+---+---+---+---+---+---+
0   I   2   3   4   5   6   7   8   9   10 II 12 13

2

Step 1

Children take a container and fill it with objects and then estimate how many they think there are.

Step 2

Model how to use a number line to check their estimate by placing one object on each number, starting by placing the first object on 1 and pointing out that you do not place an object on 0 because that means no objects (e.g. Fig. 4).

Step 3

Repeat Steps 1 and 2 frequently with different quantities of up to ten objects.

Smaller steps

Use the Numicon Large Format Table-top Number Line folded to show only 0–5. Ask children to place one object on each number. Extend to 10 as children are ready.

Activity 3: Counting how many 0–30 with number lines and Numicon Shape patterns

Have ready: Numicon 0–100 cm Number Line on display, Numicon Large Format Table-top Number Line, collections of small objects for counting (e.g. shells, 1p coins, buttons), containers (e.g. small flower pots, junk lids), that will be unlikely to hold more than thirty of the objects, circles of felt or other fabric

Step 1

Children take a container, fill it with objects and estimate how many objects there are.

Step 2

They check their estimate by placing the objects on each number along the Large Format Table-top Number Line, remembering to ignore 0 and to place their first object on 1.

Step 3

When children have completed their count, ask them if they could show the last number in the count by rearranging the objects into Numicon Shape patterns. If there are more than ten objects, children arrange them in 10-patterns first and the remaining objects into another Numicon Shape pattern (e.g. Fig. 5).

Step 4

Repeat Steps 1 and 2 frequently with different quantities of objects, including 1p coins. Extend to 30 (using the Numicon 0–31 Number Line) as children are ready.

Activity 4: How many in the box? (to follow Numbers and the Number System Activity Groups 12–16)

Have ready: Numicon 0–31 Number Line, Numicon Shapes, a small lidded box containing a number of objects for children to count (select the number of objects appropriate to children's counting range and ability to build Numicon Shape patterns)

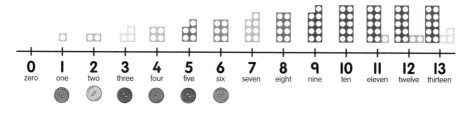

4

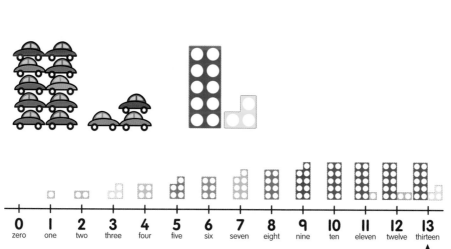

5

Counting

1

Step 1

Show children the box. Pass it round the group and ask children what they think it might contain, and how many of those objects might be in it. Discuss children's suggestions. Remove the lid to reveal the objects inside. Pass it round the group again. Ask children to estimate how many objects there are and jot down their estimate.

Step 2

Ask children for suggestions for how they might check their estimates: e.g. placing objects along the 0–31 Number Line, organizing the objects in a row, arranging the objects into Numicon Shape patterns. Try out the different methods. Discuss which is the most efficient and which one they could use if they didn't have a number line handy. Encourage them to suggest arranging the objects into Numicon Shape patterns.

Step 3

Children check their estimates against the total and find the total on the 0–31 Number Line.

Step 4

Repeat Steps 1–3 often, maintaining children's interest by varying the objects and the amounts.

Further practice

- Using Numicon Counters, Pegs or other objects for counting, point to each object as a child says the number name.
- Children say each number name out loud while counting objects from one container to another (two containers: one empty, one containing a suitable number of small objects).
- Children move each object across the table as it is counted.
- Children walk along a Numicon Display Number Line, saying the number name for each step.
- Drop objects into a tin; a child counts, with closed eyes, as objects are dropped in, and then counts to check.
- Using a counting frame (photocopy master 4), children count one object onto each circle.
- Children count objects onto the Numicon Large Format Table-top Number Line.
- Children count objects onto a number line (photocopy master 2).
- Children count up to thirty objects onto the Number Track 0–30 (photocopy master 7).
- Have a random group of objects on the table and ask a child to count all of them.
- Ask children to 'post' or drop a specific number of objects into a box (vary by giving them a written numeral to read and then count out that many objects).
- Use a sorting tray. Place different numeral cards in each section. Children count out the appropriate quantity of objects.

- Children count a given number of objects from a larger collection.
- Play board games (download Numicon Snakes and Ladders from website).

For children moving on quickly

Give children seven or eight counters to count in any order. Ask them to start at different points in the row of objects and finish at different points.

Writing numerals

This is a skill that must not take precedence over children learning other mathematics work. If the child is having difficulty with the formation of numerals, select activities suitable for their level of difficulty. If the child starts to form a numeral incorrectly, stop them as soon as you notice, otherwise the wrong habit will be reinforced. Do not allow them to 'correct' an incorrectly written numeral but encourage them to start again.

Numeral formation activities

Discuss how children find writing numerals, which ones are easy and which ones are harder. Often children find it difficult to remember which way round to write numerals as there is no visual reference as to which way they go.

- Explore shapes of numerals in PE lessons. Hold up large numeral cards one at a time for children to:
  - try making that shape with their body – invite children to share their ideas for the others to try;
  - form large numerals in air (skywrite) with both hands, ensuring that they cross the midline; with an adult describing how to form the numeral, the child says the numeral as they form it;
  - use ribbons to 'write' numerals in air describing straight actions, curved actions and round actions.
- Children 'write' numerals with a finger in sand or a glitter tray, saying the numeral as it is written.
- Children write 'rainbow numerals' by tracing over a large written numeral using different-coloured felt tip pens.
- An adult demonstrates how to write numerals on paper (the adult should sit next to the child to ensure correct formation). Use a dot to indicate the correct start point (and, if needed, an arrow to indicate the direction of movement).
- Children 'write' numerals with a finger on paper.
- Children record numerals with pencil on paper or pen on whiteboard, leaving spaces between each numeral. Numerals should be written at least six times with children quietly saying the numeral at each attempt.
- As children's counting range extends, give them opportunities to practise writing 2-digit and then 3-digit numbers.

Pattern and Algebra

Simple repeating patterns

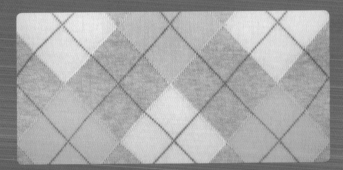

Educational context

In all the activities, children should be encouraged to notice and explain regularities and to **predict what will come next**. This lays the foundation for **identifying rules, predicting and generalizing**, which children need for success in mathematics throughout their school days and beyond. Therefore it is essential that they have plenty of opportunities to become skilful with this foundation to their mathematical thinking.

The core activities in this group focus on learning to **copy, continue and then devise repeating patterns**, but as an introduction to this it is helpful to encourage children's awareness of **regular routines** in their day, patterns they see around them and patterns in poetry, story, music and movement. Children should also have ample opportunities to create their own patterns with a range of different media including: art materials for painting, printing and collage; natural objects like shells, grasses, leaves, stones; junk objects such as bottle tops; classroom equipment such as interlocking cubes, threading beads, building blocks and small-world characters. Children can also use repeating patterns to decorate their work from other curriculum areas for display.

As often happens in mathematics, **the words and terms children will use in conversations** about pattern take on subtly different meanings from everyday use of the words. For instance, in 'What colour bead comes after the blue one?' the after describes position or direction, whereas in 'We watch television after tea,' after is used in a temporal sense. Children will need to experience many conversations using the various mathematical meanings of these words and terms before they will use them appropriately themselves.

It is strongly recommended that teachers plan for children to work regularly on independent pattern activities, even at times when the main focus may be on another activity group.

Recording patterns built with equipment are 3D and, for many children, transferring these by colouring onto squared paper in 2D is an overly challenging step. It is also time consuming. Printing or sticking shapes is a helpful step towards children **recording 2D repeating patterns**. Recording patterns by colouring is suggested for children moving on quickly.

(Note: the term **'ab'** pattern is used to describe alternating patterns where two elements are repeated, e.g. red block, blue block, red block, blue block ... ; an **'abc'** pattern has three repeated elements, and so on.)

Aims

- To recognize organized patterns and arrangements occurring naturally in the environment
- To learn to copy repeating patterns
- To begin to recognize that regular patterns follow rules
- To learn to follow rules to continue repeating patterns
- To devise simple repeating patterns

Communicating

Imagery
displays about pattern including objects, pictures that show regular patterns

Equipment
See the individual 'have ready' for each activity, various items for the activities in the 'Extending the activities' section

Words and terms for instruction (supported with signs and symbols)
copy, match, build, make, arrange, continue, 'what comes next?', 'what came before?'

Mathematical words and terms (supported with signs and symbols)
the same, pattern, too many, enough, not enough, next, before, after, regular, repeating, predict, shape, pattern

Assessment

Individual Record of Progress: Pattern and Algebra 1–7

Putting the activities into context

Set up a pattern display of objects with regular repeating patterns, e.g. cushions, T-shirts with stripes, crockery with a repeated motif, small swatches of fabric with regular patterns, necklaces, books with patterned page borders, and so on. Discuss with children the different ways that objects are decorated, and compare objects that have regular patterns with those that don't, e.g. a cushion with a picture on it, and a striped cushion. Introduce the phrase 'repeating pattern' to describe patterns where the same motif is used again and again. Ask children to suggest other situations where something is repeated, e.g. the chorus of a song, or when someone is asked to repeat what they have said. Support with signing to help children understand the word 'repeat'. Children could bring examples of patterns to add to a display.

Take children on a walk to look for regular patterns, e.g. in brick work, on paving stones, chain link fences and treads on tyres, and in natural objects (e.g. the veins on some leaves, the regular petals on flowers, patterns on snail shells), and take photographs. Display the sequence of the walk as a 'pattern map' with photos and objects from the walk shown in the order in which they were found.

Link to Number, Pattern and Calculating 1

Securing Foundations 1–3, Pattern and Algebra Activities

The activities

1

Activity 1: Copying a simple repeating pattern

Have ready: Numicon Baseboard, baskets of Numicon Coloured Pegs sorted by colour

Step 1
Explain that you are going to make a repeating pattern with Pegs on the Baseboard.

Step 2
Make a repeating pattern, e.g. yellow Peg, red Peg, yellow Peg, red Peg, and so on (e.g. **Fig. 1**).

Step 3
Discuss the pattern with children, pointing to and saying the pattern aloud – 'yellow, red, yellow, red,' and so on, with children joining in. At the end of the row of Pegs, ask children what the next coloured Peg in the pattern would be if it were to be continued.

Step 4
Children copy the pattern by building it with Pegs on the Baseboard.

Smaller steps
- If children have fine motor difficulties, these activities could be followed replacing the Baseboard with a square grid drawn on card (or enlarged from photocopy master 23) and replacing the Pegs with balls of modelling dough (e.g. **Fig. 2**) or other suitably sized objects, such as building blocks, plastic bottle tops, coloured plastic beakers, bean bags.

Activity 2: Continuing a simple repeating pattern

Have ready: one or two Numicon Baseboards, baskets of Numicon Coloured Pegs sorted by colour

Step 1
Start a simple repeating pattern of Pegs on the Baseboard and ask children what colour the next Peg will be. Children continue the pattern. The pattern can be extended across two Baseboards placed side by side.

Step 2
Discuss the pattern and encourage children to say the pattern aloud.

Smaller steps
- As for Activity 1, carry out this activity using a grid on card, and larger objects instead of Pegs, for children with fine motor difficulties.

Activity 3: Devising a simple repeating pattern

Have ready: Numicon Baseboard, baskets of Numicon Coloured Pegs sorted by colour

Step 1
Children devise their own repeating patterns; some children may wish to record them.

Smaller steps
- As for Activity 1, carry out this activity using a grid on card, and larger objects instead of Pegs, for any children with fine motor difficulties.

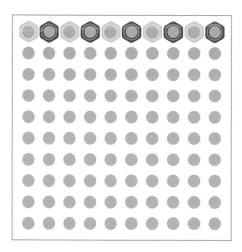

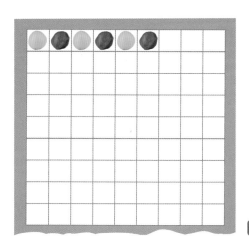

Pattern and Algebra

1

Activity 4: Responding to patterns with sounds

Have ready: cubes or blocks of different colours

Step 1
Build a pattern using two different coloured blocks, e.g. **Fig. 3**. With children, discuss and agree that they could make a sound for each colour, e.g. clap for red, tap foot for blue.

Step 2
Encourage children to join in with the sound pattern.

Step 3
Repeat with different sounds.

Step 4
Vary by using percussion instruments.

Smaller steps
• Introduce the activity with just a row of one colour of cubes for children to clap each time you point to one of the cubes.

Activity 5: Responding to patterns with movement

Have ready: cubes or blocks of different colours

Step 1
Build a pattern using two different coloured blocks, e.g **Fig. 4**. With children, discuss and agree that they could make a movement for each colour, e.g. hands on head for yellow, hands on tummy for pink.

Step 2
Encourage children to join in with the movement pattern as you point to the cubes.

Step 3
Repeat with different movements.

Smaller steps
• Introduce the activity with just a row of one colour of cubes for children to do the agreed movement each time you point to one of the cubes.

Further practice
• Continue to practise the above activities until children can recognize repeating patterns, predict what will come next to continue the pattern, and devise their own.

Extending the activities

Connecting activities
• Use different materials to devise repeating patterns, e.g. threading beads, printing, peg boards.
• Tell sound stories.
• Sing songs with repeated sequences.
• Develop patterns and sequences in movement and with percussion instruments.
• Listen to poetry and learning poems.

Connecting activities – Measures
• Time: Discuss the alternating pattern of day and night, collect children's suggestions of things that happen during the day and things that happen during the night to compile into two sets. Create a book with alternating pages for daytime and night time illustrated with children's suggestions.

For children moving on quickly
• Children devise their own patterns and movements. They may wish to record their patterns.
• Children build patterns with more than two colours of Pegs, and with different numbers of Pegs.
• Prepare collections of natural objects for children to use when creating repeating patterns, e.g **Fig. 5**.

Pattern, direction and orientation

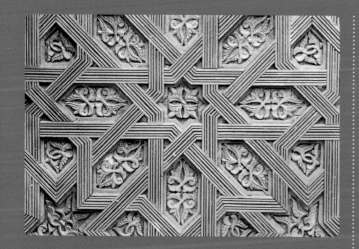

2

Educational context

Children enjoy and benefit from experimenting with Numicon Coloured Pegs on the Numicon Baseboard. In the examples given below, children explore straight lines going along and across the Baseboard from side to side and from corner to corner. They also explore arranging Pegs into different closed shapes. As children work on these activities there are also opportunities to help **develop language for position and direction** that are also used when they explore movement in forwards and backwards directions along number lines.

Aims

- To develop visual spatial perception and organizational skills
- To develop understanding of direction

Communicating

Imagery
displays of pictures that involve direction, e.g. simple mazes, arrows connecting one picture with another, simple maps, signposts

Equipment
See the individual 'have ready' for each activity, various items for the activities in the 'Extending the activities' section

Words and terms for instruction (supported with signs and symbols)
copy, match, arrange

Mathematical words and terms (supported with signs and symbols)
line, straight, turn, direction, diagonal, across, corner, edge, down, along

Assessment

Individual Record of Progress: Pattern and Algebra 2–5

Putting the activities into context

Discuss situations involving following or giving directions, e.g. giving a visitor directions for finding the way to the classroom or dining hall; describing the route taken to school; following the sequence of Numicon Shapes along the number line; counting along number lines.

Link to Geometry, Measurement and Statistics 1

Geometry 5

The activities

Activity 1: Arranging Numicon Pegs into simple shapes

Have ready: two Numicon Baseboards, baskets of Numicon Coloured Pegs sorted by colour

Step 1

Arrange Pegs in a line on the Baseboard, e.g. Fig. 1.

Step 2

Ask children to copy the arrangements of Pegs on their own Baseboard, and discuss how the Pegs have been arranged using the vocabulary of position and direction.

Step 3

Over several lessons give children opportunities to copy the arrangements of Pegs in the ways illustrated below (see Figs. 2–7).

Smaller steps

- If children have fine motor difficulties these activities could be followed by replacing the Baseboard with a square grid drawn on card (or enlarged photocopy master 23) and replacing the Pegs with balls of modelling dough or other suitable objects.

Further practice

- Over several lessons give children opportunities to copy the arrangements of Pegs in the ways illustrated below.

Extending the activities

Connecting activities

- Play 'Cover the board' activities, constraining the variety of Numicon Shapes used, e.g. use only odd Shapes that will necessitate children orientating them in order to fill the spaces.
- In PE, play games where children have to respond to directional language, e.g. running diagonally across the hall; rolling a hoop or ball in different directions.
- Use a variety of media (drawing, painting, modelling dough, craft materials such as matchsticks, string, lolly sticks) for children to create patterns where lines go in different directions, e.g. zigzags, straight line patterns, wavy line patterns.
- Use matchsticks to create triangle patterns and straight line patterns, e.g. alternating horizontal, vertical, horizontal, vertical.
- Look at mazes and track paths through them.

For children moving on quickly

- Children make their own arrangements with Pegs on the Baseboard.
- Children make the seven arrangements shown (see Figs. 1–7) using repeating patterns instead of single colours (see Fig. 8).
- Children use 5–10 counters to make different arrangements on a tabletop; these could be recorded.

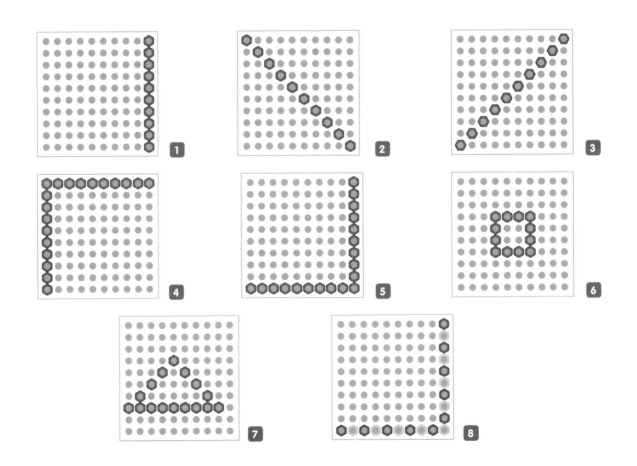

More complex repeating patterns

3

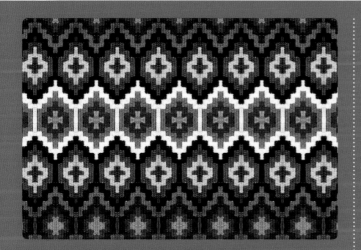

Educational context

Continue to encourage children to notice and explain regularities, to predict what will come next and to **explain the rule for patterns they make**, e.g. in a red, blue, yellow, red, blue, yellow, red, blue, yellow repeating pattern, yellow always comes between blue and red.

The core activities in this group focus on learning to **copy, continue and then devise repeating patterns with more than two elements**, and to explore different ways of responding to these with sounds or movement. They move on to building patterns where various numbers of cubes are repeated. Continue to encourage children to notice patterns in their environment and provide a wide range of media for children to create their own, more complex, repeating patterns.

It is strongly recommended that teachers continue to plan for children to work regularly on independent pattern activities, even at times when the main focus may be on another activity group.

At this stage, the focus is on **recognizing and devising patterns and finding ways of representing them through sounds, music and movement**.

Patterns built with equipment are 3D and, for many children, recording their patterns by colouring on squared paper in 2D is an overly challenging step. It is also time consuming. Printing or sticking shapes is a helpful step towards children **recording 2D repeating patterns**. Recording patterns by colouring is suggested for children moving on quickly if this is appropriate to their motor skills.

Aims

- To devise repeating patterns with more than two elements
- To recognize the rule for a pattern with more than two elements and predict what will come next
- To recognize patterns in sounds and movements
- To respond to repeating patterns built with objects with sound or movement patterns

Communicating

Imagery
displays about pattern, including objects and pictures that show repeating patterns involving different amounts, and regular patterns

Equipment
See the individual 'have ready' for each activity, various items for the activities in the 'Extending the activities' section.

Words and terms for instruction (supported with signs and symbols)
copy, match, build, make, arrange, continue, what comes next?, what came before?

Mathematical words and terms (supported with signs and symbols)
the same, pattern, too many, too few, enough, not enough, next, before, after, regular, repeating, predict, shape, pattern

Assessment

Individual Record of Progress: Pattern and Algebra 8–12

Putting the activities into context

Maintain a pattern display, refreshing it with examples of more complex repeating patterns made with different objects. Continue to provide rich opportunities for children to experience patterns in stories, poems, movement, clothes, and so on. Discuss the patterns with children, encouraging them to explain the rules they notice.

Link to Number, Pattern and Calculating 1

Securing Foundations 4–5

Pattern and Algebra

The activities

Activity 1: Copying a more complex repeating pattern

Have ready: Numicon Baseboard, baskets of Numicon Coloured Pegs sorted by colour

Step 1
Explain that you are going to make a repeating pattern with Pegs on the Baseboard, using three colours.

Step 2
Make a repeating pattern, e.g. red, yellow, green, red, yellow, green, red, yellow, green (see **Fig. 1**).

Step 3
Discuss the pattern with children, pointing to and saying the pattern aloud: 'Red, yellow, green, red, yellow, green,' and so on.

Step 4
Children copy the pattern with Pegs on the Baseboard or tabletop.

Smaller steps
- If children have fine motor difficulties, these activities could be followed by replacing the Baseboard with a square grid drawn on card (or enlarged from photocopy master 23) and replacing the Pegs with objects that are easier to handle, e.g. building blocks, plastic bottle tops, coloured plastic beakers, or bean bags (see **Fig. 2**).

Activity 2: Continuing a more complex repeating pattern

Have ready: Numicon Baseboard, baskets of Numicon Coloured Pegs sorted by colour

Step 1
Start a repeating pattern using three colours of Pegs, e.g. blue, yellow, green, blue (see **Fig. 3**), and ask children what colour the next Peg will be. Children continue the pattern on the Baseboard.

Step 2
Discuss the pattern and encourage children to say it aloud – 'blue, yellow, green, blue' – and to predict what will come next.

Step 3
Children continue the pattern with Pegs on the Baseboard or tabletop.

Smaller steps
- As for Activity 1, carry out this activity using a grid on card (or enlarged from photocopy master 23), and larger objects instead of Pegs, for any children with fine motor difficulties.

Activity 3: Devising a more complex repeating pattern

Have ready: Numicon Baseboard, baskets of Numicon Coloured Pegs sorted by colour

Step 1
Children devise their own repeating patterns using three different coloured Pegs on the Baseboard.

Smaller steps
- As for Activity 1, carry out this activity using a grid on card, and larger objects instead of Pegs, for any children with fine motor difficulties.

Activity 4: Repeating patterns with Numicon Shapes

Have ready: Numicon Shapes, Numicon Baseboard, Numicon Baseboard Overlay

Step 1
Children experiment to devise repeating patterns using Numicon Shapes (e.g. **Fig 4**). They share and discuss their patterns.

Smaller steps
- Provide the Baseboard Overlay showing a repeating pattern of 1-shapes and 2-shapes as a model for children to copy, first by matching Shapes to the Overlay, then by copying underneath and finally by building their own repeating pattern with Shapes.

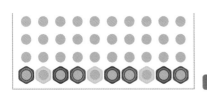

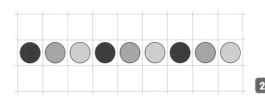

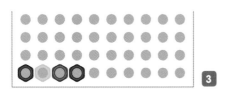

Extending the activities 3

Activity 5: Patterns where amounts of cubes are repeated

Have ready: building blocks or interlocking cubes of different colours

Step 1

Using coloured blocks or interlocking cubes, start to build a pattern where the cubes are built into towers of different heights, e.g. **Fig. 5**. Ask children to predict each time what comes next.

Step 2

Ask children to suggest and build further patterns that involve towers of different heights, e.g. **Fig. 6**.

Step 3

Share and discuss children's different patterns encouraging all children to predict how the pattern would continue.

Activity 6: Repeating patterns with number rods

Have ready: Numicon Number Rod Trays 1–10, number rods

Step 1

Children experiment to devise repeating patterns using number rods, e.g. **Fig.7**. Share their patterns, which may include repeated sequences of rods and sequences that show symmetry. If the rods are laid flat, provide a Number Rod Tray to encourage children to line them up.

Further practice for activities 5 and 6

- Give children opportunities to practise these activities, devising their own patterns until they can do so quickly and confidently. Encourage them to share their patterns and predict what the next item in each others' patterns will be.
- Show children repeating patterns of shapes or pictures on the interactive whiteboard and ask them to predict what will come next.
- Involve children in devising repeating patterns on the whiteboard.

Connecting activities

- Responding to patterns with sounds: build a pattern using two different coloured blocks. With children, discuss and agree that they could make a sound for each colour, e.g. clap for pink, click fingers for blue or tap foot for green, and encourage them to join in with the sound pattern. Repeat with different sounds. Vary by using percussion instruments instead of body sounds. Repeat using three different coloured blocks, e.g. **Fig. 8**.
- Responding to patterns with movement: build a pattern using two or three different coloured blocks. With children discuss and agree that they could make a movement for each colour, e.g. jump with feet together, arms in the air, touch toes. Encourage children to join in with the movement pattern. Repeat with different movements.

For children moving on quickly

- Children record their patterns in different ways.

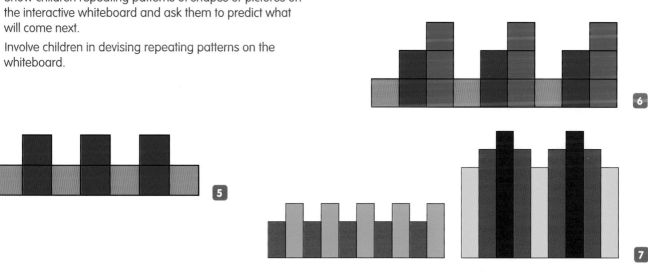

5 6 7 8

Similarities and differences – sorting

4

Educational context

This activity group encourages children, when they are making comparisons, to notice aspects that are the same and aspects that are different. Being able to explain **what is the same and what is different** is an important part of mathematical thinking. Careful questioning and conversation (with signing) will support children in developing their reasoning – when looking for similar attributes to decide **which objects go together to form a set**, and when looking for differences to be able to decide that something does not fit with the set. Once children are able to move beyond identical items being matched, e.g. sorting farm animals into cows, horses, sheep, and so on, children move on to begin to classify. Colour or size are obvious features to use when beginning to **classify**, but children then need to begin to **use further common attributes**, e.g. 'they are all thick', 'all have four sides', 'are all odd numbers'. Some children seem to be able to sort objects and notice when they are alike, but find it hard to describe the generalization.

Aims

- To be able to spot and say when something is the same colour or size
- To be able to spot and talk about other attributes that allow something to be considered 'the same'
- To find further items to be part of a given set
- To know that when something is not the same, it is different
- To be able to compile their own sets according to a chosen criterion

Communicating

Imagery
pictures and a display of sets of objects (e.g. farm animals, toy cars), pictures and displays of objects that share an attribute (e.g. all the same colour, all very small, all fruits)

Equipment
See the individual 'have ready' for each activity, various items for the activities in the 'Extending the activities' section

Words and terms for instruction (supported with signs and symbols)
sort, match, think, look carefully, put together

Mathematical words and terms (supported with signs and symbols)
same, different, because, similar, set, reason, can be part of the set, cannot be part of the set, odd one, thick, thin, long, short, wide, narrow, big, small, belong together, do not belong together, colour words

Assessment

Individual Record of Progress: Pattern and Algebra 13–20

Putting the activities into context

There are many everyday contexts in which sorting and classifying can be made meaningful to children, e.g. healthy food, clothing worn indoors, out of doors or for PE, and sorting musical instruments or PE equipment. Although contexts have been suggested for each activity, these can be varied, being mindful that some contexts might be overly distracting for some children.

Link to Number, Pattern and Calculating 1

Securing Foundations 8, 9 and 12

The activities

4

Activity 1: Noticing differences

Have ready: two very different objects, e.g. a hairbrush and a ball

Step 1
Show children the hairbrush and discuss what it is called and what it is for.

Step 2
Show and discuss the ball.

Step 3
Discuss how the objects are different, supporting the discussion with signing.

Smaller steps
- Encourage children to develop their ability to describe the attributes of different familiar objects.
- Continue to compare objects that are very different. Also compare objects that share some similarities until children are able to recognize and explain differences and similarities.

Activity 2: Noticing similarities

Have ready: two objects that are similar in some respects, e.g. a hairbrush and a toothbrush, or a tennis ball and a football

Step 1
Show children the two objects. Discuss their similarities, supporting the discussion with signing.

Step 2
Discuss the differences between the two objects, continuing to support with signing.

Smaller steps
- As for activity 1, encourage children to develop the ability to describe the attributes of different, familiar, objects.

Further practice for Activities 1 and 2
- Children compare two objects, e.g. toy cars, saying, 'They are the same because …,' 'They are different because …'. Repeat with many different objects.

Activity 3: Sorting toys

Have ready: a collection of a particular type of toy, e.g. vehicles or farm animals (for older children fruits could be used), sorting rings or circles of paper

Step 1
Put the collection of toys onto the tabletop and agree that all the objects are, e.g. toy vehicles. Explain that they are going to sort them into groups that go together.

Step 2
Children pick up the objects one by one and decide to which set they belong, e.g. cars or aircraft (see Fig. 1). Encourage children to explain their reasons, supporting by signing 'the same' when pointing out similarities between, or 'different' when pointing out differences between, the objects.

Step 3
Gradually extend the criteria for sorting, to provide opportunities for refining classification, e.g. by introducing a third type of vehicle and a third sorting ring.

Smaller steps
- Decide on a criterion, e.g. colour, and ask children to find something from around the classroom to go in the set.
- Decide on other criteria for children to make further sets, e.g. 'used for mark making', 'made of plastic'.
- Ask children to sort two very different types of object, e.g. toy vehicles and toy houses.
- Gradually extend the criteria for sorting to provide opportunities for refining classification, as in Activity 3 above.

Further practice
- Using commercial sorting equipment, ask children to take turns to decide how they will sort it, and to make a set for a friend to find the criterion. Children could draw their sets.

1

Pattern and Algebra

Activity 4: Sorting coins

Have ready: plenty of 1p, 2p, 5p, 10p, 20p and 50p coins, sorting hoops or circles of paper

Step 1

Spread out the coins on the table and ask children to look carefully at them, in order to notice similarities, and to sort them into sets. Encourage them to communicate the reasons for their choice. Children may sort according to type, e.g. **Fig. 2** or into bronze and silver, e.g. **Fig. 3**.

Smaller steps

- Provide just two types of coin, of a similar size but different colour, e.g. bronze 2p coins and silver 10p coins. Gradually extend the criteria for sorting to provide opportunities for refining classification as in Step 1.

Further practice

- Put collections of objects on interactive displays for children to sort.

Activity 5: Finding the odd one out

Have ready: sets of objects where one thing is the odd one out, e.g. a set of forks (not identical) with one knife or a set of circular things (plates, lids) with one square object, a range of other objects for children to choose from to make sets of their own

Step 1

Ask children what it would mean if someone said, 'It is the odd one out'. Listen to children's suggestions.

Step 2

With children, look at one of the sets and find the 'odd one out'. Discuss why this should be called 'odd' and agree that all the other parts of the set have something 'similar' about them whereas this is 'different'.

Step 3

Children look carefully at all the objects and choose some to put in a set; they should then include 'an odd piece'.

Step 4

Invite other children to identify the odd one out and to explain why.

Smaller steps

- Make sets of objects that are all the same colour with the odd one being a different colour.

Activity 6: Identifying a subset

Have ready: allow children to access objects in the classroom

Step 1

Decide on a criterion, e.g. 'made of wood', and ask children to find something to go in the set.

Step 2

Discuss the contributions and decide if a subset could be made, e.g. 'they are all made of wood but some also have yellow on them'. Decide together how to arrange these items.

Smaller steps

- Give children a selection of simple objects that share a common criterion, e.g. spoons. Work with children to find a subset, e.g. those that have plastic handles or those that are wooden.

Further practice

- Put collections of objects on interactive displays for children to sort and then to try to identify a subset.

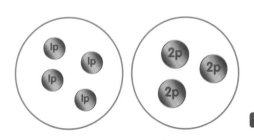

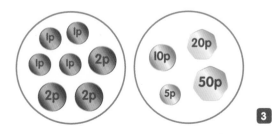

Extending the activities

4

Connecting activities

- Children sort objects by different criteria, e.g. material (wood, china, plastic, metal, etc.); colour; size (big and small); length (long and short); width (wide and narrow); capacity; function.

- Give riddles to solve, e.g. 'I have four legs. I am striped. I am a big cat. What am I?' Also include objects in the room, e.g. 'I have four legs. I am rectangular in shape. I am made of wood. You sit at me to do your work. What am I?'

- Ask children to line up, or get ready for break time, by calling out a criterion, e.g. 'Line up if you are wearing grey socks,' or, '… if you are not wearing a jumper,' or, '… if you have a brother'.

- Cut out pictures from magazines according to given criteria that will link with children's interests or current work. Children then stick them into set rings drawn on paper, or draw their own sets.

For children moving on quickly

- Introduce overlapping sets. Children sort collections of objects that display several attributes, e.g. musical instruments. They may: make sets of identical items; make sets of items of the same type but of different designs; use other criteria such as the function of the material they are made of (e.g. metal, wood, plastic). Discuss children's ideas and explore what to do when objects fit with both sets: e.g. if sorting by material, some objects may be made of both wood and metal. Introduce the idea of overlapping sorting rings (hoops). Encourage children to sort the instruments again using different criteria.

- Play the attribute game (photocopy master 1). Share out the cards and decide who will start. Place one card face up on the table. Children take turns to try to match one of their cards according to one of the attributes (it could be the same by colour, size or shape). If they can find a matching attribute, they place their card next to the one on the table (as when playing dominoes). If they cannot find a matching attribute they pass. The winner is the first to use all their cards. This game can also be played with commercially produced attribute blocks.

Labelling repeating patterns with numerals

5

Educational context

This activity group builds on and extends the ideas children have met earlier in Pattern and Algebra 3 (when they looked for and devised repeating patterns involving amounts), and also Numbers and the Number System 11, in which children labelled Numicon Shapes with numerals.

The following activities introduce children to looking for patterns in numbers, firstly by **labelling their own patterns with numerals**. In Activity 4, children are introduced to **recording their patterns** on squared paper; for some children, drawing a 2D image of their 3D pattern is a challenging step, so suggestions are made for helping children over this difficulty. As with the previous Pattern and Algebra activities, repeat the activities regularly over several sessions, until children are confidently building and recording patterns.

Knowing they can look for patterns in numbers helps to alert children that it is helpful to look for patterns when they begin to learn how to calculate – for instance, when they are adding one, or finding all the adding or subtracting facts for numbers to ten. Later, **looking for patterns** will support their learning of multiplication tables.

The pattern work with number rods is included for children moving on quickly who are able to refer to number rods by number and label them with numerals (as in Numbers and the Number System 11). However, this work is useful for all children as and when they are ready.

Aims

- To label patterns with repeated numbers with numerals
- To build patterns with apparatus in response to a numeral pattern

Communicating

Imagery
Numicon Display Number Line, Numicon 0–41 Number Rod Number Line, displays of objects that show repeated amounts, e.g. bead necklaces or children's own painted patterns

Equipment
See the individual 'have ready' for each activity, various items for the activities in the 'Extending the activities' section

Words and terms for instruction (supported with signs and symbols)
copy, match, continue, repeat, 'do again', make, build, label, predict, 'what comes next?', 'what came before?'

Mathematical words and terms (supported with signs and symbols)
the same, pattern, too many, too few, enough, not enough, next, before, after, regular, repeating, predict, shape, number words, ordinal number words (first, second, third, etc.)

Assessment

Individual Record of Progress: Pattern and Algebra 21–30

Putting the activities into context

Continue to maintain a pattern display, refreshing it with examples of patterns with repeated amounts. Continue to provide rich opportunities for children to experience patterns in stories, poems, movement, clothes, and so on. Continue to encourage children to notice patterns in their environment and to provide a wide range of media for children to create their own more complex repeating patterns. Discuss the patterns with children, encouraging them to explain the rules they notice.

Link to Number Pattern and Calculating 1

Securing Foundations 7 and 8

The activities

5

Activity 1: Simple repeating patterns with Numicon Shapes and numerals

Have ready: Numicon Shapes, Numicon Baseboards, several sets of Numeral Cards 1–10 (cut and laminated from photocopy master 11)

Step 1

Remind children about repeating patterns they have made previously using Numicon Shapes. With children, build a simple repeating pattern using two types of Shape, e.g. **Fig. 1**.

Step 2

Discuss how to label the pattern with numerals, using the numeral cards (see **Fig. 2**).

Further practice

- Invite children to devise and label other simple repeating patterns with two types of Shape.

Smaller steps

- Provide children with two Numicon Baseboards placed side by side on which they can build their patterns.

Activity 2: Repeating patterns with blocks and numerals

Have ready: different coloured cubes or blocks, several sets of Numeral Cards 1–10 (cut and laminated from photocopy master 11)

Step 1

Children experiment to devise repeating patterns with a different number of blocks for each colour, e.g. **Fig. 3**.

Step 2

Share and discuss children's patterns. With children, say the patterns aloud, e.g. 'one, two, three, one, two, three'.

Step 3

Children label the patterns with numerals using the numeral cards (see **Fig. 4**).

Further practice

- Children devise other patterns with regularly repeated amounts.

Smaller steps

- Some children may benefit from having a grid of squares drawn onto a piece of card (photocopy master 23 enlarged to A3) to help them to organize their patterns.

Activity 3: Increasing and decreasing patterns with Numicon Shapes and numerals

Have ready: Numicon Shapes, several sets of Numeral Cards 1-10 (cut and laminated from photocopy master 11)

Step 1

With children, build an increasing and decreasing pattern that shows symmetry, e.g. **Fig. 5**.

Step 2

Children say the pattern aloud: 'one, two, three, three, two, one'.

Step 3

Discuss how to label the pattern with numerals, using the numeral cards (see **Fig. 6**).

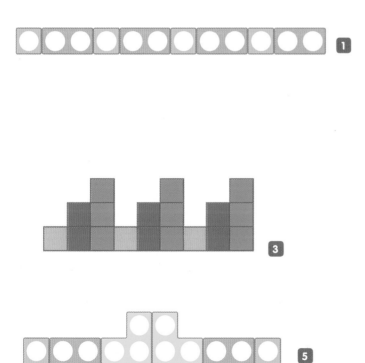

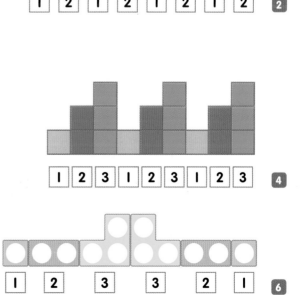

Pattern and Algebra

5

Smaller steps
- Some children may benefit from having a frame of large squares – either a grid of squares drawn onto a piece of card or photocopy master 23 enlarged to A3, or two Numicon Baseboards placed side by side to help them to organize their patterns.

Further practice
- Repeat the above steps with other increasing and decreasing patterns.

Activity 4: Recording repeating patterns of different amounts

Have ready: Numicon Shapes, several sets of Numeral Cards 1-10 (cut and laminated from photocopy master 11), printed Numicon Baseboard for drawing Numicon Shapes and Numicon Shape patterns (photocopy master 3)

Step 1
Build a pattern with Numicon Shapes and model how to record patterns built with Numicon Shapes on the printed Baseboard (e.g. **Fig. 7**).

Step 2
Children create and record a pattern of their own on the printed Baseboard.

Smaller steps
- Children continue to work practically by building their patterns and placing numeral cards underneath rather than recording by writing or drawing.

Further practice
- Children devise other patterns with regularly repeated Numicon Shapes and record these on the printed Baseboard.

Activity 5: Recording repeating patterns of different amounts on squared paper

Have ready: Numicon Shapes, several sets of Numeral Cards 1–10 (cut and laminated from photocopy master 11), squared paper (photocopy master 23)

Step 1
Build a pattern using blocks and model how to record patterns built with blocks on squared paper (see **Fig. 8**).

Step 2
Children create and record a pattern of their own.

Smaller steps
- Children continue to work practically by building their patterns and placing numeral cards underneath rather than recording by writing or drawing.

Further practice
Children devise other patterns with regularly repeated numbers of blocks and record these on squared paper.

Activity 6: Building a pattern with apparatus from a number pattern

Have ready: Numicon Shapes, number rods, a range of apparatus for building patterns (e.g. counters, interlocking cubes, blocks), a selection of number patterns similar to those children have been devising

Step 1
Show children a repeating numeral pattern, e.g. 1, 2, 3, 1, 2, 3, 1, 2, 3. Discuss how this might be represented with apparatus.

Step 2
Children choose apparatus and build the pattern.

Step 3
Discuss the patterns and encourage children to notice that in this pattern 3 always comes after 2 and before 1. Encourage children to predict what the next number would be in the repeated sequence.

Smaller steps
- Continue to provide simple patterns that use only two types of Numicon Shape. Encourage children to say the pattern aloud and support them to find the appropriate Shapes.

Further practice
- Give children other numeral patterns to build with apparatus.

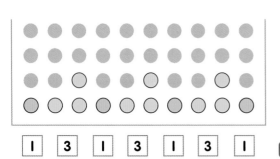

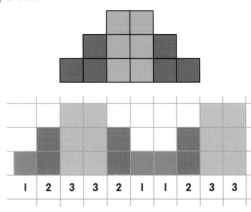

Extending the activities

5

Connecting activities

- Show children repeating patterns of shapes or pictures on the board. Ask them to predict what will come next.
- Show children repeating patterns of numerals. Ask them to suggest which Numicon Shapes would show the pattern.
- Show children patterns built with cubes or Numicon Shapes on the *Numicon Software for the Interactive Whiteboard* (if available). Ask them to suggest a numeral pattern to show it.
- Show children repeating numeral patterns and ask them to continue the pattern.
- Show children repeating numeral patterns and ask them to suggest a sound pattern that will show it.
- Show children patterns made with Numicon Shapes that use reflective symmetry and ask them to suggest how to continue the pattern.

For children moving on quickly

- Children devise different patterns using number rods, e.g. repeating patterns of rods, or sequences that show symmetry. They record one of their patterns on squared paper by drawing the number rods and writing numerals (e.g. Fig. 9).
- Show children a repeating pattern of numerals and ask them to suggest which number rods would show the pattern.

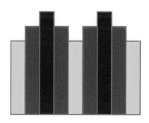

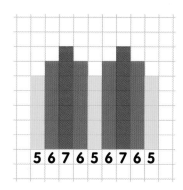

5 6 7 6 5 6 7 6 5   9

Equivalence – amounts and measures

6

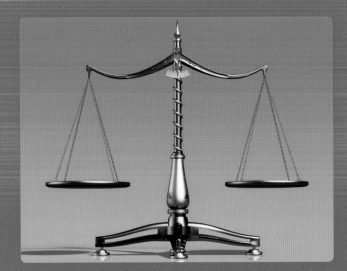

Educational context

Understanding that **equivalence means 'is of equal value'** is an essential foundation for all children's mathematics. The idea of equal value – even though the values may be represented differently – is often challenging for children. Confusion can occur with the use of language so it is important to **qualify situations**, e.g. the same length, the same weight, the same amount, rather than just saying 'the same'. When describing measures, it is helpful for children to be precise and talk about things that are 'equal in length' or 'equal in weight'. Some signing systems use the same action (sign) for 'equals' and 'the same'. Numicon has developed an action for equals to help children to understand the subtle distinction between the two: e.g. when two identical Numicon Shapes are matched together they are 'the same', and when e.g. the 3-shape and the 2-shape are shown to equal the 5-shape they are not 'the same' – they actually look very different in colour, size and the number of holes – but they are of equal value. The work on measures in Activities 3 and 4 will probably be spread over many weeks but is an essential foundation for future understanding of **equivalence in measures** (e.g. 100 cm = 1 m, 100p = £1, 1000 g = 1 kg) and is of course a basis for life skills. Further work on measures involving capacity, time and height are suggested in 'Extending the activities'. As suggested in previous activity groups teachers will need to decide when it is appropriate to introduce these activities to children.

The Numicon Pan Balance is introduced in this activity group – not just to show equal weight – but as a helpful tool for later work involving 'greater than', 'less than' and equivalence.

Number rods are used when looking at equal length and height. Some children may use colour names to describe them while others may have begun to use number names.

Activities showing equivalence with Numicon Shapes in adding situations is developed in a later activity group.

Aims

- To use the language of comparison in conversation
- To compare objects directly by length, weight, height, width and capacity
- To begin to understand that 'equals' means 'of equal value'

Communicating

Imagery
Numicon Display Number Line, Numicon 0–41 Number Rod Number Line, Numicon Large Format Table-top Number Line, Numicon Pan Balance

Equipment
See the individual 'have ready' for each activity, various items for the activities in the 'Extending the activities' section

Words and terms for instruction (supported with signs and symbols)
build, find, work out, think, talk about, explain, compare

Mathematical words and terms (supported with signs and symbols)
more, less, fewer, is greater than, is smaller than, the same, the same amount as, different amount, balances, equals, is heavier than, is lighter than, are equal in weight, is longer than, is shorter than, are equal in length, is taller than, is shorter than, are equal in height, are equal in width, is thicker than, is thinner than, is wider than, is narrower than, holds more, holds less, takes an equal amount of time

Assessment

Individual Record of Progress: Pattern and Algebra 37, Measures 14, 15, 30, 40, 49, 55, 60

Putting the activities into context

Children will need to think about contexts around both number ideas and measures. When sharing things with a friend or sibling, they talk about having an equal number of things, e.g. stickers, or an equal number of turns at a computer game. Children may compare collections with a friend and talk about having an equal number of things. When having treats at break time or in a lunch box it can be important for some to ensure that their treat is the same size as that of their sibling or friend.

Look for objects that are equal in length (shoe sizes and length of feet), height (of children) or width (if the language has been introduced to children). When talking about time and capacity the language involved is quite sophisticated. Decide which experiences are appropriate for children, e.g. talking about the same amount of time needed each day to do certain tasks, or the equal amounts of juice needed for drinks.

Link to Geometry, Measurement and Statistics 1

Measurement 1 and 3, Activities 1–3

The activities

Activity 1: Making groups equal – using identical objects

Have ready: various collections of different sorts of small object (e.g. shells, counters, bricks, small cars)

Step 1

Choose one collection of objects and arrange them into a Numicon Shape 6-pattern and 8-pattern. Ask children to point to the pattern that has more. Then ask them to point to the pattern that has fewer.

Step 2

Now explain that you want to make the two patterns have the same amount each. Talk with children about how this could be done: taking two objects away from the 8-pattern, putting two objects onto the 6-pattern, or taking one object from the 8-pattern and putting it onto the 6-pattern so they both make the 7-pattern.

Step 3

Explain to children that when two groups have the same number of objects, we can say that they are 'equal'. Show children the Numicon sign for 'equal' (see **Fig. 1**). (Agree that these groups are also 'the same' because they are identical – they have the same number, the same sort of objects, and they are arranged into the same pattern.)

Smaller steps
• Begin with 'odd' Shape patterns so only one object has to be moved to make both patterns equal.

Further practice
• Give children other collections of identical objects for them to make equal. Vary the numbers in each group according to the ability of the children.

Activity 2: Making groups equal – using different objects

Have ready: Numicon Shapes, Numicon Feely Bags, various collections of different sorts of small object (e.g. shells, counters, bricks, small cars)

Step 1

Ask one child to choose a collection and make a 5-pattern using one collection of objects, while another makes a 7-pattern with a different collection of objects.

Step 2

Ask children to make the two patterns equal by taking one object from the 7-pattern and putting it onto the 5-pattern so that both equal the 6-pattern (e.g. **Fig. 2**).

Step 3

Talk with children about the patterns looking different because of the different objects used but being of 'equal value' because they are both 6-patterns.

Step 4

Make a 4-pattern and an 8-pattern of completely random objects and ask children to make them equal. Remind children that to be equal each group will have the same value, that is, the same number of objects, and that the Shape patterns will, therefore, be the same shape.

Smaller steps
• Ensure children are secure in making random collections equal where only one object has to be moved before using collections where the gap is wider.

Further practice
• Children take two Shapes from a Numicon Feely Bag and make the patterns for both, using a collection of mixed objects. They then make the patterns equal. (Vary by having just 'odd' Shapes in the Feely Bag.)

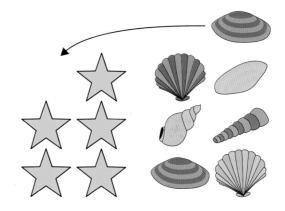

Pattern and Algebra

Activity 3: Introducing the Numicon Pan Balance and making equal weights

Have ready: Numicon Pan Balance, modelling dough objects for putting in the Pan Balance

Step 1
Even if children are familiar with pan balances from cooking, give them opportunities to learn the name 'pan balance' and to experiment to see what happens when they put things into the pans. (Initially children may enjoy using totally mixed objects in both pans.)

Step 2
Talk with children about a see-saw, and discuss why one end might be up high and the other end down low. Look at the Pan Balance and talk about how it moves up and down like a see-saw. Talk with children to decide what we know when one end of the see-saw (or one pan) is not higher than the other so they 'balance'. Agree that the things at each end of the see-saw or the things in each pan weigh the same. They are of 'equal weight'.

Step 3
Using two different-sized lumps of modelling dough, once children have compared how heavy they are by holding one in each hand, ask them to show which is heavier and which is lighter using the Pan Balance (e.g. **Fig. 3**). Ask children to make the pans 'balance'. Help them to make the two lumps of modelling dough equal in weight so they can achieve this.

Smaller steps
• Take as much time as needed with the main activity.

Further practice
• Children repeat Step 3, working independently to make different lumps of modelling dough equal.
• Give children two identical containers holding different numbers of objects. They put one container in each pan and then make the pans balance by taking some objects from one pan and placing them in the other.

Activity 4: Making equal lengths and using number rods

Have ready: number rods, strips of paper of differing lengths

Step 1
Give children two strips of paper of differing lengths. Talk about which is longer and which is shorter than the other (making sure children understand that they need to line up one end of each piece of paper at the same point to be able to compare them) and then explain to children that you want to make the strips of paper the same length. Agree that some more paper could be stuck onto the shorter piece or some could be cut off the longer piece.

Step 2
When children have made the strips of paper the same length, model the mathematical language 'equal in length'.

Step 3
Ask children to find two rods that are different in length and to say which is longer than the other and which is shorter.

Step 4
Now ask children to find two rods that are the same length. Talk with children about how they are 'equal in length'.

Smaller steps
• When children are finding rods, limit the selection to restrict the choice.

Further practice
• Show children a rod longer than the 1-rod. Challenge them to find a longer rod than one they are shown, or a shorter rod, or one that is equal in length.
• Use the Numicon Number Rod Trays 1–10. Children find the rod that fits exactly into the tray. They then find other combinations of rods that when placed end-to-end alongside are equal in length (e.g. **Fig. 4**).

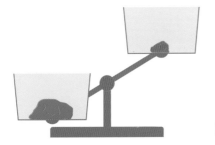

3

4

Extending the activities 6

Activity 5: Equivalence with Numicon Shapes

Have ready: Numicon Shapes, Numicon Spinner and 6–10 Shape Overlay (cut from photocopy master 20), Numicon Pan Balance, Numicon Large Format Table-top Number Line

Step 1
Children spin the Spinner, find the corresponding Shape and place it in one pan of the Pan Balance. They spin again, find the Shape and place it in the other pan.

Step 2
If children have different Shapes, they say which pan is the heaviest. They then look at the Shapes and discuss which one is heavier, also referring to the number names, e.g. 'The 8-shape is heavier than the 5-shape' (see **Fig. 5**). If they have identical Shapes, talk with them about how the 'balance of Shapes' can be seen on either side of the Pan Balance because the Shapes are the same; remind them that the Shapes are also equal.

Step 3
Children find both numbers on the Table-top Number Line, noting that the number for the heavier Shape is further along the Number Line.

Step 4
If appropriate for children, discuss that the Shape that is heavier has more holes than the Shape that is lighter, and that the number value of the Shape with more holes is greater than the number value of the Shape that is smaller or has fewer holes. Refer to the Table-top Number Line again, showing that the Shape of greater value is further along the Number Line than the one of smaller value.

Smaller steps
• Work through the steps at a pace appropriate for children.
• If the Spinners are a problem, generate numbers by taking a numeral card from a random selection spread face down on the table top, or take a Shape from the Numicon Feely Bag (or Feely Bag alternative).

Further practice
• Children repeat Activity 5 independently, keeping a record of how many times they spin identical numbers, and find Shapes that balance – and so are equal.

Connecting activities – Measures
• Height: Compare the heights of children to see if any children are equal in height.
• Children compare the heights of number rods by standing them on end.
• Children build towers with blocks or interlocking cubes that are equal in height.
• Children build structures with number rods that rely on equal-sized rods being used to make the structure secure.
• Width: In PE, talk about it being easier to balance and walk along a wide bench rather than a narrow beam.
• Weight: Provide dough (or clay) and the Pan Balance. Challenge children to make balls of dough or clay that are of equal weight.
• Provide sand (or pasta, rice) and the Pan Balance. Challenge students to adjust the amounts of sand to make the pans balance.
• Capacity: Provide identical containers containing varying amounts of liquid for students to compare to see which holds more, holds less or holds an equal amount of liquid.
• Provide identical containers for children to fill with an equal amount of liquid or dry sand.
• Provide different-shaped containers and give children the challenge of working out how they might pour equal amounts into each.
• Time: use a timer (preferably a dial) to explain that to be fair everyone should have an equal length of time to use the computer (or other favourite activity).
• Give children activities to do for just one minute, e.g. write their name, thread beads on a string, walk from one space to another and back again. Compare results to see if any children did the activity an equal number of times.

For children moving on quickly
• Some children may enjoy recording their work with rods on squared paper.
• Children compare data from pictograms.

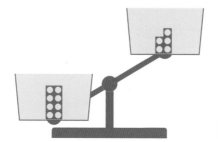

5

Odd and even

Educational context

Children might already be using the terms 'odd' and 'even' when describing Numicon Shapes, because the odd Numicon Shapes are obvious. However, it is still important for them to work through the activities in this group to help them to **generalize ideas about odd and even numbers**. These ideas lay an important foundation for much of their later learning, when they look for **patterns in multiplication tables** (leading to work on factors and prime numbers and recognizing divisibility). The first two activities focus on understanding the term 'odd', connecting odd and even to Numicon Shapes and numerals. In Activity 3, children's attention is drawn to the alternating pattern of odd and even Shapes and their connected numbers, and the regular alternating pattern of odd and even numbers.

The activities for children moving on quickly provide opportunities to make some further generalizations about odd and even numbers – firstly, through exploring odd and even numbers with number rods (children will need to be confidently naming odd and even numbers, referring to number rods by number names and labelling them with numerals, before they do this activity) and, secondly, by experimenting and looking for patterns in totals when adding odd and even Numicon Shapes.

In all the activities, children should be encouraged to organize their work systematically, helping them to realize that this makes it easier to spot patterns.

Aims

- To use the terms 'odd' and 'even' when referring to numbers and totals
- To name odd and even numbers to 10
- To begin to explore what happens when odd and even numbers are added together
- To look for patterns and notice that an odd number always follows an even number (or an even number always follows an odd number) when counting whole numbers in ones

Communicating

Imagery

Numicon Display Number Line, Numicon 0–41 Number Rod Number Line (if available), display of objects that are in pairs, objects arranged in odd and even Numicon Shape patterns

Equipment

See the individual 'have ready' for each activity, various items for the activities in the 'Extending the activities' section

Words and terms for instruction (supported with signs and symbols)

put in order, build, group, arrange, find, feel, check, sort, look carefully, label, separate, match

Mathematical words and terms (supported with signs and symbols)

pairs, partners, odd one, odd Shapes, even Shapes, odd numbers, even numbers, odd, even, set, sort, in between, match, every other, next, before, always, because

Assessment

Individual Record of Progress: Pattern and Algebra 41, 42, Numbers and the Number System 120, 121

Putting the activities into context

Talk about things that go together in pairs, e.g. shoes, socks and gloves, and explain that if we have only one of a pair we call it 'an odd shoe', 'an odd sock', 'an odd glove', and so on. Discuss working in pairs, establishing that this means there will be two children working together. Discuss working or walking with a partner, establishing that this means there will be two children working or walking together.

Link to Number, Pattern and Calculating 1

Pattern and Algebra 3

The activities

7

Activity 1: Exploring odd and even with pairs of small-world people (or children)

Have ready: Numicon Shapes, ten small-world people

Step 1
Explain to children that often people walk or dance in pairs. Discuss occasions when children work or walk in pairs at school, e.g. on school outings, for some mathematics activities and in PE or dance lessons.

Step 2
Show five small-world people (or work with five children, if the group size allows). Children arrange the small-world people into a Numicon 5-pattern to check how many there are, and find the matching 5-shape. Discuss and agree that not every person has a partner: there is an odd one (see Fig. 1).

Step 3
Show ten small-world people (or children). Children arrange the people into a 10-pattern and find the matching 10-shape. Discuss and agree that every play person has a partner: there is not an odd one.

Step 4
Continue for each number of small-world people from ten down to one. Each time, find the matching Numicon Shape and agree whether all the small-world people have partners or whether there is an odd one.

Smaller steps
- Work first on the idea of an odd one using three different coloured pairs of socks and a seventh sock of a different colour. Work with children to put the pairs of socks together and discuss that there is an odd one. This could be repeated with gloves, cutlery where there are pairs of knives and forks and an odd fork, or cups and saucers where there is an odd saucer.

Further practice
- Children take a handful of objects, from a basket of ten mixed objects, and find out whether they can be made into pairs or not by arranging them into Numicon Shape patterns. They check by finding the Numicon Shape to match the pattern.

Activity 2: Connecting odd and even Numicon Shapes with odd and even numbers

Have ready: Numicon Shapes, Numicon 0–100 Numeral Cards

Step 1
Tell children to arrange a set of Numicon Shapes in order and ask them if they can point out the Shapes which might be called 'odd'. Discuss children's ideas as to why these might be called 'odd': e.g. all the holes except the odd one are in pairs, or the odd Shapes have an odd piece sticking up.

Step 2
Point to the even Shapes and ask children what they notice about them: they have a flat or 'even' top, the holes in the Shapes are arranged in pairs and there are no odd pieces sticking up. Explain that these are called the 'even Shapes'.

Step 3
Ask children to separate the odd Shapes from the even Shapes (see Fig. 2).

Step 4
Ask children to label all the Shapes with numeral cards (see Fig. 3).

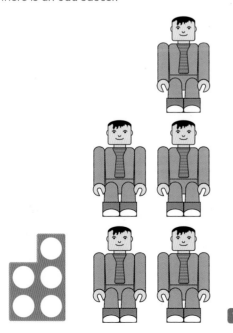

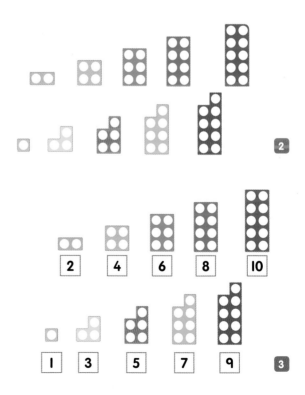

Pattern and Algebra

7

Step 5

Explain that the numbers matched to odd Shapes are called 'odd numbers' and those matched to even Shapes are called 'even numbers'.

Smaller steps

- For some children it may be helpful to do this activity first with the Numicon Large Foam Shapes (if available).

Further practice

- Working in pairs, children take turns to take a Numicon Shape from a Numicon Feely Bag and decide whether it is odd or even. Together they compile a set of odd Shapes and a set of even Shapes; they then label the Shapes with numeral cards.

- Working in pairs, children shuffle numeral cards 1–10 (from photocopy master 11) and place them face down on the tabletop. One child turns over a card and says whether it is odd or even. The second child finds the matching Numicon Shape to check.

Activity 3: Noticing the alternating pattern of odd and even numbers

Have ready: Numicon Shapes

Step 1

Ask children to put a set of Numicon Shapes 1–10 in order.

Step 2

Ask children to look carefully and say what they notice: e.g. an odd number always follows an even number and an even number always follows an odd number.

Smaller steps

- Work with Numicon Large Foam Shapes (if available) so that children can 'walk the pattern' of odd and even. Put the Large Foam Shapes in order and look carefully at the repeated sequence of odd and even. Children step along the ordered Shapes saying the pattern 'odd', 'even', 'odd', 'even' etc. as they step from Shape to Shape.

Further practice

- Working in pairs, one child puts a Shape into a Numicon Feely Bag without the other child seeing. The second child feels the Shape and says whether it is odd or even, and reveals the Shape. Together they find the two Shapes that the Shape is 'in between' and decide whether they are odd or even.

- Give children opportunities to practise building repeating patterns with odd Shapes or even Shapes.

- Give children repeating patterns or sequences of odd or even numerals to build with Numicon Shapes.

Extending the activities

Connecting activities

- Children cover the Numicon Baseboard with odd or even Shapes – decide whether children should cover the board just with odd Shapes or just with even Shapes and note which they find easier to use and why. Look for children who become systematic using the patterns of number facts to help and those who are able to adjust Shapes to make them fit.

- Children create and label repeating patterns with odd or even Shapes, e.g. Fig. 4). They may like to record their patterns in colour on a paper Baseboard (printed from photocopy master 3) and label them with numerals.

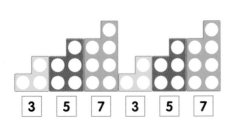
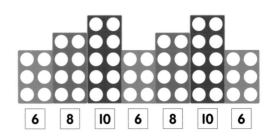
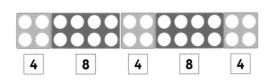
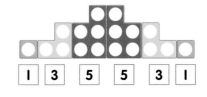

4

Pattern and Algebra

7

For children moving on quickly

- Children match number rods and numerals and try to find any ways of telling whether rods are odd or even. (Some children might realize that the even numbered rods can be covered with a pair of matching rods, whereas odd numbered rods cannot (see Fig. 5)).

- Children experiment to see what happens when they add two even Shapes together, describing their answers not just as totals but as 'even' as well. (Some children may start to realize that they can only make even numbers.)

- Children experiment to find other ways of making even numbers, describing their answers not just as totals but as 'odd' or 'even' as well. (Some children may start to realize that they can add two odd numbers together to make an even number.)

- Children experiment to find out which Shapes added together will equal an odd number, describing their answers not just as totals but as 'odd' or 'even'. (Some children may start to realize that an odd Shape added to an even Shape will always give an odd number as the total.)

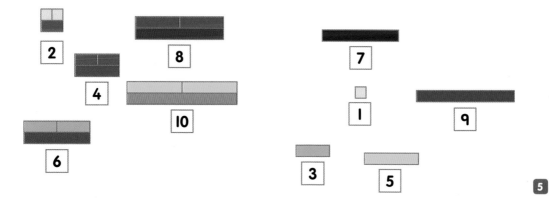

5

Reasoning about numbers

Educational context

This activity group gives children the opportunity to develop a logical approach to solving problems, which will help them to explain their conclusions confidently. The activities should only be attempted when children are able to recognize and name Numicon Shapes and patterns confidently, without hesitation.

The first two activities involve children looking carefully at **an ordered sequence** of Numicon Shape patterns, from which some Numicon Coloured Pegs have been removed, to spot the irregularities. They then have opportunities to explain what they notice and to restore the sequence.

The next two activities involve describing the properties of the Numicon Shapes. As children do so, they will be describing the properties of the numbers the Shapes represent. All four activities support and develop **the understanding of number relationships that underpins successful calculating**.

As with many of the Numicon activities, changing roles with the child provides engaging opportunities for adults to model their reasoning process by 'thinking aloud' as they solve the problem set for them by the child. Seeing the importance of being systematic and **learning to work in an organized way** are helpful life skills as well as important tools for solving mathematical problems.

The final activity requires children to organize objects (Numicon Shapes) in order to be able to solve a problem.

Aims

- To use understanding of number relationships to reason logically about numbers
- To adjust numbers to make them equal

Communicating

Imagery
Numicon Display Number Line, Numicon 0–41 Number Rod Number Line, structured apparatus

Equipment
See the individual 'have ready' for each activity, various items for the activities in the 'Extending the activities' section

Words and terms for instruction (supported with signs and symbols)
work out, think, ask, question, remember, look, see, change, adjust, imagine, find, say, explain, describe, move, arrange, hide, close your eyes, make

Mathematical words and terms (supported with signs and symbols)
one more than, one fewer than, two more than, two fewer than, etc., before, after, between, next, odd, even, pattern, less, taken away from, more, added to, in order, equal

Assessment

Individual Record of Progress: Pattern and Algebra 31–33, 37; Numbers and the Number System 18; Calculating 2

Putting the activities into context

Explain to children that knowing the Numicon Shape patterns can be helpful in many ways when they are comparing numbers and when they are thinking about adding and subtracting. Knowing how to describe Numicon Shapes in many different ways helps them to describe numbers. They can also have fun playing games where they have to work out when something is missing from a sequence of Numicon Shape patterns or Numicon Shapes.

The activities

8

Activity 1: Reasoning about Numicon Shape patterns

Have ready: two Numicon Baseboards, Numicon Coloured Pegs sorted into colours

Step 1
Put the two Baseboards side by side and ask children to choose one colour of Pegs to arrange into Numicon Shape patterns 1–7.

Step 2
Ask children to close their eyes. Remove one Peg from any pattern.

Step 3
Children open their eyes, identify the pattern that has changed (e.g. Fig. 1) and replace the missing Peg.

Step 4
Respond and model the subtracting language, saying, e.g. 'I took one Peg away from the 6-pattern, and that left five'.

Step 5
Repeat Steps 3 and 4 often, encouraging children to explain what has happened.

Smaller steps
- Work with patterns 1–4, gradually increasing the range as children are ready.

Further practice
- This activity can be repeated often by children working in pairs independently or with a group using the *Numicon Software for the Interactive Whiteboard* (if available).

Activity 2: Comparing and adjusting Numicon Shape patterns

Have ready: two Numicon Baseboards, Numicon Coloured Pegs sorted into colours

Step 1
Put the two Baseboards side by side and ask children to choose one colour of Pegs to arrange into Numicon Shape patterns 1–7.

Step 2
Ask children to close their eyes. Take away one Peg from the top of one pattern and move it to another pattern.

Step 3
Children open their eyes, identify the patterns that have changed (e.g. Fig. 2) and return the Peg to its original place.

Step 4
Respond and model the explanation, saying, e.g. 'I took one Peg away from the 6-pattern and I have added it to the four to make five'.

Step 5
Repeat often, encouraging children to explain what has happened.

Smaller steps
- Work with patterns 1–4, gradually increasing the range as children are ready.

Further practice
This activity can be repeated often by children working in pairs independently or with a group using the *Numicon Software for the Interactive Whiteboard* (if available).

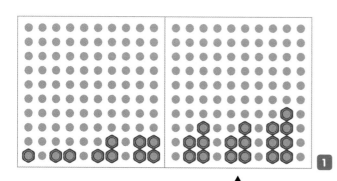

1

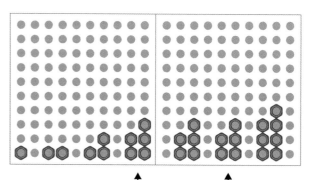

2

8

Activity 3: Comparing Numicon Shape patterns and adjusting to make them equal

Have ready: Numicon Feely Bag containing the odd Numicon Shapes, Numicon Feely Bag containing the even Numicon Shapes, Numicon Baseboard, Numicon Coloured Pegs

Step 1
Children take two Shapes from one of the Feely Bags. They say what they are and compare them to see the difference between them.

Step 2
Children build the patterns for each of the Shapes side by side on the Baseboard (leaving a gap between the patterns so that they are distinct from each other), e.g. Fig. 3.

Step 3
Children decide how to change or adjust the patterns to make them equal, by moving Pegs from one pattern to another (e.g. Fig. 4).

Step 4
Ask children to explain their reasoning. Most may have simply experimented to make the same pattern. Some may have looked at the difference between the two Shapes to work out how many Pegs they needed to move.

Smaller steps
- Start by putting in two Shapes that only require one Peg to be moved to make them equal, e.g. the 2-shape and the 4-shape, or the 3-shape and the 5-shape. When children can adjust these, introduce two Shapes that require two Pegs to be moved. Work towards children being able to adjust numbers that are further apart.

Further practice
- Repeat often until children are able to adjust numbers to make them equal with confidence and can explain what they have done.

Activity 4: Describing Shapes

Have ready: Numicon Shapes 1–10 and Numeral Cards 1–10 (cut from photocopy master 11)

Step 1
Ask children to put the Numicon Shapes and corresponding numeral cards in order (see Fig. 5).

Step 2
Point to the 5-shape and ask children to suggest ways of describing it. Encourage children to come up with as many ways as they can, which may include:
- It is an odd number.
- It is red.
- It is smaller than the 10-shape, the 9-shape, the 8-shape, the 7-shape and the 6-shape.
- It is bigger than the 1-shape, the 2-shape, the 3-shape and the 4-shape.
- It is in between the 4-shape and the 6-shape.
- It is next to the 4-shape and the 6-shape.
- It comes before the 6-shape and after the 4-shape.
- It is one more than 4.
- It is one fewer than 6.

Step 3
Repeat Step 2 for other Shapes.

Step 4
When children can confidently describe Numicon Shapes in many ways, move on to Activity 5.

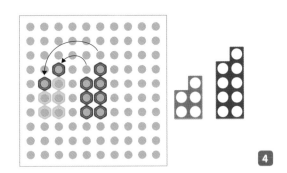

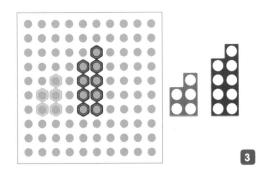

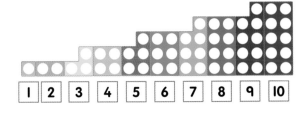

| 1 | 2 | 3 | 4 | 5 | 6 | 7 | 8 | 9 | 10 |

Pattern and Algebra

Extending the activities

8

Activity 5: Which Shape is hidden?

Have ready: Numicon Shapes 1–10 in a basket, another set of Numicon 1–10 Shapes, Numicon Feely Bag, Numeral Cards 0–10 (cut from photocopy master 11)

Step 1

Ask children to put the Numicon Shapes and corresponding numeral cards in order, as in Activity 4. Make sure children are sitting where they can easily see the Shapes and numerals in order.

Step 2

Choose one child to secretly take a Shape from the basket and hide it in the Feely Bag.

Step 3

Invite children to ask questions in order to find out which Shape is hidden in the Feely Bag. To start with, children may ask direct yes or no questions, e.g. 'Is it red?' or, 'Is it four?'

Step 4

Model indirect questions for them, e.g. 'Is it bigger than the red Shape?', and explain that these sorts of question can help them to 'work out' which Shape is hidden.

Help children to use the information gained from the answers to their questions by encouraging them to work out which ones it could it be, and which ones it couldn't be: e.g. if, in answer to the question 'Is it bigger than five?' the child answers 'no', then the adult removes the 6-, 7-, 8-, 9- and 10-shapes from the set on the table. As Shapes are eliminated, the remaining Shapes show the new (and more limited) possibilities at each stage of questioning (see Fig. 6).

Step 5

Children continue asking questions until they have worked out which Shape is in the Feely Bag.

Step 6

When children have worked out the answer, encourage them to say confidently, 'It is the … Shape.'

Smaller steps

Support children's reasoning by discussing the logical implications of the answer to each question.

Further practice

- Children take turns to feel for a Shape in the Feely Bag and describe it in their own words for others to work out which it is.
- Practise these activities until children can do them confidently.

Connecting activities

- Give reasoning activities with attribute blocks.

For children moving on quickly (Activities 1 and 2)

- Children use Numicon Pegs of mixed colours for each Numicon Shape pattern.
- Children arrange the patterns on the tabletop without using the Numicon Baseboard.
- Children work with the full range of patterns 1–10.
- Remove two Pegs from a pattern, or remove one Peg from two different patterns, for children to identify.

For children moving on quickly (Activity 5)

- Children try to work out which Numicon Shape is in the Numicon Feely Bag without a set of Shapes in front of them.

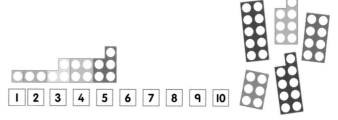

| 1 | 2 | 3 | 4 | 5 | 6 | 7 | 8 | 9 | 10 |

6

Introducing the '<' and '>' symbols – comparing amounts and measures

9

Educational context

This group continues work on comparing and ordering from earlier Pattern and Algebra, and Numbers and the Number System, activities but encourages children to realize that when we make direct comparisons between two objects or amounts, we can use what we know about one object to find out information about the other. It includes **reasoning using the word 'so'** to show this relationship, e.g. four is bigger than three so I know that three is smaller than four. Word cards are introduced to support children towards recording and then the '<' and '>' symbols replace the word cards. Whenever possible continue to use signing to support children alongside the word cards and symbols. Continue to make comparisons within all areas of measures. The **language of comparison** is expanded in this activity group to include the terms 'larger than' and 'greater than'. These will need to be introduced sensitively to take account of children's language needs.

Children have opportunities to make comparisons between number values supported by the Numicon Shapes and number rods. Some may still be using the number names as adjectives but those who have generalized these will just refer to the number names as nouns even though the Numicon Shapes or number rods are being used.

Some children may still not be using the number names of the rods fluently but using the rods in comparing situations will help to develop and establish the relationships between them even if colour names are still being used.

Further work on measures **making direct comparisons** involving height, weight, capacity and time are suggested in 'Extending the activities'. As suggested in previous activity groups, teachers will need to decide when it is appropriate to introduce these activities to children.

Aims

- To realize that when we make direct comparisons between two objects, we can use what we know about one object to find out information about the other
- To compare objects directly by length and weight
- To compare number values
- To use and read words for comparisons
- To introduce the '<' and '>' symbols

Communicating

Imagery
Numicon Display Number Line, Numicon 0-41 Number Rod Number Line, Numicon Large Format Table-top Number Line, Numicon Shapes, Numicon Pan Balance

Equipment
See the individual 'have ready' for each activity, various items for the activities in the 'Extending the activities' section

Words and terms for instruction (supported with signs and symbols)
build, find, talk about, explain, compare

Mathematical words and terms (supported with signs and symbols)
more, less, fewer, is greater than, is less than, is smaller than, the same, the same amount as, different amount, balances, equals, is heavier than, is lighter than, is equal weight, is longer than, is equal length, is taller than, is larger than, is shorter than, is equal height, equal width, is thicker than, is thinner than, is wider than, is narrower than, holds more, holds less, takes an equal amount of time, takes a longer amount of time, takes a shorter amount of time

Assessment

Individual Record of Progress: Pattern and Algebra 34–35; Measures 10, 11, 12, 13, 45, 46, 47, 48, 54, 55, 60, 61, 62

Putting the activities into context

It is important for children to make comparisons and have the opportunity to reason using 'so' throughout all areas of measures, e.g. 'Your PE bag is heavier than mine so my bag is lighter than yours', 'Your collection of toy figures is smaller than mine so my collection is larger than yours'. Comparisons between shoes sizes and heights of children could provide opportunities for some recording work and the use of the '<'and '>' symbols. Some children may be measuring using non-standard units which provides a helpful link with number comparisons.

Link to Number, Pattern and Calculating 1

Pattern and Algebra 1

Link to Geometry, Measurement and Statistics 1

Measurement 4 and 5

The activities

9

Activity 1: Introducing the use of 'so' when reasoning in comparing sentences

Have ready: a collection of ribbons of different colours and lengths

Step 1

Children choose two ribbons and after making sure one end on each is lined up, compare them and decide what they will say about them, e.g. 'The red ribbon is longer than the yellow ribbon' (see Fig. 1). Prompt them to reason further, e.g. 'The yellow ribbon is shorter than the red ribbon'. Discuss the comparison. Agree they can say, 'I know that the yellow ribbon is shorter than the red ribbon so I also know that the red ribbon is longer than the yellow ribbon.'

Step 2

Remind children of earlier work on comparisons and find objects that have previously been compared, e.g. for weight, length, height, capacity, size and width. Repeat Step 1 with these objects by asking children to choose two objects and decide what could be said. Use the comparative and deductive language – encourage children to use the appropriate comparing words for the objects and to use the word 'so' to reason about the objects, e.g. 'This bag is heavier than this marble, so the marble is lighter than the bag.'

Repeat for each area of measures as appropriate for children.

Smaller steps

- Children will need to be secure with earlier work on measures before attempting this activity. Some children find the support of the word cards helpful, in which case combining this activity with Activity 2 may be helpful.

Further practice

- Practise this activity in each area of measures.

Activity 2: Introducing word cards for comparing sentences

Have ready: a collection of ribbons of different colours and lengths (and widths if understood by the children), Words for Comparing Measures (cut from photocopy masters 27a and 27b)

Step 1

Ask children to choose two ribbons, compare them and describe the comparison, e.g. 'The red ribbon is longer than the yellow ribbon so the yellow ribbon is shorter than the red ribbon.'

Step 2

Show children the word card 'is longer than' and read (and sign) it. Place the two ribbons next to each other, longest first, then put the word card 'is longer than' between them. Read (and sign) again.

Step 3

Read out the card 'is shorter than'. Swap the ribbons; place 'is shorter than' between them. Read and sign.

Step 4

Repeat for different ribbons.

Smaller steps

- Some children find the support of the word cards helpful particularly alongside signing.

Further practice

- As appropriate, show children the words for comparing other measures, e.g. 'heavier than', 'lighter than', and use them in comparing activities.

Pattern and Algebra

Activity 3: Introducing the '<' and '>' symbols and actions

Have ready: two toy figures of differing heights, but both shorter than the 10-rod, number rods, Words and Symbols for Calculating (cut from photocopy master 26a), Words for Comparing Measures (cut from photocopy masters 27a and 27b)

Step 1
Ask children to compare the heights of the two toy figures and agree which is shorter and which is taller than the other. Agree that one is taller than the other so one is shorter. Encourage children to say the sentence.

Step 2
Place the figures next to one another and place the 'is taller than' card between them. Encourage children to also use the 'is shorter than' card, e.g. Fig. 2.

Step 3
Discuss with children that writing 'is taller than' or 'is shorter than' would take a long time and is hard work. Remind children that in mathematics we use special symbols instead of words, e.g. the adding symbol. Tell them there is a special symbol we can use to show when objects and numbers are bigger or smaller. Show children the '<' and '>' symbols and discuss which end of the symbol they think shows the biggest/largest/greatest end and which shows the 'smallest', using the signs as support.

Step 4
Remove the word card, place a card showing the '<' between the two figures, e.g. Fig. 3, and say and sign what can be seen, e.g. 'This toy is smaller than this toy'.

Smaller steps
• Illustrate the '<' and '>' symbols (some children like the idea of a crocodile mouth, others may think of their own ideas) to help children to remember which way to use them. If the size of the cards is a problem, enlarge them. If they are difficult to handle, fix them in place with adhesive tack for children to place Numicon Shapes each side of them.

Further practice
• Use the '<' and '>' symbols whenever possible in comparing situations.

Activity 4: Comparing Numicon Shapes and number rods using the '<' and '>' symbols

Have ready: Numicon Shapes, Numicon Feely Bag, Numicon Large Format Table-top Number Line, Words and Symbols for Calculating (cut from photocopy master 26a)

Step 1
Place a set of Numicon Shapes 1–10 in the Feely Bag. Ask children to take two Shapes from the Feely Bag and say which is bigger.

Step 2
Ask children to place the '>' symbol between the two Shapes. Explain to children that the name of the '>' symbol is usually 'greater than.'

Step 3
Ask children to compare the Numicon Shapes, drawing on their work in previous activities and using the word 'so', e.g. 'The 9-shape is bigger/larger/greater than the 4-shape **so** the 4-shape is smaller than the 9-shape' (see Fig. 4).

Step 4
Children take two more Shapes from the Feely Bag and say which is smaller, or has fewer holes. They place the '<' symbol between the two Shapes and compare them, e.g. 'The 5-shape is smaller than the 8-shape so the 8-shape is larger than the 5-shape' (see Fig. 5). Find both Shapes on the Number Line.

Some children may start to describe the comparisons without referring to the Shapes directly by saying, e.g. 'Five is less than eight,' rather than 'The 5-shape is less than the 8-shape.'

Step 5
Repeat with number rods, e.g. Fig. 6.

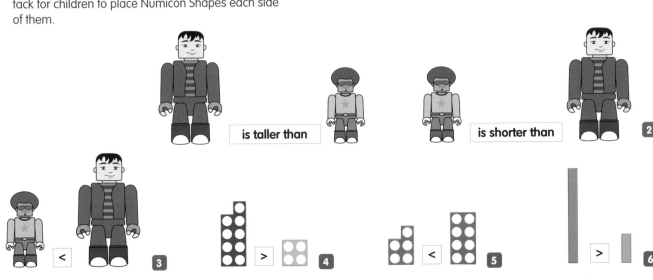

9

Smaller steps
- Attach the symbol with adhesive tack to stop it moving. Children place the Shapes appropriately.

Further practice

Have ready: Numicon Shapes, Words and Symbols for Calculating (cut from photocopy master 26a), Numicon Spinners with Numeral Overlays 1–5 and 6–10 (cut from photocopy master 20)

- Children choose any Spinner, spin a number and find the Shape. They spin again and find the Shape. They compare the Shapes and place the '<' or '>' symbol between them saying and signing the comparison number story.

Activity 5: Comparing number values using the '<' and '>' symbols

Have ready: Numicon Shapes, Numicon Pan Balance, Numicon Large Format Table-top Number Line, Words and Symbols for Calculating (cut from photocopy master 26a), Numeral Cards 1–10 (cut from photocopy master 11), number rods

Step 1

Show children two Shapes and ask them to say which 'is greater than' the other and which 'is less than' the other. Children label the Shapes with numeral cards and then place the '<' or the '>' symbol card between the two Shapes or between the numeral cards, e.g. Fig. 7). They say the comparison number story, e.g. 'Seven is greater than three so three is less than seven,' and find both numbers on the Number Line.

Step 2

Remind children about the Pan Balance. Children place one Shape on each side of the Pan Balance and put the numeral cards and relevant '>' symbol in front of the Balance, e.g. Fig. 8. They say the comparison number story, e.g. 'Seven is greater than three.'

Step 3

Repeat using number rods (see Fig. 9).

Smaller steps
- Some children may find it easier to begin with the Pan Balance (Step 2) and then work on Step 1.

Further practice

Have ready: Numicon Shapes, Numicon Pan Balance, Numeral cards 1–10 (cut from photocopy master 11), Words and Symbols for Calculating (cut from photocopy master 26a), Numicon Spinners with Numeral Overlays 1–5 and 6–10 (cut from photocopy master 20), number rods

- Children spin a number and find the numeral card. They spin again and find another numeral card. They compare them and place the '<' or '>' symbol between them. Children may like to check with the Shapes in the Pan Balance. Repeat using number rods.

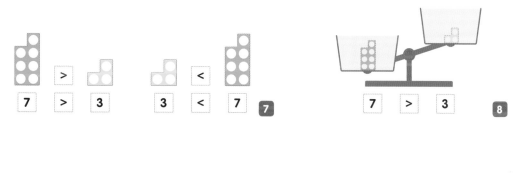

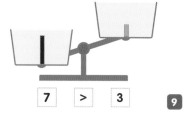

Pattern and Algebra

Extending the activities

Connecting activities – Measures

- Length: Compare the lengths of different objects around the classroom, e.g. pencils, paint brushes. Children can record their comparisons by drawing and using the '<' and '>' symbols.
- Use a measuring stick to find objects in the classroom that are longer than the measuring stick and others that are shorter.
- Height: Compare the heights of models made with blocks or interlocking cubes.
- Weight: Provide a selection of objects and the Numicon Pan Balance. Children choose one object and then compare it with others to find those that are heavier and those that are lighter than their chosen object. They could record their comparisons by drawing and using the '<' and '>' symbols.
- Capacity: Provide children with two different-shaped containers and dry sand. Set them the challenge of finding out which container holds more and which holds less.
- Provide a selection of containers and dry sand. Children choose one container and then compare it with others to find those that hold more and those that hold less. They could record their comparisons by drawing and using the '<' and '>' symbols.
- Time: Make comparisons between the length of time it takes to complete activities, e.g. it takes a long time to read a long story; it takes a short time to read a short story.
- When children are working on different tasks, discuss which tasks take longer than others to complete.
- Compare the length of time taken to do certain activities, e.g. taking the register, with the length of time taken for the sand to run through a sand timer.

For children moving on quickly

- Challenge children to find different ways to sort and order ribbons of different colours, lengths and widths.
- Repeat the activity above with different widths of ribbon.
- Using numeral cards 0–10 (cut from photocopy master 11), show children two cards for them to say which is greater and which is smaller and to place the '<' and '>' symbols between them.
- Give children three numeral cards (0–10, cut from photocopy master 11) to put in order from the smallest to the largest.

Introducing the '=' symbol

Educational context

In this activity group the idea of equal value – even though the values may be represented differently – is continued from Pattern and Algebra 6 and the '=' symbol is introduced. **Understanding that equivalence means 'is of equal value'** is an essential foundation for all children's mathematics. Children have already met the Numicon sign for 'equals' which is helpful when they need to distinguish between things that are not 'the same' but are of 'equal value', e.g. the 5-shape add the 4-shape equal the 9-shape. They are not 'the same' (they actually look very different in colour, size and the number of holes) but they are of equal value. Children have explored many activities where equivalence is embedded within another focus, e.g. adding and subtracting, but in these activities they are encouraged to use the '=' symbol as part of their recording of adding sentences. Care should be taken to avoid children thinking that the '=' symbol is just an instruction to write an answer. The use of the Numicon Pan Balance encourages children to see equivalence when looking at number values.

The work on measures in Activities 3 and 4 will probably be spread over many weeks but is an essential foundation for future understanding about **equivalence in measures**, e.g. 100 cm = 1 metre, 100p = £1, 1000 g = 1 kg, and is of course a basis for life skills. The further work on measures suggested in 'Extending the activities' includes introducing the centimetre as a standard unit for measuring length; there are further suggestions involving capacity, weight and time. As suggested in previous activity groups, teachers will need to decide when it is appropriate to introduce these activities to students and to give plenty of time for students to assimilate these ideas.

Aims

- To use the language of comparison in conversation
- To understand that equals means of equal value
- To use and read the words for equivalence
- To introduce the '=' symbol

Communicating

Imagery
Numicon Display Number Line, Numicon 0–41 Number Rod Number Line, Numicon Large Format Table-top Number Line, Numicon Shapes, Numicon Pan Balance

Equipment
See the individual 'have ready' for each activity, various items for the activities in the 'Extending the activities' section

Words and terms for instruction (supported with signs and symbols)
build, find, work out, think, talk about, explain, compare

Mathematical words and terms (supported with signs and symbols)
more, less, fewer, is greater than, is smaller than, the same, the same amount as, different amount, balances, equals, is heavier than, is lighter than, is equal weight, is longer than, is shorter than, is equal length, is taller than, is equal height, (equal width), (is thicker than, is thinner than, is wider than, is narrower than), holds more, holds less, has an equal amount, takes an equal amount of time

Assessment

Individual Record of Progress: Pattern and Algebra 38–40; Measures 14, 30, 40, 49, 56, 60

Putting the activities into context

Talk about opportunities in cooking activities, e.g. where two bun trays are needed to make jam tarts. There is enough pastry to fill one bun tray but there is not an equal amount left so the other tray cannot be completed. Also use contexts similar to these examples: 'If one netball team has 7 players, how many players will the other team have if both teams need to be equal?'; 'The tables in the hall at lunchtime have spaces for 10 seats around each table. There are only 8 seats around one of the tables. Which table does not have an equal number of seats compared to the other tables?; What will have to happen so that it has the equal number of seats?'

When children are using the Numicon Pan Balance to find combinations that equal a given number, include problems such as: 'If 10 children can sit at a table how many could be boys and how many could be girls?'; 'If there are 6 eggs in the box, how many might be white and how many might be brown?'

Link to Number, Pattern and Calculating 1

Pattern and Algebra 1

Pattern and Algebra

The activities

Activity 1: Introducing word cards for equivalence

Have ready: Numicon Pan Balance, Numicon Shapes, two Numicon Feely Bags each containing a Numicon 6-shape, Words for Calculating (cut from photocopy master 26b)

Step 1
Children feel in the Feely Bag and place the Shape that's inside, e.g. the 6-shape, in one of the pans of the Pan Balance. They then feel in the other Feely Bag and place the other 6-shape in the other pan.

Step 2
Discuss what has happened and why, ensuring that children use the terms 'balances' and 'equals' and the Numicon sign for 'equals', e.g. **Fig. 1**.

Step 3
Show children the word cards 'balances' and 'equals' and place them in front of the Pan Balance, see **Fig. 2**.

Smaller steps
- Take each step at an appropriate pace for children. Repeat the activity using different pairs of Shapes.

Further practice
- Put a selection of pairs of identical Shapes in a Numicon Feely Bag. Children feel in the Bag, choose one Shape and then feel again to find the Shape that is equal. They place the word card 'equals' between the Shapes. (If children particularly enjoy using the Pan Balance they could place the Shapes in the balance as in the activity above.) Repeat with number rods.

Activity 2: Exploring equal value with Numicon Shapes and number rods

Have ready: Numicon Shapes, Numicon Pan Balance, Words for Calculating (cut from photocopy master 26b)

Step 1
Children set out the word cards 'balances' and 'equals' in front of the Pan Balance and find two Shapes that are equal (see **Fig. 2**).

Step 2
Remove one of the 6-shapes from one of the pans. Ask children to suggest two other Shapes that could be added to the empty pan to equal the 6-shape, e.g. **Fig. 3**. Ask children to say what can be seen, e.g. 'The 6-shape is equal to, or balances, the 2- and 4-shapes.' Test out all children's suggestions.

Step 3
Discuss how the balance of Shapes can be seen on either side of the Pan Balance and that the Shapes may look different but they are of equal value: that is, both sides of the Pan Balance equal 6.

Smaller steps
- Work at a pace appropriate for children.

Further practice
- Repeat the activity with number rods, e.g. **Fig. 4**.
- Children will need plenty of practice choosing a Shape or rod to put in one pan of the Pan Balance and then finding other combinations of Shapes or rods to make the pans balance, each time saying what they have done. Include real problems as suggested in the 'Putting the activities in context' section on page 105.

1

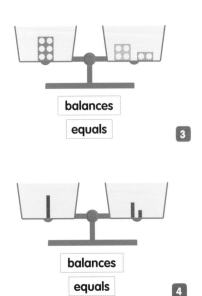

balances

equals

3

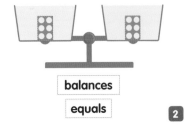

balances

equals

2

balances

equals

4

10

Activity 3: Introducing the '=' symbol

Have ready: Numicon Shapes, Words and Symbols for Calculating (cut from photocopy master 26a)

Step 1
Show children a Numicon Shape, e.g. 7-shape, and ask them to find two Shapes to equal it. Check children's suggestions in the Pan Balance, set out the word cards 'balances' and 'equals' and say what can be seen, e.g. 'Seven equals six and one.'

Step 2
Remove the Shapes from the Pan Balance and place them on the table. Position the word cards between them, e.g. **Fig. 5**. Ask children to say what they can see, e.g. 'Seven equals, or balances, six and one.'

Step 3
Talk with children about how long it would take to write the words 'balances' and 'equals' and that in mathematics we have a special symbol, as we do for adding (and 'greater than' and 'less than'). Show children the '=' symbol and exchange the word card for the symbol (see **Fig. 6**). Children repeat the number sentence, e.g. 'Seven equals six and one' and use the Numicon sign for 'equals'.

Smaller steps
• Take as much time as needed with each step.

Further practice
Have ready: Numicon Shapes, Numicon Pan Balance, Numeral cards 2–10 (cut from photocopy master 11) shuffled and face down in a pile, Words and Symbols for Calculating (cut from photocopy master 26a)

• Children turn over a numeral card, find the corresponding Shape and place it in the first pan of the Pan Balance. They then find two other Shapes to make the pans balance and put the '=' symbol in front of the balance. They say what they can see.

Have ready: Numicon Shapes, Numeral cards 2–10 (cut from photocopy master 11) shuffled and face down in a pile, Words and Symbols for Calculating (cut from photocopy master 26a)

• Children turn over a numeral card, find the corresponding Shape and place it on the table. They find two Shapes to equal it and place the '=' symbol appropriately, saying what they have done.

Activity 4: Adding sentences using '=' and '+'

Have ready: Numicon Shapes, Words and Symbols for Calculating (cut from photocopy master 26a), Numeral Cards 0–10 (cut from photocopy master 11), number rods

Step 1
Choose a Shape, e.g. 8-shape, and ask children to find two other Shapes to equal it, setting them out on the table with the '=' symbol. Say the number sentence, e.g. 'Eight equals three add five'.

Step 2
Remind children that they know the symbol for adding. Say the number sentence again using Numicon signs for '=' and '+' as they are spoken.

Step 3
Set out the whole number sentence with numeral cards and the '=' and '+' symbols, e.g. **Fig. 7**.

Smaller steps
• Take as much time as needed with each step.

Further practice
• Children choose different Shapes to start and find other Shapes to equal it. They say and sign the number sentence and set it out with the numeral and symbol cards.

Activity 5: Further adding sentences using '=' and '+'

Have ready: Numicon Shapes, Words and Symbols for Calculating (cut from photocopy master 26a), Numeral Cards 0–10 (cut from photocopy master 11), number rods

Step 1
Place a Numicon Shape, e.g. a 9-shape, in one pan of the Pan Balance and ask children to find two Shapes to equal 9 and put them in the other pan. Say and sign the number sentence, e.g. 'Nine equals four add five'.

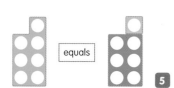

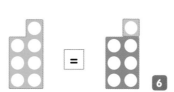

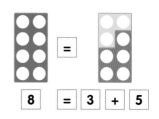

Pattern and Algebra

10

Step 2

Change the Shapes so that the 9-shape is in the other pan and the 4- and 5-shapes are in the first pan. Say and sign the number sentence, e.g. 'four and five equal nine.'

Step 3

Remove the Shapes from the Pan Balance and show the equivalence using the Shapes on the tabletop. Choose identical Shapes and set them out so that children can see, say and sign both equivalent number sentences.

Step 4

Set out both number sentences using numeral cards and symbols for calculating, e.g. **Fig. 8**. Remind children that the '=' symbol means there must be equal value on both sides of it; that like the Pan Balance both sides of the number sentence must be equal and balance.

Smaller steps

- Once children are secure with Steps 1 and 2 using a variety of Shapes to equal 9 and for other numbers, they should then move on to Step 3, again becoming secure before attempting to set out number sentences.

Further practice

- Give children as much practice as possible with this activity.

Extending the activities

Connecting activities – Measures

- Work across all areas of measures where children have opportunities to make things equal. Some may still be using direct comparison but some will include number values e.g.:
  - everyone needs an equal length of string for model making
  - an equal weight of clay is needed to make a clay pot
  - children all have an equal amount of time working on a computer program
  - children could pour drinks into cups (that are all identical in size but different colours) so that everyone has an equal amount of juice
  - bags of treats for the school fair need an equal number of treats
  - different sizes of containers need an equal number of objects (although they may look different due to the different sizes of containers)
  - children need an equal number of bricks to build a model.

- Length: Introduce centimetres. Provide children with measuring sticks marked with centimetres; discuss what they notice about the measuring sticks, drawing attention to the marks, the word centimetre and the term measuring stick. (Children may be used to calling these 'rulers' so their measuring purpose will need to be explained.) Ask children to compare a 1-rod with one space on the measuring stick so that they can see that the 1-rod is equal to 1 centimetre (see **Fig. 9**).

- Ask children to experiment with different numbers of 1-rods to show 5 centimetres, 4 centimetres and so on up to 10 centimetres.

For children moving on quickly

- In each of the activities, children could find more than two Shapes to equal the first Shape.

- Children could record their ideas shown in the Pan Balance.

- Children roll a Numicon Dice twice. They write down both scores and decide which symbol card to place between them, e.g. 4 < 5 or 3 = 3.

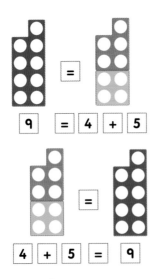

8

0 1 2 3 4 5 6 7 8 9 10 11 12 13 14 15 16 17 18 19 20 21 22 23 24 25

9

Numbers and the Number System

Exploring Numicon Shapes

1

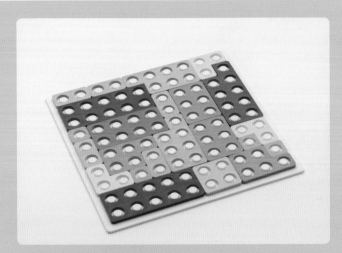

Educational context

Numicon Shapes are designed primarily to help children visualize and deal with number ideas. These activities all involve **putting parts together to complete a whole** – an important foundation for part and whole relationships in calculating and work on fractions. However, as children handle, move, combine and rearrange the Shapes they also experience **important geometrical ideas** of transformation and changes in position. They will also notice the symmetry and asymmetry of even and odd Numicon Shapes, and in fitting the Shapes together they can experiment by turning the Shapes over (reflections), turning them round (rotations), and moving them together (translations).

Children will need to **manipulate Numicon Shapes** or number rods to fill the Numicon Baseboard or a Numicon Number Rod Tray. To start with they are likely to do this by trial and error, sometimes having Shapes 'hanging over' the edge of the Baseboard and often filling a larger space with several smaller Shapes. However, in time they will begin to notice the equivalence between a space and the piece that will fill it. There are many different ways to do these activities, which can be repeated many times, incorporating some of the extension suggestions and revisited alongside all the other activity groups, giving children ample opportunity to experiment.

Children may refer to the Numicon Shapes by their size or colour, some may spontaneously use number names. The following colour names are used in the activity groups: orange, light blue, yellow, light green, red, turquoise, pink, green, purple, blue, but this is open to choice; the important thing to remember is to use whichever colour names you decide upon consistently. If children do use number names, acknowledge correct use and rectify incorrect use to avoid repetition of incorrect vocabulary. For children who find colour a distraction, grey Numicon Shapes (if available) could be substituted for the coloured Numicon Shapes.

Use activities from this group as a starter to later mathematics teaching sessions.

Aims

• To explore the Numicon Shapes freely

Communicating

Imagery
Numicon Display Number Line, Numicon Shapes

Equipment
See the individual 'have ready' for each activity, various items for the activities in the 'Extending the activities' section.

Words and terms for instruction (supported with signs and symbols)
on, in, turn over, turn round, fit in the space, gap

Mathematical words and terms (supported with signs and symbols)
big, small, the same size, the same shape, too small, too big, bigger, smaller

Assessment

Individual Record of Progress: Numbers and the Number System 4

Putting the activities into context

Show the Numicon Baseboard and Numicon Shapes. Explain and demonstrate how the Shapes fit onto the Baseboard and that fitting the Shapes onto the Baseboard is like a puzzle with many different solutions where parts are combined to complete a whole picture. Discuss other situations where pieces have to be fitted into spaces or assembled to make a whole, e.g. construction toys, jigsaw puzzles, putting correct sized lids onto jars or bottles and so on.

The activities

Activity 1: Cover the board

Have ready: Numicon Baseboard, a basket of mixed Numicon Shapes with plenty of 1- and 2-shapes

Step 1

Children cover the Baseboard with Shapes, see Fig. 1.

Smaller steps
• Use only part of the Baseboard, see Fig. 2, covering some of it with card or by making a border with 10-shapes.
• Use only 1-shapes and 2-shapes; gradually increase to include more.
• If rotating the 'odd' shapes is too challenging, first use 'even' Shapes and introduce the 'odd' Shapes gradually, including plenty of 1-shapes.
• When children are working with all the number Shapes ensure that there are more of the 1- and 2-shapes.

Further practice
• Practise the above activities often until children are able to confidently cover the Baseboard with Shapes.
• Put Shapes on a magnetic board for children to rearrange.
• Display the Numicon Display Number Line so children begin to notice the Shapes.
• Encourage children to create their own pictures and patterns with Shapes, both on and off the Baseboard.

Extending the activities

Connecting activities

• Provide puzzles where children have to look carefully at and rotate shapes, e.g. one-piece inset puzzles, multi-piece inset puzzles where two or more pieces are fitted into a shape, geometric-shape puzzles, e.g. shape posting boxes
• Children use tangrams (simplify as necessary, e.g. making 2- or 3-piece tangrams from card)

For children moving on quickly

• Limit the number of 1- and 2-shapes.
• Limit the variety of Shapes used, e.g. omit 6- and 7-shapes. Vary by omitting different sets of Shapes.
• Give children only two of each Shape.
• Encourage children to begin to identify Shapes by touch. Children take Shapes, one by one, from the Numicon Feely Bag to cover the Baseboard.

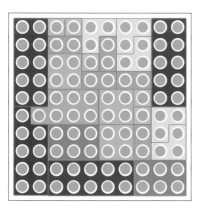

1

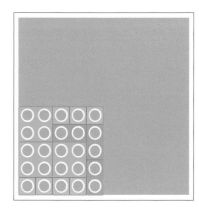

2

Matching Numicon Shapes

2

Educational context

In order to match alike Numicon Shapes or number rods, children need to look carefully to notice size, their odd or even shape (in the case of Shapes) and colour. Noticing the properties of size and oddness or evenness is a first step for children towards **constructing number meaning for these structured images**. The colours help with early identification of Shapes and number rods; when communicating about them, remember to use your chosen colour names consistently. The first activity involves matching identical Shapes by looking; the second involves feeling for Shapes from the Numicon Feely Bag. Handling and feeling the Shapes and number rods provides a sensory experience of their properties that helps children develop their own **mental imagery or visualization** of them.

Help children who are unable to pick up or handle Numicon Shapes independently to experience the 'feel' of the Shapes by helping them to press Shapes (one at a time) between their hands. Some children may have an aversion to the Numicon Feely Bag, in which case, find other ways to 'hide' the Shapes so children have to identify them by touch, e.g. in a 'feely box'.

In the third activity the Numicon Spinner is introduced. This is used extensively throughout the activities with different overlays. It is a useful alternative to dice but can be fiddly for children with motor control difficulties. For these children it may be appropriate to use a 'pocket' dice (which has a transparent pocket on each face to take different card inserts).

In all these activities, support children's thinking as they match identical Numicon Shapes or number rods by signing 'the same' (later children will learn another different sign to use when they are matching 'equivalent' combinations of Shapes). When children are matching grey Numicon Shapes to coloured Numicon Shapes qualify 'the same' to describe the matching attribute, i.e. 'the same shape' or 'the same size'.

Aims

• To learn to match Numicon Shapes by colour and shape

Communicating

Imagery
Numicon Display Number Line, Numicon Shapes

Equipment
See the individual 'have ready' for each activity, various items (including for measures) for the activities in the 'Extending the activities' section

Words and terms for instruction (supported with signs and symbols)
on top, underneath, feel, match, next to, beside, find, put together, set, spin

Mathematical words and terms (supported with signs and symbols)
the same, different, match, colour names

Assessment

Individual Record of Progress: Numbers and the Number System 5, 6, 29, 30

Putting the activities into context

Discuss situations where we have to match things that go together or that are the same, at home for example: sorting shoes or socks into pairs, sorting cutlery into sets, stacking plates of the same size; in the classroom for example: organizing equipment, e.g. pencils, crayons, pens into sets helps us to find them quickly, helps to prevent waste because equipment is looked after and helps to keep the classroom safe because things are not left lying about. Also discuss that school children often wear matching colours or uniforms that show they belong, as do members of other groups like football teams, scouts and guides, staff in shops and so on.

The activities

2

Activity 1: Match the Shapes

Have ready: two sets of 1–10 Numicon Shapes, one arranged in order and the other scattered

Step 1

Take a Shape from the scattered set and ask children to find the matching Shape from the ordered set.

Step 2

Ask children to compare the Shapes and to check that they match by placing one on top of the other.

Smaller steps

- Collect pairs of different objects. Play games where children match these objects.
- Once children can match 'real' objects gradually introduce Numicon Shapes into the games.
- If children have visual impairments that prevent them from distinguishing colours, the emphasis will be on matching by size and 'oddness' or 'evenness' of the Shape. When introducing two pairs of Shapes, start with one pair of odd shapes and one pair of even shapes that are very different in size, e.g. 3-shapes and 10-shapes. Increase the variety and difficulty (similarity in size) as children gain in confidence.
- Use two sets of the Numicon Large Foam Shapes for children to match.

Activity 2: Using the Numicon Feely Bag to find the matching Shape

Have ready: Numicon Feely Bag containing two different Numicon Shapes, 1–10 Numicon Shapes arranged in order

Step 1

Point to a Shape that is the same as one of those already in the Feely Bag, e.g. **Fig. 1**.

Step 2

A child feels in the Feely Bag to find the matching Shape. Gradually increase the challenge by increasing the number of Shapes in the Feely Bag.

Smaller steps

- Introduce the idea of identifying objects by touch by putting a familiar object into the Feely Bag, e.g. a ball, a pencil, and asking children what it is. Gradually increase to two and then three objects, asking children to feel in the Feely Bag for a specific one.
- Introduce the matching aspect of the activity by including two or more pairs of identical objects and two identical Numicon Shapes, e.g. two balls, two pencils, two Shapes. Put one of each pair in the Feely Bag and one of each on the table. Point to one of the objects on the table and ask the child to feel in the Feely Bag for the matching object.
- Repeat just with pairs of Shapes. Initially work with only two pairs of Shapes of very different sizes, e.g. two 1-shapes and two 10-shapes. Gradually increase the variety and number of Shapes used.

Activity 3: Introducing the Numicon Spinner

Have ready: Numicon Spinner with Numicon Colour Spinner Overlays (available to print and cut out from www.oxfordprimary.co.uk), Numicon Shapes

Step 1

Show the Spinner and demonstrate how to hold it steady and spin the arrow. Discuss and agree that the pointed end of the arrow points to where you need to look, e.g. **Fig. 2**.

Step 2

Children spin for a colour and then find Shapes of that colour.

Step 3

Encourage children to name the colour, modelling the agreed colour names.

Smaller steps

- Use a pocket dice (if available) with coloured cards inserted for children who have motor control difficulties that make the Spinner too difficult for them.
- Use only colours for Shapes 1–5, gradually extending the range.

Further practice

- Practise the above activities often until children are able to confidently match Shapes to pictures and explain the matching attribute (e.g. colour, shape).

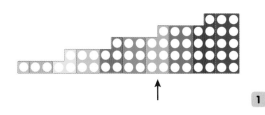

1

2

Extending the activities

Connecting activities

- To encourage children to focus on size and shape rather than colour, match coloured Shapes to grey Shapes (if available).
- Sort Shapes into sets of identical Shapes – encourage children to put the Shapes away into their box.
- Sort number rods into sets. Vary by filling Numicon Number Rod Trays 1–10 with sets of matching rods, e.g. fill the yellow tray with yellow rods.
- Colour, picture or dot dominoes.
- Colour or shape lotto.
- Use two sets of the Numicon Large Foam Shapes for children to match.
- Take opportunities for sorting equipment into sets of matching objects, e.g. classroom equipment, PE equipment – sorting bean bags into matching sets, tidying up the cutlery in the dining hall and so on.
- Use the *Numicon Software for the Interactive Whiteboard* to set up a screen with sorting hoops and a selection of Shapes or rods for children to sort virtually.

Connecting activities – Measures

- Length: Sort identical rods into sets.
- Length: Fill Numicon Number Rod Trays; with sets of matching rods 1–10 e.g. fill the yellow tray with yellow rods. Discuss that these rods match because they are all the same colour and also the same length.

For children moving on quickly

- Prepare a basket containing several of each Shape for children to sort. As children are ready, encourage them to look for criteria other than colour.

Making comparisons to understand 'bigger'

3

Educational context

The ability to **make and describe comparisons** is an essential life skill and is a cornerstone of mathematical understanding. In these activities children are learning to make comparisons between the sizes of Numicon Shapes, using the terms **'big' and 'bigger'** to describe the relationship between two Shapes and then comparing more than two Shapes to introduce the term **'biggest'**. Comparisons are made first by looking and then by feeling for the bigger or biggest Shapes in the Numicon Feely Bag to encourage children to visualize the Shapes. Children generally use 'big' before they use 'large'. To avoid confusion we suggest that 'big' is used consistently and introducing the word 'large' is delayed until children are confidently making comparisons using 'big', 'bigger' and 'biggest'.

The relative meaning of 'bigger' makes it difficult for some children to understand. Before doing these activities some children may need to work on 'big' in relation to everyday objects, toys and so on, and to use 'not big' before using 'bigger'. Refer to the Teaching Guide, 'Difficulties with the language of mathematics' (page 30). Also refer to the smaller steps suggested below each activity for these children.

The two core activities in this group should, over time, be repeated to teach further mathematical words and terms for comparing length, height, weight, capacity and time. Understanding this language is an essential part of the foundation for children's developing understanding of standard measures. Teachers will need to decide when to introduce this language to their children. Towards the end of this activity group under 'Extending the activities' there are suggested contexts for developing the language for different measures. Take opportunities as they arise to model this language supported by signs and symbols.

Aims

- To describe comparisons between Numicon Shapes using the term 'bigger'
- To make comparisons using language associated with different measures

Communicating

Imagery
Numicon Display Number Line, Numicon Shapes, number rods

Equipment
See the individual 'have ready' for each activity, various items (including for measures) for the activities in the 'Extending the activities' section

Words and terms for instruction (supported with signs and symbols)
feel, pick up, find, point to

Mathematical words and terms (supported with signs and symbols)
big, bigger, biggest;

For length: long, longer, longest

For height: tall, taller, tallest

For weight: heavy, heavier, heaviest

For capacity: full, fuller, fullest (using containers that are the same size)

For speed: fast, slow (for smaller steps use 'not fast')

Assessment

Individual Record of Progress: Numbers and the Number System 10, 32, Measures 1, 3, 8, 10, 24, 26, 43, 45, 51, 66

Putting the activities into context

Make comparisons between two similar objects that are different sizes, e.g. two toy cars of different size, two bottles, two coats, two people, identifying each time which is bigger, or larger.

The activities

Activity 1: Finding the bigger of two Numicon Shapes

Have ready: Numicon Shapes, Numicon Feely Bag

Step 1

Place a 10-shape and a 1-shape next to each other, see **Fig. 1**. Ask children to pick up the bigger Shape.

Step 2

Put both Shapes in the Feely Bag, and ask children to feel for the bigger Shape.

Step 3

Practise often with different pairs of Shapes, changing the selection to make sure that children can find the bigger Shape, e.g. of 4 and 6 or of 4 and 3.

Step 4

Ask children to work in pairs, taking turns to take on the role of the teacher by choosing two Shapes and asking, 'Can you find the bigger Shape?'

Smaller steps

- 'Big' and 'not big': Use pairs of different-sized similar objects, e.g. a big ball and a small ball; a big toy car and a small toy car. Show children the pair of different-sized objects. Ask children to pick up, point to or find the 'big' object. Ask children to pick up, point to or find the 'not big' object.

- Introducing 'bigger' with real objects: Use sets of three different-sized similar objects. To start with show children only the smallest and middle-sized objects from the set and ask children to find or point to the big or bigger one. When children can do this confidently and consistently replace the bigger object with the one that is even bigger than the 'bigger of the first two'. Ask children now to find or point to the bigger one.

- Repeat the above activity, replacing the objects with Shapes. To start with work with the 1-shape in comparison with other Shapes, and then work with the 2-shape in comparison with other Shapes.

Activity 2: Finding the biggest of three Numicon Shapes

Have ready: Numicon Shapes, Numicon Feely Bag

Step 1

Place three different Shapes next to each other, e.g. a 4-, 5- and 6-shape, e.g. **Fig. 2**. Ask children to pick up the biggest Shape.

Step 2

Ask children to take on the role of the teacher by choosing three Shapes and asking, 'Can you find the biggest Shape?'

Step 3

When children can consistently find the biggest Shape by looking, increase the challenge by asking children to find the biggest of three Shapes from the Feely Bag.

Smaller steps

- Use a set of three different-sized similar objects or toys. Ask children to find the biggest one.

Further practice

- Practise the above activities often until children are using the words 'big', 'bigger' and 'biggest' confidently and appropriately to describe comparisons.

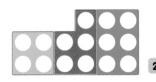

Extending the activities

3

Connecting activities – Measures

- Comparing size: Make a fishing game by attaching adhesive magnets to cut-out colour pictures of Shapes (available to download and cut out from www.oxfordprimary.co.uk). Children have to 'fish' for two Shapes and find the bigger one.
- Comparing size: Stories that involve the idea of big, such as 'Jack and the Beanstalk', 'The Enormous Turnip', 'The Giant Jam Sandwich'.
- Comparing size: Discussion about situations with which children will be familiar, e.g. big balls in PE, big chairs in the classroom, big lorries, big books and so on.
- Comparing size: Make comparisons between objects in situations of interest to children, e.g. cars, aeroplanes, trees, animals and so on.
- Comparing length: Make direct comparisons between objects of different length, e.g. string, ribbons; compare two number rods laid side by side horizontally, see Fig. 3.
- Comparing height: Make direct comparisons between heights of two children, two toy figures, two tables, two number rods standing vertically, e.g. Fig. 4.
- Comparing weight: Compare weights of two book bags or rucksacks where weights can be compared by children lifting one bag in each hand, that is, without using weighing scales.
- Comparing capacity: Children compare transparent containers of the same size (e.g. jam jars) some of which are full of dry sand or liquid and others that are not. Discuss using the words 'full' and 'not full'.
- Comparing speed: In PE ask one child to run fast on the spot while others watch; ask others if they can run faster on the spot. Use the words 'fast' and 'faster' when describing children's speed of travel.

For children moving on quickly

- Give children Numicon Shapes that are close in size, e.g. 6 and 7, for them to find the bigger one.
- Give children more than three Shapes and ask them to find the biggest.

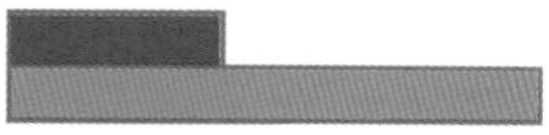

3

4

Making comparisons to understand 'smaller'

4

Educational context

In this activity group **language for making comparisons** is extended to include **'small', 'smaller' and 'smallest'**. As with 'bigger' the comparative meaning of 'smaller' makes it difficult for children to understand. Therefore, before the activities with Numicon some children may need to work on 'small' in relation to everyday objects and to compare two objects using the terms 'small' and 'not small' before using 'smaller'. Again refer to the Teaching Guide, 'Difficulties with the language of mathematics' (page 30). Also refer to the smaller steps suggested below each activity for these children.

Continue to make comparisons first by looking and then encourage development of children's mental imagery by giving them opportunities to feel for the smaller or smallest Numicon Shapes from the Numicon Feely Bag.

As in the previous activity group the two core activities in this group should, over time, be repeated to teach further mathematical words and terms for comparing length, height, weight, capacity and time. Understanding this language is an essential part of the foundation for children's developing understanding of standard measures. Teachers will need to decide when to introduce this language to children and take opportunities as they arise to model this language supported by signs and symbols. There are suggested contexts for developing the language for different measures under 'Extending the activities'.

Aims

- To describe comparisons between Numicon Shapes using the term 'smaller'
- To make comparisons using language associated with different measures

Communicating

Imagery
Numicon Display Number Line, Numicon Shapes, number rods

Equipment
See the individual 'have ready' for each activity, various items (including for measures) for the activities in the 'Extending the activities' section

Words and terms for instruction (supported with signs and symbols)
pick up, find, feel, point to

Mathematical words and terms (supported with signs and symbols)
For size: smaller, smallest

For length: shorter, shortest

For height: shorter, shortest

For weight: lighter, lightest

For capacity: less full, least full (using containers that are the same size)

For time: slow, slowest

Assessment

Individual Record of Progress: Numbers and the Number System 11, 33, Measures 2, 4, 6, 9, 11, 25, 27, 44, 46, 52, 67

Putting the activities into context

Make comparisons between two similar objects that are different sizes, e.g. two model cars of different size, two bottles, two coats, two people and so on, identifying which is smaller.

The activities

4

Activity 1: Finding the smaller of two Numicon Shapes

Have ready: Numicon Shapes, Numicon Feely Bag

Step 1
Place a 10-shape and a 1-shape next to each other, see **Fig. 1**. Ask children to pick up the smaller Shape.

Step 2
Put both Shapes in a Feely Bag, and ask children to feel for the smaller Shape.

Step 3
Work with the 1-shape in comparison with Shapes 6–10 initially and then repeat comparing the 2-shape with other Shapes.

Step 4
Practise often with different pairs of Shapes, changing the selection to make sure children can find the smaller Shape, e.g. of 4 and 6 or of 4 and 3.

Step 5
Ask children to work in pairs, taking turns to take on the role of the teacher by choosing two Shapes and asking, 'Can you find the smaller Shape?'

Smaller steps
- 'Small and 'not small': Use pairs of different-sized similar objects, e.g. a big figure and a small figure; a big toy car and a small toy car. Show children the pair of different-sized objects. Ask children to pick up, point to or find the 'small' object. Ask children to pick up, point to or find the 'not small' object.

- Introducing 'smaller' with real objects: Use sets of three different-sized similar objects. To start with show children only the smallest and middle-sized objects from the set and ask children to find or point to the small/smaller one. When children can do this confidently and consistently replace the bigger object with the one that is even smaller than the 'smaller of the first two'. Ask children now to find or point to the smaller one.

- Repeat the above activity, replacing the objects with Numicon Shapes. To start with work with the 1-shape in comparison with other Shapes, and then work with the 2-shape in comparison with other Shapes.

Activity 2: Finding the smallest of three Numicon Shapes

Have ready: Numicon Shapes

Step 1
Place three different Shapes next to each other, e.g. a 2-, 6- and 10-shape, see **Fig. 2**. Ask children to pick up the smallest Shape.

Step 2
Ask children to work in pairs, taking turns to take on the role of the teacher by choosing three Shapes and asking, 'Can you find the smallest Shape?'

Smaller steps
- Use a set of three different-sized similar objects or toys. Ask children to find the smallest one.

- When children understand small, smaller and smallest with real objects repeat with Numicon Shapes.

Further practice
- Practise the above activities often until children are confidently and appropriately using the terms 'small', 'smaller' and 'smallest'.

Extending the activities

Connecting activities

- Follow the activities above comparing number rods of different lengths.
- Put two Shapes in the Feely Bag. Children feel in the Bag for the smaller Shape.
- Tell stories that involve small characters.
- Take opportunities to make comparisons in everyday situations, e.g. comparing PE equipment, comparing chairs, comparing sizes of books.
- Make a collection of very small objects and ask, e.g. 'How many things can be fitted into a matchbox?'
- Make comparisons between objects in situations of interest to children, e.g. cars, aeroplanes, trees, animals.

Connecting activities – Measures

- Comparing length: Make direct comparisons between two objects of different lengths to say which is shorter, e.g. string, ribbons; compare number rods laid side by side horizontally, see Fig. 3.
- Comparing height: Make direct comparisons between heights of two children or objects, to say which is shorter, e.g. two toy figures, two tables, two number rods standing vertically, e.g. Fig. 4.
- Comparing weight: Compare weights of two objects to say which is lighter; e.g. two book bags or rucksacks where the weights can be compared by children lifting one in each hand, that is, without using weighing scales.
- Comparing capacity: Compare containers (some full and some empty). Discuss, using the words 'full' and 'empty'.
- Comparing speed: In PE ask one child to move slowly while others watch; ask others if they can move more slowly. Use the words 'slow' and 'slower' when describing children's speed or travel.
- Comparing speed: Look at two minibeasts that move at different speeds, e.g. a snail and a woodlouse. Discuss the speed at which they both move; they are both slow, but which is slower?

For children moving on quickly

- Give children Shapes that are close in size, e.g. 6 and 7, and ask them to find the smaller one.
- Give children more than three Shapes for them to find the smallest.

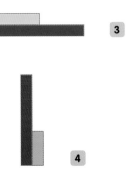

Matching Numicon Shapes to pictures of the Shapes

5

Educational context

These activities build on the matching of actual Numicon Shapes and number rods in Numbers and the Number System to matching Numicon Shapes first with actual-size printed images, e.g. on Numicon Picture Baseboard Overlays, the Numicon Display Number Line and 'mats', and then to smaller printed images on the Numicon Table-top Number Line, Numicon Spinner Overlays and pocket dice (if available). These activities can be adapted to be done on a computer or interactive whiteboard using the *Numicon Software for the Interactive Whiteboard*, which includes a virtual Spinner and Overlays.

Recognizing these images is key to children benefitting from the **number-rich environment** and a step towards developing their own **mental imagery**, as well as being necessary for engagement with many of the suggested activities.

Continue to support matching with signing but now qualify 'the same' to emphasize 'the same shape', 'the same colour'. This will help to prepare children for the sign they will use later when they are matching 'equivalent' combinations of Numicon Shapes that have 'the same value'.

Aims

- To match Numicon Shapes to coloured pictures of the Shapes

Communicating

Imagery
Numicon Display Number Line, Numicon Shapes, number rods

Equipment
See the individual 'have ready' for each activity, various items for the activities in the 'Extending the activities' section

Words and terms for instruction (supported with signs and symbols)
feel, find, match, turn over, turn round, see in your mind's eye, see in your head

Mathematical words and terms (supported with signs and symbols)
match, turn over, turn round, colour names (orange, light blue, yellow, light green, red, turquoise, pink, green, purple, blue), the same as, different, big, bigger, biggest, small, smaller, smallest

Assessment

Individual Record of Progress: Numbers and the Number System 7, 8, 9, 31

Putting the activities into context

Discuss situations where we have to match objects to pictures; e.g. when following a recipe on the internet instructions are often illustrated by pictures, as are instructions to build a model. Re-enacting illustrated stories with puppets, small world figures and objects, also makes connections between pictures and actual objects.

The activities

Activity 1: Using the Numicon Picture Overlays

Have ready: Numicon Baseboard with one of the Picture Overlays, a basket of Numicon Shapes, Numicon Feely Bag

Step 1

Children match Numicon Shapes with Shapes on the Picture Overlays.

Step 2

Vary by asking children to take the Shapes one by one from the Feely Bag and match them to complete the picture, e.g. **Fig. 1**.

Smaller steps

- Prepare 'mats' each showing only one colour Numicon Shape card (Numicon Shape, Numeral and Word 1–10 Cards Actual Size – available to print and cut out from www.oxfordprimary.co.uk)
- Ask children to match the Shapes to the mats (gradually increase the number of mats and Shapes).
- Choose one of the simpler Picture Overlays (cat or lorry) and put out only the Shapes needed.

Further practice

- Practise the above activity often until children are confidently matching Numicon Shapes to pictures and explaining matching attributes (colour and shape).

Activity 2: Matching Shapes to images on the Numicon Display Number Line

Have ready: Numicon Shapes, Numicon Display Number Line (or Numicon Large Format Table-top Number Line)

Step 1

Point to a picture of one of the Shapes on the Display Number Line (see **Fig. 2**).

Step 2

Children find the matching Shape and place it on the Display Number Line.

Smaller steps

- Work with a smaller section of the Display Number Line, e.g. 0–4, gradually increasing to 1–10, see **Fig. 2**.

Activity 3: Matching different-sized pictures of Numicon Shapes to the Shapes

Have ready: Numicon Shapes 1–10, Numicon Shape, Numeral and Word 1–10 Cards and Numicon Shape, Numeral and Word 1–10 Cards Large Size (available to print and cut out from www.oxfordprimary.co.uk), laminated and spread on the tabletop)

Step 1

Spread the Numicon Shapes and pictures of the different-sized Shapes on the tabletop.

Step 2

Children match the different-sized pictures to the Shapes (see **Fig. 3**).

Smaller steps

- Work with the range 1–4, gradually increasing to the range 1–10.

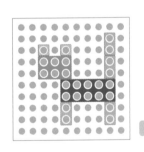

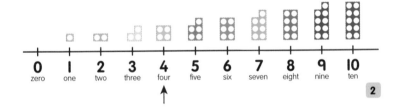

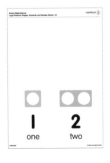
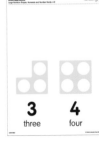
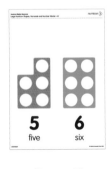
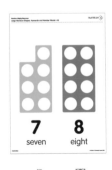
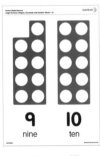

Extending the activities 5

Activity 4: Introducing the Numicon Spinner and Numicon Colour Spinner Overlays

Have ready: Numicon Shapes, two Numicon Spinners with Numicon Shape Colour Overlays (available to print and cut out from www.oxfordprimary.co.uk)

Step 1

Start with the Shape Overlay 1–5. Discuss the pictures, ensuring that children recognize the smaller versions of the Shapes.

Step 2

Point to one of the Shape pictures on the Shape Overlay. Children find the matching Shape.

Step 3

When children are confidently matching Shapes to the Shape Overlay 1–5, introduce the Shape Overlay 6–10; if appropriate, work just with this Shape Overlay before working with both together.

Smaller steps

- Use pocket dice (if available) with the Numicon Shapes 1–10 Large (available to print and cut out from www.oxfordprimary.co.uk)
- Reduce the number of Shapes by showing the same Shape on several sides of the pocket dice, or on the Spinner, by making an overlay showing fewer Shapes.

Further practice

- Practise the above activities often until children are confidently matching Shapes to variously sized pictures of these on number lines, Shape Overlays and so on.

Connecting activities

- Match coloured Shapes to the Baseboard Overlay: cover the board.
- Match grey Numicon Shapes (if available) to the Baseboard Overlay: cover the board.
- Encourage children to visualize Numicon Shapes by putting the Shapes for one of the Baseboard Overlays in the Feely Bag. Point one by one to the pictures of the Shapes on the Overlay, while children feel in the Feely Bag to find the matching Shapes.
- Use pocket dice (if available) with Numicon Shapes 1–10 Large (available to print and cut out from www.oxfordprimary.co.uk) and Large Foam Numicon Shapes. Children take turns to roll the dice and pick up corresponding Shapes.
- Prepare mats showing pictures of number rods (available to print and cut out from www.oxfordprimary.co.uk). Children match rods to their pictures.
- Play dominoes.
- Play picture lotto.

Connecting activities – Measures

- Take opportunities as they arise in the course of these activities to reinforce the language of size: big, small, bigger, smaller, biggest, smallest.

For children moving on quickly

- Give children opportunities to create their own pictures with Shapes both on and off the Baseboard.
- Use the Baseboard Overlay: cover the board on grey shapes for children to cover the board by matching Shapes to the outlines of the Shapes.
- Give children Shapes to match to the Shapes on the Numicon Large Format Table-top Number Line (see Fig. 4).

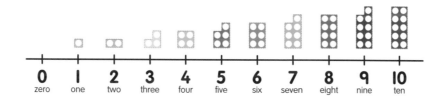

4

Using language of comparison

6

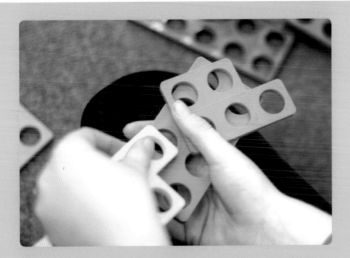

Educational context

The work on comparing continues in these activities with **a greater range of language**, now using 'bigger' and 'smaller' together and describing the Numicon Shapes in between. This gradual introduction is helpful for children who have speech, language and communication difficulties for whom signing these words is particularly important. Listen carefully for the way in which children pronounce the phrases ending in 'than'; model correct pronunciation if they say 'biggeran', 'smalleran' and so on to encourage understanding that 'than' indicates those Shapes or objects with which another is being compared.

As with previous activity groups involving comparison, the two core activities in this group should, over time, be adapted to teach further mathematical words and terms for comparing length, height, weight, capacity and time. In the 'Extending the activities' section there are suggested contexts for developing this language. Teachers will need to decide when to introduce this language to their children and should take opportunities to model it, remembering also to support it with signs and symbols.

Aims

- To use the language of comparative size with Numicon Shapes

- To use the language of comparison in conversation

- To compare objects directly by length, weight, height and capacity

Communicating

Imagery
Numicon Display Number Line

Equipment
See the individual 'have ready' for each activity, various items (including for measures) for the activities in the 'Extending the activities' section

Words and terms for instruction (supported with signs and symbols)
pick up, find, feel, point to

Mathematical words and terms (supported with signs and symbols)
Size: bigger, biggest, smaller, smallest, middle-sized, medium, larger, largest, bigger than, smaller than

Length: long, longer, longest, longer than, short, shorter, shortest, shorter than

Width: wide, wider, widest, wider than, narrow, narrower, narrowest, narrower than

Height: tall, taller, tallest, taller than, short, shorter, shortest, shorter than

Weight: heavy, heavier, heaviest, heavier than, light, lighter, lightest, lighter than

Capacity: full, empty, holds more than, holds less than, holds most, holds least

Speed: fast, faster, fastest, slow, slower, slowest, faster than, slower than

Time: long, longer, longer than, short, shorter, shorter than

Assessment

Individual Record of Progress: Numbers and the Number System 12, 34, Measures 6, 7, 12, 28, 34, 35, 36, 37, 47, 54, 58, 59, 61, 62, 66, 67

Putting the activities into context

Discuss situations in which we might need to purchase larger or smaller sizes of food or other commodities familiar to children; e.g. a family of six might buy a larger loaf of bread than a family of three, who would need a smaller loaf; a family of six might buy the largest size of milk whereas a person living alone might buy the smallest.

The activities

Activity 1: Which is the biggest? Which is the smallest?

Have ready: four different Numicon Shapes

Step 1
Ask children to pick up the biggest Shape and then the smallest one. Encourage children to use 'biggest' and 'smallest' to describe what they are doing (e.g. **Fig. 1**).

Step 2
Repeat with different Shapes until children are confident.

Activity 2: Bigger than, smaller than

Have ready: three different Numicon Shapes

Step 1
Point to the middle-sized Shape and say to children, 'Pick up the Shape that is bigger than this one' (e.g. **Fig. 2**).

Step 2
Repeat Step 1 but point to the middle-sized Shape and ask children, 'Can you pick up the Shape that is smaller than this one?'

Step 3
Repeat Steps 1 and 2, reversing roles so that children are using the language 'bigger than' and 'smaller than'.

Smaller steps for activities 1 and 2
- Prepare sets of similar objects in sizes small, medium and large. Talk about the objects, focusing on their comparative size and then use them to do activities 1 and 2.
- When children can use the language successfully with real objects, repeat activities 1 and 2; to start with use Shapes that are very different in size.

Further practice for activities 1 and 2
Practise the above activities often until children are confidently using the language of comparison when making comparisons between both real objects and Numicon Shapes.

Extending the activities

Connecting activities

(Select and adapt these activities according to the interests and ability of children.)
- Tell stories which involve small, medium and large characters.
- Repeat activities 1 and 2 above, this time comparing number rods.

Connecting activities – Measures

- Size: children order different-sized and different-shaped containers, including those that stack and nest. Introduce 'large', 'larger than', 'largest' as appropriate for the children.
- Length: Children compare three or more different lengths of ribbon, string or three number rods laid side by side horizontally, e.g. **Fig. 3**.
- Capacity: As children work on filling the Numicon Number Rod Trays take opportunities to discuss that the big trays hold more rods than the smaller trays.
- Height: Compare heights of three or more toy figures, tables or number rods standing vertically, to say which is tallest, which is shorter, which is shortest, e.g. **Fig. 4**.
- Width: Children compare ribbons of two different widths. Give children opportunities to build constructions with blocks to make wide doorways and narrow doorways, wide gaps and narrow gaps.
- Width: In PE talk about it being easier to balance and walk along a wide bench rather than a narrow beam.
- Weight: Comparing more than two weights requires the use of a pair of balances. Children can compare weights in the balances by finding out which is the heavier and then comparing that with the third weight. This involves reasoning that may be challenging. Support children by careful preparation of three items: one heavy, one lighter and one very light. Children may be able to deduce which is heaviest, which is lighter and which is lightest without the use of the balance and can then check using the weighing scales.
- Capacity: Compare three identical containers holding different quantities of dry sand or liquid (e.g. jam jars) so children can see which is full, which is less full and which is empty.

1

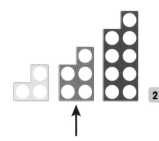

2

3

4

Numbers and the Number System

- Speed: Compare fast and slow. In music ask children to clap hands in fast time; contrast this with clapping hands in slow time. In writing discuss speed of handwriting, writing quickly and writing slowly, described as fast writing and slow writing.

- Time: Introduce the idea of a long and a short time as children work on filling number rod trays. Take opportunities to discuss whether it took a long time or a short time to fill the trays. Encourage the connection that a tray with lots of rods takes longer to fill.

- Time: As different groups of children work on various tasks discuss which tasks take a long time and which take a shorter, or longer time.

For children moving on quickly

- When comparing three Shapes, when the smallest and biggest have been identified talk about what to call the one that is left; introduce the words 'middle-sized' and 'medium'.

- Extend the number of Shapes to give further opportunities for comparison.

Learning to order Numicon Shapes

Educational context

Putting Numicon Shapes or number rods in size order is another important step towards **understanding and describing number relationships**; although at this stage some children may have started to use number names for some of the Shapes, the emphasis here is on **using comparative and positional language**. As children arrange Shapes in order of size, they will be comparing sizes to find the next Shape in the series. They will also be using words such as 'first', 'last', 'before', 'after' and 'next'. Children may well be familiar with these in everyday temporal contexts as they discuss their day – 'We do maths work after break time', 'We read our books before we go home', 'We will be singing next' – and where a visual timetable is used each day to help children understand 'before' and 'after' in the sequence of their daily routines (see photo above). They may also have used them to describe position, e.g. when standing in line waiting for their lunch or to leave the classroom: 'Tom is first in the line'; 'Tanya is last in the line'. Now they will be using these words to describe positions of Numicon Shapes in relation to each other.

Children usually learn 'first' and 'last' prior to learning 'before' and 'after' because 'first' and 'last' are **absolute** within a particular series, whereas 'next', 'before' and 'after' are **relative** to each particular item in the series. Signing these words will be helpful – as will having the Numicon Display Number Line as a permanent feature of the teaching space (displayed at children's eye level where they can touch it and match Numicon Shapes to it) and having Numicon Large Format Table-top Number Lines to hand. Both offer a model of the Numicon Shapes in order from left to right.

It is not unusual for children to be able to order Numicon Shapes 1–5 and then have more difficulty with Shapes 6–10, often misplacing the 6-shape and 7-shape. See suggestions for 'Smaller steps' below.

Towards the end of this activity group under 'Extending the activities' there are suggested contexts for developing the language relevant to different measures. Teachers will need to decide when to introduce these activities to their children. They should take opportunities as they arise to model this language supported by signs and symbols.

Aims

- To put Numicon Shapes 1–10 in order of size
- To put objects in order of length, height, weight, capacity, time

Communicating

Imagery
Numicon Display Number Line, visual timetable

Equipment
See the individual 'have ready' for each activity, various items (including for measures) for the activities in the 'Extending the activities' section

Words and terms for instruction (supported with signs and symbols)
put in order of size, put in size order, start with

Mathematical words and terms (supported with signs and symbols)
first, last, next, after, before, in between, bigger, biggest, smaller, smallest, larger, largest, bigger than, smaller than, larger than
Length: long, longer, longest, longer than, short, shorter, shortest, shorter than
Height: tall, taller, tallest, taller than, short, shorter, shortest, shorter than
Width: wide, wider, widest, wider than, narrow, narrower, narrowest, narrower than
Weight: heavy, heavier, heaviest, heavier than, light, lighter, lightest, lighter than
Capacity: full, empty, holds more than, holds less than, holds most, holds least
Time: long time, short time, longer than, shorter than, before, after, next, in between

Assessment

Individual Record of Progress: Numbers and the Number System 13, 15, 35, Measures 16, 31, 38, 41, 47, 54, 61, 62

Putting the activities into context

Discuss collections of objects that are stacked or stored in order of size. Adapt the objects chosen according to the age and interests of children. For example, for younger children you might look at puzzles where pieces have to be placed in order, or stacking toys such as sets of beakers. For older individuals you might look at stacks of kitchen weights, a set of socket spanners, or arrangements of bottles and jars in cupboards with the smallest at the front and largest at the back. Whatever the context, discuss that we have to compare objects so that we can arrange them in order of size and that keeping things in an organized way helps us to find things quickly when we need them. For older individuals it might be helpful to discuss the ways in which tools are stored in garage workshops.

The activities

Activity 1: Jumbled Shapes

Have ready: Numicon Shapes 1–10 scattered on the table

Step 1

Explain that the activity is putting the Shapes in order starting with the smallest, and then show children what to do.

Step 2

Jumble the Shapes, pick out the first one and ask children to find the next one. Continue until all Shapes are ordered.

Smaller steps

- Focus on one temporal concept at a time before using them together. Use 'after' and, when children are confident, introduce the word 'next'. Then introduce 'before'.
- Give children an Ordering Frame (photocopy master 16) to help them organize the Shapes in order. Work initially from 1–3, gradually including further Shapes one at a time until children can order the series up to 10 (e.g. **Fig. 2**).
- Use Baseboard Overlay: Numicon Shapes in order. Children match Numicon Shapes to the Baseboard Overlay.

Further practice

- Practise the above activity often until children are confidently putting Numicon Shapes in order of size.
- Using the Numicon Magnetic Strip (if available), put Shapes on a magnetic board for children to order independently.
- Cut out the Outlines of Numicon Shapes (photocopy master 18) for children to glue onto paper in order of increasing size and decreasing size.
- Match the Shapes to Baseboard Overlays: Grey Numicon Shapes in order (e.g. **Fig. 3**).

Extending the activities

Connecting activities

- Repeat these activities using number rods.
- Provide nesting and stacking puzzles that involve ordering by size.
- Provide magazines or catalogues for children to cut out pictures of different-sized objects to glue onto paper in order of increasing size and decreasing size.

Connecting activities – Measures

- Length: Provide objects of different lengths for children to compare and order.
- Height: Provide collections of small world figures of various heights for children to compare and put into increasing or decreasing order of height.
- Width: Provide three items of different widths for children to compare and order.
- Weight: Provide three objects of different weights and a pair of balancing scales for children to compare the heaviness and put them in increasing or decreasing order of weight.
- Capacity: Provide various different-sized containers and dry sand or liquid. Children experiment to find which holds more and which holds less.
- Time: Discuss the order of the school day using the visual timetable. Use children's experiences of time to make comparisons. Discuss what is a 'long time'; e.g. the lunch time break is longer than morning break, which is shorter. Ask if their journey to school takes a long time or a short time.

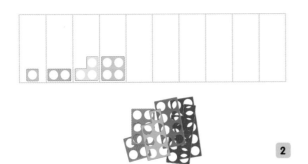

2

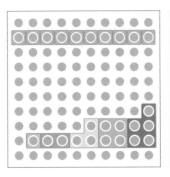 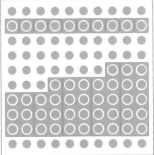

3

7

For children moving on quickly

- Children order the Numicon Shapes and number rods independently.
- Children find the next Shape or rod starting anywhere in the series.
- Children find the previous Shape from any point in the series.
- Children put Shapes in reverse order from the largest to the smallest, e.g. **Fig. 4**.
- Some children might like to build an increasing and decreasing pattern with two sets of Shapes, e.g **Fig. 5**.

4

5

Securing ordering of Numicon Shapes

8

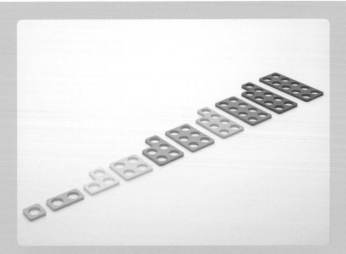

Educational context

These activities involve children's understanding of the 'whole set' of Numicon Shapes 1–10, **recognizing the pattern in the ordered sequence of Shapes** and noticing when one part of that set is missing. It is important to encourage children to explain how they know **what is missing from, or is misplaced in, the ordered set**.

Many children will benefit from the adult modelling explanations, using signing as necessary. Note that while some children may refer to the Numicon Shapes by their number names, for others the emphasis will be on size, colour and pattern. If children are using number names, remember to correct them if they use the wrong number name to avoid repetition of misunderstanding.

When an activity is familiar to children, change the teacher and child roles so that children swap or remove Numicon Shapes for the adult to restore the ordered set. This provides useful opportunities for modelling aloud the process and language for solving the problem.

In the 'Connecting activities' section it is suggested that the ordering activities for measures in the previous activity group are continued. Teachers will need to decide when to introduce these activities to children. They should take opportunities as they arise to model the associated language, supported by signs and symbols.

Aims

- To order Numicon Shapes confidently and securely

Communicating

Imagery
Numicon Display Number Line

Equipment
See the individual 'have ready' for each activity, various items for the activities in the 'Extending the activities' section.

Words and terms for instruction (supported with signs and symbols)
order, arrange, swap, change over, look, find, what's wrong?, put right

Mathematical words and terms (supported with signs and symbols)
reinforce language of size, order and position – first, last, next, after, before, in between

Assessment

Individual Record of Progress: Numbers and the Number System 13, 14, 15, 16, 35, 36

Putting the activities into context

Extend the conversations about situations where sets of collections are stored in order of size, to include discussion about how we can recognize that one part of an ordered set is missing. Adapt the context according to the age and interests of children. For example, for younger children you might look at a set of Russian dolls or nesting boxes – for older individuals you might look at a set of measuring spoons or socket spanners. Whatever the chosen context, put the set in order and remove one; then discuss how we know that one is missing, emphasizing the incremental increase in size and the importance of noticing the regularity and that where this is broken indicates where one of the set is missing.

The activities

8

Activity 1: Fill the gap

Have ready: two sets of Numicon Shapes 1–10

Step 1

Scatter one set of Shapes on the table nearby and ask children to arrange the second set of Shapes in order from 1–10.

Step 2

Ask children to close their eyes. Remove a Shape from the ordered set.

Step 3

Children pick up the Shape from the scattered set to fill the gap.

Step 4

Repeat, removing different Shapes.

Step 5

Change roles so children remove a Shape for the adult to explain what has happened and correct the order.

Smaller steps

- Have a set of Numicon Shapes 1–10 in order nearby to which children can refer.
- Use a limited range of Shapes, e.g. Shapes 1–5, gradually increasing to working with the full set.

Activity 2: Swaps

Have ready: Numicon Shapes 1–10

Step 1

Ask children to arrange the Shapes in order of size, 1–10, starting with the smallest.

Step 2

Ask children to close their eyes; swap the order of two Shapes (e.g. Fig. 1).

Step 3

Ask children to open their eyes and explain or indicate which Shapes have been moved. Children move the two Shapes back to their correct places.

Step 4

Repeat, swapping different Shapes.

Step 5

Change roles so children swap two Shapes for the adult to explain what has happened and correct the order.

Smaller steps

- Have a set of Shapes 1–10 in order nearby to which children can refer.
- Use a limited range of Shapes, e.g. Shapes 1–5, gradually increasing to working with the full set.
- To start with, swap Shapes that are far apart, e.g. 3-shape and 9-shape, working gradually towards swapping adjacent Shapes.

Activity 3: Which Shape is missing?

Have ready: two sets of Numicon Shapes 1–10

Step 1

Scatter one set of Shapes on the table nearby and ask children to arrange the second set of Shapes in order from 1–10.

Step 2

Ask children to close their eyes; remove one Shape from the ordered set and close the gap.

Step 3

Ask children to open their eyes and to explain or indicate which Shape is missing. Children then pick up a Shape from the scattered set to complete the ordered set.

Step 4

Repeat, removing different Shapes.

Step 5

Change roles so children remove a Shape for the adult to explain which Shape is missing and find the correct Shape to restore the series.

Smaller steps

- Do not attempt Activity 3 until children are able to do activities 1 and 2 confidently. Support by helping children to look for the break in the pattern.

Further practice for activities 1–3

- Practise the above activities often until children are able to do them confidently. Continue to vary by changing roles.

1

Extending the activities

Connecting activities

- Continue the ordering activities for measures from Numbers and the Number System, Activity Group 7.
- Set up play situations where something is in the wrong place or position, and encourage children to describe 'what's wrong'.
- Look at 'spot what's wrong' pictures and discuss how children know what's wrong.
- Use a sequence of pictures that tell a story, remove one picture, and ask children to describe what is wrong or missing.

For children moving on quickly

- Do these activities with number rods.
- Encourage children to explain which Shapes are missing or swapped and give them opportunities to play these games in pairs.
- Children put a set of rods 1–10 in order starting with the largest. Emphasize that this is a full set of rods (see Fig. 2).
- Some children might like to build an increasing and decreasing pattern with two sets of rods, e.g. Fig. 3.

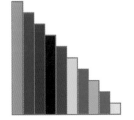

2

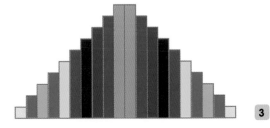

3

Beginning to learn Numicon Shape patterns

9

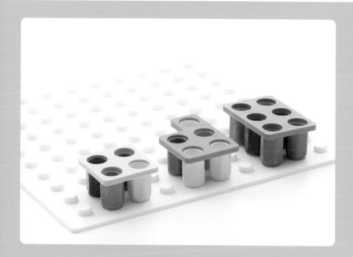

Educational context

In these activities children start to learn to build the patterns for the Numicon Shapes. This work continues in Numbers and the Number System 12 and in many of the later activities as it is fundamental to their Numicon work. Building Numicon Shape patterns helps children to **understand numbers as composite ideas in themselves, each having cardinal and ordinal value**. Although counting is an important initial skill to master, if they are to learn to calculate successfully children need to move beyond thinking of numbers as words they hear, or numerals they see in the counting sequence. Therefore, at this stage, the emphasis is on building the Numicon Shape pattern. Although some children may use number names to label their Numicon Shape patterns and want to count the Numicon Coloured Pegs when they have built them, they should be encouraged not to count while they are actually placing Pegs to build the patterns.

Model how to build the Numicon Shape patterns (for numbers higher than 1) by taking a Numicon Coloured Peg in each hand and placing them side by side, starting at the bottom. When children copy the patterns in Activities 1 and 2, they check that they have copied correctly by looking at the original, and in Activity 3 they check with the matching Numicon Shape and not by counting.

Aims

- To learn the patterns of the Numicon Shapes

Communicating

Imagery
Numicon Display Number Line

Equipment
See the individual 'have ready' for each activity, various items for the activities in the 'Extending the activities' section.

Words and terms for instruction (supported with signs and symbols)
look, make, arrange, copy, match, check, fit, put

Mathematical words and terms (supported with signs and symbols)
shape, pattern, the same, different, enough, not enough, bigger, smaller

Assessment

Individual Record of Progress: Numbers and the Number System 17, 18

Putting the activities into context

Discuss situations in which we recognize particular arrangements, e.g. laying a table, recognizing patterns on dice or dominoes. Look at the regular arrangements of holes in the Numicon Shapes and explain that these are called Numicon Shape patterns and that, like dice and domino patterns, they are a way of showing (representing) numbers.

The activities

Activity 1: Copying Numicon Shape patterns

Have ready: Numicon Baseboards, Numicon Coloured Pegs sorted into baskets by colour

Step 1
Take the 5-shape and explain to children that you are going to build its pattern. To encourage focus on the pattern of holes in the Shape and avoid children matching by colour, do not use red Pegs for the 5-shape, e.g. **Fig. 1**.

Step 2
Taking a Peg in each hand, start building the pattern, two Pegs at a time from the bottom up, and then the odd one.

Step 3
Tell children that you are going to build another pattern for them to copy. Build the pattern for the 3-shape (not with yellow Pegs).

Step 4
Ask children to copy the pattern on their Baseboard.

Smaller steps
- Work with Numicon Shape patterns from 1–4 only; gradually extend until children can arrange Pegs into the patterns of all the Shapes.
- If fitting Pegs onto the Baseboard is too fiddly for children, provide them with larger counters and enlarge and laminate the Baseboard for Drawing Numicon Shapes and Numicon Shape Patterns (photocopy master 3) on which they can build the patterns.

Activity 2: Find the Shape

Have ready: Numicon Shapes in order, Numicon Baseboard, baskets of Numicon Coloured Pegs sorted into colours

Step 1
Arrange the Pegs on the Baseboard to make a Numicon Shape pattern. Ask children to pick up the corresponding Shape and place it on top of the arranged Pegs to check the pattern (e.g. **Fig. 2**).

Step 2
Repeat Steps 1 and 2, making patterns of different Shapes. Sometimes change roles so the child builds a pattern for the adult to copy.

Smaller steps
- Work with Numicon Shape patterns from 1–4 only; gradually extend until children can arrange Pegs into the patterns of all the Numicon Shapes.
- If fitting Pegs onto the Numicon Baseboard is too fiddly for children, provide them with larger counters and enlarge and laminate Baseboard for Drawing Numicon Shapes and Numicon Shape Patterns (photocopy master 3) on which they can build the patterns.

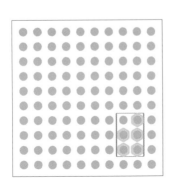

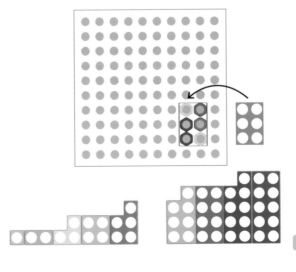

Extending the activities

Activity 3: Make a Numicon Shape pattern

Have ready: Numicon Shapes 1–10 in order, Numicon Baseboard, Numicon Coloured Pegs sorted into colours

Step 1
Ask children to choose the colour of Pegs they would like to use.

Step 2
Take a Shape of a different colour from the Pegs the children have chosen.

Step 3
Ask children to look at the Shape carefully and to make the pattern of the Shape by arranging some of their Pegs on the Baseboard.

Step 4
Encourage children to check that they have built the pattern correctly by fitting the matching Shape over it.

Step 5
Repeat Steps 1–4, using different Shapes and making different Numicon Shape patterns. Sometimes change roles, so the child chooses a Shape for the adult to make the pattern.

Smaller steps
- Work with Numicon Shape patterns from 1–4 only; gradually extend until children can arrange Pegs into the patterns of all the Shapes.
- If fitting Pegs onto the Baseboard is too fiddly for children, provide them with larger counters and enlarge and laminate Baseboard for Drawing Numicon Shapes and Numicon Shape Patterns (photocopy master 3) on which they can build the patterns.

Further practice
- Practise the above activities often. Continue to vary by changing roles, revisiting them (even after they have moved on to the later activities) until children are able to do them confidently.

Connecting activities

- Children print Numicon Shape patterns with a round sponge or cork.
- Children paint the patterns in dots by painting through the holes in the Shapes.
- Children spin a Numicon Shape pattern using a Numicon Spinner with Numicon Shape Overlay, then make the Numicon Shape pattern with Pegs on the Baseboard.
- Children use the Baseboard for Drawing Numicon Shapes and Numicon Shape Patterns, to draw Shape outlines and colour the patterns.
- Give children geometric shape puzzles.
- Give children collage activities.
- Give children 6–9 Numicon Coloured Counters and ask them to arrange them in different ways or patterns; e.g. 6 could be arranged into the dice pattern, in a row, as a triangle, as a circle. These arrangements can be recorded if appropriate.

For children moving on quickly

- When children are confident with Activities 1, 2 and 3 as described, repeat them using a mixture of Pegs. Give children opportunities to arrange Pegs into a Numicon Shape pattern from memory. To choose a pattern they could either feel for a Shape in the Numicon Feely Bag or look closely at a Shape that is subsequently hidden.

Giving Numicon Shapes their number names

Educational context

It is likely that many children will by now have been counting the holes in the Numicon Shapes and referring to some of the Shapes by number names spontaneously. However, it is essential to **ensure that children have made connections between their counting and the ordered sequence of patterns seen in the Shapes**, as these will help them to understand the **cardinal values of numbers** and to notice relationships between them. Therefore, the work in this activity group now focuses on giving the Shapes number names. At this stage children are only naming the Shapes in preparation for the next activity group, when they label them with numerals. Those children who have phonological memory difficulties, who are still finding it difficult to remember the count sequence, may find it helpful if numerals are introduced at the same time as number names for the Shapes. This will give them two **visual prompts** on which to hang their memory of the sounds of the number words.

In Activities 2 and 3, children are encouraged to connect the count sequence and the ordered sequence of Numicon Shapes with the **number line**, as they are asked to find the Shapes they have filled with Numicon Coloured Pegs and named on the Numicon Display Number Line.

In Activity 3, children begin to make comparisons between two Numicon Shapes to find which has more holes and which has fewer holes. They also find each Numicon Shape on the Numicon Display Number line, giving them the opportunity to begin to **connect the order of the forward count sequence with the increasing size of the Shapes**.

Teachers are faced with a genuine dilemma as to whether to use **'fewer' or 'less'**, because 'less' is commonly (and incorrectly) used instead of 'fewer', probably because it is phonologically easier. Bearing this in mind, teachers need to decide which vocabulary they will use and then use it consistently, at least until children have grasped the idea, although children will need to be able to use both eventually. 'Less' should be used when comparing continuous substances; e.g. 'You have less tea in your cup than I have in

mine'. 'Fewer' is used when comparing collections of discrete objects; e.g. 'You have fewer biscuits than I'. Teachers will need to decide when it is appropriate to introduce the correct vocabulary to individual children, though it is strongly recommended to use the correct terms from the start wherever possible and to support this by signing.

Activities 4 and 5 provide opportunities for children to consolidate the number names of Numicon Shapes as they use them in a variety of playful situations.

Aims

- To give number names to the Numicon Shapes
- To count objects one by one

Communicating

Imagery
Numicon Display Number Line, Numicon Large Format Table-top Number Line

Equipment
See the individual 'have ready' for each activity, various items for the activities in the 'Extending the activities' section.

Words and terms for instruction (supported with signs and symbols)
match, find, estimate, count

Mathematical words and terms (supported with signs and symbols)
how many, more, number names, enough, less, fewer, not enough, the same size as, the same pattern as, count, different, next, before, after

Assessment

Individual Record of Progress: Numbers and the Number System 20, 21, 25

Putting the activities into context

Discuss with children their names and names of other objects. Talk about how it is important that we all use the same name for the same person or object so we all know who or what we are talking about. Discuss how, up until now, we have been calling Numicon Shapes by colour names and some number names and explain that now we are going to agree the number name for each of the Shapes.

The activities

10

Activity 1: Reasoning to give the Shapes number names

Have ready: Numicon Shapes, Numicon Coloured Pegs, Numicon Display Number Line (if available)

Step 1

Ask children to put Shapes 1–10 in order, starting with the smallest.

Step 2

Point to the 1-shape and ask, 'If this is one, what is this?' pointing to the 2-shape (see **Fig. 1**).

Step 3

Point to the 2-shape and ask, 'If this is two, what is this?' pointing to the 3-shape.

Step 4

Continue in this way until children have said the number name for each Shape.

Step 5

Point to different Shapes in turn, each time asking the question, 'If this is ... , what is this?' Sometimes point to the previous Shape; e.g. when pointing to the 6-shape say, 'If this is six, what is this?' pointing to the 5-shape.

Step 6

Repeat Steps 1–5 often until children are able to name all the Shapes in order with confidence.

Smaller steps

- For children for whom analogical reasoning is too challenging, signing may help them to understand the question.

- Point to each Shape in turn and ask directly, 'What shall we call this Shape?' Reinforce by explaining when pointing to the 1-shape; for example, 'We call this Shape "one" because it has one hole.'

- If necessary, initially work with Shapes 1–5 and gradually extend to include all Shapes 6–10.

Activity 2: Fill the holes

Have ready: Numicon Coloured Pegs, Numicon Shapes 1–10, Numicon Display Number Line (if available)

Step 1

Ask children to put the Shapes in size order and then choose a Shape and count one Peg at a time into the holes (see **Fig. 2**).

Step 2

Ask children to find the matching Shape on the Display Number Line and say the number name (see **Fig. 2**).

Step 3

When children show confidence with this activity, ask them to estimate how many objects they will need to fill the Shape and then to check by filling the holes.

Smaller steps

- If necessary, initially work with Shapes 1–5 and gradually extend to include all Shapes 6–10.

- If children have fine motor difficulties, substitute the Shapes and Pegs with laminated versions of the Numicon Shapes (enlarged and cut from photocopy master 18) and either modelling dough or large counters such as plastic milk bottle tops.

Activity 3: More or less, or fewer

Have ready: Numicon Shapes, Numicon Coloured Pegs, Numicon Large Format Table-top Number Line

Step 1

Ask children to choose two Shapes and to fill both with Pegs.

Step 2

They compare the Shapes to say which has more Pegs and which has fewer or less.

Step 3

Children point to each of their Shapes on the Large Format Table-top Number Line.

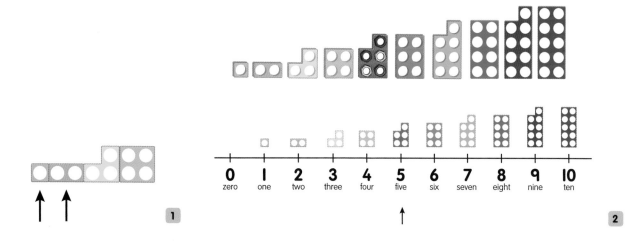

Numbers and the Number System

10

Activity 4: Spin a pattern – a game for 2–4 players

Have ready: Numicon Shapes, Numicon Spinner and Numeral Overlays 1–5 and 6–10 (cut from photocopy master 20)

Step 1
Explain to children that the object of the game is for each player to collect their own set of Shapes (1–5 or 1–10) and put them in order.

Step 2
Children take turns to spin a pattern, say the number name and pick up the Shape to match. Before play starts, decide whether players should spin again or miss a turn if a number is spun more than once.

Step 3
Children build an ordered number line with the Shapes as they collect them.

Smaller steps
- Children who have organizational difficulties may find it helpful to collect the Shapes and match them onto Baseboard Overlay: grey Numicon Shapes in order.
- Children may also find it easier to organize the Shapes in order using the Ordering Frame (photocopy master 16).
- Work on these activities first with Shapes 1–5 and gradually extend to 1–10.

Activity 5: Build it up

Have ready: Numicon Shapes, Numicon Baseboard, Numicon Coloured Pegs, Numicon Display Number Line

Step 1
Ask children to choose a Shape, name it and put it on the Baseboard.

Step 2
Children put a Peg into each hole in the Shape and then find the Shape on the Display Number Line.

Step 3
Children then find combinations of Shapes to fit on top of the Pegs, naming them as they do so.

Step 4
Children continue to build a tower with different combinations of Shapes (e.g. Fig. 3), naming the Shapes used and finding each Shape on the Display Number Line.

Smaller steps
- For children who find building towers too fiddly, the activity can be done without Pegs, by simply placing combinations of Shapes on top of one another.

Further practice
- Practise the above activities often until children are confidently naming Shapes with number names.

Extending the activities

Connecting activities
- Give children other objects, e.g. 1p coins, buttons and so on to count into the holes in the Shapes.
- Children choose a Shape, fill it with Pegs and name it. They then build a Numicon Shape pattern using interlocking cubes, noticing that they need the same number of cubes as Pegs. If appropriate, these could be recorded by colouring onto Squared Paper (photocopy master 23).
- Put a collection of Shapes 1–10 into the Numicon Feely Bag, say a number name and ask children to find that Shape in the Feely Bag. Adjust the range of Shapes used as appropriate for the needs of the children.

For children moving on quickly
- Children identify Shapes by touch. Put a collection of Shapes 1–10 in the Numicon Feely Bag. Children feel for a Shape and name it. They remove the Shape from the Bag to check that they are correct.

3

Labelling Numicon Shapes with numerals

11

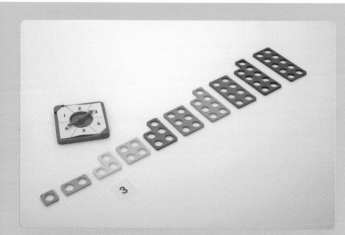

Educational context

Children may already have noticed the connection between Numicon Shapes and numerals on the Numicon number lines on display. In this activity group children learn to make this connection explicitly. Once they have labelled the Shapes in order, move on to play the 'swaps' and 'fill the gap' games, which will be familiar from the previous activity group. When playing swaps, it is helpful for you to model **strategies for solving the problem**; e.g. counting along the sequence of Shapes and noticing when you are saying a number name but the Shape and numeral do not match it; looking carefully at the sequence of Shapes and noticing when the pattern is broken; then describing what has happened and moving the Shapes and numeral cards back to their correct positions.

All of these activities will need to be repeated many times until children are confidently labelling Numicon Shapes with numerals. They are also useful as starter activities at the beginning of a mathematics lesson. Once children are confident, they often enjoy doing the activities with a friend.

Suggestions for **numeral formation** are included in the 'Connecting activities' section, but these should be included in handwriting sessions rather than mathematics lessons. Important though it is for children to write numerals legibly, this is a skill that does not move them on in their mathematical understanding.

Children who are moving on quickly could now label number rods with numerals. There are three activities in this section. Before doing these activities, children will need to have worked through the number rod activities in previous activity groups. Teachers may decide that it is appropriate that some children focus on the activities with Numicon Shapes. However, it is important to bear in mind that children's ability to use both number rods and Numicon Shapes to represent numbers is a useful indication of the extent to which they have **generalized number ideas**, such as that '5' can represent 'five anythings' and that it has relationships with other number ideas; e.g. it is one more than 'four' and one less than 'six'. Children will need to have covered these rod activities so that they can confidently and consistently refer to number rods by name, before they will be able to attempt the rod activities going forward from Numbers and

the Number System 13. Number rods are also widely used in calculating activities as children move on to work with higher numbers, fractions, multiples and divisors. Teachers may therefore decide to return to these activities later when children are confidently working with Numicon Shapes.

Aims

• To match numerals with Numicon Shapes in order
• To order numerals on a number line

Communicating

Imagery
See the individual 'have ready' for each activity, various items for the activities in the 'Extending the activities' section.

Equipment
See the individual 'have ready' for each activity, various items for the activities in the 'Extending the activities' section

Words and terms for instruction (supported with signs and symbols)
put in order, swap, change, move, look for, read, find, match, turn over, label, spin, find, feel

Mathematical words and terms (supported with signs and symbols)
next, after, first, last, before, smaller, bigger, more, less, number names, numeral, ordinal number names (i.e. first, second, third and so on) how many

Assessment

Before writing numerals for each Numicon Shape, children learn to say the number name and then label each Shape with its numeral using a numeral card.

Individual Record of Progress: Numbers and the Number System 22, 37, 38, 39, 40, 41, 42

Putting the activities into context

Ask children about situations when they notice numbers in order, e.g. numbered storage trays in the classroom, pages in a book, house numbers, levels in a multi-storey car park, lockers in changing rooms. Discuss that the purpose of numbering things in order is to help us find things and to know where to put them. Ask children for examples; e.g. the postman uses house numbers to make sure letters are delivered to the correct house; we can remember where we have read to in a book by making a note of the page number, and the number helps us to find that page again; in the classroom we can find the equipment we need quickly when we know the number of the storage tray, and so on. Explain that Numicon Shapes and number rods give us a picture of numbers, and that labelling them with numerals helps us to remember the order of numbers.

The activities

Activity 1: Give it a number

Have ready: Numicon Shapes, Numeral Cards 0–10 (cut from photocopy master 11) in order in a pile

Step 1
Ask children to arrange Shapes in order 1–10.

Step 2
Ask children to take the 1 numeral card, read the number aloud and put it under the 1-shape. Continue until each Shape is matched with its numeral card (see **Fig. 1**).

Step 3
Discuss that there is no Shape for zero.

Smaller steps
- Initially work only with the numeral cards and Shapes 1 and 2. Gradually increase the Shape numbers used until children are ready to work with Shapes and numeral cards 1–10.

Activity 2: Swap the Shape, swap the numeral

Have ready: Numicon Shapes 1–10, Numeral Cards 1–10 (cut from photocopy master 11)

Step 1
Ask children to arrange a set of Shapes 1–10 and numeral cards in order.

Step 2
Ask children to close their eyes. Swap two Shapes and their corresponding numeral cards e.g. **Fig. 2**.

Step 3
Ask children to open their eyes, look carefully and explain what has happened.

Step 4
Children move the Shapes and numeral cards back to their correct positions.

Step 5
Repeat, swapping other numbers. Sometimes change roles, so the child swaps Shapes and numeral cards for the adult to correct.

Smaller steps
- Initially swap Shapes that are further apart (e.g. swap the 2-shape and the 9-shape) as these are easier to spot, but avoid swapping the 1-shape and the 10-shape until children are confident with the activity.

Activity 3: Number the Shapes

Have ready: Numicon Shapes 1–10 arranged in order, Numeral Cards 0–10 (cut from photocopy master 11) shuffled and in a pile face down

Step 1
Ask children to take turns to turn over a card, say the number and match it to its corresponding Shape, e.g. **Fig. 3**. When the 0 numeral card is turned, discuss that there is no Shape for zero.

Step 2
Continue until all Shapes and numeral cards are matched.

Activity 4: Spin a number

Have ready: Numicon Spinners with Numicon Numeral Overlays 1–5 and 6–10 (cut from photocopy master 20), Numicon Shapes, Numeral Cards 1–10 (cut from photocopy master 11) spread about on the table, Numicon Display Number Line.

Step 1
Ask children to take turns to spin a number, find the appropriate numeral card and match it to the correct Shape, e.g. **Fig. 4**.

Step 2
Children find the Shape and number on the Display Number Line.

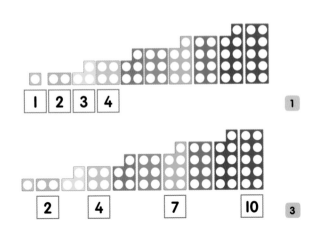

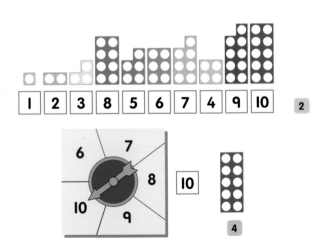

Extending the activities

Smaller steps

- Work initially with a limited range of Shapes and numeral cards and gradually extend the range of numbers used. For instance, some children may start using only Shapes and numeral cards 1 and 2. Make spinner overlays showing the range of numbers required using photocopy master 22.

Activity 5: Feel and find

Have ready: Numicon Shapes 1–10 in the Numicon Feely Bag, Numeral Cards 1–10 (cut from photocopy master 11) scattered on the tabletop, two Numicon Spinners with Numicon Numeral Overlays 1–5 and 6–10 (cut from photocopy master 20), Numicon Display Number Line

Step 1

Ask children to take turns to spin a numeral, feel for the Shape in the Feely Bag and match it with its corresponding numeral, e.g. Fig. 4.

Step 2

Children then find the number on the Display Number Line.

Step 3

Continue until all the numerals have been matched with their corresponding Shapes.

Smaller steps

- Work initially with a limited range of Shapes and numeral cards and gradually extend the range of numbers used. For instance, some children may start using only Shapes and numeral cards 1 and 2. Make spinner overlays showing the range of numbers required using photocopy master 20.
- Work with one Spinner and the matching range of Shapes in the Feely Bag.
- If children have an aversion to the Feely Bag, the Shapes can be put in a box instead. Alternatively, ask children to close their eyes and then place a Shape in their hands.
- Working without the Feely Bag, spread the numerals and Shapes on the tabletop. Children spin a numeral and match the numeral shown with its Shape.

Connecting activities

- Children make books about numbers. On each page they include Shapes, numerals, number rods, number words, collections of objects and individual details such as their age, house or flat number, the number of siblings they have and so on.
- Go on a 'numeral spotting' walk, take photographs, e.g. of door numbers, car number plates, calendars, scales and so on, and compile a numeral display in the classroom.
- Look for numerals in the classroom: in pictures, on drawers, on clocks, on calendars and so on.
- Get children to match numerals to collections of objects.
- Give children number jigsaw puzzles.
- Give children practical numeral formation activities, e.g. 'writing' numerals in the air with ribbons or in the sand with their finger. For younger children roll 'ball shapes' and 'sausage shapes' from modelling dough and form into Numicon Shape patterns and numerals (see Fig. 5).
- Play target games where children record the score by picking up the Shape.
- In PE, hold up a Shape and ask children to respond with different actions; e.g. for the 6-shape, 6 jumps, 6 hops, 6 rolls and so on.

For children moving on quickly

- For Activity 1, give children numeral cards 1–10 (cut from photocopy master 11) to put in order, then ask them to match the Shapes to the numeral cards.
- When children are confident with Activity 2 as shown, try swapping only the numerals. Some children may be ready to extend to work with 'teen' numbers.

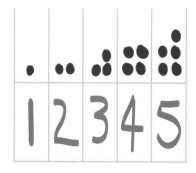

Numbers and the Number System

11

Extension activities

Activity 6: Finding how many 1-rods equal each of the other rods

Have ready: number rods (for children who find the rods fiddly provide a metal board and magnetize rods with the Numicon Magnetic Strip, if available)

Step 1

Children investigate how many 1-rods fit alongside each of the other rods. Discuss what children notice and model saying, e.g. 'Eight 1-rods will fit alongside the brown rod, so we can call the brown rod "eight".'

Step 2

Repeat for other rods.

Activity 7: Naming number rods

Have ready: number rods, Numicon Number Rod Trays 1–10, Numicon 0–41 Rod Number Line (if available)

Step 1

With children build a staircase pattern with rods in the orange 10-tray, starting with the smallest rod. Discuss, encouraging connections with stairs going up one step at a time, in the same way that the pattern increases evenly by one each time (see Fig. 6).

Step 2

Point to the 1-rod. Ask, 'If we call this the 1-rod, what shall we call this rod?' (pointing to the 2-rod). Look and listen for children who suggest 'two' or 'the 2-rod'. Then point to the 2-rod and ask, 'If we call this two, what shall we call this?' (pointing to the 3-rod). Look and listen for children who suggest 'three'. Continue to point to each rod in the staircase in turn asking each time, 'If we call this ... , what shall we call this?' pointing to the next rod.

Step 3

Point to rods randomly, asking children, 'If this is ... what is this?' (pointing to the next rod) until children can consistently give a number name to each rod.

Step 4

Point to rods and ask children to find them on the 0–41 Rod Number Line.

Activity 8: Labelling number rods with numerals

Have ready: Numeral Cards 1–10 (cut from photocopy master 11), number rods

Step 1

Spread out an ordered set of 1–10 rods and ask children to match a numeral to each rod (see Fig. 7).

Further practice

Have ready: Numeral Cards 1–10 (cut from photocopy master 11), number rods

- Activity 1: Children spread out the numeral cards on the table and match a rod to each numeral.
- Activity 2: Children play the 'swaps' game with rods and Numeral Cards.
- Activity 3: Children play the 'Fill the Gap' game with rods and Numeral Cards.
- Activity 4: Children play the 'Which rod is missing' game with rods and Numeral Cards.

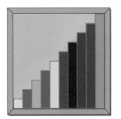

6

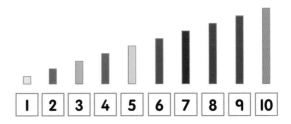

7

Seeing how many without counting from Numicon Shape patterns

Educational context

Building the pattern for each Numicon Shape is a fundamental skill for all pupils working with Numicon, both for the immediate work in the *Breaking Barriers Teaching Handbook* and for their further mathematics work. It is important for several reasons:

- The system of patterns seen in the Numicon Shapes supports understanding of the cardinal value of each number from 1–10 and helps children to connect this to their ordinal value.

- Learning to build the patterns for all the Numicon Shapes 1–10 with a variety of different objects helps children to make the important generalization about numbers – that 'five', for example, can represent five of anything and is also an idea in itself that has many relationships with other number ideas; e.g. it is one more than 4 and one less than 6; it is between 3 and 7 in a sequence of odd numbers; it is half of 10; it equals 3 plus 2.

- When a random collection of objects is organized into Numicon Shape patterns the quantity can be recognized without counting in ones, beyond the usual perceptual range for subitizing (the ability to recognize small collections of objects, up to five for most people, without counting them one by one). Subitizing is the first step towards developing an understanding of numbers as whole ideas in themselves.

- The ability to group objects into Numicon Shape patterns is used where larger collections are grouped into tens and the remaining units, to introduce first the structure of teen numbers, then higher 2-digit numbers. The quantity and column values of numbers and the place value of the digits are clearly seen when numbers are represented by Numicon Shapes and Numicon Shape patterns. Understanding these provides a firm foundation for the development of efficient calculation strategies. It also prepares children for using other structured representations, e.g. base-ten apparatus and number rods.

- Learning to build the patterns provides a mathematical context rich in opportunities to develop understanding of the mathematical words and terms needed for communicating about number relationships. For children with speech, language and communication difficulties it is important to sign these words, particularly where the sounds involved are difficult, e.g. the fricative sounds in 'fewer'.

Because these activities are fundamental to children's understanding of number, they will need to be practised often until children can quickly confidently build the patterns for each Numicon Shape. The emphasis on doing so without counting is to enable them to see numbers as whole entities which will support their success with calculating. This in turn will enable them to add and subtract whole numbers without having to rely on inaccurate counting strategies.

Making connections between Numicon Shape patterns and other structured representations of numbers, such as number rods, supports children's generalizing; other useful connections can be made with domino patterns and towers of interlocking cubes. However, number rods are a particularly useful representation since they can be used interchangeably with Numicon Shapes in nearly all the activities in *Breaking Barriers Teaching Handbook* and are used increasingly instead of Numicon Shapes in the on-going programme of Numicon teaching activities. We recommend an activity to encourage these connections with number rods, particularly for children moving on quickly at this stage, but these connections should be made later for all children as they are ready.

Aims

- To reliably recognize Numicon Shape patterns and label them with number names and numerals without counting

- To reliably and quickly build Numicon Shape patterns for Shapes 1–10 without counting in response to hearing the number name and from reading the numeral

- To compare two Numicon Shape patterns and say which pattern has more objects and which has fewer using the terms 'fewer than' and 'more than'

Communicating

Imagery
Numicon Display Number Line

Equipment
See the individual 'have ready' for each activity, various items for the activities in the 'Extending the activities' section.

Words and terms for instruction (supported with signs and symbols)
match, choose, find, 'see in your head', visualize, remember, estimate, guess, arrange, find out, check, compare

Mathematical words and terms (supported with signs and symbols)
number names, pattern, how many, more, fewer, more than, fewer than, larger, smaller

Assessment

Individual Record of Progress: Numbers and the Number System 18, 19, 23, 24, 25, 26, 43, 57

Putting the activities into context

Discuss situations in which we may need to count and the need to count accurately, asking children for their suggestions. Model counting in ones making a deliberate mistake, then re-count, arriving at a different total. Ask children for their suggestions about how to check and be sure that the count is accurate. Discuss their suggestions, prompting, if necessary, to suggest that if objects are grouped into Numicon Shape patterns the total can be seen and, if necessary, the Shapes can be used to check.

The activities

Activity 1: Picture the pattern 1

Have ready: Numicon Baseboard, Numicon Coloured Pegs, two Numicon Spinners with Numicon Numeral Overlays 1–5 and 6–10 (cut from photocopy master 20), Numicon Display Number Line

Step 1

Ask children to take turns to spin a number and say it out loud.

Step 2

Children arrange Pegs on the Baseboard to make the Numicon Shape pattern for that number and then find the corresponding number on the Display Number Line, e.g. **Fig. 1**.

Smaller steps

- Some children may need to work initially with a limited range, starting with small numbers of Pegs and other objects to be arranged into Numicon Shape patterns, eventually extending to 10.

Activity 2: Picture the pattern 2

Have ready: Numicon Display Number Line, two Numicon Spinners with Numicon Numeral Overlays 1–5 and 6–10 (cut from photocopy master 20), various collections of different sorts of small objects or counters (e.g. shells, counters, bricks, small cars)

Step 1

Ask children to choose a Spinner, spin a number and read it out loud.

Step 2

Children choose objects to arrange into the Numicon Shape pattern for that number and then find the number on the Display Number Line.

Smaller steps

- Some children may need to work initially with a limited range, starting with small numbers of Pegs and other objects to be arranged into Numicon Shape patterns, eventually extending to 10.
- Some children may like to have a Counting or an Ordering Frame (photocopy master 4 or 16) to help them organize their patterns.

Activity 3: Which pattern has more? Which has fewer?

Have ready: two Numicon Spinners with Numicon Numeral Overlays 1–5 and 6–10 (cut from photocopy master 20), various collections of different sorts of small objects or counters (e.g. shells, counters, bricks, small cars)

Step 1

Children spin both Spinners and read the numbers aloud.

Step 2

Children choose objects, e.g. shells, to arrange into Numicon Shape patterns for each number.

Step 3

Ask children to point to the pattern that has more shells. Ask them to point to the pattern that has fewer shells.

Step 4

Children repeat Steps 1 and 2. Ask them to compare the two Numicon Shape patterns and explain the comparison, e.g. 'This pattern has more shells', 'This pattern has fewer shells', e.g. **Fig. 2**.

Smaller steps

- Some children may need to work initially with a limited range, starting with small numbers of Pegs and other objects to be arranged into Numicon Shape patterns, eventually extending to 10.

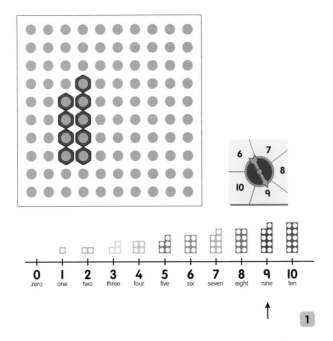

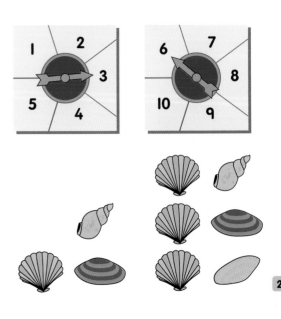

Activity 4: More than, fewer than

Have ready: Numicon Display Number Line, two Numicon Spinners with Numicon Numeral Overlays 1–5 and 6–10 (cut from photocopy master 20), various collections of different sorts of small objects or counters (e.g. shells, counters, bricks, small cars)

Step 1

Children spin each Spinner and read the numbers aloud. They find the two numbers on the Display Number Line.

Step 2

Children choose objects, e.g. shells, to arrange into Numicon Shape patterns for each number.

Step 3

They compare the two Numicon Shape patterns and, pointing to the larger Numicon Shape pattern, say, 'This pattern has more shells than this pattern', pointing to the smaller pattern.

Step 4

They compare the two Numicon Shape patterns again, this time pointing to the smaller pattern and saying, 'This pattern has fewer shells than this pattern', pointing to the larger Numicon Shape pattern, e.g. **Fig. 2**.

Smaller steps
• Some children may need to work initially with a limited range, starting with small numbers of Pegs and other objects to be arranged into Numicon Shape patterns, eventually extending to 10.

Activity 5: Finding how many by recognizing Numicon Shape patterns

Have ready: Numicon Shapes, Numicon Baseboard, Numicon Coloured Pegs, Numeral Cards 1–10 in order (cut from photocopy master 11)

Step 1

Place between one and ten Pegs randomly on the Baseboard and ask children, 'How can we find out how many there are, without counting?' Encourage children to remember that they can group the Pegs into Numicon Shape patterns to see how many there are altogether, e.g. **Fig. 3**.

Step 2

Ask children to group the Pegs into Numicon Shape patterns and ask them, 'Can you see which Numicon Shape pattern you have made with the Pegs without counting them?'

Step 3

Children can check by placing the corresponding Shape over the arranged Pegs. Ask them to point to the numeral card that shows that number, read it aloud and label their pattern with the numeral card, e.g. **Fig. 4**.

Smaller steps
• Some children may need to work initially with a limited range, starting with small numbers of Pegs and other objects to be arranged into Numicon Shape patterns, eventually extending to 10.

Activity 6: Building a pattern from hearing the number name

Have ready: Numicon Shapes, Numicon Baseboard, Numeral Cards 1–10 (cut from photocopy master 11), baskets of small objects

Step 1

Say a number name between 1 and 10.

Step 2

Children choose objects and quickly arrange them into the Numicon Shape pattern for that number. They label the Numicon Shape pattern with the corresponding numeral card.

Step 3

Repeat Steps 1 and 2 for other numbers until all the Numicon Shape patterns have been built.

Smaller steps
• Some children may need to work initially with a limited range starting with small amounts of Pegs and other objects to be arranged into Numicon Patterns, eventually extending to 10.

Further practice
• Repeat Activities 1–6 often, until children can build the patterns for all the Shapes confidently and quickly without counting.

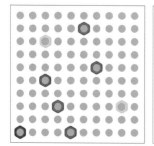

3

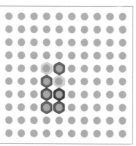

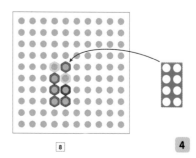

8   4

Extending the activities

12

Connecting activities

- Children roll a numeral dice, collect the corresponding number of objects and arrange them into Numicon Shape patterns.

- If plastic numerals are available children could generate numbers by taking them one at a time from a Numicon Feely Bag and arranging that number of objects into Numicon Shape patterns.

- Put out three Shapes for children to look at carefully, and then cover them. Can children remember which Shapes are hidden?

- Arrange stickers into Numicon Shapes patterns and label them with a numeral. Alternatively, if their motor skills allow, children could draw pictures of objects arranged into Numicon Shape patterns and label them with a numeral. Some children may like to have an Ordering Frame (photocopy master 16) to help them organize their patterns in order.

For children moving on quickly

Have ready: Numeral Cards 1–10 (cut from photocopy master 11), number rods

Step 1
Children turn a numeral card over and build the Numicon Shape pattern for the number shown using 1-rods.

Step 2
Children pick up the rod for the number shown and check that the Numicon Shape pattern for the number is correct by placing the 1-rods along the length of the rod, e.g. Fig. 5.

Step 3
Repeat Steps 1 and 2 until all the numeral cards have been turned and patterns built for numbers 1–10.

Further practice
Have ready: two Numicon Spinners with Numicon Numeral Overlays 1–5 and 6–10, number rods

Children spin a number from their chosen Spinner and repeat Steps 1 and 2 from the above activity.

5

Building and naming teen numbers

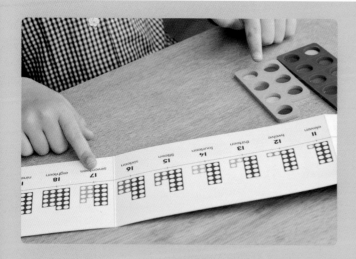

Educational context

Children have generally spent a considerable amount of time learning about numbers to 10 and understanding the relationships between them. They need similar opportunities with the teen numbers, especially as they are now meeting the two new ideas essential to understanding our number system: grouping and place value. The following activities will help children gain understanding of the **structure of teen numbers and how they are named**. Children will also begin to develop their understanding about the relationships between these numbers and numbers to 10.

While on Numicon number lines the Numicon Shapes are placed side by side in tens and units to support grouping and place value, in this activity group **children are introduced to 'increase' in the ordered sequence of numbers by seeing the Numicon Shapes in a 'growing pattern' 0–20**.

There are no Numicon Shapes or number rods specifically for the teen numbers (since building them helps to understand their structure) but for some children, once the Numicon Shapes (or number rods) have been built it can be helpful to use adhesive tack to join the 10-shape and a unit Numicon Shape (or number rod) together or to use the grey Numicon Shapes, if available.

When building teen numbers with Numicon Coloured Pegs, children may need a reminder to start at the bottom of the Numicon Shape pattern and to use two hands. They may also need to be shown how to leave a space beside the 10-pattern after completing it, to make it easier to see the final amount. If children use too few or too many Numicon Coloured Pegs when building the 10-pattern they should check with the 10-shape and be encouraged to self-correct.

Activities from the Counting Activity Group, where objects are counted one-to-one along number lines and then arranged into Numicon Shape patterns, should support work on teen numbers.

Aims

- To see that arranging objects into patterns or grouping is an efficient way to find out 'how many'
- To name and pronounce correctly numbers 11–20
- To build teen numbers with structured apparatus
- To connect number names 11–20 with structured apparatus
- To learn about relationships between numbers 1–20

Communicating

Imagery
Numicon Display Number Line, Numicon 0–41 Number Rod Number Line, Numicon Large Format Table-top Number Line

Equipment
See the individual 'have ready' for each activity, various items for the activities in the 'Extending the activities' section.

Words and terms for instruction (supported with signs and symbols)
build, find, work out, think, talk about, explain, compare

Mathematical words and terms (supported with signs and symbols)
number names zero to twenty, order, more, growing pattern, next, before, after, in between

Assessment

Individual Record of Progress: Numbers and the Number System 65, 66, 67, 68, 69

Putting the activities into context

Talk with children about their ages and how old they will be on their next birthday. Ask if they know anyone who is 10 years old and discuss how old they will be next. Talk about 'teenagers' and agree that they could be aged 13–19. Explain that it is important to pronounce (or sign carefully) the numbers ending in 'teen'. Count along the Numicon Display Number Line pointing to each number as it is spoken (or signed), particularly emphasizing the 'teen' numbers. (Look at the spelling of 'teen' if appropriate for children.)

The activities

Activity 1: Estimating how many Pegs

Have ready: Numicon Shapes, Numicon Coloured Pegs, Numicon Baseboard, Numicon Display Number Line, number rods

Step 1
Randomly place between 11 and 20 Pegs on the Baseboard, e.g. Fig. 1. Explain that you need to find out how many there are and ask children to estimate how many Pegs. Keep a record of their estimates.

Step 2
Children arrange the Pegs into the Numicon 10-pattern and other Numicon Shape patterns for any left over, e.g. Fig. 2.

Step 3
Children find the corresponding Shapes to fit over the Pegs, e.g. Fig. 3. Some may be able to say how many they have by looking at the Shapes; others may need to take the matched Shapes off the Pegs and match to the Display Number Line, then say how many; others may still need support to name the number.

Step 4
Sensitively look back at children's estimates. Some children will need encouragement to understand that an estimate does not have to be exactly right.

Smaller steps
- At Step 2, before beginning to group the Pegs, place a 10-shape on the Baseboard. Children fill the Shape and then start a new Numicon Shape pattern for the Pegs that are left.

Further practice
- Practise Activity 1 often, varying the number of Pegs.

- This activity can be worked on in pairs. Children have 20 Pegs in a basket. They take turns to take a quantity of Pegs from the basket and place them randomly on the Baseboard for the other to find out how many.

Activity 2: Building and naming teen numbers

Have ready: Numicon Shapes, Numicon Number Rod Trays 11–20 (if available), number rods

Step 1
With children, order and count Shapes from 1–10. Talk about the 'staircase' pattern seen in the sequence of Shapes. Ask children what the next number will be. Talk about the Shapes that will be needed to show 11, and then place them in position in the growing pattern.

Step 2
Continue to involve children in building the number line up to 20 with Shapes (see Fig. 4).

Step 3
Children count along the sequence of Shapes. Check that they are saying 'teen' correctly (not 'ty').

Step 4
Point to 16 and run a finger down the 6-shape of the 16, saying 'six', then down the 10-shape, saying 'teen'.

Step 5
Repeat Step 4 for numbers 17, 18, 19 and 14.

Step 6
Talk about the strange names for 13 and 15 (sometimes it helps children to call them 'three-teen' and 'five-teen' in the process of learning 'thirteen' and 'fifteen').

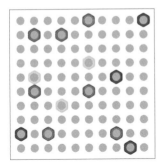

1

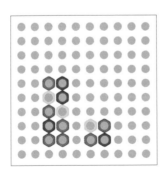

2

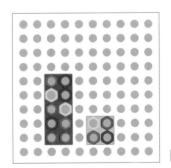

3

4

Step 7
Discuss how best to remember 11 and 12. Agree that they should be part of the set of numbers 11–19 because they do have one 10-shape like the others but they do have strange names that have to be remembered.

Step 8
Call out random numbers in the range 11–19 and ask children to point to the Shapes for that number in the staircase.

Step 9
Repeat with rods in the Number Rod Trays 11–20.

Smaller steps
- Wait until children are confident with 14, 16, 17, 18 and 19 before tackling 11, 12, 13 and 15.
- Alternatively, build a number line with Shapes from 1–12 and practise until children are confident before moving on.
- If appropriate, use Activity 3 to support the range of numbers being practised.

Further practice
The adult says a number from 11–20 and the child builds it with Shapes or rods
- The adult puts Shapes for three different numbers 11–20 in the Numicon Feely Bag, says one of the number names and the child finds the Shapes in the Feely Bag to make that number.

Activity 3: Connecting and identifying numbers 1–10 with 11–20

Have ready: Numicon Shapes, Numicon Number Rod Trays 11–20 (if available), number rods

Step 1
Ask children to order Shapes from 1–20 as a staircase or growing pattern.

Step 2
Point to, e.g. the 6-shape, saying 'six'. Then point to Shapes showing 16, running your finger from the top of the 6-shape down to the bottom of the 10-shape, saying '**six**-teen'. Say numbers 1–9 one at a time in random order and ask children to find each corresponding 'teen' number.

Step 3
Point to Shapes for 11–20 in random order and ask children to say the number name.

Step 4
Repeat with rods in the Number Rod Trays 11–20.

Smaller steps
- Initially work with numbers 14, 16, 17, 18 and 19.
- Use a Numicon blank spinner overlay (cut from photocopy master 22). Fill in three of the spaces by drawing Shapes for a number to be practised and the other three spaces with Shapes for a number known by the child. The child spins, finds Shapes for those shown and says the number name.
- Put Shapes for a number in the range 11–20 in the Numicon Feely Bag. Children feel, describe the Shapes and say the number name. They check by removing the Shapes and matching them to the number on the Numicon Display Number Line.
- Children use the Baseboard for Drawing Numicon Shapes and Numicon Shape Patterns (photocopy master 3) to draw a 'teen' number from memory. They say the number name and check with Shapes.

Further practice
- Build a number 11–20 with Shapes or rods, and ask the child to say the number name.
- Put five 10-shapes and five other different Shapes from 1–9 in a Feely Bag. The child has to find a 10-shape and a different Shape from the Bag, place them on the table, say the number name and find it on the Display Number Line.
- Using two Numicon Spinners with Numicon Numeral Overlays 1–5 and 6–10, children begin with a 10-shape or 10-rod in front of them. They spin a number, find the Shape or rod, place it with the 10-shape or 10-rod and say the number made.

Extending the activities
Connecting activities
- Encourage children to listen for teen numbers when reciting counting or counting objects one-to-one.
- Encourage children to listen for teen numbers being spoken during daily activities.
- Refer to numbers of eggs in boxes, e.g. twelve, fifteen or eighteen, and to other collections involving teen numbers.
- Set out Numicon Shapes 11–20 and play 'swaps' (see Numbers and the Number System 8, Activity 2).

For children moving on quickly
- Discuss with children the patterns within the number words on the Numicon Large Format Table-top Number Line.
- When working on Activity 1, after Step 3 children can show the amount represented by Shapes with rods.

Teen numbers notation

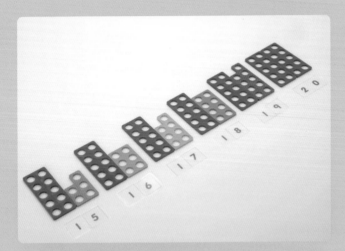

Educational context

This activity group builds on the work in Numbers and the Number System 13. Children are introduced to teen notation and the term **'units'**. If you feel that it is not appropriate to use this term with the children you are working with, you may prefer to use the term **'ones'**. Whichever term is chosen should be used consistently.

The relationship between teen numbers continues to be developed and children have opportunities to begin to compare and order numbers to 20. Some of the steps may seem very small, but unless children can meet all of the assessment points in the Individual Record of Progress Numbers and the Number System 65–75 they may have gaps in their understanding that could become a stumbling block in later work with 2-digit numbers. Although 'twenty' is included within this group of numbers it is not the main focus (developed in later activity groups). It is essential that 'teen' is spoken (or signed) correctly and not confused with 'ty'.

Once children have given number names to the number rods it is possible to use number rods for all of the activities in this group.

Aims

- To build teen numbers with structured apparatus and label them with numerals
- To learn to read and write numbers 11–20
- To learn about relationships between numbers 1–20

Communicating

Imagery
Numicon Display Number Line, Numicon 0–41 Number Rod Number Line, Numicon Large Format Table-top Number Line

Equipment
See the individual 'have ready' for each activity, various items for the activities in the 'Extending the activities' section.

Words and terms for instruction (supported with signs and symbols)
build, find, work out, think, talk about, explain, compare

Mathematical words and terms (supported with signs and symbols)
number names zero to twenty, order, more, growing pattern, next, before, after, in between

Assessment

Individual Record of Progress: Numbers and the Number System 70, 71, 72, 73, 74, 75, 76

Putting the activities into context

Remind children about 'teenagers' and explain that they are now going to learn how to read and write the 'teen' numbers. Count along the Numicon Display Number Line pointing to each number as it is spoken (still emphasizing the 'teen' pronunciation), but looking closely at the written numerals.

The activities

14

Activity 1: Labelling teen numbers with numerals

Have ready: Numicon Shapes, Numicon Large Format Table-top Number Line, Numeral Cards 0–20 (cut from photocopy masters 11 and 12), number rods

Step 1

Children build the growing pattern 1–20 with Shapes. Explain that they are going to label the growing pattern with numerals and, beginning with zero, place the 0 numeral card before the first Shape, agreeing that there is no Shape for zero. Continue with numeral cards to 10, saying each number name.

Step 2

Using numeral cards 11–20 in order, children take the 11 numeral card, read the number aloud and put it under the 11-Shape. Continue until all the Shapes are matched with numeral cards (see **Fig. 1**).

Step 3

Make connections between numerals below 10 and those above 10; e.g. '4' repeated in '14', and that each number from 10–19 has one 10-shape and a numeral '1' as part of the number, whereas 20 (and 21 on the Large Format Table-top Number Line) has two 10-shapes and a numeral '2'.

Step 4

Say different numbers for children to point to, and point to random numbers for children to read aloud.

Step 5

Repeat with rods.

Smaller steps

- When labelling Shapes with numeral cards, initially work to 12, gradually increasing to 20.
- Use a Numicon Blank Spinner Overlay and fill in three of the spaces with a numeral to be practised and the other three spaces with known numerals. Children spin and read the number.

Further practice

- Play 'swap the Shape, swap the numeral' (see Numbers and the Number System 11, Activity 2) using Shapes and numerals 11–20.

- Using a Numicon Spinner with Numicon Numeral Overlay 11–15, children spin a number, say the number name and find the corresponding Shapes from the Numicon Feely Bag. Repeat with rods (not in the Feely Bag.)
- Repeat for 16–20 with Numicon Numeral Overlay 16–20.
- Make a 'teen' number with Shapes or rods. Children say the number and find the numeral card.

Activity 2: Comparing the growing pattern with the Numicon Table-top Number Line

Have ready: Numicon Shapes, Numicon Large Format Table-top Number Line, Numeral Cards 0–20 (cut from photocopy masters 11 and 12)

Step 1

Children build the growing pattern 1–20 with Shapes and label with numeral cards.

Step 2

Place the Large Format Table-top Number Line below the growing pattern and count with children, pointing along the number line and the growing pattern at the same time.

Step 3

Compare the two arrangements, noticing the same Shapes and numerals but different arrangements of the Shapes.

Step 4

Beginning with the Shapes for 11 in the growing pattern, move the 1-shape and place it beside the 10-shape so it matches the Large Format Table-top Number Line. Agree that whichever way the Shapes are arranged, a 10-shape and a 1-shape still represent 11 and have the same numeral card.

Step 5

Repeat Step 4 with numbers 12–20.

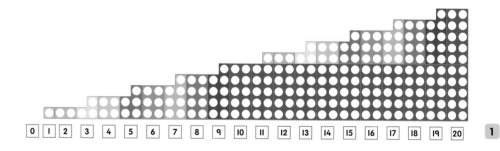

0 1 2 3 4 5 6 7 8 9 10 11 12 13 14 15 16 17 18 19 20   **1**

14

Smaller steps

- Build 11 twice with Shapes: once with the 1-shape above the 10-shape and once with the 1-shape beside the 10-shape. Ask children to say the number name, find the numeral card and say what is the same and what is different. Agree that both show 11. Repeat with other numbers 12–20.

Further practice

- Prepare Numeral Cards 11–20 (cut from photocopy master 12), shuffled and placed face down in a pile. Ask children to turn over a card, read the number aloud and, with Shapes, to build it as if it were part of the growing pattern 11–20. Children then find the number on the Table-top Number Line and rearrange to match the way it is shown on the number line.

Activity 3: Introducing 'units' and recording teen numbers with numeral cards

Have ready: Numicon Shapes, Numeral Cards 0–9 (cut from photocopy master 11), number rods

Step 1

Put out Shapes 1–9 with numeral cards 0–9. Ask children to suggest other numbers they know. Write the numbers they have suggested and show children that the numbers only use the numerals 0–9.

Step 2

Set out the 1 and 0 numeral cards to show 10. Ask children to read the number and find the 10-shape (see **Fig. 2**). Talk about 10 being very special because it has two 'digits', the 1 and 0, as compared with 0–9 Shapes that only have one digit. Explain that in mathematics there is a special name for the numbers 0–9: they are called 'units'. The numeral 10 has no units, since none of the 1–9 Shapes have been used, so '0' is used to show no units. (Remind children about the '1' showing one 10-shape.)

Step 3

Ask children to show 19 with Shapes, encouraging them to use the 10-shape already in place. Then talk about the need to replace the 0 card with a 9 (see **Fig. 3**) because the 9-shape has been used, so we need to show 9 units not 0 units.

Step 4

Read the number name together. Establish that numerals for teen numbers are written and read in the opposite order from the way they are written; e.g. for 19 we see 'ten' then 'nine' but we read aloud 'nine' then 'teen'.

Step 5

Ask children to change 19 to 17, so they replace the 9-shape with a 7-shape and the numeral 9 with a 7 and read aloud 'seventeen'.

Step 6

Repeat Step 5 for numbers 14, 16 and 18, followed by 13 and 15 and finally 11 and 12.

Step 7

Repeat with rods.

Smaller steps

- Spend as much time as needed on each step in Activity 3 and play 'games' to emphasize each point, e.g.:
  - Using Numicon 0–100 Numeral Cards, choose a selection of 1- and 2-digit numbers for children to sort into sets of 1-digit numbers and 2-digit numbers.
  - Using a Spinner with Numicon Numeral Overlay 6–10 (cut from photocopy master 20) children guess whether a 'ten' or a 'unit' might be spun. They spin and see if they are correct.
  - Make cards with a picture of a Shape at the top and numeral underneath for children to sort into tens or units.

Further practice

- The adult calls out 'unit' and the child has to find any 'unit' Shape. The adult calls out 'ten' and the child finds a 10-shape. Repeat with rods.

- The adult builds a teen number using Shapes. Using Numeral Cards 0–9 (cut from photocopy master 11) the child labels the Shapes and says the number name. Repeat with rods.

Extending the activities 14

Activity 4: Writing teen numbers

Have ready: Numicon Shapes, Numicon Display Number Line, Numeral Cards 11–20 (cut from photocopy master 12)

Step 1

Following the arrangement of the Shapes on the Display Number Line, children build a teen number line with Shapes and label it with numeral cards.

Step 2

Point to, e.g. 14, and write '14'. Draw children's attention to the 1 being written first and then the 4 – which is the opposite way round from how we say 'fourteen'.

Step 3

Repeat Step 2, modelling 16, 17, 18 and 19, then 13 and 15, emphasizing the same 'peculiarity' for each number.

Step 4

Agree that 11 and 12 are part of this set of numbers because they too have just one 10-shape each and children have to learn that, like 10, the 1 is written first followed by the other numeral.

Step 5

Repeat with rods (see **Fig. 4**).

Smaller steps

- See 'Supporting children with writing numerals' in 'Developing Counting'.
- Colour code 'teen' numerals to help children remember which digit to write first.

Further practice

- Children build a teen number line with Shapes or rods and write their own labels for each number.

Connecting activities

- Ask children to look for teen numbers in other situations, e.g. on pages in books, on calendars, as drawer labels and so on.

For children moving on quickly

- Children need to work through each of the above activities, at a faster pace.
- Discuss the patterns within the number words on the Large Format Table-top Number Line.
- Play 'swap the Shape, swap the numeral' (see Numbers and the Number System 11, Activity 2) using Shapes and numerals 11–20, but try swapping only the numerals.
- Give children Numeral Cards 11–20 (cut from photocopy master 12) and ask them to put these in order and then match Shapes to the cards.
- Children make their own number line by drawing Numicon Shape patterns for each number, e.g. **Fig. 5**.

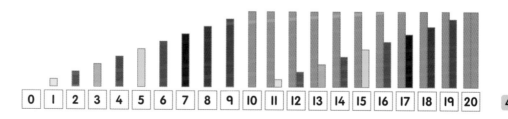

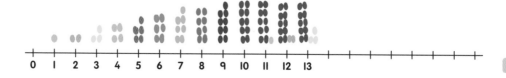

Comparing and ordering numbers to 20

15

Educational context

The experience children gained when comparing and ordering numbers to ten should benefit them when working with numbers in the range 0–20. The Numicon Shapes and number rods continue to make visible the important **regularity in the order of numbers** and, as children develop their understanding of the relationships between numbers 1–10 and 11–20, as well as their own mental imagery of the Numicon Shapes and number rods, they will support the understanding children need to compare and order numbers.

It is still important to encourage children to explain how they know what is missing from or is misplaced in the ordered set, so they do need to **understand that there is a 'whole set' of Numicon Shapes 1–10 and how the pattern in the whole set is repeated for the range 11–20**. Unless children can recognize the pattern in the ordered sequence of Numicon Shapes it will be difficult for them to notice when one part of that set is missing.

Continue to listen carefully and sensitively for children with speech and language difficulties to ensure that they understand and use **'than'**, as it is a key word used in a comparison, rather than not being clear and running 'than' into the previous words, e.g. saying 'biggeran' instead of 'bigger than'.

The further work on **measures** suggested in the 'Extending the activities' section focuses on developing the work on centimetres introduced in Pattern and Algebra 10 to measure objects up to 20 cm long. Connections with the structure of teen numbers are used as ten 1-rods are exchanged for one 10-rod. This work will probably be spread over many weeks. It is developed further in Numbers and the Number System 17 when the metre rule is introduced. As suggested in previous activity groups, teachers will need to decide when it is appropriate to introduce these activities to children and to give plenty of time for children to assimilate these ideas. There are also some further suggestions for using arbitrary units for measuring capacity and the height of larger objects.

Aims

- To recognize when it is helpful to use the order of numbers to organize or find things
- To use the '<' and '>' symbols when comparing Numicon Shapes, number rods and numerals
- To compare and order numbers to 20

Communicating

Imagery
Numicon Display Number Line, Numicon 0–41 Number Rod Number Line, Numicon Large Format Table-top Number Line

Equipment
See the individual 'have ready' for each activity, various items (including for measures) for the activities in the 'Extending the activities' section

Words and terms for instruction (supported with signs and symbols)
build, find, think, talk about, explain, organize

Mathematical words and terms (supported with signs and symbols)
growing pattern, growing sequence, order, tens, units, more, less, between, nearly, before, after, forwards, backwards, larger than, greater than, bigger than, smaller than, more than, less than, fewer than, higher, lower, 'I know this, so I know that', centimetre, measuring stick

Assessment

Individual Record of Progress: Numbers and the Number System 77, 79, 80, Measures 19, 20, 23, 31, 32

Putting the activities into context

Discuss situations where numbers are shown in order and remind children that keeping things organized helps us to find them quickly when we need them; e.g. numbered pages in books enable us to find the page we want. Look at situations where numbers are still used in order but presented in different orientations, e.g. a clock face, numbers in a lift. Talk about situations where knowing the order of numbers helps us to predict situations, e.g. being the fifth person in a queue, having number 10 in the ticket system in a shop when the person being served is number 6. Remind children that Numicon Shapes and number rods give us a picture of numbers; labelling them with numerals helps us to remember the order of numbers. Extend the conversations about situations where sets or collections are stored in order of size to include discussion about how we can recognize that one part of an ordered set is missing, emphasizing the incremental increase in size and the importance of noticing that where the regularity is broken it indicates where one of the set is missing.

Discuss situations where it is important to be able to compare numbers, e.g.:

- If a sweet bar costs 17p and I have 15p, do I have enough money to buy it?
- If I need 18 g of chocolate powder to make the drink and there is 15 g left, will there be enough to make the drink?
- I like to have a fruit string 14 cm long after my lunch. The fruit string in the packet is 12 cm long. Is it long enough?
- It takes me 16 minutes to walk to the park and it takes my friend 13 minutes. If we leave at the same time, who will get to the park first?

Link to Number, Pattern and Calculating 1

Numbers and the Number System 1

The activities

15

Activity 1: Playing a game

Have ready: Numicon Display Number Line, Numicon Snakes and Ladders Game (photocopy master 15), Numicon Spinner with Numicon Numeral Overlay 1–5 (cut from photocopy master 20) or Numicon 0–5 Dice, a counter for each player

Step 1

Talk with children about giving and following instructions (from a game, recipe, shampoo bottle, train set) and the importance of them being in order.

Step 2

Play a game where you start at zero and follow along a track to the end, e.g. Numicon Snakes and Ladders (photocopy master 15).

Step 3

Compare the snakes and ladders track with the Display Number Line and agree that the numbers are in the same order but the tracks go in different directions. Talk about how having things in order or putting them in order can help us – refer back to the context conversations you had at the start of the lesson.

Smaller steps

• Spend as long as necessary on each step in Activity 1.

Further practice

• With children, write instructions for playing a game, a procedure they need to follow during their day or something else of their choice. Number the instructions and remind children that the numbering shows the order in which the instructions should be followed.

Activity 2: Ordering numerals to 20

Have ready: Numicon Display Number Line, or Large Format Table-top Number Line, Numicon Shapes, Numeral Cards 0–20 (cut from photocopy masters 11 and 12), number rods

Step 1

Discuss with children whether they prefer to order the Shapes or rods 1–20 as growing patterns or as seen on the Display Number Line. Order them as per children's preference and label with numeral cards (see **Fig. 1 & 2**). Remind children that, whether in a growing pattern or as a number line image, the Shapes and rods give us a picture of numbers, which helps us to remember the order of numerals.

Step 2

Ask children to close their eyes. Remove a Shape(s) or rod(s) and the corresponding numeral card, then close the gap. Children open their eyes and say what is missing. Replace the Shapes or rods and the numeral card.

Step 3

Repeat Step 2 but remove two consecutive numbers. Discuss whether it was easier to spot what was missing and why.

Step 4

Cover the Shapes (or rods) so only the numerals can be seen. Remove a numeral card, close the gap and ask children to say what is missing.

Step 5

Repeat Step 4 often, talking with children about how to solve the problem. Encourage them to use the order of the numerals and then the repeated pattern in the order of the numerals for the teen numbers, as well as encouraging them to imagine which Shapes (or rods) represent the numbers to help them solve the problem.

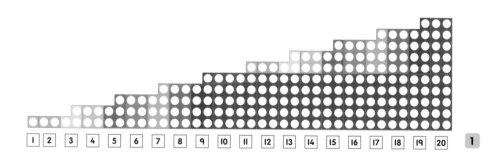

15

Smaller steps

- For Step 2, do not close the gap when removing Shapes (or rods) and numerals. From another pile of Shapes (or rods) and another set of numeral cards, children choose those needed to fill the gap. They check by looking at those that have been removed.
- Play 'swap the Shapes, swap the numerals' from Numbers and the Number System 11, Activity 2 using Shapes and numerals 11–20, but try swapping only the numerals.

Further practice

- Give children numeral cards 11–20 (cut from photocopy master 12) to put in order and then match the Shapes to the cards.
- Ask children questions about which numbers come between other numbers, e.g. 'Which numbers come between 16 and 18?' and '… between 14 and 17?'
- Children order numerals 0–20 by setting out numeral cards, by writing on an empty number line and by making their own board game.
- Give children numeral cards for 4 or 5 consecutive numbers. Shuffle them and ask children to put them in order, e.g. 9, 10, 11, 12, 13.

Activity 3: Comparing teen numbers built with apparatus using the '<' and '>' symbols

Have ready: Numicon Shapes, Numicon Pan Balance, Words and Symbols for Calculating (cut from photocopy master 26a), Numeral Cards 1–20 (cut from photocopy masters 11 and 12), number rods

Step 1

Children build two different teen numbers with Shapes (or rods), e.g. 13 and 17, and label them with numeral cards.

Step 2

Now ask which 'is greater than' the other and which 'is less than' the other. Children place the '<' or '>' symbol between the Shapes and numeral cards and say, e.g. '17 is greater than 13, so 13 is less than 17' (see **Fig. 3**).

Step 3

Use the Pan Balance to check and place the '<' or the '>' symbol between the numeral cards (see **Fig. 4 & 5**). Repeat the comparison.

Smaller steps

- Work initially with 'is greater than' before reminding children about 'is smaller than'.
- Remind children about earlier work when comparing number values.
- Place the Shapes in the Pan Balance at Step 2, and then remove them and repeat the comparison.

Further practice

Have ready: Numicon Shapes, Words and Symbols for Calculating (cut from photocopy master 26a), Numeral Cards 1–20 (cut from photocopy masters 11 and 12)

Step 1

Using two Numicon Spinners with Numicon Numeral Overlays 11–15 and 16–20 (cut from photocopy master 21) and the Numicon Pan Balance, children spin a number, find the corresponding Shapes and place them in one of the pans. They spin again and place the Shapes in the other pan. They say the number story and set out the numeral cards and '<' or '>' symbols (cut from photocopy master 26a).

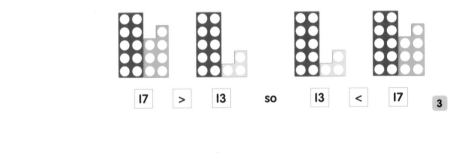

17 > 13   so   13 < 17   3

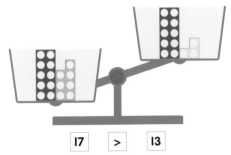

17 > 13   4

17 > 13   5

Activity 4: Comparing the size of two collections in the range 0–20

Have ready: Numicon Shapes, Numicon Large Format Table-top Number Line, number rods, two collections of objects (e.g. 14 objects in one collection, 18 in the other), Words and Symbols for Calculating (cut from photocopy master 26a).

Step 1

Talk with children about finding out which collection has more. Depending on the size of the objects in the collection they could be placed along the number line or counted, but remind children of how they should group objects to find how many and ask them to group the objects in each collection.

Step 2

Discuss the totals: which has more and which has fewer; which 'is greater than' so which 'is smaller than'. Children show the totals with Shapes or rods and find the numbers on the Large Format Table-top Number Line.

Step 3

Children find the relevant numeral cards and use the '<' or '>' symbol to show the comparison.

Smaller steps

- If children find using the '<' or '>' symbols challenging, revisit their introduction in Pattern and Algebra 9.

Further practice

- Children compare the sizes of collections of objects of interest to them.

- Ask children to point to two numbers on the Large Format Table-top Number Line and to say which 'is greater than' and which 'is smaller than'.

- Hold up two numeral cards for children to say which 'is greater than' and which 'is smaller than' or to place the '<' or '>' symbol between them and say the number story.

Activity 5: Comparing and ordering more than two numbers in the range 0–20

Have ready: Numicon Shapes, Numicon Large Format Table-top Number Line, Numeral Cards 0–20 (cut from photocopy masters 11 and 12), number rods

Step 1

Build four numbers with Shapes or rods, e.g. 12, 8, 16, 5 (not in order) and ask children to rearrange the Shapes or rods to put them in order from the smallest to the largest.

Step 2

Label the numbers with numeral cards (or write numerals on small pieces of paper) and find each number on the Large Format Table-top Number Line. Talk about how the numbers increase as you move along the line and how each number is more than the previous one.

Step 3

Show children four numeral cards, e.g. 4, 7, 13, 15 (not in order) and ask them to rearrange them to put them in order from the smallest to the largest.

Step 4

If children hesitate, remind them that they can think about what the numbers look like when built with Shapes or rods. Ask questions to find out what children are not sure about. Some may not have recognized the numerals correctly and only seen the '3' in '13', so place it before the 4; others may see the '5' in '15' and think it should come before the 7 because 7 is bigger than 5. If necessary, place the Shapes or rods with their respective numeral card and then put them in order.

Smaller steps

- Ask children either to order three numeral cards in the range 0–20 or, using only number range 0–10, try to order four cards.

Further practice

- Give children 4 or 5 Shapes or numeral cards to put in order. Ask them to find them on the Large Format Table-top Number Line.

- Show children numeral cards with two non-consecutive numbers. Ask them to find the numeral cards for the numbers that come between them.

Extending the activities

Connecting activities

- If children still need help sequencing numbers, look back at Numbers and the Number System 7, 8 and 11 and Pattern and Algebra 9.
- Children organize a jumbled pack of playing cards into suits to see if any are missing.
- Children fill in the missing numbers on number lines with some numerals missing (but a mark for every number).

Connecting activities – Measures

- Length: Make connections between ten 1-rods and 10 cm. Provide measuring sticks (measuring up to 20 cm) and ask children to check how many 1-rods would fit along it. Agree that it is 20 cm in length. Ask children how many 10-rods would fit. Agree 2 and that this also shows 20 cm: twenty 1-rods are equal to two 10-rods, (see Fig. 6). (Some children may like to check this in the Pan Balance.)
- Provide objects up to 20 cm in length for children to measure using one 10-rod and other rods. Some children may use a 10-rod and 1-rods, others who are confident with rod values may use other rods. Children can record the lengths of the objects in centimetres.
- Provide a collection of different objects measuring up to 20 cm in length. Children can put these in order, and then measure and record their lengths in centimetres, e.g. Fig. 7.

- Height: For larger objects use non-standard units of measurement; e.g. stack building blocks to measure bean plants children have grown. Make connections, e.g. between the greater number of blocks and the tallest plant. Keep a record of the number of blocks for each plant on small squares of paper. Children compare and order the heights of the plants.
- Provide small objects e.g. small-world people, small wood toys, small plastic bottles etc. Children measure their heights in centimetres by comparing with number rods.
- Capacity: Children compare the capacity of two different containers by counting how many cupfuls of sand or liquid each holds.
- Measuring scales: Show children an example of a simple scale, e.g. on a measuring jug where intervals are marked but not all are labelled with a numeral. Provide a very simple scale from 0–20 where there is a mark for every number but not every numeral is written, as on some block graphs or pictograms where even numbers are marked but odd numbers are not. Children complete the scale by filling in the missing numbers.

For children moving on quickly

- Ask questions about which numbers come between backwards sequences, e.g. 18 and 15.
- Children mark the positions and numbers on empty number lines.

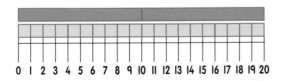

0 1 2 3 4 5 6 7 8 9 10 11 12 13 14 15 16 17 18 19 20

6

14 centimetres   7

Counting by grouping in 10s

16

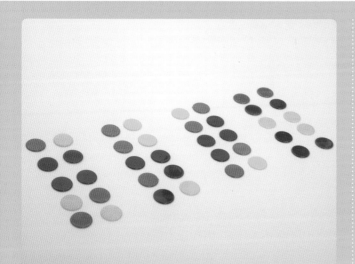

Educational context

These activities build upon earlier 'finding how many without counting' activities and will help children continue to extend their understanding of the size and quantities involved in 2-digit numbers **(quantity value)** as well as supporting place value **(column value)** of 2-digit numbers. They will also establish firmly the understanding that grouping in 10s is a more efficient way to find out 'how many' than counting in 1s or in small groups such as 2s or 5s.

Remind children to build the Numicon Shape patterns from the bottom, placing two objects at a time. Some children may need the support of a frame to help them group the objects in an organized way, leaving a gap between each pattern so the number of ten patterns and the remaining pattern can be seen and the total can be seen clearly.

Connections between Numicon Shape patterns and number rods are encouraged in Activity 2, where children group 1-rods into Numicon 10-patterns and exchange each group of ten 1-rods for a 10-rod. Knowing that the same number may be represented by either number rods or Numicon Shapes will also be helpful when base-ten apparatus is introduced. Some children may not be ready yet to cope with Numicon Shapes and number rods, which would suggest that they have not yet generalized number ideas 1–10; in which case continue with work in earlier activity groups (Numbers and the Number System 8–12). Limiting children to using only Numicon Shapes will also limit their access to some of the later activities, so connections with number rods should be made for all children as they are ready.

Children have not yet been introduced to the term 'multiples', so in these activities multiples of 10 are called 'tens numbers'.

Aims

- To reinforce understanding that arranging counters into patterns and groups is an efficient way to find out 'how many' without counting
- To extend counting range
- To begin to understand place value

Communicating

Imagery
Numicon Display Number Line, Numicon 0–41 Number Rod Number Line, Numicon 0–31 Number Line, Numicon 0–100 cm Number Line

Equipment
See the individual 'have ready' for each activity, various items for the activities in the 'Extending the activities' section.

Words and terms for instruction (supported with signs and symbols)
estimate, guess, arrange, find out, check

Mathematical words and terms (supported with signs and symbols)
how many, patterns, groups of, tens, units, count

Assessment

Individual Record of Progress: Numbers and the Number System 88, 97

Putting the activities into context

Discuss situations in which we estimate whether we have the amount needed and then count to check. For example, when preparing equipment for a sports day we know that there is a large box of bean bags in the PE store but we need to check that there are at least thirty; when preparing a meal with baked potatoes for a group of friends we can see there are lots of potatoes in the bag but we need to check that there are enough potatoes for each friend to have one. Explain that estimating means how many you think there are and model by showing children a bag of objects for the example you have chosen and saying your estimate. Ask children for their suggestions about how to check whether your estimate is correct. Discuss their suggestions, prompting if necessary to suggest that if objects are grouped into Numicon Shape patterns the total can be seen and if necessary the Numicon Shapes can be used to check.

Link to Number, Pattern and Calculating 1

Numbers and the Number System 2

The activities

Activity 1: Finding 'how many' by grouping objects

Have ready: Numicon Shapes, between 20 and 30 Numicon Coloured Counters in a small pot, Numicon 0–100 Numeral Cards, Numicon 0–31 Number Line

Step 1
Show children the pot of Counters and explain that you need to find out how many there are; tip them out. Children estimate how many Counters. Keep a record of their estimates.

Step 2
Explain that they are not going to count one at a time but that they need to arrange the Counters into the Numicon 10-patterns and other Numicon Shape patterns for any left over.

Step 3
Children start to group the Counters into the Numicon 10-patterns. When one 10-pattern is complete, children label it with the 10 Numeral Card and find the number on the 0–31 Number Line.

Step 4
Continue to guide children through grouping their Counters into Numicon 10-patterns. Each time they make a new 10-pattern agree the new total, record it by showing the matching 10s Numeral Card and find it on the 0–31 Number Line. When all the 10s have been grouped, arrange the last few Counters into a Numicon Shape pattern. Children can now see how many have been grouped altogether, say the total and find it on the 0–31 Number Line.

Step 5
Find the corresponding Shapes to show 'how many' and find the total on the number line.

Step 6
Look back at children's estimates, being positive about their attempts. Some children will need encouragement to understand that an estimate does not have to be exactly right.

Smaller steps
- Some children may need to use Squared Paper – 2 cm (photocopy master 23, enlarged if necessary) or the circles on Baseboard for Drawing Numicon Shapes and Numicon Shape Patterns (photocopy master 3) to help them organize their objects into patterns.
- Children fill the outlines of the 10-shapes with objects, using photocopy master 17.
- Work with amounts up to 20 first and gradually increase.

Further practice
- Repeat Activity 1 often, using different equipment.
- Put out baskets of objects and a selection of different-sized containers. Children choose a container, fill it with objects and then find out how many by grouping the objects, not counting them in ones.
- Extend to the 30–40 range.
- Turn a 0–100 Numeral Card (from within children's counting range). Children say the number and arrange objects into the Numicon Shape pattern for that number.

Activity 2: Finding 'how many' without counting in ones, using 1-rods

Have ready: Numicon Shapes, Numicon 0–31 Number Line, Numicon 0–100 Numeral Cards, number rods, between twenty and thirty 1-rods in a small pot

Step 1
Show children the pot of 1-rods and explain that, just as in Activity 1, you need to find out how many there are. Tip them out. Children estimate how many rods and keep a record of their estimates.

Step 2
Children start to group the 1-rods into the Numicon 10-pattern, label each Numicon 10-pattern with the appropriate 10s Numeral Card and arrange the last few 1-rods into a Numicon Shape pattern.

Step 3
Children find the corresponding Shapes to show 'how many' and find the number on the 0–31 Number Line.

Step 4
Now ask children to rearrange each 10-pattern of 1-rods into a 10-rod length (and the 'units' amount into the 'unit' rod length).

Step 5
Find the corresponding 10-rods (and unit rods) and talk about the connections and equivalence between the Shapes and rods.

Smaller steps
- Depending on the range children are working in, work with ten 1-rods, then twenty 1-rods, or work with ten 1-rods, then between eleven and nineteen 1-rods.

Further practice
- Repeat Activity 2 using different amounts of 1-rods (initially still in the 20–30 range, then extend).

16

Activity 3: Finding 'how many' without counting in ones

Have ready: Numicon Shapes, Numicon Coloured Pegs, Numicon 0–31 Number Line, Numicon 0–100 Numeral Cards, a sheet of gift wrap with a repeating picture pattern no higher than 31

Step 1

Talk with children about finding out how many objects are in drawn pictures or patterns. Discuss the difficulty that they cannot be moved to be counted. Explain that they could use Pegs to tag or mark each object.

Step 2

Show children the sheet of gift wrap. Ask them to estimate how many pictures there are and write their estimates.

Step 3

Children put one Peg on each picture, e.g. **Fig. 1**. When all pictures have a Peg on them, ask children to group the Pegs into the Numicon 10-patterns, labelling each one with the 10s Numeral Card and finding each number on the 0–31 Number Line, e.g. **Fig. 2**.

Step 4

When all the 10s have been grouped, arrange the last few Pegs into a Numicon Shape pattern. Children can now see how many have been grouped altogether and say how many pictures are on the sheet of gift wrap.

Step 5

Find corresponding Shapes (and, or, rods) for each pattern and say the total.

Step 6

Children check the total against their estimate and find both numbers on the 0–31 Number Line.

Smaller steps

- Choose wrapping paper with only a small number of pictures, cut down the sheet, or prepare a sheet with only a small number of pictures.
- Arrange the Pegs on a Numicon Baseboard (leave a gap between each pattern).

Further practice

- Repeat Activity 3 often, but vary by using different gift wrap with different numbers of motifs and use different objects for tagging.
- As children become more familiar with the activity, extend questioning to include asking how many tens and how many units in the grouped patterns of Pegs and in the Shapes showing the total.

Extending the activities
Connecting activities

- Whenever opportunities for counting arise, remind children that an efficient way to count is to group objects into tens with Numicon Shape patterns.
- Bring in collections of different objects for children to estimate and then find how many by grouping into Numicon Shape patterns.

For children moving on quickly

- Once children are able to complete Activities 1–3 independently they should be ready to work with higher numbers and find them on the Numicon 0–100 cm Number Line.

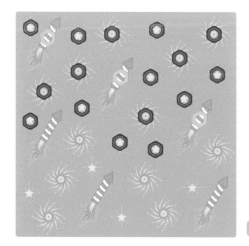

1

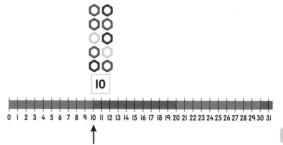

2

Exploring number lines and counting in steps of 10

17

Educational context

Some children may be able to recite the sequence of 10s numbers, but these activities support children counting by the structure of the Numicon Shapes, number rods and number lines to encourage them to **understand the relationships between the numbers within the sequence**. The use of different number lines helps children to realize that all number lines show numerals in order. The Numicon 10s Number Line is introduced in this activity group and becomes a very useful tool to further work with 2-digit numbers, for counting in steps of other numbers and in future work on multiplying and dividing. Only the numerals for 10s numbers are shown on the Numicon 10s Number Line, which encourages children to visualize the imagery when they are calculating mentally.

When children are finding numbers on number lines it can be very revealing to see where they look, e.g. if a child is looking for 40 and they begin to look towards 100 it shows they have not grasped the cardinal or ordinal value of 40 in relation to 100.

Continue to listen for any confusion between 'teen' and 'ty'.

Aims

- To be able to use the Numicon 10s Number Line
- To practise finding numbers on the Numicon 0–100 cm Number Line
- To describe and extend number sequences when counting in steps of 10

Communicating

Imagery

Numicon Display Number Line, Numicon 0–41 Number Rod Number Line, Numicon 0–100 cm Number Line, Numicon 10s Number Line

Equipment

See the individual 'have ready' for each activity, various items for the activities in the 'Extending the activities' section.

Words and terms for instruction (supported with signs and symbols)

build, find out, check, arrange

Mathematical words and terms (supported with signs and symbols)

tens numbers, units, before, after, next, between, nearly, more than, less than, pattern

Assessment

Individual Record of Progress: Numbers and the Number System 99, 100, 111, 112, 117, 122, Measures 21, 22, Money 12

Putting the activities into context

Children may have noticed multipacks of ten box drinks, ten breakfast cereals, ten packets of crisps and so on in supermarkets. Take several multipacks (or show a picture) and ask children to suggest what we might do to find out how many single bags of crisps or box drinks there are altogether. Discuss their suggestions, encouraging them to make connections with the work in Numbers and the Number System 16 when they were grouping objects into Numicon 10-patterns. Older children may have noticed bank cashiers counting £10 notes – discuss and suggest that they also count in tens until they reach £100 when the notes are bundled and another ten notes counted.

Link to Number, Pattern and Calculating 1

Numbers and the Number System 3

The activities

17

Activity 1: Making a 10s Number Line

Have ready: Numicon Shapes, Numicon 10s Number Line, sheet of paper about 150 cm long by 25 cm wide, metre stick (for drawing an empty line), felt-tip pen

Step 1

Explain that together you are going to make a new number line using Numicon 10-shapes. Draw an empty number line on the long sheet of paper. Mark and label '0' at the left-hand side of the line.

Step 2

Start to construct a 10s number line by placing a 10-shape horizontally on the line from '0', drawing round it and marking and labelling the point where 10 is reached on the line. Leave the 10-shape in place.

Step 3

Continue to 100. At each step, place a 10-shape along the line, draw round it, mark and label the next 10s number (see **Fig. 1**). Leave the 10-shapes in place.

Step 4

Remove the 10-shapes so children can see the sequence of 10s numbers. Count in tens, placing a 10-shape back on the line as each number is spoken (or signed), making sure children pronounce (or sign) 'ty' correctly.

Step 5

Show children the Numicon 10s Number Line. Compare it with the one made. Look at the sequence of 10s numbers and the number words, in order. Discuss with children that counting in 10s can be helpful with larger amounts of objects as it is much quicker than counting in ones.

Step 6

Children practise finding tens numbers, in any order.

Smaller steps
- Only construct the 10s Number Line to 30. Continue to work on Steps 1–6 and gradually extend as appropriate.

Further practice
- Practise counting in 10s often, placing a 10-shape on the 10s Number Line as each number is spoken (or signed) and making sure children pronounce (or sign) 'ty' correctly.
- Shuffle tens Numicon 0–100 Numeral Cards and place them face down in a pile. Children turn a card, say the tens number and build it with Shapes. They place the Shapes along the 10s Number Line to check they reach the same 10s number.

Activity 2: Connecting 10-rods with the Numicon 0–100 cm Number Line

Have ready: Numicon 0–100 cm Number Line, Numicon 0–100 Numeral Cards, number rods, dry wipe pen

Step 1

Look at the 0–100 cm Number Line and notice the alternating colours, the numerals where the colours change and the 10s numbers. Agree that they are useful when trying to find numbers on the 0–100 cm Number Line.

Step 2

Place a 10-rod along the 0–100 cm Number Line from 0. Highlight the numerals for 10 and place a 10s Numeral Card under the mark for 10.

Step 3

Continue to place 10-rods along the 0–100 cm Number Line, highlighting each 10s number and placing the relevant 10s Numeral Card beneath it (see **Fig. 2**).

Step 4

Call out tens numbers in any order for children to find on the 0–100 cm Number Line.

Smaller steps
- Initially just work to 30, extending as appropriate.

Further practice
- Children practise counting in tens often, placing a 10-rod on the 0–100 cm Number Line as each number is spoken (or signed) and making sure children pronounce (or sign) 'ty' correctly.
- Spread the 10s Numeral Cards randomly and face down on the table. Children turn a Numeral Card, say the number, find the corresponding rods and place them along the 0–100 cm Number Line, checking that they reach the appropriate 10s number.

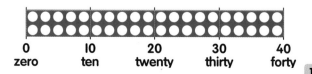

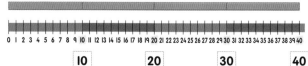

Numbers and the Number System

17

Activity 3: Writing 10s numbers and looking for patterns

Have ready: Numicon 10s Number Line, paper, felt-tip pen

Step 1
Ask children to look closely at the numerals on the 10s Number Line as you point to each one and they count in tens.

Step 2
Explain to children that it is sometimes easier to look for patterns when numbers are written down as numerals, one under the other. Ask children to count in tens again while you write the numerals, one below the other (see Fig. 3). Notice that, after 0, the first numerals follow the 1–10 sequence and are all followed by 0.

Step 3
Children count in tens again while you write the words for the 10s numbers in a list one below the other. Notice that, after zero and ten, all the words end in 'ty' until one hundred.

Smaller steps
- Decide whether children should wait until they have completed Activities 1 and 2 to 100 before trying this activity or whether it is beneficial for them to see the beginning of the pattern, e.g. 0–50, written in this way.

Further practice
- Children write their own list of 10s numbers by copying them from the 10s Number Line as each 10-shape is placed on it. Repeat using rods along the 0–100 cm Number Line.
- Call out a tens number for children to write. Repeat for each tens number 0–100 in random order.

Activity 4: Finding how many 1p coins by grouping and counting in tens

Have ready: Numicon Shapes, Numicon 0–100 Numeral Cards, Numicon 0–100 cm Number Line, four 10p coins and forty 1p coins in a small pot

Step 1
Explain to children that you have been saving 1p coins and need to find out how much you have saved. Tip out the coins and ask children to estimate how many coins there are. Jot down their estimates.

Step 2
Remind children of how they have previously grouped objects and ask them to arrange the first 10 coins into the Numicon 10-pattern. Check with the 10-shape and label the pattern with a 10 Numeral Card. Find 10 on the 0–100 cm Number Line.

Step 3
Continue to arrange the coins into Numicon 10-patterns (see Fig. 4). As each pattern is made, agree the new total, record it by showing the matching tens Numeral Card and find it on the 0–100 cm Number Line.

Step 4
When all the tens have been grouped (see Fig. 5), sensitively look back at children's estimates and find both numbers on the 0–100 cm Number Line.

Step 5
Agree with children that a 10p coin could be exchanged for each Numicon 10-pattern. Replace each group of 10 with a 10-shape then place a 10p coin on each 10-shape (see Fig. 6).

Step 6
Count in tens, pointing to each 10-shape with its coin and find the total on the 0–100 cm Number Line.

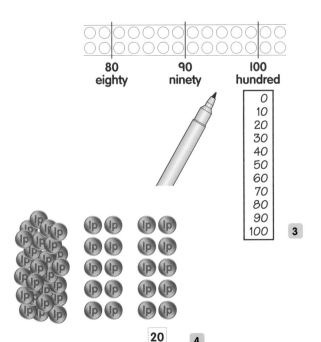

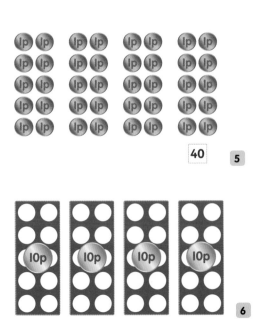

Smaller steps
- Work with just ten 1p coins and one 10p, gradually extending. Once children can work with 10p and 20p they could try the 'Further practice' ideas.

Further practice
- Give children different amounts of 10p coins for them to find the total, which they can write if appropriate.
- Ask children to give you the right number of 10p coins for different amounts from 10p to 100p, e.g. 50p.
- Show children different amounts written, e.g. 60p, for them to read and give you the right number of 10p coins.

Activity 5: Finding numbers on the Numicon 10s Number Line

Have ready: Numicon Shapes, Numicon 10s Number Line, Numicon 0–100 Numeral Cards, dry wipe pen

Step 1
Place a 1-shape on the 10s Number Line and talk with children about how the numeral for 1 is not written on the number line but how the Shape shows the number. Take the 1-Shape off and repeat for each Shape to 10.

Step 2
Now place a 1-shape next to the 10-shape and agree that it shows 11 although the numeral is not there. Continue to 20.

Step 3
Now place a 1-shape next to the two 10-shapes and agree the Shapes now show 21. Explain that children are going to be looking for a pattern: which number comes after a 10s number.

Step 4
Remove the 1-shape, make 30 by placing another 10-shape on the 10s Number Line, and then place the 1-shape to show 31 (see **Fig. 7**). Try with other examples and then see if children can generalize for other numbers with 1 unit. Agree that the next whole number after a 10s number always ends in '1'.

Step 5
Begin again with two 10-shapes but this time place a 9-shape next to them and agree it is 29 (see **Fig. 8**). Agree there is space for a 1-shape showing there is one more to make 30, so 29 must be the number just before 30. Try with other examples and then see if children can generalize for other numbers. Agree that the previous whole number before a 10s number always ends in '9' (and you have to think of the correct 'tens' name as well; e.g. before the thirties are the twenties).

Smaller steps
- Children build a 10s number with Shapes and place along the 10s Number Line, saying 'how many'. Add a 1-shape and say how many altogether. Some children will benefit from matching the corresponding Numeral Card.

Further practice
- Call out 10s numbers for children to find on the 10s Number Line and say what the next number will be.
- Call out 10s numbers for children to find on the 10s Number Line and say what the previous number is.

Activity 6: Finding numbers on the Numicon 0–100 cm Number Line

Have ready: Numicon 0–100 cm Number Line, Numicon 0–100 Numeral Cards, number rods, dry wipe pen

Step 1
Place a 1-rod on the 0–100 cm Number Line and agree with children that it reaches to where the numeral '1' is shown. Replace with a 2-rod and agree it reaches '2'. Continue for each rod to 10.

Step 2
Ask children to suggest the rods needed for numbers 11–21. Explain that children are going to be looking for the pattern that shows which number comes after a 10s number, but this time with rods.

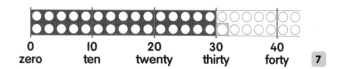

0	10	20	30	40	
zero	ten	twenty	thirty	forty	7

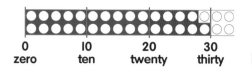

0	10	20	30	
zero	ten	twenty	thirty	8

Numbers and the Number System

17

Step 3
Find 31, then 41 and 51. Ask children if they can see the pattern and look for other numbers in the sequence. Write out the pattern if appropriate.

Step 4
Now ask children to find 29. Talk about the 'twenties' coming before the 'thirties' and knowing that '29' is the last of the twenties so will be found close to '30'. Place rods along the 0–100 cm Number Line to check (see Fig. 9). Repeat for 39 and 49, then see if children can generalize and find 79 easily.

Step 5
Talk with children about being able to see each number marked along the 0–100 cm Number Line and how the rods can be used to check.

Smaller steps
- Just find numbers ending in 1 and notice that they are always after a 10s number. When secure, begin to explore where to find numbers ending in 9.

Further practice/overlearning
- Call out numbers ending in 1 or 9 for children to find on the 0–100 cm Number Line.
- Ask children to find numbers ending in 5 on the 0–100 cm Number Line.

Extending the activities

Connecting activities
- Take opportunities to count in steps of 10 as they occur, e.g. school benches seating 10 children, tables seating 10 in the dining hall, counting 10p coins.
- Give children numeral cards for 10s numbers for children to put in order.

Connecting activities – Measures
- Length: Introduce a metre rule: Ask students to compare a metre rule and a Numicon Number Rod Track, noticing both show numbers to 100 in order. Discuss the use of the metre rule. Give students opportunities to compare the length of the metre rule with objects in the classroom, challenge them to find objects that they think will be about a metre in length.
  Compare the length of the metre rule with the 0–100 cm Number Line and the Number Rod Track. Discuss similarities and any differences children notice. Ask children how many 10-rods will fit along the metre rule. Encourage them to count in tens as they place each 10-rod.

For children moving on quickly
- Children continue to find other numbers on the 0–100 cm Number Line and discuss patterns seen according to which numbers are found; e.g. numbers ending in 6 are roughly in the middle between two 10s numbers, or next to a number ending in 5.
- Using both the 10s Number Line and 0–100 cm Number Line, count backwards in 10s pointing to each number.
- Give children three consecutive tens numbers, e.g. 30, 40, 50. Ask children to look carefully and continue the sequence.

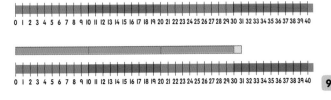

Structure of 2-digit numbers

18

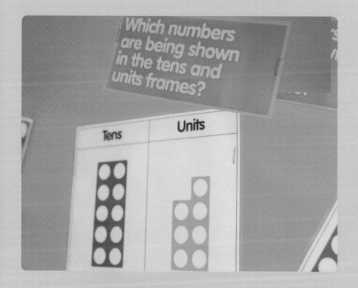

Educational context

The activities build on earlier work but now look closely at the structure of 2-digit numbers. Continue to ensure that children pronounce (or sign) 'teen' and 'ty' correctly. The initial focus is on numbers 20–30, but it is then important to see whether children have **generalized numbers to 40** and what they have learned about the structure of 2-digit numbers before moving to higher numbers (up to 100).

If children are asked to show, e.g. 31, with Numicon Shapes and they pick up a 3-shape and a 1-shape, it is a clear indication that they do not understand that the numeral 3 means '3 tens'. Also, if children make the common error of describing a number, e.g. 24 as '2 and 4', correct this by discussing what the first 2 represents. Address both **'quantity value'** and **'column value'** by modelling the phrases 'twenty and four' and 'two tens and four' (i.e. the quantity value of the 2 in 24 is 'twenty' and its column value is '2 tens'). It is important for children to understand that these column and quantity values are equivalent – the Numicon Shapes and number rods illustrate this distinction very clearly, **enabling children to see the size of the number as well as its structure of tens and ones**.

Activity 5 has some revision but also includes building higher 2-digit numbers from hearing the number name. It could be used for assessment.

Some children may be able to access these activities and learn to recognize 2-digit numbers and build them with apparatus but as yet be unable to recite the count sequence to 100.

Aims

- To extend counting range
- To learn to build and say 2-digit numbers
- To begin to learn to read 2-digit numbers
- To begin to understand the quantity and column value of 2-digit numbers

Communicating

Imagery
Numicon Display Number Line, Numicon 0–41 Number Rod Number Line, Numicon Large Format Table-top Number Line, Numicon 0–100 cm number line, Numicon 10s Number Line

Equipment
See the individual 'have ready' for each activity, various items for the activities in the 'Extending the activities' section.

Words and terms for instruction (supported with signs and symbols)
build, find, explain, arrange, check

Mathematical words and terms (supported with signs and symbols)
how many, patterns, groups of, tens, units, 1-digit, 2-digit

Assessment

Individual Record of Progress: Numbers and the Number System 83, 84, 85, 86, 87, 88, 89, 90, 91, 92, 98

Putting the activities into context

Explain to children that school stationery and writing materials usually come in packs of ten. Show them some complete packs of ten pens or pencils and one incomplete pack. Ask children how they might work out quickly how many pens or pencils there are altogether. Discuss their suggestions and follow these to work out the total, encouraging them to make connections with previous activities where they have been counting in steps of 10 and grouping objects into Numicon 10-patterns. Other examples where goods are supplied in packs of ten include cleaning materials and paper towels, as well as various food items. There are also ten-seater cars and minibuses, so there is plenty of scope for finding a context that is within the children's interest and experience.

Link to Number, Pattern and Calculating 1

Numbers and the Number System 4

The activities

Activity 1: Introducing the tens and units frame

Have ready: Numicon Shapes 1–10 in order, nine Numicon 10-shapes, Numerals Cards 0–10 (cut from photocopy master 11), Tens and Units Frame (photocopy master 25)

Step 1
Ask children if they can remember which Shapes show 'units'. Order the Shapes and numeral cards 0–9. Remind children that each numeral 0–9 is written with only one digit and they are called 'units'.

Step 2
Put the 10-shape and numeral card in place and remind children about 10 having two digits. Ask children for examples of other 2-digit numbers. Check by writing them for children to see.

Step 3
Show children the Tens and Units Frame (photocopy master 25) and check that they can read the words. Agree with them which Shapes could be placed on the 'units' side and that only the 10-shapes can be placed on the 'tens' side.

Step 4
Ask children to build 16 with Shapes and then to place the 10-shape and 6-shape on the tens and units frame and say the number (see **Fig. 1**). Agree that there are 1 ten and 6 units.

Step 5
Repeat Steps 1–4 with rods (see **Fig. 2**).

Smaller steps
• Place the 'unit' Shapes in a set and the 10-shapes in another set. Call out either 'units' or 'tens' for children to find different amounts, e.g. 5 tens, 7 units. Repeat using numerals for the units.

Further practice
• Ask children to build numbers 11–19 with Shapes or rods and place them on the tens and units frame, saying how many tens and how many units.

Activity 2: Building, naming and labelling numbers 20–30 with Numicon Shapes/ number rods

Have ready: Numicon Shapes, 21–30 from Numicon 0–100 Numeral Cards, Numicon Large Format Table-top Number Line

Step 1
With children, count along the Large Format Table-top Number Line pointing to each number as it is spoken. When you reach 21, set out the number with Shapes and the corresponding Numeral Card. Ask children what the next number will be and how they could build it with Shapes. Set out a two 10-shapes and a 2-shape and find the corresponding Numeral Card.

Step 2
Continue to ask children to say each next number, build it with Shapes and find the Numeral Card (see **Fig. 3**).

Step 3
Point to 21 and ask children to say the number. Then ask, 'How many tens?' and, 'How many units?' Make the connection between the Shapes and the written numerals showing '2 tens' and '1 unit'.

Step 4
Repeat for each number, particularly noticing that 30 has '3 tens' and '0 units'.

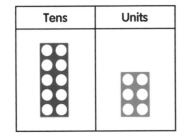

1

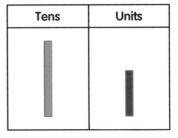

2

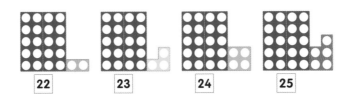

3

Numbers and the Number System

18

Smaller steps

- Allow plenty of time to work on Steps 1–3. Work initially to, e.g. 24, repeating until children are secure before moving on. Print and cut out colour pictures of Numicon Shapes (available to download and cut out from www.oxfordprimary.co.uk) and, with children, at an appropriate pace, make a number line 20–31 alongside building each number with Shapes.

Further practice

- Children set out their own number line 21–30 with Shapes and 0–100 Numeral Cards. Play 'swaps' from Numbers and the Number System 8.
- Children turn a Numeral Card 21–30 (or call out a number) and build it with Shapes.
- Children turn a Numeral Card and build the Numicon Shape pattern using Numicon Coloured Pegs on the Numicon Baseboard or other objects on the tabletop.
- Children build a 21–30 number line with rods (see Fig. 4).

Activity 3: Looking at quantity value and column value with Numicon Shapes

Have ready: Numicon Shapes, Numicon Pan Balance, Numicon 10s Number Line, Numicon 0–100 cm Number Line, number rods

Step 1

Put two 10-shapes into one pan of the Pan Balance. Ask children how many 1-shapes will be needed to make the pans balance.

Step 2

Once the pans have balanced with twenty 1-shapes agree with children that twenty 1-shapes equals two 10-shapes. Remove the 1-shapes and ask children to arrange them into two Numicon 10-patterns. Check by placing the two 10-shapes over them and agree again that they are both equal.

Step 3

Place the two 10-shapes along the 10s Number Line and then arrange the 1-shapes on top of the 10-shapes, again showing that 'twenty 1s' is equal to 'two 10s' and that both reach 20 on the 10s Number Line.

Step 4

Hold up the two 10-shapes and look closely at them. Ask children if they can see that there are 20 holes (showing the quantity value, 'twenty') and at the same time that there are 'two 10s' (showing the column value). Remind children that the two 10-shapes reached 20 on the 10s Number Line.

Step 5

Repeat Step 4 for other 2-digit numbers (not just 10s numbers); e.g. build 27 with Shapes and ask, 'How many holes altogether?', 'How many tens?', 'How many units?' If children have any difficulty naming the number, count in tens to establish 20 then encourage them to add on the 7 by identifying the Numicon 7 pattern, not counting in ones. Place along the 10s Number Line and talk about how far along the 10s Number Line the Shapes have reached. This will need to be repeated and practised often using different 2-digit numbers.

Smaller steps

- Work on one or two steps at a time, at a pace appropriate for children, repeating until children are secure before moving on.

Further practice

- Hold up Shapes to show different 2-digit numbers and ask children to say 'how many altogether' and then how many tens and how many units. Initially ensure that children are secure with numbers to 30, and then see if they can generalize to 40.

Activity 4: Looking at quantity value and column value with number rods. Equivalence between Numicon Shapes and number rods

Have ready: Numicon Pan Balance, Numicon 0–100 cm Number Line, number rods

Step 1

Put two 10-rods into one pan of the Pan Balance. Ask children how many 1-rods will be needed to make the pans balance (see Fig. 5).

Step 2

Once the pans have balanced with twenty 1-rods and children agree that twenty 1-rods equal two 10-rods, remove the 1-rods and ask children to arrange them into two Numicon 10-patterns. Check by placing the two 10-rods over them and agree again that they are both equal.

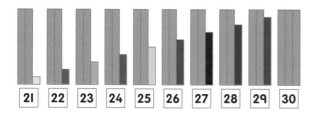

21 22 23 24 25 26 27 28 29 30

4

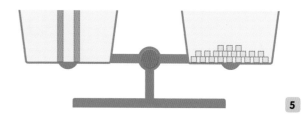

5

18

Step 3

Place the two 10-rods along the 0–100 cm Number Line and then arrange the 1-rods alongside the 10-rods, again showing that 'twenty 1s' is equal to 'two 10s' and that both reach 20 on the 0–100 cm Number Line.

Step 4

Place two 10-shapes on the table and remind children about the two 10-shapes and twenty 1-shapes being equal to 20. Remove the 1-rods from the 0–100 cm Number Line and put them into the holes of the two 10-shapes. Talk with children about the equivalence of the 10-shape and the 10-rod when representing the number values.

Smaller steps

- Work on one or two steps at a time, at a pace appropriate for children, repeating until children are secure before moving on.

Further practice

- Repeat Steps 3 and 4 for other 2-digit numbers (not just 10s numbers).

Activity 5: Extending understanding of 2-digit numbers to 40

Have ready: Numicon Shapes, Numicon 10s Number Line, Numicon 0–100 cm Number Line, Tens and Units Frame (photocopy master 25), number rods

Step 1

Build a 2-digit number with Shapes or rods, e.g. 36 (see **Fig. 6**). Ask children to say the number name, that is, 'thirty-six'. Children then say how many tens and how many units.

Step 2

If using Shapes, lay them along the 10s Number Line and discuss that the Shapes have reached between the 30 and 40 that are marked, because 36 is more than 30 but less than 40. Find 36 on the 0–100 cm Number Line.

If using rods, find 36 on the 0–100 cm Number Line first; then lay the rods along it to check that they reach 36.

Step 3

Repeat Steps 1 and 2 for other numbers 30–40.

Step 4

This time say a 2-digit number name, e.g. 'thirty-five', and ask children to build the number with Shapes or rods. They place the Shapes or rods on the tens and units frame and find the number on the 0–100 cm Number Line. (Check that children are confident about placing more than one 10-shape in the 'tens column' but only one unit Shape in the 'units column'.)

Step 5

Repeat Step 4 for other numbers 30–40.

Smaller steps

- Work with numbers in the range 21–30.

Further practice

- Place, e.g. three 10-shapes and a 4-shape, in a Numicon Feely Bag. Children feel in the Feely Bag and say how many 10-shapes they can find and then find any other Shapes. They say the number, remove the Shapes to check and find 34 on the 0–100 cm Number Line.

Extending the activities
Connecting activities

- Take and create opportunities to point out 2-digit numbers in the environment. Encourage children to recognize, read, name and compare them, e.g. page numbers in books, prices on different objects, comparing shoe sizes, numbers of children in classes, amount of money raised at fundraising events.

For children moving on quickly

- Children set out their own number line 21–30 with Shapes, labelling each number by writing the numerals on small squares of paper and placing them below each of the Shapes.

- When children find numbers on a number line, extend by looking at and saying the numbers before and after the number being found.

- Build a 2-digit number using Shapes and rods, e.g. a 10-shape, a 10-rod and a 5-shape. Ask children to say the number, then 'how many tens' and 'how many units'.

6

Structure of 2-digit numbers – notation

19

Educational context

The activities look closely at notation for 2-digit numbers and the **importance of the place of each digit**. Although children are aware of 2-digit numbers and have been reading and finding them on number lines, as notation is introduced there are further opportunities to notice if children still have misconceptions about the value of each digit. When children are recognizing and reading 2-digit numbers, if they respond to a number, e.g. 36, by picking up a 3- and a 6-shape, it is a clear indication that they do not understand that the numeral 3 means '3 tens'. It can help some children to use notation alongside the Numicon Shapes and number rods, but continue to be aware of the common error of describing a number, e.g. 24, as '2 and 4'. As in earlier work, address both 'quantity value' and 'column value' by modelling the phrases 'twenty and four' and 'two tens and four'. It is vital for children to understand that these **column and quantity values are equivalent**.

Some activities may seem to have very small steps, but if children have difficulty with any one of these they will not have a sufficiently firm foundation for future work. Although the focus is with numbers to 40, once children are confident, each activity can be easily extended to 100. Continue to ensure that children pronounce (or sign) 'teen' and 'ty' correctly.

Numeral cards are used throughout this activity group but, if possible, writing 2-digit numbers should be introduced where suggested. However, if fine motor difficulties persist, continue to use the numeral cards, as being unable to write numerals should not prevent children moving on with the activities and mathematical thinking.

Before attempting Activity 5, check that children have mastered coin equivalence activities (Calculating 11) and Numbers and the Number System 17, Activity 4.

Some children may be able to access these activities and learn to recognize 2-digit numbers and build them with apparatus but, as yet, be unable to recite the count sequence to 100.

Aims

- To extend counting range
- To read, write and build 2-digit numbers
- To understand the importance of the place of each numeral in 2-digit numbers
- To understand the equivalence between quantity value and column value

Communicating

Imagery
Numicon Display Number Line, Numicon 0–41 Number Rod Number Line, Numicon 0–100 cm Number Line, Numicon 10s Number Line

Equipment
See the individual 'have ready' for each activity, various items for the activities in the 'Extending the activities' section.

Words and terms for instruction (supported with signs and symbols)
build, find out, explain, arrange, check

Mathematical words and terms (supported with signs and symbols)
how many, patterns, groups of, tens, units, 1-digit, 2-digit, more, less, fewer

Assessment

Individual Record of Progress: Numbers and the Number System 100, 101, 102, 103, 104, 109, 110, Money 13

Putting the activities into context

Discuss with children the need to recognize 2-digit numbers that are used as labels, e.g. 'When I go to the shops I need to catch a number 12 bus. If I get on a number 25 bus it does not go the shops.'

Talk about times when understanding the size and quantity of higher numbers is important, e.g. 'The chocolate bar I like costs 40p but sometimes I decide to spend less, so I buy a chocolate bar for only 10p.'

When buying packs of toy figures, stickers, sweets in packs or collecting feature cards, children need to understand that if they need, e.g. 16 more and the item comes in packs of 10, they will need to buy two packs to have enough, and 'The space in the kitchen for a new washing machine is 55 cm, but the machine is 60 cm wide. We will need to find a narrower washing machine to fit the space.'

Link to Number, Pattern and Calculating 1

Numbers and the Number System 4

The activities

Activity 1: Labelling 2-digit numbers built with Numicon Shapes

Have ready: Numicon Shapes, Numicon 0–100 cm Number Line, 30–40 from Numicon 0–100 Numeral Cards, Numicon 10s Number Line, number rods

Step 1
Build a 2-digit number with Shapes or rods, e.g. 38, and ask children to say the number name.

Step 2
Looking at the Shapes or rods, children say how many tens and how many units.

Step 3
Spread out the Numeral Cards, reading them aloud with the children; then ask children to find the corresponding card and place it with the Shapes, e.g. **Fig. 1**.

Step 4
Place the Shapes along the 10s Number Line. Talk about how far along the 10s Number Line the Shapes reach, e.g. that they have passed 30 so the number is greater than 30, but do not reach as far as 40 so the number is less than 40. Find the number on the 0–100 cm Number Line.

Step 5
Repeat Steps 1–4, initially within this number range. (Children write a list of the numbers found using the Numeral Cards or 0–100 cm Number Line as a prompt.)

Smaller steps
• Work within the number range of the children.

Further practice
• Check that children are able to identify any 2-digit number to 40 built with Shapes or rods and label it with the corresponding Numeral Card.

Activity 2: Building 2-digit numbers from reading the number

Have ready: Numicon Shapes, Numicon 0–100 cm Number Line, 30–40 from Numicon 0–100 Numeral Cards, Numicon 10s Number Line, number rods

Step 1
Show children a Numeral Card and ask them to say the number name and build the number with Shapes or rods.

Step 2
Children say how many tens and how many units.

Step 3
Place the Shapes along the 10s Number Line and talk about how far along the 10s Number Line the Shapes have reached. Find the number on the 0–100 cm Number Line.

Step 4
Repeat Steps 1–3, initially within this number range. (Children write a list of the numbers found using the Numeral Cards or 0–100 cm Number Line as a prompt.)

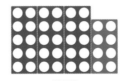

19

Smaller steps

- Spread out a small selection of Numeral Cards for the range being worked on (or several Numeral Cards for those children know and one they need to learn). Read them aloud with the children. Build one of the numbers with Shapes and then ask children to find the corresponding Numeral Card and place it with the Shapes.

Further practice

- Give children a selection of Numeral Cards (appropriate to the range they are working on). Numeral cards could be placed face down. Children turn a Numeral Card, say the number and build it with Shapes or rods.

- Show children a Numeral Card and challenge them to find Shapes for that number from a selection of Shapes in a Numicon Feely Bag.

- Put a Numicon Coloured Peg on a number on the 0–100 cm Number Line. Children say the number, build it with rods and check by placing them along the number line, e.g. **Fig. 2**.

Activity 3: Beginning to understand 2-digit notation

Have ready: Numicon Shapes, 0–9 from Numicon 0–100 Numeral Cards, Tens and Units Frame (photocopy master 25), number rods

Step 1

Ask children to place two 10-shapes on the Tens and Units Frame (photocopy master 25). Talk with them about there being 'two' 10-shapes and that it is possible to place them both in the 'tens column' (as they are both 'tens'). Agree that there are no units.

Step 2

Name the two 10-shapes as 'twenty'. Model writing twenty as 20 and ask children to show this with Numeral Cards (2 and 0). Agree that the 2 should go in the 'tens column' because there are 2 tens, and that the 0 should go in the units column because there are no units.

Step 3

Remind children about the two 10-shapes having 20 holes (pointing to the Numeral Cards 2 and 0 together as 'twenty' and the '20 holes' in the Shapes), and about 20 having 'two 10-shapes' (pointing to the numeral 2 in the tens column and the two 10-shapes), and that there are no units (pointing to the numeral 0 and the empty units column). Talk about 'twenty' and '2 tens' being equal.

Step 4

Repeat this activity often with tens numbers 20–90. (Children begin to write the numerals needed on small pieces of paper and use them as the labels on the tens and units frame.)

Smaller steps

- Take as much time as necessary with each step.

- Practise each step with different numbers before moving on.

- Play the game in 'Further practice' with fewer Shapes in the Feely Bag.

Further practice

- Place nine 10-shapes in a Numicon Feely Bag. Give instructions to children, e.g. 'Find five tens'. A child takes out five 10-shapes but then has to say the total number 'fifty'. Or reverse the game by asking children to find 50 with Shapes. Children have to then say, 'It's 5 tens'.

Activity 4: Recording 2-digit numbers built with Numicon Shapes

Have ready: Numicon Shapes, Numicon 0–100 cm Number Line, 30–40 from Numicon 0–100 Numeral Cards, Tens and Units Frame (photocopy master 25), Numeral Cards 0–9 (cut from photocopy master 11), number rods

Step 1

Say a 2-digit number, e.g. 35. Ask children to build it with Shapes or rods and find the corresponding Numeral Card (from 0–100 Numeral Cards).

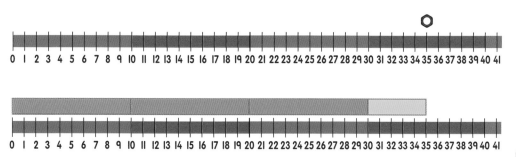

Numbers and the Number System

19

Step 2
Children place the Shapes or rods on the tens and units frame. (Check that they are confident about placing more than one 10-shape in the 'tens column' but only one unit Shape in the 'units column'.)

Step 3
Spread out numeral cards 0–9 (from photocopy master 11) and ask children to find the numeral cards that illustrate the number on the tens and units frame and then place them below the frame (see **Fig. 3**). Talk about the relationships between the Shapes or rods and the Numeral Cards, the columns and the positions of the Shapes or rods and numeral cards on the frame. Always find the number on the 0–100 cm Number Line.

Step 4
Repeat with other numbers within children's number range. (Once children are confident about labelling the Shapes on the tens and units frame they could write their own labels.)

Smaller steps
- Work through the steps at a pace appropriate for children, working within the children's number range.

Further practice
- Give children a selection of 30–40 Numeral Cards from 0–100 Numeral Cards, shuffled and face down in a pile. Children turn a Numeral Card, build the number with Shapes or rods and place them on the tens and units frame. They then find the corresponding numeral cards from 0–9 and find the number on the 0–100 cm Number Line.

- A game to play in pairs: Shuffle numeral cards 0–9 and place them face down in a pile. Player 1 turns a card and decides whether to place it on the tens or units side of the tens and units frame. Player 2 takes a turn. Player 1 turns a second card and has to place it in the remaining space. Player 2 takes a turn. The player with the highest number is the winner.

   Build numbers with Shapes or rods if necessary and find numbers on the 0–100 cm Number Line to check.

- Vary the game above by having the lowest number as the winner.

- Vary the game further by allowing children to pick two numeral cards and, looking at them both, decide where to place them on the frame.

- Call out 2-digit numbers for children to write.

Activity 5: Connecting Numicon Shapes and number rods with money

Have ready: Numicon Shapes, number rods, coins (1p, 2p, 5p, 10p), thirty-four 1p coins in a purse

Step 1
Ask children to find out how much money you have in your purse. If necessary, remind them about grouping in 10s to find out how much. When they have grouped the coins into three Numicon 10-patterns, again, if necessary, remind them about arranging the last few coins into a Numicon Shape pattern. Agree that you have 34p.

Step 2
Exchange the three Numicon 10-patterns of 1p coins for three 10p coins and ask children to show the amount with Shapes or rods (some children may wish to exchange the four 1p coins for two 2p coins). Talk about how the Shapes or rods can help to represent amounts of money.

Step 3
This time show children 39 built with Shapes or rods and ask them to find coins; to show the amount. Some children may use only 1p coins, some may use three 10p coins and nine 1p coins; some may use three 10p coins and then other combinations to make 9p.

Smaller steps
- Build 11 with Shapes and find coins for 11p. Continue to 20. Extend to higher numbers as appropriate.

Further practice
- Give children different amounts of money using 10p coins and 1p coins for them to find the Shapes or rods for the amount.

- Give children different numbers built with Shapes or rods for them to find how much in coins (use coins appropriate for the ability of children, e.g. just 10p and 1p coins).

- Children choose a 2-digit number and build it with Shapes or rods. They find coins for the amount and write how much.

- Use 'shopping' items with different prices. Children find the exact amount in coins to pay. (Some children may still need to build with Shapes or rods first.)

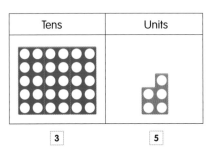

Tens	Units
3	5

Extending the activities

19

Activity 6: Putting numerals in the right places

Have ready: Numicon Shapes, Numeral Cards 0–9 (cut from photocopy master 11), number rods, coins (1p, 10p)

Step 1
Write '13p' and '31p' and ask children to build each amount with coins (see Fig. 4). Discuss the differences they can see between the two amounts (and which they would prefer to have and why).

Step 2
Ask them to build the amounts with Shapes or rods (see Fig. 5). Talk about which set of Shapes or rods shows more and which shows fewer (or less) and agree that the one with the higher number of tens shows the amount with more.

Step 3
Find the 1 and 3 numeral cards, place them to show 13 and ask children to match the corresponding Shapes. Then change the places of the numeral cards to show 31 and ask children to match the corresponding Shapes. Discuss that it matters in which place we write the numerals.

Step 4
Using numeral cards 1 and 4, ask children to place the cards to make the highest number. If children reverse the places of the digits they will need further practice with earlier activities.

Smaller steps
- Establish that children understand 'more' and 'fewer'. With children, build 13 and 31 with Shapes and talk about a context appropriate for children; then ask which they would prefer to have, 13 or 31. Work on Step 3 of Activity 6.

Further practice
- Give children two Numeral Cards from 0–100 Numeral Cards and ask them to make the highest number. Support with Shapes or rods and find on the 0–100 cm Number Line.
- Give children two Numeral Cards from 0–100 Numeral Cards and ask them to make the lowest number. Support with Shapes or rods and find on the 0–100 cm Number Line.
- Choosing a suitable context for the age of children, e.g. stickers, collections of football cards and so on, choose pairs of numbers where the digits are reversed, e.g. 35 and 53. Ask children to say either the number that would be the most or the number that would be the least. Write the number.

Connecting activities
- Children read 2-digit numbers in the environment, e.g. house numbers, labelled trays in school, page numbers in books
- Children read 2-digit prices in the supermarket.
- Children begin to understand that a higher number of tens denotes the highest amount; e.g. when someone has 42 of something they have more than someone else who only has 38.
- Involve children in making a display of all the different ways they could show, e.g. 23 (see Fig. 6). (Include further collections of real objects.)

For children moving on quickly
- For Activity 3, show quantity and column value in a 'chart' e.g. Fig. 7.

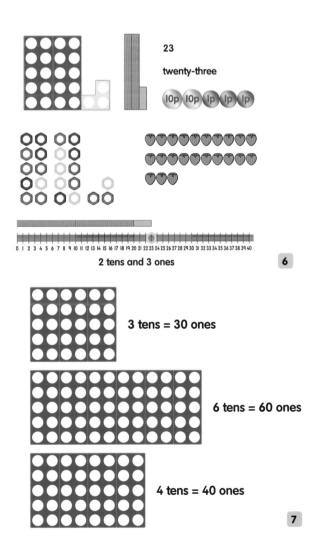

23
twenty-three

2 tens and 3 ones
6

3 tens = 30 ones

6 tens = 60 ones

4 tens = 40 ones
7

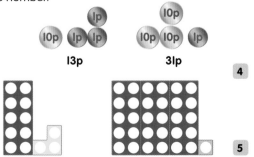

13p   31p
4

5

Comparing and ordering higher numbers

20

Educational context

As children compare and order higher numbers they will need to have a clear understanding of **place value, that is that the place of a digit tells us its value**. Comparing and ordering Numicon Shapes and number rods makes visible the **important regularity in the order of numbers**, which is a crucial step towards understanding the system of whole numbers. Whatever problem is being considered, the numbers being compared can still be shown with Numicon Shapes or number rods, providing continuity and supporting understanding and confidence for children when working with higher numbers.

These activities include work on reasoning to make comparisons between number values in the context of **measures**. As in earlier work, when making comparisons remind children to say (or sign) clearly 'bigger than' (not running 'than' into the previous word, e.g. saying 'biggeran'), as 'than' is a key word used in comparisons. These activities can easily be repeated to include numbers to 100. The further work on measures suggested in 'Extending the activities' focuses on developing the work on using standard measures of length in Numbers and the Number System 3 and 15 to compare and order objects up to 1 metre long by length. In the work on weight, pupils compare and weights up to 100 grams.

The decision will need to be made as to when it is appropriate for children to experience the type of problem when, e.g. there are two bags, and one of the bags is heavier than the other but it may not contain the most items. They could be bigger items and fewer of them. In the capacity work, they compare and order amounts less than 100 millilitres.

This work on these different measures will need to be spread over many weeks. As suggested in previous activity groups, teachers will need to decide when it is appropriate to introduce these activities to children and to give plenty of time for children to assimilate these ideas.

Aims

- To recognize when it is helpful to use the order of numbers to organize or find things
- To use the '<' and '>' symbols when comparing Numicon Shapes, number rods and numerals
- To compare and order numbers to 40 (then to 100)

Communicating

Imagery
Numicon Display Number Line, Numicon 10s Number Line, Numicon 0–100 cm Number Line, Numicon 0–31 Number Line

Equipment
See the individual 'have ready' for each activity, various items (including for measures) for the activities in the 'Extending the activities' section

Words and terms for instruction (supported with signs and symbols)
build, check, continue

Mathematical words and terms (supported with signs and symbols)
tens, units, more, less, between, nearly, before, after, forwards, backwards, larger than, greater than, bigger than, smaller than, more than, less than, fewer than, higher, lower, 'I know this, so I know that', compare

Assessment

Individual Record of Progress: Numbers and the Number System 93, 94, 95, 96, 105, 106, 107, 108, 109, Measures 13, 22, 29, 39, 42, 48, 50, 55, 57, 63, 64, Money 14, 15

Putting the activities into context

Children need to experience comparing problems using 2-digit numbers throughout the whole range of measures (that is, money, length, weight, capacity and time), as well as in data handling situations and general day-to-day questions that arise (e.g. 'are more people having a school dinner than a packed lunch?'). Example questions:

- 'It takes Alisha 14 minutes to walk to school and Elena 23 minutes. Who takes the longest time to get to school?'
- 'I spent 35p of my pocket money last week and 26p this week. Which week did I spend less?'
- 'Toby had to take 20 ml of medicine a day. Ellen had to take 15 ml. Who had to take the most?'
- 'When playing marbles, if I can get as close as 20 cm I know I might win on my next shot, but if I am 35 cm away it is more difficult. Why?'
- 'The recipe needed 25 g of nuts and 18 g of seeds. Which was the smallest quantity?'

Problems involving weight and capacity can sometimes be quite challenging due to the size of the numbers, so, as with all measures, millilitres and grams will need to be restricted to those within the children's working number range.

Link to Number Pattern and Calculating 1

Numbers and the Number System 4, Activity 7

The activities

20

Activity 1: Comparing the size of two collections

Have ready: Numicon Shapes, Numicon 10s Number Line, Numicon 0–100 cm Number Line, Numicon 0–100 Numeral Cards, two bags each containing between twenty and thirty 1p coins, Words and Symbols for Calculating (cut from photocopy master 26a), number rods

Step 1

Talk with children about finding out which collection of 1p coins has more. Remind children of how they grouped objects to find 'how many' and ask them to group the coins in each collection.

Step 2

Discuss the totals and which is more and which is fewer, then which 'is greater than' so which 'is smaller than'.

Step 3

Find the numeral cards and use the '<' or '>' symbol to show the comparison between the coins, e.g. **Fig. 1**.

Step 4

Children show the totals with Shapes or rods and compare both numbers by placing the Shapes along the 10s Number Line, e.g. **Fig. 2 & 3**. Discuss that one reaches further along the 10s Number Line than the other and, although they both have the same number of 10s (that is, two 10s), 7 units are more than 4 units so 27 is greater than 24.

Step 5

Find the numbers on the 0–100 cm Number Line, discussing again that one number is further along the number line than the other and making the connection with which number 'is greater than' so which 'is smaller than'.

Step 6

Also discuss which numbers come in between the two numbers being compared.

Smaller steps

- Using Numicon Coloured Pegs and two Numicon Baseboards, group one amount of Pegs on each Baseboard for children to compare.
- Children check which number is greater using the Numicon Pan Balance.

Further practice

- Children group and compare other collections of interest to them.
- Give children sets of numerals to put in order, e.g. 24, 25, 26, 27, 28.

Activity 2: Comparing and ordering numbers in the range 0–40

Have ready: Numicon Shapes, Numicon Pan Balance, Numicon 10s Number Line, Numicon 0–100 cm Number Line, Numicon 0–100 Numeral Cards, Words and Symbols for Calculating (cut from photocopy master 26a), number rods

Step 1

Build a pair of 2-digit numbers with structured apparatus, e.g. 28 and 35 (see **Fig. 4**) and talk with children about what is the same and what is different about them; e.g. both have tens and units, both are 2-digit numbers, 35 is larger than 28, 28 is smaller than 35, and 35 has more tens but fewer units than 28.

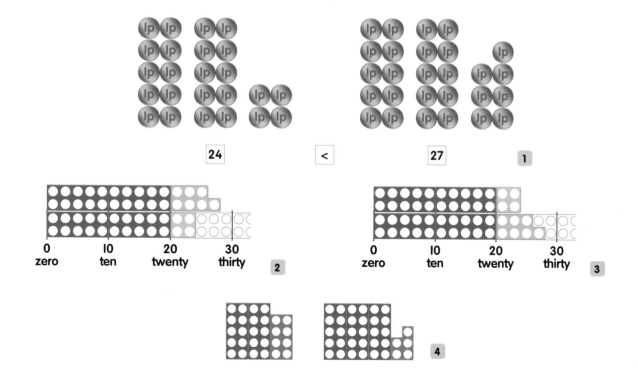

Numbers and the Number System

20

Step 2

Compare both numbers by placing the Shapes along the 10s Number Line. Discuss that the Shapes showing the largest number go further along the 10s Number Line than the Shapes showing the smaller number.

Step 3

Write both numbers on small squares of paper and place the '<' or '>' between them, e.g. **Fig. 5**.

Step 4

Find 28 and 35 on the 0–100 cm Number Line. Talk with children about what happens to the numbers as you move forwards or backwards along a number line.

Smaller steps

- Children check by putting Shapes in the Pan Balance.
- Children may still need reminding that the Shapes showing the largest number have more holes in total than the Shapes showing the smallest number.
- Ensure that children are secure with each step using the range 0–30.

Further practice

- Partners each take an 11–40 Numeral Card. They each build their number with Shapes (or with rods) and compare them, deciding which number is larger and which is smaller. Children check using the Numicon Pan Balance and put the '<' or '>' symbol in the appropriate place.
- Partners each take an 11–40 Numeral Card. They each build their number with Shapes (or with rods) and compare them by laying the Shapes along the 10s Number Line (or rods along 0–100 cm Number Line). They write both numbers on small squares of paper and place the '<' or '>' between them.

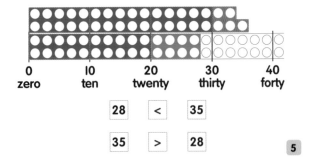

5

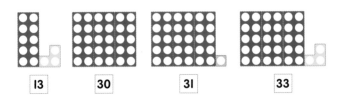

6

Activity 3: Comparing and ordering more than two numbers in the range 0–40

Have ready: Numicon Shapes, Numicon 0–100 cm Number Line, Numicon 0–100 Numeral Cards, Numicon Coloured Pegs, number rods

Step 1

Show children Numeral Cards for 31, 13, 33 and 30. Ask children to put them in order from the smallest to the largest.

Step 2

Build each number with Shapes or rods and place the Numeral Cards below them. Compare the values shown with the apparatus, referring to 13 only having one 10 and the others all having three 10s; so 13 is the smallest number. Then move on to the units digits to order the remaining numbers. Agree on the order (see **Fig. 6**).

Step 3

Check on the 0–100 cm Number Line by marking each number with a Peg.

Smaller steps

- Only use three numeral cards. Work in the range 0–30 initially.

Further practice

- Give children any four 0–40 Numeral Cards for them to put in order. (Use apparatus to help if needed.) Increase the number of numeral cards as children are ready.
- Give children two numeral cards from adjacent decades for them to say the numbers that come between them.

Activity 4: Comparing and ordering with money

Have ready: Numicon Shapes, Numicon 0–31 Number Line, number rods, coins (1p, 2p, 5p, 10p, 20p)

Step 1

Give children the coins to put in order of value (only using the 20p coin if appropriate).

Step 2

Children find Shapes to show each coin value and put them in order from the smallest to the largest. They check that the order of coin values and Shapes both coincide.

Step 3

Mark each coin value along the 0–31 Number Line and talk with children about how the monetary values can be ordered in the same way as number values (see Fig. 7).

Step 4

Give children problems to solve, e.g. 'Jack has a 20p coin and Heidi has a 10p coin. Who has the most (or least)?' Restrict to 10p and 5p coins if necessary.

Smaller steps

• Take time to work through each step, restricting coins to those up to 10p.

Further practice

• Share further stories where children are given amounts like 29p and 37p and need to decide who has the most (or the least). If support is needed to order the amounts, children use Shapes or rods rather than coins.

Extending the activities

Connecting activities

• Include the comparison and order of 2-digit numbers in all areas of measures.

Connecting activities – Measures

• Length, height and width: Use number rods to measure up to 1 metre. Give children a collection of objects whose dimensions measure less than 1 metre. Children measure the objects by placing 10-rods end to end along on length and then placing an appropriate rod for any remaining distance less than 10 cm.

  Children can then check their measurements by placing the rods on the Numicon 0-100 cm Number Rod Track and then record them in centimetres.

  Children can order and compare the measurements using the '<' and '>' symbols, such as: 19 cm < 21 cm < 29 cm

• Weight: Make a collection of different small containers or packets that are labelled with weights up to 100 g.

  Children can read the weights and order the packets by weight from lightest to heaviest or heaviest to lightest. They can record their comparisons by drawing and labelling the objects and using the '<' and '>' symbols.

  Look at how the weights are written and discuss the term 'gram' Explain that 'g' as the initial letter of 'gram' is used to represent the whole word.

Use sets of 1 g 2 g 5 g 10 g, 20 g, 50 g and 100 g weights. Ask children to look carefully at the amounts written on each weight and to put the weights in order.

• Weight: Prepare sealed bags containing different amounts up to 100 grams of dry material (such as sand, rice, beans). Children weigh the bags in the Numicon Pan Balance. They can record the weights.

  Pupils can order and compare the weights of the bags using the '<' and '>' symbols, e.g:

  15g < 25g < 30g < 50g < 75g < 100g

  Vary the number of bags and the combinations of weights required according to the needs of the pupils.

• Capacity: Discuss when we need to measure small amounts of liquid accurately, e.g. for medicine and cooking. Look at a collection of measuring spoons or a medicine syringe that is labelled 5ml, 10ml, and so on. Look at how the capacities are written and discuss the term 'millilitre'. Explain that 'ml' is used to represent the whole word.

• Capacity: Make a collection of different small containers or packets that are labelled with amounts up to 100 millilitres, e.g. bath products, cosmetic samples, essential oils bottles, food colouring. Children can read the capacity and order the containers from holding the least or most, or most to least. They can record their comparisons by drawing and labelling the objects and using the '<' and '>' symbols.

• Time: Discuss when it is important to know how long an event takes and that we call this timing, e.g. timing sports races, timing cooking, knowing how long it will take us to walk to the station to catch a train etc. Show children recipe books or food packets and look for instructions on timing.

• Time: Introduce a digital stop watch and a cooking timer. Use these to measure and compare the time taken for tasks within the school day.

• Time: Children can keep a record of time taken and compare the lengths of time taken on different days for similar events, e.g. on Monday Assembly lasted for 12 minutes, on Tuesday it lasted for 15 minutes.

For children moving on quickly

• Extend the range to 100 for all activities.

• Children try recording along an empty number line.

• Extend the range to 100p when working with monetary values.

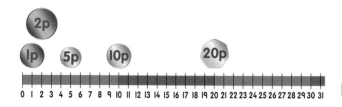

Counting in steps of 2 and 5

21

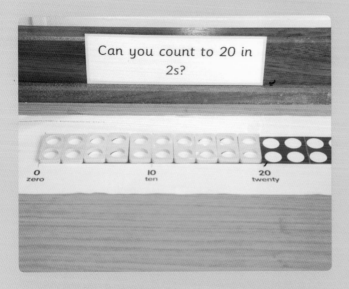

Can you count to 20 in 2s?

0 zero   10 ten   20 twenty

Educational context

Some children may be able to recite some numbers in these sequences, but in this activity group counting in steps of 2 and steps of 5 is supported by the structure of the Numicon Shapes, number rods and number lines, to encourage children to understand the **relationships between the numbers within each sequence**. Activities 1 and 2 build on the work on even numbers in Pattern and Algebra 7. The activities in this group are a very helpful foundation for future work when the relationships between steps of 5 and 10 are explored, when learning to tell the time and for multiplying through repeated adding.

Aims

- To describe and extend number sequences when counting in steps of 2 and 5.

Communicating

Imagery

Numicon Display Number Line, Numicon 0–41 Number Rod Number Line, Numicon 0–31 Number Line, Numicon 0–100 cm Number Line, Numicon 10s Number Line

Equipment

See the individual 'have ready' for each activity, various items for the activities in the 'Extending the activities' section.

Words and terms for instruction (supported with signs and symbols)

find, along, fill, check, label, continue, look carefully, notice

Mathematical words and terms (supported with signs and symbols)

before, after, between, count, twos, fives, more, counting in steps, pattern, pair

Assessment

Individual Record of Progress: Numbers and the Number System 113, 114, 115, 116, 118, 119, 121, 123

Putting the activities into context

Discuss counting in ones and saying a number name for each object; then remind children that when they count in tens there are 10 objects in a group each time and so it is a quicker way to count (not having to say every number name). Explain they are now going to learn to count in groups of 2 and then in groups of 5. Talk about pairs of shoes (check that children understand the term 'pair') needing to fit on a shoe rack but because there are 2 shoes in each pair extra (or double) space will be needed. Explain that if children have saved lots of 5p pieces, it would be helpful to count in fives to know how much they have saved.

Link to Number Pattern and Calculating 1

Numbers and the Number System 3

The activities

21

Activity 1: Counting in twos

Have ready: Numicon Shapes, Numicon 0–31 Number Line, Numicon 0–100 cm Number Line, Numicon 0–100 Numeral Cards

Step 1

Show children a growing pattern built with even Shapes up to 20 (see **Fig. 1**). Talk about the Shapes that have been used and agree that it is only the even numbers.

Step 2

Count, with children, pointing to each even number in turn. Explain that this is called 'counting in twos' or 'counting in steps of two'.

Step 3

Discuss and agree that the pattern increases by two each time and illustrate with the 2-shape.

Step 4

When appropriate, support the counting with numerals by pointing to each step of the growing pattern of even Shapes and labelling it with the corresponding Numeral Card (see **Fig. 2**).

Step 5

Find these numerals on the 0–31 Number Line or 0–100 cm Number Line.

Step 6

Count in twos, pointing to the sequence of Shapes and to each number along the 0–31 Number Line at the same time.

Smaller steps

- Work up to 10 first until children are secure with the sequence 2, 4, 6, 8, 10 before extending to 20. Always support children with limited auditory memory with the imagery of the sequence of Shapes.

Further practice

- Repeat with rods (see **Fig. 3**).
- Children count in steps of 2 pointing at a number line as they do so.

Activity 2: More counting in twos

Have ready: Numicon Shapes, Numicon 10s Number Line, a collection of items that can be counted in twos, e.g. pairs of socks or shoes

Step 1

Children place a 2-shape on the 10s Number Line and say 'two'. They then place another 2-shape, look at the combined total and say 'four'. (Some children may need to check with the 4-shape.) They continue to place 2-shapes along the 10s Number Line saying the total each time (see **Fig. 4**), that is, each twos number (and, if necessary, finding the Shape to check).

1

| 2 | 4 | 6 | 8 | 10 | 12 | 14 | 16 | 18 | 20 |

2

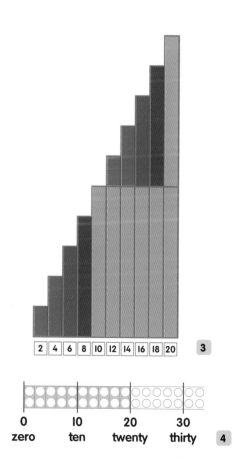

| 2 | 4 | 6 | 8 | 10 | 12 | 14 | 16 | 18 | 20 |

3

0   10   20   30
zero   ten   twenty   thirty

4

21

Step 2

Have a collection of items, using a context suitable for the children, e.g. pairs of shoes, socks, gloves, 2p coins, and find out how many are in the collection by counting in twos. Agree to keep check of the count by placing a 2-shape on the 10s Number Line as each 'two' is counted. (It can be helpful to place a 2p coin over each 2-shape, e.g. **Fig. 5**).

Smaller steps

• Again, work up to 10 first until children are secure with the sequence 2, 4, 6, 8, 10 before extending to 20. Always support children with limited auditory memory with the imagery of the sequence of Shapes. Children may need to build each step of 2 with 2-shapes and find the total, e.g. **Fig. 6**.

Further practice

• Count in twos placing a 2-rod on the 0–100 cm Number Line as each number is spoken, or by placing 2-shapes along the 10s Number Line.

• Select the 'multiple of 2' cards from the 0–100 Numeral Cards and place them shuffled and face down in a pile. Children turn a card and read the number name. They place 2-shapes to reach that number on the 10s Number Line or place 2-rods to reach that number on the 0–100 cm Number Line.

• Using the 0–100 cm Number Line for support, children write the numbers for the sequence of twos.

Activity 3: Counting in fives with Numicon Shapes

Have ready: Numicon Shapes, Numicon 10s Number Line, Numicon 0–100 Numeral Cards

Step 1

Talk with children about 'counting in fives' and what they think it means. Some children may be able to recite some of the sequence of 5s. Agree that it means counting in steps of 5.

Step 2

Discuss that the 5-shapes might help when counting in fives and lay a 5-shape on the 10s Number Line, saying 'five'. Place another 5-shape on the 10s Number Line, noticing that the two 5-shapes equal 10 and reach 10 on the 10s Number Line.

Step 3

Continue to place 5-shapes along the 10s Number Line, pausing to look closely and say the total each time. Continue to 50 (see **Fig. 7**).

Step 4

When appropriate, support the counting with numerals, pointing to each step of the growing pattern of Shapes and labelling the numbers with the corresponding Numeral Card. Notice that, on the 10s Number Line, all the 10s numbers are already written so, beginning with the first 5-shape, label this with the Numeral Card for '5'. The card for '10' is not needed so agree the next label needed is '15'. Continue counting in steps of 5 and labelling the numbers with Numeral Cards to 50 (see **Fig. 8**).

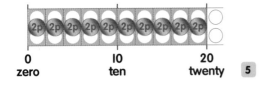

5

6

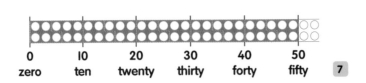

7

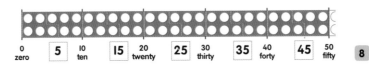

8

21

Smaller steps

- Build up the sequence of fives with Shapes before placing them along the 10s Number Line, beginning with a 5-shape, then adding another 5-shape to show the 10-shape. Then add another 5-shape to show 15, and so on, each time allowing children time to say the total (see Fig. 9).

- Work up to 25 first until children are secure with the sequence 5, 10, 15, 20, 25 before extending to 50. Always support children with limited auditory memory with the imagery of the sequence of Shapes.

Further practice

- Whenever children count in fives, support their counting by placing 5-shapes along the 10s Number Line.

- Select the 'multiple of 5' cards from the 0–100 Numeral Cards and place them shuffled and face down in a pile. Children turn a card and read the number name. They place 5-shapes to reach that number on the 10s Number Line.

- Count a collection of 5p coins by placing them on top of 5-shapes (see Fig. 10).

Activity 4: Counting in fives with number rods

Have ready: Numicon 0–100 cm Number Line, Numicon 0–100 Numeral Cards, number rods

Step 1

Explain to children that they are now going to use 5-rods to help when counting in steps of 5. Lay a 5-rod on the 0–100 cm Number Line, saying 'five' and place the 5 Numeral Card below the 5 on the 0–100 cm Number Line.

Step 2

Place another 5-rod on the 0–100 cm Number Line noticing that the two 5-rods equal 10 and reach 10 on the 0–100 cm Number Line. Place the 10 Numeral Card below the 10 on the 0–100 cm Number Line. Continue to lay 5-rods along the 0–100 cm Number Line pausing to look closely. Say the total

each time and place the corresponding Numeral Card below. Continue to 50 (see Fig. 11).

Smaller steps

- Initially work to 25.

Further practice

- Select the 'multiple of 5' cards from the 0–100 Numeral Cards and place them shuffled and face down in a pile. Children turn a Numeral Card and read the number name. They place 5-rods to reach that number on the 0–100 cm Number Line.

- Using the 0–100 cm Number Line for support, children write the numbers for the sequence of 5s.

- Children count in steps of 5, pointing at numerals in the fives sequence on the 0–100 cm Number Line as they do so.

Extending the activities
Connecting activities

- Where pairs of things need counting, children count them in twos.

- Children make connections with 5 fingers and 5 toes when counting in fives.

- Children count different amounts of 2p and 5p coins.

For children moving on quickly

- Using shuffled 0–100 Numeral Cards for the sequence of twos, children put them in order.

- Using shuffled 0–100 Numeral Cards for the sequence of fives, children put them in order.

- Give children three consecutive fives numbers, e.g. 15, 20, 25. Ask children to look carefully and continue the sequence.

- Repeat for the twos sequence.

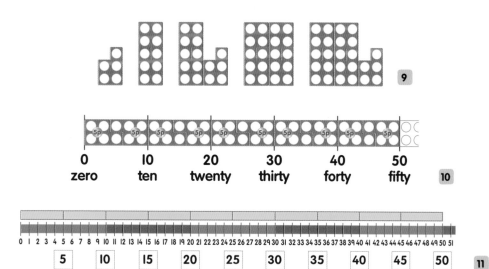

Calculating

Practical adding: starting with the total

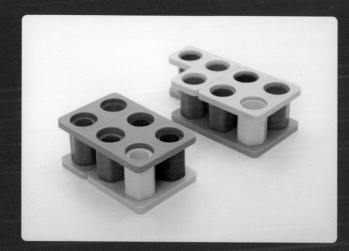

Educational context

In this activity group children are introduced to the terms **'wholes' and 'parts'**. They have met the ideas before informally but now they encounter specific adding activities where the focus is on part-whole relationships. In these activities children begin with the 'whole' (or the total) and find 'parts' that together equal the total. Numicon Shapes and number rods support this idea very well. Children can also see the **equivalence** between the 'parts' added together and the whole, as the smaller Numicon Shapes or number rods are combined to equal the Numicon Shape pattern of a larger Numicon Shape or number rod length. Through these activities children will notice and may begin to remember some adding combinations. Exploiting and creating opportunities for children to hear mathematical language for adding throughout the day provides an essential model which they can then be encouraged to copy. In this activity group only use combined Numicon Shapes with a total of 10 or less.

Aims

- To experience situations in which it is useful to add
- To understand that a 'whole' can be made of different-sized 'parts' or parts that are the same size
- To understand that the whole is larger than either of the parts
- To use Numicon Shapes and number rods to add whole numbers
- To begin to generalize, starting to use number words as nouns, not just as adjectives
- To begin to understand that adding can be done in any order

Communicating

Imagery
Numicon Display Number Line, Numicon 0–41 Number Rod Number Line

Equipment
See the individual 'have ready' for each activity, various items for the activities in the 'Extending the activities' section.

Words and terms for instruction (supported with signs and symbols)
build, find, talk about, explain, put together, combine, same way, different way

Mathematical words and terms (supported with signs and symbols)
same number, same as, more, less, fewer, larger Shape, larger amount, smaller Shape, smaller amount, add, and, makes, equals, altogether, together, adding, adding sentence, adding story, add, and, total, compare, equals, facts, pattern

Assessment

Individual Record of Progress: Calculating 2, 3 and towards 5.

Putting the activities into context

The contexts for the first activity are included within it. For other activities, discuss with children that if 8 of them were choosing PE equipment, some might choose a ball, some a bean bag, some a quoit, some a hoop. The 8-shape could represent the total (the whole) of all the equipment used and the smaller Numicon Shapes (the parts) how many children were choosing a particular item; e.g. a 3-shape for 3 balls, a 3-shape for 3 bean bags and a 2-shape for 2 quoits (not all of the equipment might be used at one time). There could be different choices each time. Children could think about different fillings for sandwiches; e.g. 'If 9 people were going on a picnic, 5 might like egg sandwiches and 4 might prefer jam, or 3 might like egg, 4 might like cheese and 2 jam'.

Calculating

The activities

Activity 1: Wholes and parts of everyday objects

Have ready: a jigsaw puzzle, an apple or orange, a loaf of bread (sliced or unsliced), a pizza or cake or pictures of some items that can be cut into parts (e.g. several identical pictures of cupcakes so that each one can be cut into a different number of parts), scissors, knife (optional)

Step 1

Remind children about things that are 'whole', e.g. a jigsaw puzzle that has been completed though it has been put together using smaller parts; a sliced loaf of bread has many 'parts' that make the 'whole' loaf.

Step 2

Now talk about things that are whole, such as an apple or orange, a pizza or a cake that could be cut into parts. (Do this practically, if possible.) Show that the things might be cut into two parts, or three or four (or lots more) and that each part might look different, some bigger than others, some quite small or the parts might be the same size – they might be equal. The cutting should be done so that the parts can be reassembled and held together to show the whole again.

Smaller steps

- Guide children through cutting something into parts.
- Use the terms precisely, e.g. 'I am using the "parts" of this jigsaw and putting them together to make the "whole" jigsaw'.

Further practice

- Give children a ball of modelling dough that they can cut into parts and then squeeze back together.
- Give children pictures, e.g. old greetings cards, that can be cut into parts and reassembled.
- Children work with a jug of water that can be poured into cups.

Activity 2: Showing wholes and parts using Numicon Shapes

Have ready: Numicon Baseboard, Numicon Baseboard Overlays: number bonds, Numicon Shapes, Numicon Coloured Pegs

Step 1

Put a Baseboard Overlay: number bond on the Baseboard and ask children what they notice. Talk about how there is one Shape by itself (a whole) whereas the other pictures have two or more Shapes together (parts).

Step 2

Children match Shapes to the Baseboard Overlay, thus making different combinations of the number, e.g. **Fig. 1**.

Step 3

Children fill the 'whole' single Shape with Pegs and place one of the combinations on top. In this way children progressively build a tower, e.g. **Fig. 2**, until all the combinations are used.

Step 4

Ask children to describe the combination for each layer of the tower, e.g. for the 8-tower combinations are 'four and four', 'seven and one', 'two and two and two and two', and so on.

Step 5

Make the most of opportunities as they arise to ask questions and talk with children about how they have made 8:

- Ask, 'How many Shapes have been used in each layer to make the total (how many 'parts' to make the 'whole')?'
- Compare layers, e.g. 'You have used three Shapes in this layer but two Shapes in this layer.'
- Ask, 'In which layer have you used the most Shapes, or the least?'
- Model the language, e.g. 'You have used a 3-shape and another 3-shape and a 2-shape to make eight' or, 'You have used two 3-shapes and a 2-shape to make eight' (language for adding).
- Repeat the language for adding saying the Shapes used in a different order. Ask children whether they think it matters in which order the Shapes are described.

1

2

- Extend by just using nouns, e.g. 'so three and three and two equals eight'.
- For even Shapes, e.g. for 8, look at the two 4-shapes and talk about the two Shapes (parts) being the same size (equal or equivalent).
- Refer to Shapes that are repeated in one layer, e.g. two 4-shapes, four 2-shapes (multiplicative thinking).

Smaller steps

- If children have fine motor difficulties that may make using Pegs frustrating, ask them to build towers by simply placing different combinations of Shapes on top of one another, like a 'sandwich'.
- On the Baseboard set out three combinations of Shapes that equal 6 for children to place on top of one another, or to use in building a tower.
- Use the Numicon Large Foam Shapes (if available) and place combinations on top of one another. Begin by using the even Shapes.

Further practice

- Children repeat this activity often, choosing their own Shape to start a tower and choosing their own combinations to build it up. They describe the combination for each layer of the tower.
- Once children are confident about building the towers, further questioning whilst children are actually building and describing their combinations, could include, e.g. 'What Shape do you need to complete that layer?'or, 'How many more will you need to make eight?'

Activity 3: Combining 'parts' to equal the 'whole' with Numicon Shapes

Have ready: Numicon Shapes, two Numicon Spinners with Numeral Overlays 1–5 and 6–10 (cut from photocopy master 20)

Step 1

Children spin one of the Spinners, read out the number (if they spin '1' they have another go) and find the corresponding Shape.

Step 2

They find two or more Shapes to make that Shape and say what they have made using the language of adding, e.g. 'I have made the 7-shape by adding a 3- and a 4-shape together' or, 'I have a 3-shape and a 4-shape and together they equal the 7-shape' (see Fig. 3).

Step 3

Talk with children about adding situations, e.g. if they had 7 reward stars, 3 might be gold and 4 might be silver.

Smaller steps

- Give children a 2-shape or a 4-shape and ask them to find two (or more) Shapes to cover it. Gradually introduce the other even Shapes and then the 'odd' Shapes.

Further practice

- Children should practise the activity often until they are confidently finding two or more shapes to cover another whole shape.
- Children take a Shape from a Numicon Feely Bag containing 4–10 Shapes and make that number by finding two or more Shapes to cover it.

Activity 4: Combining parts to equal the whole with number rods

Have ready: number rods

Step 1

Ask children to find, e.g. a 6-rod. Then ask them to find smaller rods which, when placed end-to-end, equal the length of the 6-rod (so the parts will equal the whole); e.g. Fig. 4.

Step 2

Children say what they have done. Some children may be able to use number names for the rods; others will still use colour names, e.g. 'The pink rod and the red rod together equal the dark green rod' or, 'The 4-rod and the 2-rod equal the 6-rod'. Some children may say, 'Four add two equals (makes) six.'

Step 3

Some children may continue to find different ways to equal their first rod, to create a 'wall' or 'mat', e.g. Fig. 5.

Smaller steps

- Some children may find it easier to use the Numicon Number Rod Trays (if available) for the 'whole' activity.

Further practice

- Children choose a Number Rod Tray (if available). They begin with the rod that fits exactly in the Number Rod Tray and then find other combinations to fill it. They describe what they have done using the language of adding. Practice often with different Trays.

Calculating

1

Activity 5: Beginning to think about commutativity

Have ready: Numicon Shapes, Numeral Cards 2–10 (cut from photocopy master 11) spread out randomly on the tabletop

Step 1

Children choose a numeral card, say the number and find the corresponding Shape.

Step 2

They find two smaller Shapes to equal that Shape and place them on top, saying what they have done, e.g. 'The 2-shape and the 4-shape equal the 6-shape' (see **Fig. 6**).

Step 3

Children now rearrange the positions of the smaller Shapes, e.g. **Fig. 7** and say what they have done, 'The 4-shape and the 2-shape equal the 6-shape'. Talk with children about the Shapes still being equal to 6 whichever way they are added together.

Smaller steps

- Children should take as much time as needed with each step.

Further practice

- Children practise the activity often until they are confidently describing combinations of shapes to equal different totals.
- Children also repeat the activity often with rods.

Extending the activities

Connecting activities

- Give children jigsaw puzzles.
- Give children 3D cube puzzles.
- Give children pictures with something missing.
- Give children pretend food that can be put together and taken apart (with hook-and-loop fasteners).

For children moving on quickly

- Children say which numbers can be combined to make any number from 2–10 just by looking at the 'whole' Shape.
- Children may record the Shapes they have used either by drawing the Numicon Shape patterns or using a Baseboard for Drawing Numicon Shapes and Patterns (photocopy master 3).

 6   7

Practical adding: combining to find how many altogether

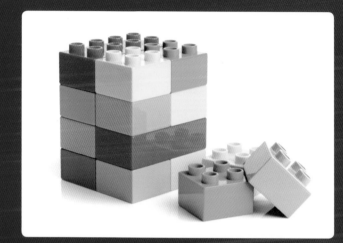

Educational context

Exploiting and creating opportunities for children to hear **mathematical language for adding** throughout the day provides an essential model which they can then be encouraged to copy. Children have met the ideas and terms 'and', 'add' and 'equals' in previous activity groups but now the focus on adding uses them together. Decide which language should be used when describing adding situations. Some children obviously benefit from concentrating on a specific term before others are introduced, whilst other children cope with hearing a range of terms in context. Unless children are well on their way to having fluent recall of the number names for the Numicon Shapes and Numicon Shape patterns they will have difficulty saying (or signing) the mathematical language for the adding sentences.

When children combine the Shapes or Numicon Shape patterns they need to be able to identify the larger Numicon Shape or Numicon Shape pattern made ('the whole') without counting the holes in the Numicon Shapes or the objects used to make the Numicon Shape pattern. Initially they can find the larger Numicon Shape, place it over the combined Numicon Shapes and say the answer (finding the whole of the combined parts) but they should be encouraged to try to answer from just looking at the larger pattern of the combined Shapes and then finding the larger Shape to check. This helps them gain confidence and make progress in using the **imagery for larger and smaller numbers**.

Many children will need to repeat Activity 4, Step 5 and the activities in the 'Further practice' section frequently and for some children this may be over a long period of time.

By this stage of the teaching programme, children have had much practice in manipulating the Numicon Shapes. However, for some, rotating the 'odd' Shapes may still be very challenging. These children may benefit from an introduction to adding using combinations of 'even' Shapes.

If children have fluent recall of the number names for number rods they can use them alongside the Shapes. Otherwise work on the number rod activities from Calculating 1 where children use number rods in adding situations whilst continuing to attach the number names.

Although the term 'total' has been used in the activities it is not being suggested that children should use this term immediately. Once children are confident with speaking an adding sentence, adults should then decide when to introduce this term to them.

In this activity group only use combined Numicon Shapes with a total of 10 or less.

Aims

- To experience situations when it is useful to add
- To relate adding to combining and to use the language of adding
- To know that adding is used to answer 'How many altogether?'
- To add whole numbers without counting, using Numicon Shapes
- To begin to generalize, starting to use number words as nouns, not just as adjectives, and recall some adding facts
- To begin to understand that adding can be done in any order

Communicating

Imagery
Numicon Display Number Line, Numicon 0–41 Number Rod Number Line

Equipment
See the individual 'have ready' for each activity, various items for the activities in the 'Extending the activities' section.

Words and terms for instruction (supported with signs and symbols)
build, find, remember, think, look closely, talk about, same way, different way

Mathematical words and terms (supported with signs and symbols)
add, and, makes, equals, altogether, together, same number, same as, larger Shape, larger amount, adding, adding sentence, adding story

Assessment

Individual Record of Progress: Calculating 1, 2, 3, 4, 6, 8, 10

Putting the activities into context

Very simple contexts have been used to illustrate how to encourage children in their understanding of the activity but adapt these to suit the interests and ability of the children you are working with. Initially keep contexts very simple and direct as in Activity 1, then gradually introduce questions, e.g. 'There are six children in our group. We need to find out if we have enough pieces of fruit for everyone in the group. There are two apples and four oranges in the fruit bowl. How shall we find out?'

Calculating

The activities

Activity 1: Exploring adding opportunities throughout the day

Have ready: Numicon Shapes

Step 1

Use practical opportunities within the day to involve children in adding situations and questions, e.g. 'There are two apples and three oranges in the fruit bowl. How many pieces of fruit are there altogether?'

Step 2

Explain that it is possible to use Numicon Shape patterns to find answers to adding questions to save counting in ones. Arrange the apples into the Numicon 2-pattern and the oranges into the Numicon 3-pattern. Combine them to form the Numicon 5-pattern and talk about how the two Numicon Shape patterns together have formed a larger Numicon Shape pattern and a larger number, that is, 5 (see **Fig. 1**).

Step 3

Model the adding sentence, e.g. 'Two apples and (add) three apples equals (makes) five apples altogether', and encourage children to join in.

Step 4

Whilst pointing to the apples, model the adding sentence, 'two and (add) three equals (makes) five'.

Further practice

- Children continue to use practical opportunities every day, whenever possible, even when they have understood, as it will increase confidence and support them in becoming fluent with adding facts.

Activity 2: Introducing Numicon Shapes and number rods when adding

Have ready: Numicon Shapes, number rods

Step 1

Choose a scenario where it is not sensible (or possible) to move objects; e.g. tables. Explain that it is possible to use Shapes to find answers to adding questions to save counting in ones. Find the corresponding Shapes for the amounts to be added, referring to the items they are representing, e.g. for 2 circular tables and 5 rectangular tables, find a 2-shape and a 5-shape and ask children to combine them.

Step 2

Children find and match the larger Shape, that is, the 7-shape that fits over the combined Shapes and say 'how many altogether' (see **Fig. 2**). Again, talk about how the two smaller Shapes have been combined to form a larger Shape and a larger number, that is, 7.

Step 3

Together with children, reinforce the language, e.g. 'A 2-shape and a 5-shape equal a 7-shape', so 'two tables and five tables equal seven tables altogether'.

Smaller steps

- With children, find the corresponding Shapes for an adding situation. Model the activity and the mathematical language: take the 2-shape and 4-shape and say, 'We can find out how many these Shapes make altogether by putting them together'. Combine the Shapes whilst modelling the mathematical language, 'I am putting the 2-shape and 4-shape together to make ... ?' Ask children to look at the combined Shapes and find the larger Shape that shows how many altogether. Repeat, 'The 2-shape and the 4-shape together make the 6-shape'. Refer to the adding situation and agree that two objects and four objects together make six objects.

Further practice

- Children repeat with rods (see **Fig. 3**).
- Repeat Activity 2 often with different combinations of numbers, giving children opportunities to find Shapes to solve adding problems.

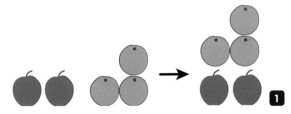

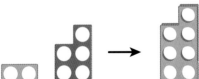

2

Activity 3: Finding how many altogether

Have ready: Numicon Shapes, number rods, small-world figures, toys, other 'real objects' (e.g. buttons, bottle tops, pens)

Step 1

Explain to children that you are going to tell them a number story but it is different from other stories because it has a question. Tell children an adding story using an appropriate context, e.g. model ducks on a paper 'pond'. Ask, 'If there are four ducks on this pond and two ducks beside the pond, how could we find out how many ducks there are altogether?' (see Fig. 4).

Step 2

Agree that the two amounts need to be combined and arrange the two groups into the Numicon 4- and 2-patterns. Combine them to make the Numicon 6-pattern. Say clearly, 'four ducks add (and) two ducks equals (makes) six ducks' (see Fig. 5).

Step 3

Find Shapes to represent four ducks and two ducks and the Shape showing the total and say clearly, 'A 4-shape add (and) a 2-shape makes (equals) a 6-shape' or 'four add (and) two makes (equals) six' (see Fig. 6).

Step 4

Repeat using the same context but different numbers.

Smaller steps

- Work with even amounts first, then either add an odd pattern of objects above an even pattern of objects or try two odd amounts.

Further practice

- Make up other adding stories for children to illustrate with props and Shapes or rods. Children say the adding sentences.

Activity 4: Creating adding stories with Numicon Shapes or number rods and generalizing adding facts

Have ready: Numicon Shapes, number rods, props for illustrating adding stories

Step 1

Model an adding story using Shapes, e.g. holding the 6-shape and 3-shape say, 'In the fruit bowl there are six apples and three pears. How many pieces of fruit are there altogether?'

Step 2

Children combine the Shapes and find the Shape showing the total.

Step 3

Children say the adding sentence, 'A 6-shape add (and) a 3-shape equals (makes) a 9-shape, so six apples add (and) three pears equals (makes) nine pieces of fruit'. Some may say, 'Six add (and) three equals (makes) nine'.

Step 4

Keeping the same Shapes, children decide what other things they could represent (it could be anything and usually children are keen to choose their own 'things' but occasionally it is helpful to provide a 'props' bag where children can choose an item and make up a story about that item). Children say the adding sentences for the different objects.

Step 5

Repeat with other objects to help children generalize, and say that whenever this pair of numbers is added together, (that adding 6 of anything and 3 of anything) they always equal 9 things. Some may be able to generalize further and use the number words as nouns, e.g. 'six add (and) three equals (makes) nine'.

Step 6

Repeat with rods.

4

5

6

Calculating

2

Smaller steps

- Show children, e.g. a toy car. Let them choose two Shapes from 1–5, add them together and say an adding story about cars. Gradually introduce the mathematical words and terms for the adding sentence.

Further practice

- Children repeat on other occasions for other number pairs until they are confident.

- Using two sets of Shapes or rods 1–5, children choose two Shapes or rods, decide on the context and say their own adding story. (Use props as prompts if children find it hard to decide on a context.) They combine the Shapes or rods, find the larger Shape or rod that shows the total and say the answer to the adding story. Encourage children to say the answer from the combined Shapes or rods and then find the Shape or rod that shows the total to check.

- Put two sets of Shapes or rods 1–5 in a Numicon Feely Bag. Children take out two Shapes or rods, combine them, say the total and find the Shape or rod showing the total to check. They say the adding sentence.

Extending the activities

Connecting activities

- Draw children's attention to adding opportunities, and 'organize' some, e.g. put out 3 chairs at one table and 4 chairs at another table and ask children to find out how many children can work at the activities. Remind children that instead of counting to find 'how many altogether' they can find the Shapes or rods and put them together.

For children moving on quickly

- Show children different combinations of Shapes or rods and ask them to say the adding sentence, including the total (because they can see the larger Numicon Shape pattern when both Shapes are combined), e.g. show a 3-shape and a 5-shape, they say 'three add five equals (makes) eight' and find the Shape to check.

- Children choose two Shapes or rods totalling 10 or less, decide on the context and say their own adding story. They combine the Shapes or rods and complete the story with the answer. Check by finding the Shape or rod that shows the total and place it over the combined Shapes or rods.

- Children could record their stories in words and pictures, including drawing the Shapes. Children can use the Baseboard for Drawing Numicon Shapes and Patterns (photocopy master 3) to help with drawing the Shapes.

Practical adding: adding more

Educational context

In this activity group the increase structure of adding is introduced, so continue to exploit and create opportunities for children to hear mathematical language for adding throughout the day, particularly choosing an emphasis on **the increase structure of adding where 'more' are needed**. Some children may need to include the word 'more' in their adding sentence until they are able to generalize and use the number words as nouns.

As in the previous activity group, unless children are well on their way to having fluent recall of the number names for Numicon Shapes and Numicon Shape patterns they will have difficulty saying (or signing) the mathematical language for the adding sentences.

Children will also have the opportunity to focus on the pattern of 'adding one more' to each number from 1–9 in practical situations. Through these opportunities and through conversations and questioning, some children may show that they are able to generalize about 'one more' within their whole number range but for most children this work is likely to need much repetition over a long period of time.

By now, when children add Numicon Shapes or Numicon Shape patterns to show more being added they should be able to identify the larger Numicon Shape or Numicon Shape pattern made ('the whole') without counting the holes in the Numicon Shapes or the objects used to make the Numicon Shape pattern. Obviously they can still find the larger Numicon Shape, place it over the combined Numicon Shapes and say the answer (finding the 'whole' of the 'combined parts') but it is important that they are encouraged to try to answer from just looking at the larger pattern of the combined Numicon Shapes and then finding the larger Numicon Shape to check. This helps them gain confidence and make progress in using the imagery.

If children have fluent recall of the number names for number rods they can use them alongside the Numicon Shapes. If not, children should work on activities building the 'staircase' patterns (as suggested in the 'Connecting activities'

section) where they will have opportunities to connect their knowledge of the order of number names to the order of the staircase pattern. Children should also continue to work on Calculating 1 where they are using number rods in more introductory adding situations.

In this activity group only use combined Numicon Shapes with a total of 10 or less.

Aims

- To introduce the increase structure of adding
- To find 1 more than a number from 1–9
- To add whole numbers without counting, using Numicon Shapes
- To begin to generalize, starting to use number words as nouns, not just as adjectives

Communicating

Imagery
Numicon Display Number Line, Numicon 0–41 Number Rod Number Line

Equipment
See the individual 'have ready' for each activity, various items for the activities in the 'Extending the activities' section.

Words and terms for instruction (supported with signs and symbols)
build, find, talk about, explain, put together, combine

Mathematical words and terms (supported with signs and symbols)
add, and, more, makes, equals, altogether, together, same number, same as, larger Shape, larger amount, adding, adding sentence, adding story

Assessment

Individual Record of Progress: Calculating 7, 9, 11, 12

Putting the activities into context

Very simple contexts have been used to illustrate how to encourage children in their understanding of the activity but adapt these to suit the interests and ability of the children you are working with. It can sometimes be quite challenging for children to devise adding stories using this structure of adding so children may need plenty of modelling and prompting. When adding 1 more, use rhymes familiar to children or stories where one more character is added each time.

Calculating

The activities

Activity 1: Exploring 'adding more' opportunities throughout the day and using Numicon Shapes or number rods

Have ready: Numicon Shapes, number rods

Step 1
Use practical opportunities throughout the day to involve children in adding situations and questions where more are added, e.g. ask, 'Four pencils were in the pot then two more were put in. How many pencils were in the pot altogether?'

Step 2
Find the 4-shape and then add the 2-shape to it, referring to the pencils they are representing, and ask children to say the total.

Step 3
Children find the larger Shape that fits over the combined Shapes to check.

Step 4
Talk about the increase and reinforce the language, e.g. 'A 4-shape and a 2-shape equals a 6-shape, so four pencils and two more pencils equals six pencils altogether'.

Step 5
Repeat with rods.

Smaller steps
- 'Organize' opportunities using appropriate 'props' and amounts that are suitable for children you are working with.

Further practice
- Children continue to use practical opportunities every day illustrating them with Shapes or rods. Even when they have understood, it will increase confidence and support them in becoming fluent with adding facts.

Have ready: Numicon Shapes 1–7 in a Numicon Feely Bag, Numicon 1-, 2- and 3-shapes in a basket, number rods

- Children choose a Shape from the Feely Bag and begin the adding sentence. They then take a Shape from the basket and join it to the first Shape saying the whole 'adding more' sentence. Repeat with rods.

- If children are still finding rotating the 'odd' Shapes challenging place just the 2-, 4- and 6-shapes in the Numicon Feely Bag.

Activity 2: Adding more using Numicon Shape patterns

Have ready: small-world props or other props suitable for children's interest and ability

Step 1
Explain to children that Numicon Shape patterns can help to find answers to adding more questions to save counting in ones. Model an adding story where 'more' are added using props, e.g. use 'play figures' and arrange them into the Numicon 4-pattern saying, 'Four children were going to do a cooking activity then two more asked if they could join in. How many children were now going to cook?'

Step 2
Add 2 more figures to the Numicon 4-pattern and ask children what pattern has been made. They should identify the 6-pattern by looking at the arrangement of the play people without counting them. Talk about the increase and the larger Numicon Shape pattern and larger number, that is, 6.

Step 3
After children have said the whole number sentence, reinforce the language. Some children may need to include the word 'more' in their adding sentence until they are able to generalize and use the number words as nouns.

Smaller steps
- Continue to use signing and, if appropriate, display the number sentence using the words cut from photocopy master 26b and numeral cards cut from photocopy master 11.

- Retain the Numicon 4-pattern for the initial number but change the amount of increase each time.

Further practice
- Give children further scenarios using props where more is added. Change the amount in the starting group and the amount of increase.

- Children make up their own 'increase' stories, illustrating with small-world equipment or real things.

- Play a 'game' with children: Ask them to build a Numicon 2-pattern with Numicon Coloured Pegs. Then ask them to add 3 more and say what the total is by looking at the Peg pattern and not counting in ones. Then ask them to add 1 more and again say the total. The aim is not to begin with, or reach, any particular number but to add more using the structure of the Numicon Shape patterns (not by adding 1 at a time).

3

Activity 3: 'Adding more' stories with Numicon Shapes/number rods and generalizing adding facts

Have ready: Numicon Shapes, number rods, props for illustrating adding stories

Step 1

Model an adding story using Shapes. Hold, e.g. a 6-shape say, 'There were six apple juice drinks in the tray but three more were needed.' Add a 3-shape to the 6-shape. Ask, 'How many drinks were needed altogether?'

Step 2

Children look at the Shapes, say the total and check by finding the Shape showing the total (see **Fig. 1**).

Step 3

Children say the whole adding sentence; e.g. 'A 6-shape add (and) a 3-shape equals (makes) a 9-shape, so six drinks add (and) three more drinks equals (makes) nine drinks'. Some may say, 'six add (and) three equals (makes) nine'.

Step 4

Keeping the same Shapes, children decide what other things they could represent (it could be anything and usually children are keen to choose their own 'things' but occasionally it is helpful to provide a 'props' bag where children can choose an item and make up a story about it). Children say the adding sentences for the different objects.

Step 5

Repeat with other objects to help children generalize and say that whenever 3 more are added to 6 they always make 9 things. Some may be able to generalize further and use the number words as nouns, e.g. 'Six add (and) three equals (makes) nine'. Some may also notice the connection with the combining structure of adding that whether you are adding 6 and 3 more or combining 6 and 3 they always make 9.

Step 6

Repeat with rods.

Smaller steps

- Show children, e.g. an orange. Let them choose a 2- or 4-shape and start their story; e.g. 'There were four oranges in the bowl ... '. They then choose from Shapes 1–5, add, e.g. a 3-shape to a 4-shape, saying, ' ... and three more makes seven oranges'. Gradually introduce the mathematical words and terms for the adding sentence.

Further practice

- Children repeat on other occasions for other number pairs until they are confident.

Have ready: Numicon Shapes, Numicon Spinner with Numeral Overlay 1–5 (cut from photocopy master 20), number rods, props to help with story contexts

- Children decide on the context for their adding story. They spin the Spinner, find the Shape and begin the adding story, e.g. 'I had four marbles in my bag ... '. They then spin again and find the corresponding Shape and continue their story, ' ... and I won three more'. They add the 3-shape to the 4-shape and say their total. They find the Shape to check. Repeat with rods.

Activity 4: Adding 1 more

Have ready: Numicon Shapes, 0–10 from the Numicon 0–100 Numeral Cards, an extra 1-shape, number rods, an extra 1-rod

Step 1

Order the Shapes 1–10 and label with Numeral Cards. Take an extra 1-shape and put it beside the 1-shape in the ordered row so that it looks like the 2-shape.

Step 2

Point to the two 1-shapes and ask children to say what has been made. Model the mathematical language by saying, 'Yes, 1 more than 1 is 2' or '1 and 1 more is 2.'

Step 3

Continue to add an extra 1-shape to each Shape in the ordered row in turn, each time asking what has been made (see **Fig. 2**). Continue to model and encourage children to use the correct language.

Step 4

Repeat with rods.

Smaller steps

- If children have difficulty with the language use visual prompts, including signing and displaying the number sentence using word cards cut from photocopy master 26b and numeral cards cut from photocopy master 11.

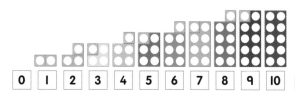

Calculating

3

Further practice

Have ready: Numicon Shapes, Numeral Cards 1–9 (cut from photocopy master 11), Numicon Spinners with Numeral Overlays 1–5 and 6–10 cut from photocopy master 20), number rods

- Children order the Shapes and label with numeral cards. They spin a number and point to the corresponding Shape. They then say what '1 more' will be and point to the equivalent Shape and numeral card. Some children will need to continue to add the extra 1-shape for some time before they can do this just by looking (see **Fig. 3**).

Have ready: Numicon Shapes, Numicon Feely Bag, number rods

- Children take a Shape out of a Feely Bag containing Shapes 1–9. They say the '1 more' adding sentence, e.g. for the 8-shape 'eight add one more equals nine.' Some children may also need to show it with shapes.

Have ready: Numicon Shapes, Numeral Cards 1–9 (cut from photocopy master 11), number rods

- Children turn a numeral card from a pile of shuffled and face down cards 1–9 and say the '1 more' adding sentence. Repeat the three further practice activities above with rods.

Extending the activities

Connecting activities

- If it is not appropriate for children to work on Activity 4 with rods, continue to build staircases with the rods and talk about increasing size. Introduce numeral cards as appropriate. Continue to use the Number Rod Trays 1–10 (see **Fig. 4 & 5**).

- Continue to use the word 'more' in many contexts, e.g. 'We need one more biscuit', 'Please get one more paintbrush', 'Would you like one more turn?'

For children moving on quickly

- Ask children to explain what happens when you 'add one' to any number.
- Ask children to give 'one more' answers when looking only at the numerals.
- Ask children to 'add one' to any number within their counting range.

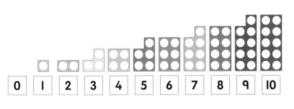

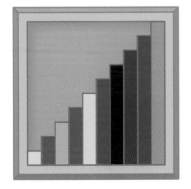
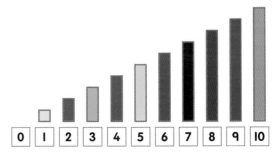

Practical subtracting: take away

Educational context

Exploiting and creating opportunities for children to hear **mathematical language for subtracting** throughout the day provides an essential model that they can then be encouraged to copy. Children will have experienced in some form the idea of loss and things being taken away so the term 'take away' and the idea of 'what is left' should not be unfamiliar; however, the terms 'subtract' and 'minus' probably will be and it will need to be decided when best to introduce these terms for children you are working with. Some children obviously benefit from concentrating on a specific term before others are introduced, whilst others can cope with hearing a range of terms in context. Children should be familiar with the term 'equals' from earlier activities even if they need to extend their understanding.

The 'take away' structure of subtracting is introduced first for which children may either cover the holes of Numicon Shapes with their fingers or use the Subtracting Covers (cut from photocopy master 24). When using their fingers, encourage children to cover the Numicon Shape pattern for the number being subtracted from either the top or the bottom of the Numicon Shape rather than a random pattern of holes. If using the Subtracting Covers (or later when finding the difference), encourage children to match up the 'sticking-up bits' or the 'straight edges' to reveal the Numicon Shape pattern that is left. **Remind children that instead of counting 'to find how many are left', they can look and see the Numicon Shape pattern of holes that is left**.

It is important for children to be able to illustrate taking away with the Numicon Shapes (or number rods) and to be able to say clearly the corresponding number sentence without omitting any words (initially many children omit the first number, e.g. when holding the 7-shape and showing 7 take away 4, they may say, 'take away four leaves three'). Being encouraged to refer to the Numicon Shapes can help, e.g. 'the 7-shape take away the 4-shape equals the 3-shape'.

When taking away with number rods it is helpful if children find the number rod showing the amount to be taken away. Once it has been placed alongside the starting number rod,

they cover it with their hand to illustrate the loss. They can then see the length of number rod left showing the amount remaining and can find the corresponding number rod to check. We would strongly recommend that until children are secure using number rods in adding situations they do not attempt the number rod work for subtracting.

In this activity group children will only be subtracting from 10 or below.

Aims

- To recognize situations when it is useful to subtract
- To be able to say a take away number story and illustrate it with 'objects' and structured apparatus
- To understand subtracting as take away
- To take away whole numbers, without counting, using Numicon Shapes
- To begin to generalize, starting to use number words as nouns, not just as adjectives and begin recall of subtracting facts.

Communicating

Imagery
Numicon Display Number Line, Numicon 0–41 Number Rod Number Line

Equipment
See the individual 'have ready' for each activity, various items for the activities in the 'Extending the activities' section.

Words and terms for instruction (supported with signs and symbols)
build, find, talk about, look carefully, explain, check

Mathematical words and terms (supported with signs and symbols)
take away, subtract, minus, compare, smaller amount, smaller Shape, leaves, equals, how many left?, subtracting, subtracting story, subtracting number sentence

Assessment

Individual Record of Progress: Calculating 29, 30, 33, 38, 39

Putting the activities into context

Very simple contexts have been used to illustrate how to encourage children in their understanding of the activity but adapt these to suit the interests and ability of the children you are working with.

Calculating

The activities

Activity 1: Exploring subtracting opportunities throughout the day

Have ready: Numicon Shapes

Step 1

Use practical opportunities throughout the day to involve children in subtracting situations and questions, e.g. 'There are six pieces of fruit in the bowl. Two children would like a piece each. How many pieces will be left?'

Step 2

Explain that it is possible to use Numicon Shape patterns to find answers to subtracting questions to save lots of counting in ones. Arrange the pieces of fruit into the Numicon 6-shape and then take away two pieces (in the pattern of the 2-shape) (see **Fig. 1**). Identify the Numicon Shape pattern left and talk about it being smaller because some have been taken away. Say the subtracting sentence and encourage children to join in.

Smaller steps

- Organize simple subtracting opportunities that can be modelled and where children can join in.

Further practice

- Draw children's attention to subtracting opportunities and organize some, e.g. put out six chairs at a table, explain that two are needed at another table and ask children how many will be left.

Activity 2: Taking away

Have ready: Numicon Shapes, small-world figures, toys, other objects such as pens and books

Step 1

Remind children about number stories that have a question and tell them a subtracting story, e.g. 'If there were ten children playing football, then four had to go home for dinner, how could we find out how many were left playing football?'

Step 2

Agree they need to arrange the figures into the Numicon Shape pattern for 10 and then take away 4 of the figures, not randomly, but in the Numicon 4-pattern arrangement (see **Fig. 2**). Children look at the pattern of figures left and say the amount without counting in ones.

Step 3

Say the subtracting sentence, 'ten footballers take away four footballers equals six footballers' or 'ten take away four equals six'. Talk about the amount left being smaller than the starting amount when you take something away; that is, there were fewer left playing football than when the game started.

Step 4

Repeat using the same context but with different numbers.

Smaller steps

- Children work with even amounts first, then subtract an odd pattern of objects from an odd pattern of objects.

Further practice

- Make up other subtracting stories for children to illustrate with props and say the subtracting sentence.
- Children make up their own subtracting stories, illustrate with props and say the whole subtracting number sentence.

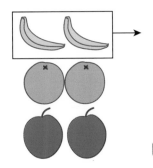

1

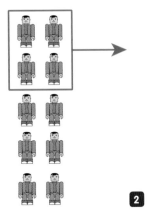

2

4

Activity 3: Introducing subtracting covers

Have ready: Numicon Shapes, Numeral Cards 0–10 (cut from photocopy master 11), Subtracting Covers 1–5 and 6–10 (cut from photocopy master 24)

Step 1

Children order Shapes 1–10 and label them with numeral cards.

Step 2

Show children the subtracting covers and, one at a time, place them over the corresponding Shapes.

Step 3

Play a 'game': say a number and children find the corresponding subtracting cover and remove it, e.g. **Fig. 3**. Continue until all subtracting covers have been removed.

Step 4

Ask children to place the subtracting cover for the 4-shape over the 6-Shape. Decide whether they place it from the top or the bottom of the 6-shape. Talk about and identify the Numicon Shape pattern of holes they can still see. Children find the 2-shape to check (see **Fig. 4**).

Step 5

Children now place the subtracting cover for the 3-shape over the 7-shape. Some may need help to align the 'sticking up pieces'. Again, talk about and identify the Numicon Shape pattern of holes that is left and that they can still see, and find the Shape to check (see **Fig. 5**).

Step 6

When subtracting an even from an odd Shape or Numicon Shape pattern children will need to align both straight edges of the Shapes and subtracting covers so the remaining 'sticking up bit' and Numicon Shape pattern is clearly seen (see **Fig. 6**).

Step 7

When subtracting an odd from an even Shape or Numicon Shape pattern children will need to align both straight edges of the Shapes and subtracting covers. This is probably best done from the top (so the subtracting cover is upside down) so the remaining Numicon Shape pattern is clearly seen (see **Fig. 7**).

Smaller steps

- Children use the 'even' subtracting covers with 'even' Shapes first, then 'odd' subtracting covers with 'odd' Shapes.

Further practice

- Show children different subtracting covers for them to identify with the number name.
- Shuffle numeral cards 1–10 and place them face down in a pile. Children turn over a numeral card and find the corresponding subtracting cover.

Activity 4: Using subtracting covers when taking away using Numicon Shapes

Have ready: Numicon Shapes, Subtracting Covers 1–5 and 6–10 (cut from photocopy master 24), props for illustrating subtracting stories

Step 1

Choose a scenario where it is either impractical or not possible to move the objects and tell children a take away subtracting story. Explain that it is possible to use Shapes to find answers to subtracting questions, e.g. 'There were five school buses waiting to take children home at the end of the day. Three buses were full and drove off. How many were left?' Find a 5-shape for the starting amount.

Step 2

Agree that 3 need to be taken away from the 5 so find the 3-shape subtracting cover and place it over the 5-shape. Children look at the pattern of holes left, and say the answer 'two', without counting the holes (see **Fig. 8**). Agree that there were 2 buses left. Check by finding the Shape and talk about it being a smaller amount left.

Step 3

After children have said the whole number sentence, reinforce the language for subtracting, e.g. 'A 5-shape take away a 3-shape equals a 2-shape, so five take away three equals (leaves) two'.

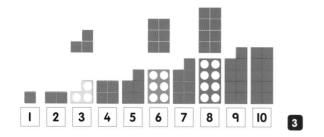

| 1 | 2 | 3 | 4 | 5 | 6 | 7 | 8 | 9 | 10 |

3

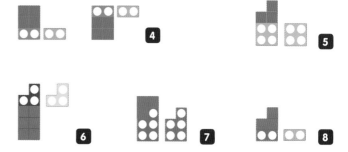

4 **5** **6** **7** **8**

Calculating

4

Step 4

Keeping the same Shapes, children decide what other things they could represent (it could be anything and usually children are keen to choose their own 'things' but occasionally it is helpful to provide a 'props' bag where children can choose an item and make up a story about that item). Children say the take away sentences for the different objects.

Step 5

Repeat with other objects to help children generalize and say that whenever this pair of numbers is subtracted, (taking away 3 of anything from 5 of anything) they always equal 2 things (or always leave 2 things). Some may be able to generalize further and use the number words as nouns, e.g. 'five take away three equals (leaves) two.'

Smaller steps

- Children begin with the even Shapes and even subtracting covers.

Further practice

- Children repeat the activity on other occasions for other number pairs until they are saying the full subtracting sentence confidently and automatically without being reminded and recalling some subtracting facts.

Have ready: Numicon Shapes, paper, crayons, scissors

- Children choose a Shape, draw round it and cut it out. They decide how many to take away, cut the corresponding Numicon Shape pattern from their paper Shape and say the subtracting sentence.

Have ready: Numicon Shapes, two Numicon Spinners with Numeral Overlays 1–5 and 6–10 (cut from photocopy master 20), Subtracting Covers 1–5 and 6–10 (cut from photocopy master 24)

- Children spin a Spinner and use subtracting covers to take away the amount from a 10-shape, saying the subtracting number sentence.

Have ready: Numicon Shapes 1–9, Numicon Feely Bag, Subtracting Covers 1–5 and 6–10 (cut from photocopy master 24)

- Children feel in the Feely Bag for a Shape (1–8) and then take that amount away from a 9-shape, saying the subtracting number sentence.
- They repeat for taking Shapes 1–7 away from an 8-shape, then Shapes 1–6 from a 7-shape and so on until children have subtracted from all the Shapes.

Have ready: Numicon Shapes, props for ideas (optional)

- Children decide on a context and make up their own subtracting story whilst illustrating it using Shapes. They say the whole subtracting sentence.

Extending the activities

Connecting activities

- Draw children's attention to take away opportunities, and organize some, e.g. put out 6 chairs at a table and explain to children that you need to take 3 chairs away to use at another table; ask how many will be left. Remind children that instead of counting to find 'how many left' they can find the 6-shape or rod and take 3 away.
- Give children opportunities to practise 'taking away' with rods (by covering part of the rod to be subtracted, saying how much is left and finding the rod to check). Some children may initially need to find the rod showing how much is left before saying the number value. They say the number sentence.

For children moving on quickly

- Show children a Shape then cover some of the holes. Ask them to say the subtracting number sentence, including the answer (because they can see the Numicon Shape pattern left), e.g. show a 7-shape, then cover 5 holes; they say 'seven take away five equals (leaves) two'. Find the Shape to check.
- Children choose a Shape or rod of 10 or less, decide on the context and how many to take away, covering the holes or part of the rod as they say their own subtracting story, including the answer. They check by finding the Shape or rod that shows the answer.
- Children could record their stories in words and pictures, including drawing Shapes. Children can use the Baseboard for Drawing Numicon Shapes and Patterns (photocopy master 3) to help with drawing the Shapes.

Practical subtracting: decrease

Educational context

For the decrease structure of subtracting, as with 'take away', children may either cover the holes of the Numicon Shapes with their fingers or use the Subtracting Covers (cut from photocopy master 24). Continue to remind children that instead of counting 'to find how many are left', they can look and identify the Numicon Shape pattern of holes that is left.

When looking at the decrease structure of subtracting with number rods it is still helpful if children find the number rod showing the amount to be taken away. Once it has been placed alongside the starting number rod, they cover it with their hand to illustrate the loss. They can then see the length of number rod left, showing the amount remaining, and can find the corresponding number rod to check.

This activity group builds on Numbers and the Number System 12 where the use of the terms 'more' and 'fewer', in relation to Numicon Shape patterns, have been introduced, so **children have already met the often difficult language associated with decrease**. However, there is a dilemma around **the terms 'less' and 'fewer'**. Less should be used when comparing continuous substances, e.g. 'You have less tea in your cup than I have in mine'. Fewer should be used when comparing collections of discrete objects, e.g. 'You have fewer biscuits than I'. It will need to be decided when it is appropriate to introduce the correct vocabulary to individual children.

Aims

- To be able to illustrate a subtracting number story or rhyme with objects and structured apparatus
- To understand subtracting as decrease
- To subtract whole numbers, without counting, using Numicon Shapes
- To begin to generalize, starting to use number words as nouns, not just as adjectives

Communicating

Imagery
Numicon Display Number Line, Numicon 0–41 Rod Number Line, Numicon Large Format Table-top Number Line

Equipment
See the individual 'have ready' for each activity, various items for the activities in the 'Extending the activities' section.

Words and terms for instruction (supported with signs and symbols)
build, find, work out, remember, think, talk about, explain

Mathematical words and terms (supported with signs and symbols)
fewer, less, compare, smaller amount, smaller Shape, leaves, equals, how many left?, one fewer, one less, subtracting, subtracting story, subtracting number sentence

Assessment

Individual Record of Progress: Calculating 37, 42

Putting the activities into context

Discuss with children the food they enjoy, particularly things that come in packets, e.g. biscuits, packs of fairy cakes or multi-packs of crisps. Sometimes the multi-packs might have 10 packs inside but sometimes they have fewer packs and there might only be 6. Perhaps the family might eat five fairy cakes but on another day they might not eat so many, maybe two fewer. For Activities 2 and 3 using a tube of sweets or bar of chocolate, where one sweet or one square of chocolate can be eaten at a time, will help illustrate the decrease structure. Some children may enjoy beginning with a rhyme or song where the numbers are decreasing one by one, e.g. 'Five Currant Buns', 'Five Little Ducks' or 'Ten Green Bottles', where the end result is none.

Calculating

The activities

Activity 1: Revising fewer

Have ready: Numicon Coloured Pegs

Step 1
Children build Numicon Shape patterns with Pegs for, e.g. 5 and 8. Ask which pattern has fewer Pegs. Agree it is the Numicon 5-pattern. (If children are unsure, repeat this Step comparing other Numicon Shape patterns or return to earlier activity groups.)

Step 2
Ask children to build the Numicon 10-pattern. Now ask them to change the pattern so it has two fewer Pegs. Encourage them to remove the 2 Pegs as the Numicon 2-pattern either from the top or bottom of the Numicon 10-pattern. Agree that the pattern of Pegs is now showing the Numicon 8-pattern. Say, 'Two fewer than ten is eight'.

Step 3
Now ask children to change the Numicon 8-pattern so it has 4 fewer Pegs (again removing them as a Numicon 4-pattern) and say, 'Four fewer than eight is four'. Finally ask them to change the Numicon 4-pattern so it has 3 fewer Pegs and say the number sentence.

Step 4
There is no significance in having 1 Peg left. When repeating this activity ensure that different amounts are left. Some children may be ready to understand that when you have, e.g. 4 fewer than 4, you have none left.

Smaller steps
- Just work on Steps 1 and 2 (possibly using the Numicon Baseboard). Start with the Numicon 6-pattern and remove 2 Pegs. Again start with the Numicon 6-pattern and remove, e.g. 4 Pegs. Continue to remove a specific number from the Numicon 6-pattern. When children are secure removing different numbers of Pegs from the Numicon 6-pattern choose another Numicon Shape pattern and repeat the activity.

Further practice
- Practise from Step 2 starting with different Numicon Shape patterns. Remove different amounts of Pegs until children are confidently using the language and are removing Pegs in different Numicon Shape patterns, not one by one.

Activity 2: One fewer, one less than

Have ready: Numicon Shapes, Numeral Cards 0–10 (cut from photocopy master 11), Subtracting Covers 1–10 (cut from photocopy master 24), number rods

Step 1
Children set out Shapes 1–10 and label them with numeral cards.

Step 2
Cover one hole of the 10-shape (using fingers or the subtracting cover for 1, see **Fig 1**) so that the Numicon 9-pattern can be seen. Ask children to say what they can see. Model the correct language by saying, 'Yes, one fewer, or less, than ten is nine'. Children can pick up the 9-shape to check.

Step 3
Continue to cover one hole of all the Shapes in turn, each time asking children to say what they can see and encouraging them to say the full number sentence.

Step 4
Repeat with rods.

Smaller steps
- Support children's understanding of the language of fewer or less by signing.
- With Shapes 1–10 in order, talk about the decreasing pattern, linking it to going down stairs.
- Work with Shapes 1–5 initially, gradually extending to 10.

Further practice
Have ready: For each child: Numicon Shapes, Numicon Feely Bag, Numeral Cards 0–10 (cut from photocopy master 11), one set of Numicon Shapes in a basket

- Children each have an ordered set of Shapes 1–10 labelled with numeral cards. One child or adult takes a Shape from the basket and hides it behind their back saying, e.g. 'I have nine, what number is one fewer, or less?' Children choose the Shape to show the answer. The caller reveals the hidden Shape and children check to see if the Shape they have chosen is one fewer, or less.
- Children take a Shape from a Feely Bag containing 1–10 Shapes. They subtract 1 from the Shape they choose and say the subtracting number sentence.

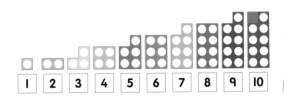

Calculating

Extending the activities

5

Activity 3: Using Numicon Coloured Pegs to show one fewer or less

Have ready: Numicon Large Format Table-top Number Line, Numicon Coloured Pegs, Numeral Cards 0–10 (cut from photocopy master 11), another set of Numeral Cards 0–10 shuffled and placed face down in a pile

Step 1

With children, arrange the Pegs into the Numicon Shape patterns 1–10 and label them using one of the sets of numeral cards. (If children have collections of small objects that are of interest to them these could be arranged into the Numicon Shape patterns and used for this activity.)

Step 2

Children turn over a card from the second set of numeral cards and point to the corresponding Numicon Shape pattern, e.g. **Fig. 2**.

Step 3

They then take one Peg away from that Numicon Shape pattern so that a remaining Numicon Shape pattern is left. They should say what is left by looking at the whole Numicon Shape pattern, without counting the Pegs one by one.

Step 4

Find both numbers on the Large Format Table-top Number Line.

Step 5

Replace the Pegs before turning over the next numeral card. Continue until all numeral cards have been turned.

Step 6

Talk with children about what happens when you remove one Peg from a number (that you always make the Numicon Shape pattern of the previous number).

Smaller steps

- Work in the range 1–5.
- Use one colour of Pegs for all the Numicon Shape patterns or use different coloured Pegs next to each other to make each Numicon Shape pattern very distinct, e.g. 1-pattern red, 2-pattern green, 3-pattern blue, 4-pattern yellow and so on.

Further practice

- Use two Numicon Spinners with Numeral Overlays 1–5 and 6–10 (photocopy master 20). Children spin and point to that number (if 1 is spun, check children understand that one less is 0). Children look at the pattern and say what one fewer or less will be before removing a Peg. Remove one Peg to check.

Connecting activities

- Order sets of rods 1–10 and talk about the decreasing pattern. Some children may benefit from ordering the rods in the Numicon 10-rod Rod Tray first.

For children moving on quickly

- Ask children to explain what happens when 1 is subtracted from any number.
- Some children may be able to subtract 1 from any number within their counting range.

2

Practical subtracting: difference

6

Educational context

This activity group builds on earlier work about 'the same' and 'different' both from the Numbers and the Number System strand and the Pattern and Algebra strand where children had the opportunity to sort objects into sets and categorize them. It also draws on the language used when comparing measures, Numicon Shapes, Numicon Shape patterns and number rods. The subtracting term 'the difference between' will need to be clearly spoken (or signed) to avoid confusion.

The idea of 'the difference between' can be difficult, although it is made clear with the Numicon Shapes and number rods, since they are particularly helpful in showing clearly **the difference between number values** in any real-life situation or word problem. When comparing the Numicon Shapes it is important (as with previous subtracting with Numicon Shapes) that the Numicon Shapes are used so the remaining Numicon Shape pattern is always revealed.

Conversations about 'the difference between', 'take away' and 'decrease' all being connected due to being subtracting terms should happen carefully and at a time appropriate for individual children.

Aims

- To recognize situations when it is useful to find 'the difference between'
- To be able to say a difference number story and illustrate it with 'objects' and structured apparatus
- To understand subtracting as difference
- To find the difference between whole numbers, without counting, using Numicon Shapes
- To begin to generalize, starting to use number words as nouns, not just as adjectives

Communicating

Imagery
Numicon Display Number Line, Numicon 0–41 Number Rod Number Line

Equipment
See the individual 'have ready' for each activity, various items for the activities in the 'Extending the activities' section.

Words and terms for instruction (supported with signs and symbols)
build, find, think, talk about, explain

Mathematical words and terms (supported with signs and symbols)
difference, the difference between, compare, smaller amount, leaves, equals, how many left?, subtracting, subtracting story, subtracting number sentence

Assessment

Individual Record of Progress: Calculating 31, 34, 40

Putting the activities into context

Remind children about how they compared their heights, lengths of different objects, and so on (and other comparisons suggested in Numbers and the Number System 3). Explain that they are now going to learn about 'the difference between' number values. Children may be familiar with the term 'minutes' and so the difference between short amounts of time can be represented with the Numicon Shapes or number rods, as can finding the difference between children's ages (or ages of siblings). Length and height are easily compared by using the number rods since there is a direct correlation. The numbers involved in length and height measurements can of course also be represented with Numicon Shapes. In this activity group 'the difference between' is shown only between numbers 1–10. Comparing amounts of discrete objects of interest to children is helpful for finding the difference. Again very simple contexts have been used to illustrate the ideas but change these according to the interests of children. Using real-life examples when finding the difference for situations involving mass and capacity can be challenging, due to the size of the numbers involved and the need to read scales or even digital displays, so at this stage children will probably still be working on making direct comparisons in these areas.

The activities

Activity 1: What is the same and what is different?

Have ready: Numicon Shapes, pairs of objects different in size, colour or design (e.g. one large and one small spoon, or toy, two hats of different design, two different number rods)

Step 1

Look at a pair of objects and talk with children about what is the same and what is different using the language of comparison.

Step 2

Hold up two Shapes, e.g. the 9-shape and the 5-shape. Discuss the similarities and differences, e.g. they both have a bit sticking up, one is bigger or smaller, one is purple or red.

Step 3

Hold up two rods, e.g. the 9-rod and the 5-rod. Discuss the similarities and differences, e.g. they are both rods, one is longer or shorter, one is blue or yellow.

Smaller steps

- Choose objects where the comparison is very obvious, e.g. a big and a small spoon, and gradually extend.
- Use signing for 'looks different' in preparation for making the distinction between things that 'look different' in the real world and 'finding the difference' in a mathematical sense.

Further practice

- Encourage children to find other objects and make comparisons between them.
- Compare other Shapes. Ask children to choose two Shapes to compare.
- Compare other rods. Ask children to choose two rods to compare.

Activity 2: Finding the difference between two collections using Numicon Shapes and number rods

Have ready: Numicon Shapes, number rods, two bags each containing different numbers (ten maximum) of the same 'collectables' (e.g. model cars, football stickers, fridge magnets or anything of interest to children)

Step 1

Show children the two bags and explain that you want to find out which bag has more. Let children suggest how to work this out then model arranging the collections into Numicon Shape patterns so children can see easily which is larger and which is smaller, e.g. **Fig. 1**.

Step 2

Explain that children are now going to find the difference between the size of the two collections. Talk with them about what is known: that one collection has, e.g. 7 objects and one has 9 objects. Remind children that the Shapes can help when finding the difference in size or the number difference and ask children to find the Shapes for those numbers.

Step 3

Place, e.g. a 7-shape on top of a 9-shape, lining up the 'odd bits' to show the remaining Numicon Shape pattern not covered. Ask children to look closely at the remaining Numicon Shape pattern and to say 'how many' without counting. They then find the 2-shape to check (see **Fig. 2**).

Step 4

Model the mathematical language, e.g. 'The difference between the 9-shape and the 7-shape is the 2-shape,' or 'The difference between the 7-shape and the 9-shape is the 2-shape'. Some children may say, 'The difference between nine and seven is two,' or 'The difference between seven and nine is two'. Refer back to the collections and agree that the difference between them is 2.

Step 5

Repeat from Step 2 using rods.

Smaller steps

- Children will need to take as much practice over time as necessary to understand this.
- Use signing to make the distinction between things that 'look different' in the real world and finding 'the difference' in a mathematical sense.

My Friend's Collection   My Collection

  1

  2

Calculating

Further practice

- Children practise the activity using different objects and different amounts to help them become confident using the language of difference. Organize opportunities for children to find the difference between different objects in each collection so they understand it is the number values they are finding the difference between.

Have ready: Numicon Shapes, two Numicon Spinners with Spinner Overlays and 1–5 and 6–10 (photocopy master 20), number rods

- Children spin both Spinners once each or spin one of them twice. They find the corresponding Shapes or rods and find the difference between them. Check and say both difference number sentences.

Have ready: Numicon Feely Bag, lots of Numicon Shapes, lots of number rods

- Children place either one set of Shapes 1–10 or one set of rods 1–10 in the Feely Bag. They feel and select two Shapes (or rods) and find the difference between them. Check and say the difference number sentence.

Activity 3: Finding the difference using Numicon Shapes and number rods

Have ready: Numicon Shapes, number rods

Step 1
Choose two Shapes, e.g. 6- and 10-shapes and, with children, decide what they will represent, e.g. the amount of PE balls in two baskets.

Step 2
Children find out the difference between the number of balls in one basket and the other. They place the 6-shape on top of the 10-shape and, looking at the Numicon Shape pattern remaining uncovered, without counting, say 'four'.

Step 3
Check by placing the 4-shape over the remaining holes (see **Fig. 3**), and agree that the difference between the number of balls in both baskets is 4 balls.

Step 4
Repeat with rods (see **Fig. 4**).

Smaller steps

- Work at a slower pace and use scenarios that will engage children.

Further practice

- Use other scenarios as they occur everyday and devise some new ones, e.g.' Zachary takes three minutes to walk to school and Pat takes seven minutes. What is the difference in the time it takes them to walk to school?' Children find Shapes or rods to illustrate the problem and find the difference between them.

- Children make up their own 'difference' stories illustrating them using Shapes and rods. Generate the numbers by taking Shapes from a Feely Bag, spinning Numicon Spinners, rolling Numicon Dice or turning over numeral cards.

Extending the activities
Connecting activities

- Children use modelling dough to make snakes or minibeasts the same length as different rods and compare them, finding the rod that shows the difference. Some children may have attached number names to the rods, which will extend the comparison to number ideas.

For children moving on quickly

- Make pictograms and block graphs and use the language of comparison and difference when comparing different sets of data and when answering questions about results shown in the graphs.

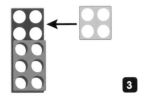

3

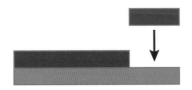

4

Practical subtracting: comparing numbers to say how many more to equal

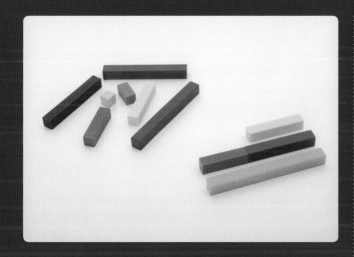

Educational context

This activity group builds on earlier work about 'more' and 'fewer' (or 'less') and 'more than' and 'fewer than' (or 'less than') and the language used when comparing measures, Numicon Shapes, Numicon Shape patterns and number rods. Ensure that children are secure with the language of 'more' and 'fewer' or 'less' and 'more than' and 'fewer than' or 'less than'. It can be very confusing that the language 'how many more to reach … ?' is subtracting, as 'more' has until now been associated with adding. Conversations about this with children will need to take place over a long period of time.

When using Numicon Shapes and number rods to show the subtracting ideas, some children may be able to make connections with 'the difference between' structure of subtracting. When comparing to find **'how many more to reach'**, the Numicon Shapes and number rods may be placed on top of each other or side by side. As in previous activity groups the number rods can be used alongside the Numicon Shapes or activities that use the Shapes can be repeated using number rods.

Aims

- To recognize situations when it is useful to find how many more, fewer or less
- To be able to say a 'how many fewer' (or 'less') or 'how many more' subtracting number story and illustrate it with 'objects' and structured apparatus
- To understand subtracting as how many more, how many fewer or less
- To find how many more, how many fewer or less, without counting, using Numicon Shapes
- To begin to generalize, starting to use number words as nouns, not just as adjectives

Communicating

Imagery
Numicon Display Number Line, Numicon 0–41 Number Rod Number Line, Numicon Large Format Table-top Number Line

Equipment
See the individual 'have ready' for each activity, various items for the activities in the 'Extending the activities' section.

Words and terms for instruction (supported with signs and symbols)
build, find, arrange, look closely, think, talk about, explain

Mathematical words and terms (supported with signs and symbols)
how many more?, how many fewer?, how many less?, the difference between, compare, smaller amount, how many left?, subtracting, subtracting story, subtracting number sentence

Assessment

Individual Record of Progress: Calculating 32, 35, 36, 41, 43

Putting the activities into context

Talk with children about collections of things they may have. If two friends are collecting the same things, they talk about who has more, or fewer, and often how many more one of them has to collect to have the same amount in their collection as their friend. Other situations involve collecting a specific number of things, e.g. children may be collecting mini figures. There are 10 in the complete set and they may have collected 6 so far. They want to know how many more they have to collect to complete the set.

Calculating

The activities

Activity 1: How many fewer (or how much less)?

Have ready: Numicon Shapes, Numicon Large Format Table-top Number Line, number rods, two bags each containing different numbers (ten maximum) of the same 'collectables' (e.g. model cars, football stickers, fridge magnets or anything of interest to the child)

Step 1
Children arrange the two collections of the same objects into Numicon Shape patterns and say which has fewer.

Step 2
Explain to children that they are going to find out how many fewer objects one collection has than the other and that the Shapes can help. Ask them to find Shapes to show how many there are in each collection.

Step 3
Place, e.g. the 6-shape on top of the 8-shape. Children look closely to see the Numicon Shape pattern of holes left uncovered and say, 'two' and then find the 2-shape to check.

Step 4
Model the language, 'The collection of six is two fewer than the collection of eight', and 'Six is two fewer (or less) than eight'.

Step 5
Find both numbers on the Large Format Table-top Number Line.

Step 6
Repeat with rods.

Smaller steps
- Support children's understanding of the language needed with signing. The Shapes do help to make the comparisons clear but children will need to take as much time as necessary to practise using the correct language.

Further practice
- Children practise the activity using different objects and different amounts to help them become confident in finding out how many fewer there are and using the language of fewer.

Have ready: Numicon Shapes, two Numicon Spinners and 1–5 and 6–10 Shape Overlays (cut from photocopy master 20), number rods
- Children spin both Spinners once each or spin one of them twice. They find the corresponding Shapes or rods and compare them to find out how many fewer holes one number has than the other. Check and say the number sentence.

Have ready: Numicon Shapes, Numicon Feely Bag, number rods
- Children place either one set of Shapes 1–10 or one set of rods 1–10 in the Feely Bag. They feel and select two Shapes (or rods) and find how many fewer holes one has than the other. Check and say the number sentence.

Activity 2: How many more?

Have ready: Numicon Shapes, Numicon Large Format Table-top Number Line, number rods, two bags each containing different numbers (ten maximum) of the same 'collectables' (e.g. model cars, football stickers, fridge magnets or anything of interest to the child)

Step 1
Children arrange the two collections of the same objects into Numicon Shape patterns and say which has more objects.

Step 2
Explain to children that they are going to find out how many more there are in one collection than the other and that the Shapes can help. Ask them to find Shapes to show how many are in each collection.

Step 3
Place, e.g. the 5-shape on top of the 9-shape. Children look closely to see the Numicon Shape pattern of holes left uncovered and say 'four' and then find the 4-shape to check.

Step 4
Model the language, 'The Shapes show the collection with nine has four more objects than the collection with five, so we can see that nine is four more than five'.

Step 5
Find both numbers on the Large Format Table-top Number Line.

Step 6
Repeat with rods.

Smaller steps
- Support children's understanding of the language needed with signing. The Shapes do help to make the comparisons clear but children will need to take as much time as necessary to practise using the correct language.

Further practice
- Children practise the activity using different objects and different amounts to help them become confident in finding out how many more and using the language of how many more.

Calculating

7

Activity 3: How many more, how many fewer?

Have ready: Numicon Shapes, Numicon Large Format Table-top Number Line, number rods, two bags each containing different numbers (ten maximum) of different 'collectables' (e.g. model cars, football stickers, fridge magnets or anything of interest to the child)

Step 1
Children arrange two collections each of different objects into Numicon Shape patterns and say which has more and which has fewer, e.g. **Fig. 1**.

Step 2
Explain to children that they are still going to find out how many more objects in one collection than the other and how many fewer objects in one collection than the other even though the collections are using different objects. Children find the Shapes as before to show how many there are in each collection, place one Shape on top of the other and then find the Shape that shows how many more and how many fewer, e.g. **Fig. 2**.

Step 3
Model the language, e.g. 'There are three fewer apples than oranges, so there are three more oranges than apples.'

Step 4
Find both numbers on the Number Line and model the language, 'Six is three fewer than nine' or 'Nine is three more than six', encouraging children to notice the gap between the numbers.

Step 5
Repeat with rods.

Further practice
- Fold the Large Format Table-top Number Line so only 1–10 is showing. Children point to two numbers. They find the Shapes for those numbers and compare them to find out how many more and how much less one number is than the other.

Activity 4: How many more to reach ... ?

Have ready: Numicon Shapes, Numicon Large Format Table-top Number Line, number rods, a bag containing a collection (ten maximum) of different 'collectables' (e.g. model cars, football stickers, fridge magnets or anything of interest to the child)

Step 1
Children arrange the collection into the Numicon Shape pattern and say the number. Talk with children about their collection and how many there are in the complete set, e.g. they have 7 but the complete set is 10.

Step 2
Find the two Shapes that correspond, e.g. 7-shape to represent their collection and 10-shape showing how many in the set. Ask children how many more would be needed to make the collection complete, that is, to reach 10.

Step 3
Children place the 7-shape on top of the 10-shape, or place them side by side, and look closely at the Numicon Shape pattern of holes left, agreeing that it shows how many more are needed. They say how many without counting and then find the Shape to check.

Step 4
Model the language, e.g. 'If I have seven, I need three more to equal ten (or to reach ten)', relating it to their collection.

Step 5
Find both numbers on the Large-Format Table-top Number Line.

Step 6
Repeat with rods.

Smaller steps
- Take as much time as needed to work through the steps.

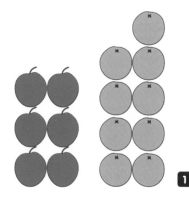

1

2

Calculating

7

Further practice

Have ready: a set of Numicon Shapes 1–10 placed in a random order, e.g Fig. 3, a second set in a pile

- Children look at the first Shape, e.g. the 8-shape. Ask, 'How many more to reach ten?' Children find the Shape that goes with the 8-shape to equal the 10-shape (compare with the 10-shape if necessary), that is, the 2-shape, and say 'eight and two more equal ten' or 'it's two more to reach ten from eight', see Fig. 4. Repeat for each Shape.

Have ready: Numicon Number Rod Trays 1–10, number rods

- Children choose a Rod Tray and build a staircase pattern beginning with the 1-rod, e.g. Fig. 5. They then jumble the rods up and find each rod to fill the gaps, e.g. Fig. 6. Each time they say the number sentence for how many more to fill the gap.

Extending the activities

Connecting activities

- Compare towers built with interlocking cubes (up to ten cubes).
- Make pictograms and block graphs and use the language of comparison and difference when comparing different sets of data and when answering questions about results shown in the graphs.

For children moving on quickly

- Roll two Numicon 0–5 and 5–10 Dice and say how many more and how many fewer one number is than the other by just looking at the Shapes, instead of physically comparing them.

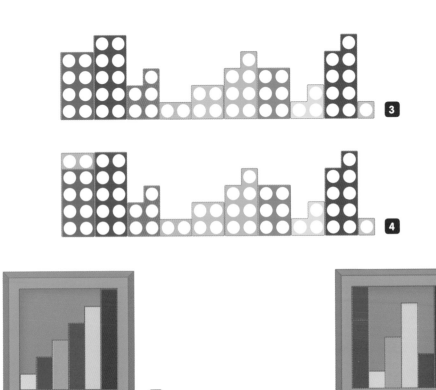

Introducing the '+' symbol

8

Educational context

In this activity group children are introduced to the idea that **a symbol can be used instead of words to tell us something**. To help children understand that symbols tell us something it is suggested that children go for a walk to look for symbols in the environment. **The '+' symbol is introduced alongside the Numicon adding action** and then familiar adding activities are revisited using '+', providing important practice to help children begin to memorize and become fluent with adding facts for each number to 10. Children usually need to be able to say (or sign) a complete adding sentence when using apparatus before attempting to set out the word cards. Insights into their understanding and any misconceptions they may have are often revealed when they first set out cards to show a number sentence. For some children setting out the word cards supports auditory memory difficulties. However, it is not recommended that children move on to using the '+' symbol until they are secure in setting out an adding sentence with the word cards.

Number rods can be used alongside the Numicon Shapes or activities that use the Shapes can be repeated using number rods.

Aims

- To experience situations when it is useful to add
- To consolidate understanding and use of the language of adding
- To add whole numbers without counting, using Numicon Shapes and number rods
- To begin to understand that adding can be done in any order
- To use and read the words 'and', 'add' 'plus', 'makes' and 'equals' in adding sentences
- To recognize and use the adding symbol, '+'

Communicating

Imagery
Numicon Display Number Line, Numicon 0–41 Number Rod Number Line

Equipment
See the individual 'have ready' for each activity, various items for the activities in the 'Extending the activities' section.

Words and terms for instruction (supported with signs and symbols)
build, find, work out, talk about, explain, put together, combine

Mathematical words and terms (supported with signs and symbols)
add, and, plus, makes, equals, altogether, together, total, more, larger Shape, larger amount, adding, adding sentence, adding story

Assessment

Individual Record of Progress: Calculating 13, 14, 24

Putting the activities into context

Very simple contexts have been used in the activities to help explain the ideas but adapt these according to the interests and ability of the children.

Calculating

The activities

Activity 1: Introducing word cards for adding sentences

Have ready: Numicon Shapes, Numeral Cards 0–10 (cut from photocopy master 11), Words for Calculating (cut from photocopy master 26b), number rods, small-world figures, toys, other 'real objects', e.g. pens or pictures of objects to be used as ideas for adding stories

Step 1
Use equipment or pictures to tell children an adding story that involves combining two amounts. They then find Shapes or rods to illustrate it.

Step 2
Children say the adding sentence and check the total with the appropriate Shape or rod.

Step 3
Children find the corresponding numeral cards for the Shapes or rods. They say the adding sentence again pointing to the numeral cards as they say the number names. As they do this, the adult combines the Shapes or rods to match the number sentence.

Step 4
Take time to introduce the word cards 'and', 'add, 'makes' and 'equals'. Decide which cards are going to be used for the adding sentence.

Step 5
Children say the adding sentence again placing the numeral and word cards in position as they are spoken, e.g. **Fig. 1**. Children read their adding sentence.

Step 6
Using the same context, vary the numbers used for children to create different adding sentences.

Smaller steps
- Introduce and use word cards for either 'and' or 'add', and either 'makes' or 'equals' according to which terms are most familiar to children.
- Create a 'frame' or 'stand' in which to place each card as it is used.
- Use Makaton® symbols and signs to illustrate mathematical words and terms.

Further practice
- Use either small-world figures, toys, other objects or pictures and encourage and guide children to choose their own contexts.
- Give children two Shapes or rods that total 10 or less. They say an adding story using the Shapes or rods and context chosen. They then set out the adding sentence using the numeral and word cards.
- Repeat often with other totals.

Activity 2: Reading adding sentences and finding apparatus

Have ready: Numicon Shapes, number rods, Numeral Cards 0–10 (cut from photocopy master 11), Words for Calculating (cut from photocopy master 26b)

Step 1
Set out numeral and word cards in an adding sentence for children to read.

Step 2
Children then find the Shapes or rods that correspond to the story, add them together and check the total.

Smaller steps
- Children who sign will obviously 'read' the sentence in the way that is appropriate for them.

Further practice
- Repeat with other adding sentences.

Activity 3: Reading adding sentences and making up adding stories

Have ready: Numicon Shapes, Numeral Cards 0–10 (cut from photocopy master 11), Words for Calculating (cut from photocopy master 26b), number rods, small-world figures, toys, other 'real objects', e.g. pens or pictures of objects to be used as ideas for adding stories

Step 1
Set out numeral and word cards in an adding sentence. Children read it and then make up an adding story using those numbers (use props as needed).

Step 2
Set out numeral and word cards as an adding expression (without the total), e.g. **Fig. 2**. Children read it and make up an adding story (some children may know the total from memory or be able to think of the total mentally).

8

Step 3

Children then find the Shapes or rods that correspond to the story, add them together and say the total. Check by finding the appropriate Shape or rod.

Smaller steps

• Use props to illustrate the adding story as it is being told.

Further practice

• Repeat with other examples and practise often.

Activity 4: Adding 'more'

Have ready: Numicon Shapes, Numeral Cards 0–10 (cut from photocopy master 11), Words for Calculating (cut from photocopy master 26b), number rods, small-world figures, toys, other items 'real objects', e.g. pens or pictures of objects to be used as ideas for adding stories

Step 1

Using equipment or pictures, tell children an adding story where 'more things' are added. They find Shapes or rods to illustrate it.

Step 2

Children say the adding sentence and check the total with the appropriate Shape or rod.

Step 3

Decide with children which numeral and word cards are needed for the adding sentence (some children may need to include the word card 'more', e.g. '6 and 2 more makes 8') and set them out. Children read the sentence.

Step 4

Children make up and share their own adding stories. They find Shapes or rods to illustrate them and set out the adding sentences using the numeral and word cards.

Step 5

Explain to children that, e.g. '6 and 2 makes 8' could mean either a combining situation or a situation where 'more things' are added.

Smaller steps

• Use props to illustrate the adding story as it is being told.

Further practice

• Set out an adding sentence using numeral and word cards. Children read it, illustrate it with Shapes or rods and make up an adding story using the numbers. Encourage children to devise both combining stories and those where 'more things' are added.

Activity 5: Symbol spotting

Have ready: pictures of road signs, exit signs, Makaton® symbols known to the child

Step 1

Help children to understand the usefulness of signs and symbols by taking them on a 'maths walk' around the local environment. Look for signs that use symbols to give instructions, warnings or directions; also notice some signs that use words. Or, look around the classroom and school and spot any written directions, instructions, labels, signs or symbols. Talk with children about how signs and symbols can be a way of communicating something without using words.

Step 2

Play a game: show children either a word or symbol (written or drawn on a card), which they can do the action for, e.g. sit, clap, stand up, turn around.

Activity 6: Introducing the '+' symbol and action

Have ready: Numicon Shapes, Numeral Cards 0–10 (cut from photocopy master 11), Words and Symbols for Calculating (cut from photocopy master 26a), number rods, small-world figures, toys, other 'real objects', e.g. pens or pictures of objects to be used as ideas for adding stories

Step 1

With children, decide on an adding story, record it using numeral and word cards, read it and illustrate it with Shapes or rods.

Step 2

Remind children about the symbol game (or symbol-spotting walk) and show them the '+' symbol. Replace 'and' or 'add' with the '+' card and re-read the adding sentence, continuing to use the written word 'makes' or 'equals', e.g. **Fig. 3**.

Step 3

Say there is an action to help remember the '+' symbol. Model (see **Fig. 4**) saying, 'I'm putting them together. I'm adding.' Children repeat the words as they do the action.

| 3 | + | 5 | equals | 8 | **3** |

4

Calculating

8

Step 4
Point to each card in the adding sentence and ask children to say the adding sentence again and include the action for 'add' as the word is spoken.

Smaller steps
• Take as much time with each step as needed.

Further practice
Have ready: Numicon Feely Bag containing two of each Numicon Shapes or number rods 1–5, Numeral Cards 0–10 (cut from photocopy master 11), Words for Calculating (cut from photocopy master 26b)

• Children take two Shapes/rods from the Feely Bag, add them together and say the adding sentence. They set out the numeral, '+' symbol and word cards to show it.

Have ready: Numicon Shapes, Numicon Spinner and 1–5 Spinner Overlay (cut from photocopy master 20), Numeral Cards 0–10 (cut from photocopy master 11), Words for Calculating (cut from photocopy master 26b), number rods

• Children spin twice, find both Shapes or rods for the numbers spun and add them together. They say the adding sentence and set out the numerals, '+' symbol and word cards to show it.

Activity 7: Adding has a commutative property

Have ready: Numicon Shapes, Numeral Cards 0–10 (cut from photocopy master 11), Words and Symbols for Calculating (cut from photocopy master 26a), number rods

Step 1
Say an adding problem that involves combining, e.g. 'There were four blue pens in a pot and five green pens in another pot. How many pens altogether?' Children find a 4-shape and a 5-shape and combine them, finding the 9-shape to check.

Step 2
They say the adding sentence clearly, e.g. 'Four pens add five pens equals (makes) nine pens' and set out the adding sentence using numeral and word and symbol cards.

Step 3
Ask, 'What would happen if there were five blue pens and four green pens? How many pens altogether?' Find the Shapes and set out the adding sentence.

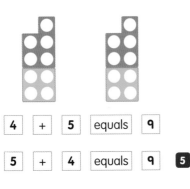

Step 4
Look at both sets of Shapes and both adding sentences. Talk with children about what they can see. Look at the first problem set out with Shapes. Point to the 4-shape first and then the 5-shape whilst saying the adding sentence, then for the second problem point to the 5-shape first, then the 4-shape whilst saying that adding sentence. Agree that whether you add the 5- to the 4-shape or the 4- to the 5-shape it always equals 9 (see **Fig. 5**).

Step 5
Show the commutative property by rearranging the 4 and 5 numeral cards and reading both adding sentences.

Step 6
Repeat with rods.

Smaller steps
• It may help some children if the combined 4- and 5-shape is rotated so the 4-shape is above the 5-shape (which now has the 'sticking up bit' pointing down) to reinforce that whichever way the Shapes are placed they still equal 9.

Further practice
• Set out an adding expression (without the total, e.g. 4 + 3) for children to find the corresponding Shapes or rods and find the numeral card for the total. Children then use numeral cards and symbol and word cards to set out the related adding sentence that shows the commutative property, e.g. 3 + 4 equals 7.

• Repeat all the activities with different numbers to support development of fluent recall of adding facts.

Extending the activities

Connecting activities

• Continue to use opportunities throughout the day to involve children in adding situations.

• Play board games using two dice, which children can add together to score their move.

For children moving on quickly

• Introduce the 'plus' word card when telling a new story.

• Encourage children to begin to work mentally when answering adding questions. Suggest that they look at images of the shapes on the Numicon Display Number Line (if available) or Shapes in order on the tabletop and then 'use their eyes' to try and work out the answer before using the actual Shapes to check.

Introducing the '−' symbol

9

Educational context

In this activity group children are introduced to the '−' symbol following the use of word cards, as with the introduction of previous symbols. Remind children that symbols tell us something. The '−' symbol is introduced alongside the Numicon subtracting action and then familiar subtracting activities are revisited, now using '−', providing important practice to help children begin to memorize and become fluent with subtracting facts for each number to 10. Children usually need to be able to say (or sign) a complete subtracting sentence when using apparatus before attempting to set out the word cards, though insights into their understanding and any misconceptions they may have are often seen when they first set out the cards. For some children setting out the word cards supports auditory memory difficulties; however, it is not recommended that children move on to using the '−' symbol until they are secure in setting out a subtracting sentence with the word cards, since these help to make the **connection between what they are saying and what they have recorded**. Some children may be able to record by writing.

Decisions will need to be taken about when it is appropriate for children to write down their mathematics learning, though we would strongly advise that children do not spend time learning to write during mathematics sessions when they could be communicating in other ways and moving forward in their mathematics learning.

Number rods can be used alongside the Numicon Shapes or activities can be repeated using number rods instead of Shapes.

Aims

- To experience situations when it is useful to subtract
- To consolidate understanding and use of the language of subtracting
- To subtract whole numbers without counting, using Numicon Shapes and number rods
- To use and read the words 'take away', 'minus', 'subtract', 'the difference between', 'leaves' and 'equals' in adding sentences
- To recognize and use the subtracting symbol, '−'

Communicating

Imagery
Numicon Display Number Line, Numicon 0–41 Rod Number Line

Equipment
See the individual 'have ready' for each activity, various items for the activities in the 'Extending the activities' section.

Words and terms for instruction (supported with signs and symbols)
build, find, work out, talk about, explain, left over

Mathematical words and terms (supported with signs and symbols)
take away, fewer, subtract, minus, the difference between, compare, smaller amount, leaves, equals, pattern, how many more to reach?

Assessment

Individual Record of Progress: Calculating 43, 44, 46, 47, 48, 49, 50

Putting the activities into context

Very simple contexts have been used in the activities to help explain the ideas, but adapt these according to the interests and ability of the children.

Calculating

The activities

Activity 1: Introducing word cards for calculating sentences

Have ready: Numicon Shapes, Numeral Cards 0–10 (cut from photocopy master 11), Words and Symbols for Calculating (cut from photocopy master 26a), Subtracting Covers 1–5 and 6–10 (cut from photocopy master 24), number rods, small-world figures, toys, other 'real objects' (e.g. pens) or pictures of objects to be used as ideas for subtracting take away stories

Step 1
Tell children a take away subtracting story using equipment or pictures. They find the Shape and subtracting cover or rod to illustrate it.

Step 2
Children say the subtracting sentence and check the answer by finding the appropriate Shape or rod.

Step 3
Explain that, just as for adding, children are going to set out a number sentence for 'take away' stories. Take time to introduce the word cards 'take away' and 'leaves'. Remind children that they already know the symbol for 'equals'. Decide which cards are going to be used for the take away number sentence.

Step 4
Children say the take away sentence again, placing the numeral cards and word and symbol cards in position as they say them. They read their number sentence, e.g. **Fig. 1**

Step 5
Using the same context, vary the numbers used for children to create different take away sentences.

Smaller steps
- Only introduce and use the word cards for 'take away'. Children know the symbol '='.
- Create a 'frame' or 'stand' in which to place each card as it is used.
- If children are used to using symbols such as Makaton® to support mathematical language, use those that they are familiar with.

Further practice
- Use either small-world figures, toys, other objects or pictures and encourage and guide children to choose their own contexts.

- Give children a Shape and subtracting cover. They say a take away story using the Shape, subtracting cover and context chosen. They then set out the take away sentence using the numeral and word and symbol cards.
- Give children a rod (from 2–10) and then a smaller rod to show how much to take away. They say a take away story using the rods and context chosen. They then set out the take away sentence using the numeral, word and symbol cards.

Activity 2: Recording number sentences using 'subtract' and 'minus'

Have ready: Numicon Shapes, Numicon Spinner and 1–5 Shape Overlay (cut from photocopy master 20), Numeral Cards 0–10 (cut from photocopy master 11), Words and Symbols for Calculating (cut from photocopy master 26a), Subtracting Covers 1–5 and 6–10 (cut from photocopy master 24), number rods

Step 1
Give children either a 6-, 7-, 8-, 9- or 10-shape or rod. They spin the Spinner and find the corresponding subtracting cover or rod to show the amount to be taken away. Children say and record the take away sentence using numeral, word and symbol cards.

Step 2
Show children the 'subtract' and 'minus' word cards. Read the take away number sentence from Step 1 twice, first using 'subtract' instead of 'take away', then using 'minus' instead of 'take away', e.g. **Fig. 2**

Step 3
Talk about how the words 'take away', 'subtract' and 'minus' can be used interchangeably.

Smaller steps
- Just introduce 'subtract'. When children are secure with this then introduce 'minus'.

Further practice
- Generate other subtracting sentences, as in Step 1, for children to say and record 'subtract' and 'minus' sentences using numeral, word and symbol cards.

| 7 | take away | 2 | = | 5 | **1** |

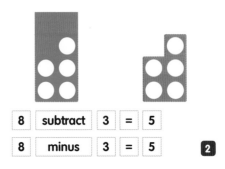

| 8 | subtract | 3 | = | 5 | |
| 8 | minus | 3 | = | 5 | **2** |

Calculating

9

Activity 3: Reading subtracting sentences and finding apparatus

Have ready: Numicon Shapes, Numeral Cards 0–10 (cut from photocopy master 11), Words and Symbols for Calculating (cut from photocopy master 26a), Subtracting Covers 1–5 and 6–10 (cut from photocopy master 24), number rods

Step 1
Set out numeral, word and symbol cards in a take away sentence and ask children to read it.

Step 2
Children then find the Shape and the subtracting cover or rods that correspond to the subtracting sentence. They take away the appropriate amount using the subtracting cover or rod, say the answer and check by finding the Shape or rod that shows the remainder.

Step 3
Repeat Steps 1 and 2 using 'subtract' and 'minus' word cards.

Smaller steps
- Children who sign will obviously 'read' the sentence in the way that is appropriate for them.

Further practice
- Repeat Activity 3 with other subtracting number sentences.

Activity 4: Reading subtracting sentences and making up subtracting stories

Have ready: Numicon Shapes, Numeral Cards 0–10 (cut from photocopy master 11), Words and Symbols for Calculating (cut from photocopy master 26a), Subtracting Covers 1–5 and 6–10 (cut from photocopy master 24), number rods, small-world figures, toys, other 'real' objects (e.g. pens) or pictures of objects to be used as ideas for take away stories

Step 1
Set out numeral and word cards in a subtracting number sentence. Ask children to read it and then make up a take away story using those numbers (use props as needed or just as a prompt for the context).

Step 2
Set out numeral and word cards as a subtracting expression (without the answer), e.g. **Fig. 3**. Ask children to read it and make up a subtracting story (some children may know the answer from memory or be able to think of the answer mentally).

Step 3
Children then find the Shape and subtracting cover that correspond to the story, subtract the appropriate amount using the subtracting cover and say the answer, relating it to the context they chose if they have not already done so. They check by finding the appropriate Shape.

Step 4
Repeat with rods.

Smaller steps
- Use props to illustrate the take away story as it is being told.

Further practice
- Repeat Activity 4 with other examples and practise often.

Activity 5: Introducing the '–' symbol and action

Have ready: Numicon Shapes, Numeral Cards 0–10 (cut from photocopy master 11), Words and Symbols for Calculating (cut from photocopy master 26a), Subtracting Covers 1–5 and 6–10 (cut from photocopy master 24), number rods, small-world figures, toys, other 'real' objects (e.g. pens) or pictures of objects to be used as ideas for take away stories

Step 1
With children, decide on a take away story. Record it using numeral and word cards, read it and illustrate it with a Shape and subtracting cover or rods.

Step 2
Remind children about the symbols they know, i.e. '<', '>', '+' and '=' and explain that they are now going to learn the symbol for take away. Show them the '–' symbol. Replace 'take away' with the '–' card and re-read the take away sentence, e.g. **Fig. 4**.

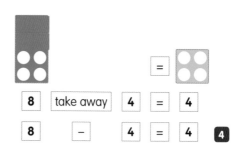

| 8 | take away | 3 | = | **3** |

Calculating

9

Step 3

Say that there is an action to help remember the '–' symbol. Model saying, 'I'm taking them away. I'm subtracting.' Children repeat the words as they do the action (see Fig. 5).

Step 4

While you point to each card in the take away sentence children say it again and include the action for 'take away' as the word is spoken.

Step 5

Repeat Step 4 using 'subtract' and 'minus'.

Smaller steps

- Work at a pace appropriate for the children.

Further practice

- Children spin a Numicon Spinner and 1–5 or 6–10 Shape Overlay (cut from photocopy master 20) and take away that amount from the 10-shape or 10-rod. They say the subtracting sentence and set it out using numeral, word and symbol cards.

- Children choose a Shape then choose which subtracting cover to subtract from the Shape. They say the subtracting sentence and set it out using numeral, word and symbol cards. Repeat with rods.

Extending the activities

Connecting activities

- Continue to use opportunities throughout the day to involve children in subtracting situations, and encourage them to use the sign each time they say a subtracting sentence.

For children moving on quickly

- Encourage children to look at images of the Shapes and 'use their eyes' when answering subtracting questions before using the Shapes themselves to check.

- Remind children about equivalence. It is difficult to show subtracting using Shapes and rods in the Numicon Pan Balance, but an understanding of equivalence will enable children to solve problems like $4 = 9 - 5$ (see Fig. 6).

- Use the word cards for 'the difference between', talking with children about it being subtracting.

5

4 = 9 – 5 6

Adding and subtracting 1

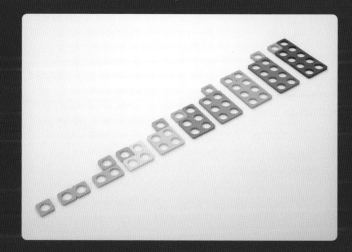

Educational context

This activity group gives children the opportunity to explore relationships and patterns in adding and subtracting within numbers to 10, and looks at the 'decrease' structure when subtracting. It builds on children's earlier work with '1 more' and '1 fewer/less' and the labelling of patterns with numerals to support them in noticing patterns in written calculations. Children are helped to begin to move from concrete examples towards more abstract reasoning and are given the opportunity to begin to make generalizations about the **increase and decrease of numbers in our number system**. This is an important step in the development of their mathematical thinking. These ideas should be referred to whenever possible within daily routines and everyday situations.

Aims

- To understand that adding 1 to a whole number equals the next number and that subtracting 1 from a whole number equals the number before
- To begin to understand that it is helpful to look for patterns, and that it is easier to spot them when work is organized systematically
- To begin to look for patterns in a systematic way

Communicating

Imagery
Numicon Display Number Line, Numicon 0–41 Number Rod Number Line, Numicon 0–100 cm Number Line

Equipment
See the individual 'have ready' for each activity, various items for the activities in the 'Extending the activities' section.

Words and terms for instruction (supported with signs and symbols)
build, find, talk about, explain

Mathematical words and terms (supported with signs and symbols)
one more, next, the same, equals, after, one fewer, one less, before, pattern, add, plus, total, more, compare, subtract, take away, minus, difference, systematic, always, because

Assessment

Individual Record of Progress: Calculating 15, 27, 45, 53

Putting the activities into context

Use rhymes like 'There were ten in the bed and the little one said, "Roll over"', 'Ten green bottles standing on the wall', 'One man went to mow' or stories where one more is added or subtracted. Talk with children about situations where one more is needed, e.g. one more juice at break time, one more place for dinner because a friend is coming, or where one fewer or less is needed, e.g. one fewer child will be taking part in the activity as they are absent today, one fewer piece of toast because Isla is having cereal today.

Link to Number, Pattern and Calculating 1

Calculating 2

Calculating

The activities

Activity 1: Using apparatus to add 1

Have ready: Numicon Shapes

Step 1

Sing or say a rhyme where one more is added each time.

Step 2

Children set out Shapes to show what is happening in the rhyme. Begin with the 1-shape and add another 1-shape, then put the 2-shape in place.

Step 3

Add a 1-shape to the 2-shape (to show the 3-Shape pattern) and put the 3-shape in place. Continue to 10 (see **Fig. 1**).

Smaller steps

- Use a rhyme that stops at five.

Further practice

- Try setting out Shapes for other rhymes or songs where one more is added each time.
- Repeat with number rods.

Activity 2: Looking at the written pattern when adding 1

Have ready: Numicon Shapes, slips of paper

Step 1

Children set out Shapes as a staircase pattern from the 1-shape to the 10-shape.

Step 2

Beginning with the 1-shape, add another 1-shape and say the adding sentence, 'one add one equals two'.

Write what has been spoken on a slip of paper, $1 + 1 = 2$, and place it under the two 1-shapes.

Step 3

Continue to add a 1-shape to each Shape, each time saying the adding sentence, writing it on a slip of paper and placing it under the corresponding Shapes (see **Fig. 2**).

Step 4

Beginning with $1 + 1 = 2$, move each slip of paper to rearrange them into a vertical pattern (see **Fig. 3**). Talk with children about the patterns they can see in the adding

sentences and about what happens when you add 1 to a whole number (you always get the next whole number).

Smaller steps

- Use word and symbol cards (cut from photocopy master 26a) for the main activity or scribe for children.
- Work to 5 only.

Further practice

- Children turn a card from Numeral Cards 1–9 (cut from photocopy master 11, shuffled and face down in a pile). In their heads they add 1 to the number. They say the adding sentence and record it either by writing or setting out the numeral, word and symbol cards (cut from photocopy master 26a) or in writing.
- Children build their own staircase of rods 1–10 and colour the pattern onto squared paper. Beginning with 1 they add an extra 1-rod, draw in the new square and write $1 + 1 = 2$. They continue to add 1 to each step, drawing in each new square and recording each adding sentence as they go (see **Fig. 4**).
- Give children the slips of paper with all 'add 1 adding sentences' from Activity 2 for them to put in order independently.

$0 + 1 = 1$
$1 + 1 = 2$
$2 + 1 = 3$
$3 + 1 = 4$
$4 + 1 = 5$
$5 + 1 = 6$
$6 + 1 = 7$
$7 + 1 = 8$
$8 + 1 = 9$
$9 + 1 = 10$ **3**

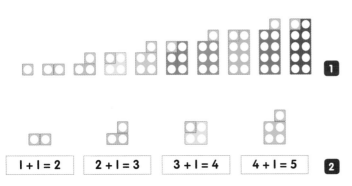

1

$1 + 1 = 2$ $2 + 1 = 3$ $3 + 1 = 4$ $4 + 1 = 5$ **2**

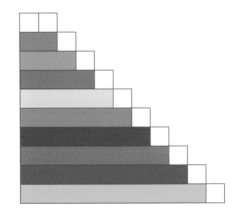

$1 + 1 = 2$
$2 + 1 = 3$
$3 + 1 = 4$
$4 + 1 = 5$
$5 + 1 = 6$
$6 + 1 = 7$
$7 + 1 = 8$
$8 + 1 = 9$
$9 + 1 = 10$

4

Calculating

10

Activity 3: Using apparatus to subtract 1

Have ready: Numicon Shapes, Subtracting Cover for 1 (cut from photocopy master 24)

Step 1
Talk about a situation or sing or say a rhyme where one more is subtracted each time.

Step 2
Children set out Shapes 1–10. Beginning with the 10-shape and using the 1-shape subtracting cover, show 10 subtract 1 equals 9. Look at the Numicon Shape pattern of holes left and point to the 9-shape. Relate it to what is happening in the rhyme.

Step 3
Continue to illustrate the rhyme by subtracting 1 from the 9-shape (looking at the Numicon Shape pattern of holes left and pointing to the Shape showing the answer) (see **Fig. 5**). Continue to 1.

Smaller steps
• Use a rhyme that works back from five.

Further practice
• Try setting out Shapes for other rhymes or songs where one more is subtracted each time.
• Repeat with rods.

Activity 4: Looking at the written pattern when subtracting 1

Have ready: Numicon Shapes, Words and Symbols for Calculating (cut from photocopy master 26a), slips of paper

Step 1
Children set out Shapes as a staircase pattern from the 1-shape to the 10-shape.

Step 2
Beginning with the 10-shape, subtract 1 and say the subtracting sentence, 'ten subtract one equals nine'.

Write the spoken sentence on a slip of paper, 10 – 1 = 9, and place it under the 10-shape.

Step 3
Continue to subtract 1 from each Shape, each time saying the subtracting sentence, writing it on a slip of paper and placing it under the corresponding Shape (see **Fig. 6**).

Step 4
Beginning with 10 – 1 = 9, move each slip of paper to rearrange them into a vertical pattern (see **Fig. 7**). Talk with children about the patterns they can see in the subtracting sentences. Rearrange the slips of paper again into a vertical pattern, this time beginning with 1 – 1 = 0, and again talk about patterns that can be seen.

Step 5
Talk with children about what happens when you subtract 1 from a whole number (you always get the previous whole number).

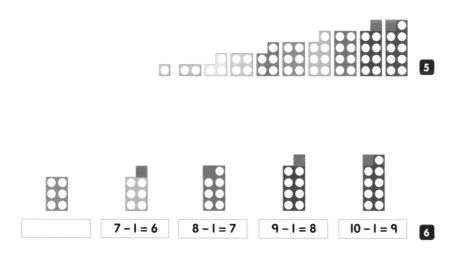

5

6

10 – 1 = 9
9 – 1 = 8
8 – 1 = 7
7 – 1 = 6
6 – 1 = 5
5 – 1 = 4
4 – 1 = 3
3 – 1 = 2
2 – 1 = 1
1 – 1 = 0

7

7 – 1 = 6   8 – 1 = 7   9 – 1 = 8   10 – 1 = 9

Calculating

10

Smaller steps
- Use word and symbol cards for the main activity or scribe for children.
- Work back from 5 only.

Further practice
- Children turn a card from Numeral Cards 1–10 (cut from photocopy master 11, shuffled and face down in a pile). In their heads they subtract 1 from the number. They say the subtracting sentence and record it using the numeral, word and symbol cards (cut from photocopy masters 26a and 26b) or in writing.
- Children build their own staircase of rods 1–10 and colour the pattern onto squared paper. Beginning with 1, they subtract 1, cross out 1 square and write 1 – 1 = 0. They continue to subtract 1 from each step, crossing out each new square and recording each subtracting sentence as they go (see **Fig. 8**).
- Give children the slips of paper with all 'subtract 1 subtracting sentences' from Activity 4 for them to put in order independently.

Extending the activities

Connecting activities
- Use interlocking cubes and make a staircase pattern 1–10. Add or subtract 1 to or from each tower. Children could record the pattern of adding sentences.
- In PE, include 1 more jump or hop, e.g. jump three times and then jump once more. Repeat but with 1 fewer jump or hop (use clapping, tapping and so on in music sessions).
- Hold up different Shapes or rods and ask children to say or find the Shape or rod that is 1 more or 1 less.

For children moving on quickly
- Use the Numicon 0–100 cm Number Line. Children find different numbers within their counting range and then find 1 more or 1 less.

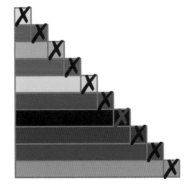

1 – 1 = 0
2 – 1 = 1
3 – 1 = 2
4 – 1 = 3
5 – 1 = 4
6 – 1 = 5
7 – 1 = 6
8 – 1 = 7
9 – 1 = 8
10 – 1 = 9   **8**

Money – coin equivalence

11

Educational context

In this activity group the idea of equal value – even though the values may be represented differently – is continued in the context of money. The activities use and develop ideas that children have met in previous activity groups and with which they should be secure before attempting these activities. These are: counting 1p coins by grouping them into Numicon Shape patterns (Numbers and the Number System 12), recognizing and naming different coins (Pattern 4), understanding equivalence (Pattern 6 and 10), adding (Calculating 2, 3 and 8), subtracting (Calculating 6, 7 and 9).

There is a progression within the activity group, initially working on **finding equivalent combinations of coins** (explicit connections are made between Numicon 1-, 2-, 5- and 10-shapes and coin values by sticking 1p, 2p, 5p and 10p coins onto the corresponding Numicon Shapes with adhesive tack), then moving on to **understanding 'p' in money notation**; adding amounts of money up to 10p. The first subtracting activity, taking smaller from larger amounts of money (take away structure), is relatively straightforward. However the final two activities, comparing amounts of money to find the difference and beginning to work out change are more challenging, so we recommend that these two activities are taught after Activity Group 12 when children are more fluent with adding and subtracting facts. Solving change problems quickly becomes complicated as they involve several steps and these challenges should not be underestimated. At this point children have not met the idea of counting up in combinations of ones, twos, fives and tens to calculate change but the ground work is laid for future understanding.

Throughout the activities there is an emphasis on the idea of **fair exchange** which is the key idea for children to understand in money transactions.

There are also many opportunities for developing fluency with adding and subtracting facts in the context of money.

Aims

- To connect coin values with cardinal number values
- To work out equivalent values of coins up to 10p
- To continue to develop fluency with adding and subtracting facts through using money

- To know when to use an equivalent value of a different selection of coins
- To take away smaller amounts of money from larger amounts
- To compare amounts of money to find the difference
- To understand that paying for something is a fair exchange transaction
- To meet the idea that change is calculated by finding the difference between the amount paid and the cost of the item

Communicating

Imagery
Numicon Display Number Line, Numicon 0–41 Number Rod Number Line, a money number line, i.e. the Numicon 0–100 cm Number Line with 1p, 2p, 5p, 20p, 50p and £1 coins matched appropriately, Numicon Large Format Table-top Number Line

Equipment
See the individual 'have ready' for each activity, various items for the activities in the 'Extending the activities' section.

Words and terms for instruction (supported with signs and symbols)
label, match, stick, post, arrange, group, make, find, talk about, explain, compare, combine, put together

Mathematical words and terms (supported with signs and symbols)
money, coin, penny, pence, make, exchange, change, add, take away, comparison, difference, total, pattern, combination, equal, how much more than?

Assessment

Individual Record of Progress: Money 2–11

Putting the activities into context

Children may be used to buying small items at their local shop when they see an exchange of money for goods, e.g. milk, newspapers and sweets, even though they might not often see their parents shopping with cash. The key idea for them to understand is that buying something is an exchange transaction. They will see this happening when tickets are bought to take them swimming, or for the bus, or train. Ask children for suggestions about when they have paid for something or seen someone pay for something, e.g. buying stamps at the post office, parking tickets or drinks from vending machines, and discuss this idea of exchange.

Link to Geometry, Measurement and Statistics 1

Measurement 2

Calculating

The activities

Activity 1: Connecting 1p, 2p, 5p and 10p coins with Numicon Shapes

Have ready: Numicon 1-, 2-, 5- and 10-shapes, coins (1p, 2p, 5p and 10p), Numeral Cards 0–10 (cut from photocopy master 11), Numicon 0–100 cm Number Line with 1p, 2p, 5p, 20p, 50p and £1 coins matched appropriately, adhesive tack

Step 1
Ask children to spread out the Shapes, in order, and label them with numeral cards.

Step 2
Ask children to look carefully at the 1p coin and to look at what is written on it. When they have found the numeral 1, ask them to match it to the relevant Shape and numeral card.

Step 3
Repeat for the 2p, 5p and 10p coin until each coin is matched with the corresponding Shape (see **Fig. 1**).

Step 4
Discuss why only the 1- 2- 5- and 10-shapes are used and agree that these are the only Shapes that have a matching coin. Refer to the money number line on display.

Step 5
Use adhesive tack to stick the coins onto their corresponding Shapes. Keep these for the further activities.

Activity 2: Exchanging 1p coins (attached to 1-shapes) for 2p, 5p and 10p coins (attached to Numicon Shapes)

Have ready: Numicon 1-, 2-, 5- and 10-shapes with 1p, 2p, 5p and 10p coins attached (saved from Activity 1)

Step 1
Choose a coin with a Shape attached, e.g. the 5p coin and 5-shape. Ask children to exchange this for 1p coins.

Step 2
Children take five 1-shapes with 1p coins attached and arrange them into the 5-pattern (see **Fig. 2**).

Step 3
Discuss that both the 5p coin and the five 1p coins are equal to 5p.

Step 4
Repeat for 10p and 2p.

Further practice
- Children work in pairs. The first child chooses a Shape with coin attached and posts it through the Numicon Post Box to their partner.

  The second child posts back the correct number of 1-shapes with 1p coins attached.

  Together the two children arrange the 1-shapes into the Numicon Shape pattern to check they have exchanged an equal amount.

   **1**

 2

11

Activity 3: Finding combinations of coins to equal 5p

Have ready: Numicon 1-, 2- and 5-shapes with 1p, 2p and 5p coins attached (saved from Activity 1)

Step 1

Show children a 5p coin attached to a 5-shape. Ask them to investigate different combinations of 1p and 2p coins that could be exchanged for 5p, because they are equal to it.

Step 2

Share and discuss their suggestions, e.g. **Fig. 3**.

Step 3

Agree how they could display their findings, e.g. as **Fig. 3** or **Fig. 4**.

Further practice

• Children work in pairs. The first child selects a 5-shape with coin attached and posts it through the Numicon Post Box to their partner.

  The second child chooses an equivalent combination of coins to post back. Together the two children arrange their Shapes with coins into the Numicon 5-pattern, to check they have exchanged an equal amount.

For children moving on quickly

• Some children will be ready to do these activities just with coins, having made the connections with the Shapes and having generalized the number ideas.

Activity 4: Reading amounts using 'p' notation

Have ready: a collection of suitable objects labelled with different amounts up to 10p, coins (1p, 2p, 5p and 10p)

Step 1

Ask children to name each coin. Some may say '1 pence', '2 pence', and so on; others '1p', '2p', and so on. Discuss and model the correct language: '1 pence coin', '5 pence coin'.

Step 2

Write the word 'pence'. Discuss that 'p' is the initial letter for pence and so we say 'p' as a quick way of saying and writing 'pence'.

Step 3

Show the items labelled with different amounts. Children read aloud each amount.

Further practice

• Give children labels or small pieces of paper and objects for them to write their own price labels. Children swap labels with a partner and read each other's.

Activity 5: Finding equivalent combinations of coins for amounts up to 9p

Have ready: Numicon 1-, 2- and 5-shapes, some with 1p, 2p, 5p coins attached plus extra 1p, 2p and 5p coins, a collection of suitable objects labelled with different amounts up to 10p

Step 1

Take an object labelled 3p and ask children what coins could be used to pay for it. Work with children to investigate the different combinations.

Step 2

Ask children what coins could be used for an object labelled 4p, encouraging children to experiment to find different combinations of coins, e.g. **Fig. 5**.

Smaller steps

• Encourage children to use 1-, 2- and 5-shapes with coins attached until they are ready to work with coins alone.

Further practice

• Continue to explore equivalent combinations of coins for other amounts up to 9p.

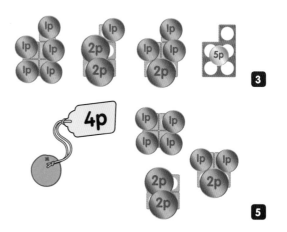

3

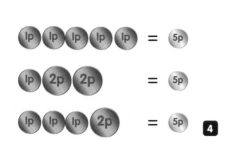

4

5

Calculating

11

Activity 6: How much money in the purse? Adding two coins.

Have ready: Numicon Shapes, a purse containing two coins (choose combinations of 1p, 2p, 5p, e.g. Fig. 6).

Step 1
Show the purse and ask children how much money is in it. Discuss that they will need to find the total by adding.

Step 2
Children experiment to work out the total, using Shapes to help them if they wish.

Step 3
Model how to write the adding sentence using 'p' notation, e.g. 1p + 5p = 6p.

Step 4
Give children other combinations of two coins in the purse for them to work out the total.

Smaller steps
• Children continue to use coins attached to Shapes to calculate the totals.

For children moving on quickly

• Give children combinations of three or four coins that equal less than 10p. They calculate the totals and record the adding sentences.

Activity 7: Finding the largest amount

Have ready: Numicon Shapes, Numicon Display Number Line or Numicon Large Format Table-top Number Line, small containers or purses containing different combinations of coins totalling up to 10p, '<' and '>' symbols (cut from photocopy master 26a)

Step 1
Show children the containers and ask them to find out which purse or container holds the most money.

Step 2
Give them time to investigate and ask them to keep a record of the totals.

Step 3
Children find out which purse holds the most.

Step 4
Share answers and find each total on the Display Number Line, or the Large Format Table-top Number Line. Agree which purse has the most money, that is to say, holds the largest total, e.g. Fig. 7.

Smaller steps
• Give children only two containers or purses to compare. Gradually increase the number of totals they are comparing as they are ready.

For children moving on quickly

• Children keep a record of the totals of each container or purse and record them, in order.

• Children then compare the totals of two containers or purses and record the comparison using the '<' and '>' symbols, e.g. Fig. 8.

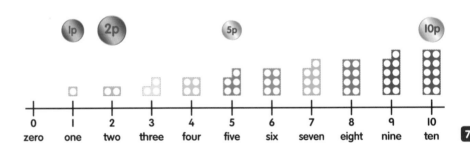

| 0 | 1 | 2 | 3 | 4 | 5 | 6 | 7 | 8 | 9 | 10 |
| zero | one | two | three | four | five | six | seven | eight | nine | ten |

7

6

8

11

Activity 8: Finding combinations of coins to equal 10p

Have ready: Numicon 1-, 2- and 5-shapes with 1p, 2p, 5p and 10p coins attached (saved from Activity 1)

Step 1

Show children a 10p coin attached to a 10-shape. Ask them to investigate different combinations of 1p, 2p and 5p coins that could be exchanged for 10p, because they are equal to it.

Step 2

Share and discuss their suggestions.

Step 3

Agree how they could display the findings, as in Activity 3.

Further practice

• Children work in pairs. The first child posts a 10-shape with coin attached through the Numicon Post Box to their partner.

  The second child chooses an equivalent combination of coins to post back. Together the two children arrange their Shapes with coins into the Numicon 10-pattern to check they have exchanged an equal amount.

For children moving on quickly

• Some children will be ready to do these activities just with coins, having made the connections with the Shapes and having generalized the number ideas.

• Some children may enjoy the challenge of finding how many combinations they can find and organizing them systematically so they can be sure they have found all of them.

Activity 9: Shopping for two items

Have ready: Numicon 1-, 2-, 5- and 10-shapes, coins (1p, 2p, 5p and 10p), various items labelled with amounts up to 5p

Step 1

Children choose two items and work out the total amount they will have to pay.

Step 2

Children then investigate different combinations of coins they could use to pay. Encourage them to use coins for the total amount and not just for the separate items, and to avoid using only 1p coins, e.g. **Fig. 9**.

Step 3

Discuss how children might check they have added the amounts correctly, and that the total will be the same whichever way round they add the prices.

For children moving on quickly

• Ask children to work out which pairs of items would cost the most when added together. Vary by asking which would cost the least.

• Give children one item labelled 10p and give them the choice of one other item. Ask them to calculate the total cost, encouraging them to make connections with the work on teens numbers in Numbers and the Number System 13 and 14.

Activity 10: Subtracting amounts of money

Have ready: Numicon Shapes, one item labelled 5p, a purse containing 8p made up of a 5p, a 2p and a 1p coin

Step 1

Tell children that you have 8p in your purse. Ask them to check and agree the amount (see **Fig. 10**).

Step 2

Say that you want to buy the item (labelled 5p) and ask children to read the label and the amount. Ask, 'Have I got enough money in my purse to pay?'

5p + 4p = 9p

5p + 2p 2p   **9**

2p + 1p + 5p = 8p   **10**

Calculating

11

Step 3
Show children 8p built with Shapes with coins attached. Ask them to work out how much you will have left in your purse after paying 5p for the item.

Step 4
Discuss and remove the 5-shape with attached 5p coin to show the remaining 3p (see **Fig. 11**).

Step 5
Repeat, putting different amounts in the purse and with different priced items. Always subtract an amount involving whole coins that are in the purse, e.g. start with 9p represented with 5p, 2p and 2p, buy an item costing 2p, so that children will just be removing one 2p coin, and calculate that there is 7p left.

Smaller steps
* Work with only two coins in the purse and buy an item the value of one of the coins, e.g. 7p represented with 2p and 5p, and buy an item costing 2p.

For children moving on quickly
* Select combinations of coins that will involve using coin equivalence and taking two steps to solve the problem, e.g. 10p in the purse represented with 2p, 2p, 2p, 2p, 1p and 1p and buy an item costing 5p. This will involve children working out the combination of coins that will equal 5p and recall of the subtracting fact 10 − 5 = 5.

Activity 11: Comparing amounts of money

Have ready: Numicon Shapes, coins (1p, 2p, 5p and 10p), two purses: one containing 5p; one containing 10p, '<' and '>' symbols (cut from photocopy master 26a)

Step 1
With children, compare the amounts in the two purses, using the '<' and '>' symbols, and with Shapes as well. Help children to make the connection by sticking coins to the Shapes (see **Fig. 12**).

Step 2
Ask children how much more money is in the purse with 10p.

Discuss and encourage children to compare the Shapes and to find the Shape to show the difference.

Step 3
Find the 5-shape to show the difference, and then stick a 5p coin to it. Discuss that this shows us there is 5p more in the purse with 10p.

Step 4
Repeat with other examples involving whole coins, e.g. comparing 2p with 5p; 1p with 5p; 2p with 10p; 1p with 10p.

For children moving on quickly
* Compare amounts made up with different coins, e.g. compare 10p with 5p + 2p; or compare 5p + 2p + 1p with 5p + 2p. Some children may be ready to find the difference between the two amounts (see **Fig. 13**).

8p − 5p = 3p

11

10p > 5p

12

7p < 8p   10p > 7p

11

Activity 12: Beginning to relate how much more to giving change

Have ready: a classroom shop with shopping items priced 1p, 2p, 5p and 10p

Step 1

Discuss that when we buy something we exchange money for what we want to buy. The exchange has to be fair.

Give children a 10p coin. In the shop they can buy one item costing 10p. Children exchange their 10p coin for an item costing 10p. Agree that this is a fair exchange (see Fig. 14).

Step 2

Give children a 10p coin. Ask them to go to the shop and buy an item that costs 5p. Ask, 'When you pay, what will have to happen to make the exchange fair?' Discuss the idea of change being needed and ask children how they will work out how much change they should have.

Step 3

Remind children that they are buying something that costs 5p and they are giving the shopkeeper 10p to pay for it. Ask, 'How much more is this than what you are buying?'

Step 4

Discuss children's ideas and agree that they have to find out the difference between the cost of the item and how much they have paid the shopkeeper. The shopkeeper has to give the difference back to the shopper to make the exchange fair. The shopper keeps the item costing 5p and receives 5p change. The shopkeeper keeps 10p. Demonstrate with Shapes with coins attached and the item labelled 5p (see Fig. 15).

Step 5

Repeat, giving children a 2p coin and buying an item costing 1p (see Fig. 16).

Smaller steps

- Repeat the idea of a fair exchange so that children are exchanging 1p, 2p, 5p or 10p coins for items that are labelled for one of these amounts, that is, no change is given.

Further practice

- As children are ready, practise all these activities until they show understanding by working confidently and accurately.

For children moving on quickly

- Select exchanges that involve using understanding of coin equivalence to calculate change and taking two steps to solve the problem, e.g. paying with a 10p to buy an item that costs 7p, e.g. Fig. 17.

14

16

15

17

Further ideas for developing fluency – adding and subtracting with each number to 10

12

Educational context

These activities move on to exploring the adding and subtracting facts for 6 but it is vital that each number to 10 is explored in the ways illustrated with 6. As they work on this activity group, children should make some important steps towards developing fluency. The activities begin by looking at zero when adding and subtracting. **Children experience that, if zero is added or subtracted, it just leaves everything as it was.** It is important for children to have opportunities to explore and make discoveries when finding combinations for each number, as well as learning **the importance of being systematic.** There are no 'Further practice' activities when exploring the facts for each number as the activities themselves should be repeated (with different numbers) to provide the practice needed to develop fluency, independence and confidence.

Children should be encouraged to notice the triadic (three-way) associations between numbers (e.g. 4 + 2 = 6, 6 – 2 = 4, 6 – 4 = 2) and to explain these relationships in their own way. This provides opportunities for them to begin to notice the inverse relationship between adding and subtracting, although at this stage it is not taught explicitly.

The activities will also provide assessment opportunities related to perseverance, understanding and systematic ways of working, as well as the extent to which children are able to **recall known facts.** As these facts are such an important foundation for children's ongoing calculating, children should start to build a repertoire of known facts. Exploring all the numbers with both number rods and Numicon Shapes gives further important practice.

Once children are confident with the activities in this group it is recommended that the activities are 'kept bubbling' alongside other work to continue to develop and maintain fluency with all the number facts for each number to 10.

Aims

- To understand what happens when zero is added or subtracted
- To become fluent with adding and subtracting facts for numbers to 10 and to recognize that these can be useful in many different situations
- To experience situations when it is useful to use adding and subtracting facts for numbers to 10

- To begin to know when to look for patterns and that it is easier to spot them when work is organized systematically
- To begin to see when to use the inverse relationship between adding and subtracting to solve problems

Communicating

Imagery
Numicon Display Number Line, Numicon 0–41 Number Rod Number Line, Numicon 0–100 cm Number Line, Numicon 10s Number Line

Equipment
See the individual 'have ready' for each activity, various items for the activities in the 'Extending the activities' section.

Words and terms for instruction (supported with signs and symbols)
build, find, work out, remember, think, talk about, explain, organize, how many ways, systematic

Mathematical words and terms (supported with signs and symbols)
add, plus, total, compare, subtract, take away, minus, the difference between, how many more to make?, equals, facts, pattern, similar, different, combination, parts, wholes, adding sentences, subtracting sentences

Assessment

Individual Record of Progress: Calculating 16–23, 25, 26, 28, 51, 52, 54

Putting the activities into context

When adding and subtracting zero, games where children gain a score can be a helpful context, but use examples relevant for the children you are working with.

For Activities 3–7 contexts are needed where there are two connected but different possibilities, e.g. boys or girls, yellow balls or red balls, blue pens or black pens, circular road signs or triangular road signs, chocolate cupcakes or vanilla cupcakes.

For Activities 8–13 the contexts need to begin with a collection where children can decide how many should be subtracted each time or where one can be subtracted each time, e.g. a group of children working on an activity, a pack of stickers, a group of birds in a tree, a pot of pencils, a plate of cupcakes and so on.

Link to Number, Pattern and Calculating 1

Calculating 4, 7 and 8; Pattern and Algebra 5

Link to Number, Pattern and Calculating 2

Pattern and Algebra 7; Calculating 1 and 3

Link to Number, Pattern and Calculating 3

Calculating 1

Calculating

The activities

12

Activity 1: Adding with zero

Have ready: Numicon Shapes, Numicon Feely Bag, Numeral Cards 0–10 (cut from photocopy master 11), Words and Symbols for Calculating (cut from photocopy master 26a), number rods

Step 1

Tell children a number story where no more are added, e.g. 'Six people got on the bus at the station but no one got on at the next stop. How many people were on the bus?' Children say the adding sentence.

Step 2

Find the Shapes or rods to represent the story and set out the numeral and symbol cards below the Shapes (see **Fig. 1**).

Step 3

Repeat using other contexts and numbers. Include scenarios where, e.g. there were no passengers at the first bus stop, then 6 got on at the next stop.

Step 4

Talk with children about what happens when zero is added to any number or a number is added to zero.

Smaller steps

- Children may need to work with more everyday opportunities or small-world equipment at the same time as using structured apparatus to illustrate what happens when zero is added.

Further practice

- Place Shapes 1–10 in a Feely Bag. Children feel for a Shape and add zero. They say and write the number sentence.
- Once children have been introduced to the Numicon 10s Number Line and the Numicon 0–100 cm Number Line they can develop adding zero further by placing the Shape or rod along the appropriate number line and saying and recording the adding sentences.

Have ready: Numicon Shapes, two Numicon Spinners and 1–5 and 6–10 Numeral Overlays (cut from photocopy master 20), number rods

- Children spin a number, add zero, then say and write the adding sentence.

Activity 2: Subtracting with zero

Have ready: Numicon Shapes, Words and Symbols for Calculating (cut from photocopy master 26a), Subtracting Covers 1–5 and 6–10 (cut from photocopy master 24), number rods

Step 1

Tell children a number story where none are subtracted, e.g. 'There were five apples in the fruit bowl and none were eaten at snack time. How many were still in the bowl?' Children say the number sentence.

Step 2

Find the 5-shape and agree with children that they do not need a subtracting cover as none are being taken away.

Step 3

Set out the numeral and symbol cards for the subtracting sentence (see **Fig. 2**).

Step 4

Repeat using other contexts and numbers. Talk with children about what always happens when zero is subtracted from any number.

Step 5

Once children are secure with subtracting zero ask what the number sentence would be if, 'There were five apples in the fruit bowl and all of them were eaten. How many would be left in the bowl?' Children say the number sentence. Illustrate the number sentence with apparatus and set out the numeral and symbol cards for the subtracting sentence. Repeat with other examples and discuss what always happens when the same number is subtracted from the amount they started with.

Smaller steps

- Children may need to work with more everyday opportunities or small-world equipment at the same time as using structured apparatus to illustrate what happens when subtracting with zero.

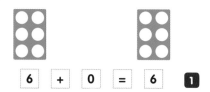

6 + 0 = 6 **1**

5 − 0 = 5 **2**

Calculating

12

Further practice

Have ready: Numicon Shapes, Numicon Feely Bag

- Place Shapes 1–10 in a Feely Bag. Children feel for a Shape and take away zero. They say and write the number sentence.

Have ready: Numicon Shapes, two Numicon Spinners and 1–5 and 6–10 Numeral Overlays (cut from photocopy master 20), number rods

- Children spin a number, take away zero, then say and write the subtracting sentence.
- Once children have been introduced to the Numicon 10s Number Line and the Numicon 0–100 cm Number Line, place a Shape or rod on the appropriate number line to practice subtracting where zero remains, e.g. 6 – 6 = 0, and where zero is subtracted, e.g. 6 – 0 = 6. Say and record the subtracting sentence.

Activity 3: Finding adding facts

Have ready: Numicon Shapes, number rods, mini figures or appropriate small-world apparatus

Step 1

Explain that there are six spaces available for some children to do a cooking activity. They need to think how many might be boys and how many might be girls. Talk with children about their ideas so that they realize there is not just one answer and that different ideas could all be possible answers.

Step 2

With children decide what apparatus might be helpful for illustrating the problem. Some may prefer to use mini figures to represent boys and girls; some may prefer to draw the boy and girl combinations. Children should try their own ideas first but then suggest using Shapes or rods.

Step 3

With children, agree that the 6-shape or 6-rod could represent the total number of children doing the activity. Ask children to use Shapes or rods to show how many could be boys and how many could be girls. Initially children may suggest random combinations that equal 6. Decide how to keep a record of suggestions. This could be by setting out each combination suggested with Shapes or rods or by writing the adding sentence for each combination.

Step 4

Talk with children about whether they think they have found all the possible combinations of boys and girls for the cooking activity. Some children may have been systematic when finding combinations. When appropriate, discuss how children might find all the possibilities and guide them into putting the Shapes or rods in order so that they can see that no combinations have been omitted (see **Fig. 3**).

Step 5

Beginning with the first combination, write the adding sentence: 1 + 5 = 6, then continue to write the adding sentences for each combination using the patterns shown by the ordered Shapes or rods (see **Fig. 4**). Write the adding sentences vertically so the patterns can be seen in the numerals as well as the apparatus.

Step 6

For another session, repeat the activity using a different context.

Activity 4: Learning adding facts by building towers

Have ready: Numicon Shapes, Numicon Coloured Pegs

Step 1

Beginning with the 6-shape, children put a Peg in each hole and then find two Shapes (that together equal 6) to fit exactly over the Pegs (see **Fig. 5**).

Step 2

Put Pegs in each of those holes, then choose two more Shapes that equal 6 and place them over the Pegs.

Step 3

After a few combinations some children may decide they have finished whereas some children may be able to continue to build the tower until no other different combinations can be found. Discuss with children how 1 + 5 and 5 + 1 are the same and different.

Step 4

Children say the adding sentences for each combination shown in each layer of the tower. If appropriate, write the adding sentences. Some children may have been systematic as they built the tower.

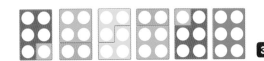

3

$1 + 5 = 6$
$2 + 4 = 6$
$3 + 3 = 6$
$4 + 2 = 6$
$5 + 1 = 6$
$6 + 0 = 6$

4

5

Calculating

12

Activity 5: Learning adding facts by filling the rod trays

Have ready: Numicon Number Rod Trays 1–10, number rods

Step 1

Using the 6-rod Tray children find two rods that equal 6 and place them in the Tray. If the rods are too long or too short to fit exactly, children should self-correct. (Some children may need to place one rod in the Tray first and then look for the other that goes with it to equal 6.)

Step 2

They then find two different rods that will also fit together to equal 6 and place them in the Tray.

Step 3

Children continue to find two rods that equal 6 each time until the Tray is full. Agree with children that 1 + 5 and 5 + 1 shown in the Trays do look sufficiently different in orientation and can be read differently. Also remind children that (thinking about the example in Activity 1) they could represent 1 boy and 5 girls or 5 boys and 1 girl so they do need to show both possibilities.

Step 4

Children say and then write the adding sentences for each combination shown in the Trays. Some children may have been systematic as they filled the Trays.

Step 5

If there is time, or in a different session, children use the 6-rod Tray to build a staircase pattern 1–6 with rods. They then fill in the gaps so each combination equals 6. Say each adding sentence and then write them, each one underneath the previous number sentence. Discuss the number patterns seen in this vertical arrangement.

Activity 6: Using the Numicon Pan Balance to learn adding facts

Have ready: Numicon Shapes, Numicon Pan Balance

Step 1

Put a 6-shape in one side of the Pan Balance. Children find different ways of making 6, using just two Shapes, so that the pans balance each time.

Step 2

Children write or draw what they find. Encourage them to write the adding sentences and talk about whether it matters if they write 4 + 2 = 6 or 2 + 4 = 6 (depending on which Shape they choose first from the pan).

Step 3

Turn the Pan Balance round so that the 6-shape is in the first pan (or put the 6-shape in the first pan and the Shapes that equal 6 in the second pan). Write the adding sentences: 6 = 2 + 4 or 6 = 4 + 2 (see **Fig. 6**).

Step 4

Talk about what can be seen. Agree that provided there is the same value on both sides of the '=' symbol it does not matter which way round the sentence is written.

Step 5

Some children will be able to extend the activity to show the equivalence of two adding sentences, e.g. **Fig. 7**.

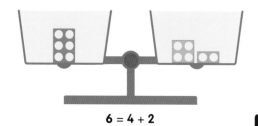

6 = 4 + 2   **6**

3 + 3 = 4 + 2   **7**

Calculating

12

Activity 7: Parts and wholes

Have ready: Numicon Shapes, Parts and Wholes (photocopy master 19), number rods

Step 1
Remind children about previous work on parts and wholes. Explain to them that they are going to play a game where they need to find three 'parts' to make a 'whole set'. In these sets one part is always bigger than the other two. The two smaller parts together equal the biggest part.

Step 2
Show children the 6-shape and say, 'If this is the biggest part, what might the two smaller parts be?' Illustrate children's suggestions with Shapes, e.g. placing the smaller Shapes over the 6-shape, e.g. **Fig. 8**.

Step 3
Show children a parts and wholes sheet. Decide where they could place the three Shapes, remembering the rules: there are three parts; one part is bigger than the others; the smaller parts together equal the biggest part, and place the three Shapes that form a 'whole set' into the three 10-outlines on the parts and wholes sheet, e.g. **Fig. 9**.

Step 4
Talk with children about the relationships they can see between the three Shapes or numbers (each Shape could be labelled with the appropriate numeral), that is, the adding number facts (some children may notice the subtracting facts).

Step 5
Illustrate the part-whole relationship using rods.

Activity 8: Finding subtracting facts

Have ready: Numicon Shapes, Subtracting Covers 1–5 and 6–10 (cut from photocopy master 24)

Step 1
Say, e.g. 'Six children were working at a craft activity but one finished so went away to do something else.'

Step 2
Using the 6-shape and 1-subtracting cover, illustrate what happened, say the number sentence and record it as a subtracting sentence, 6 – 1 = 5.

Step 3
Repeat the scenario with a different number of children finishing and leaving the activity. Ask children how many should be taken away and write the subtracting sentence. Children continue to choose different numbers that could be subtracted and each time they write the corresponding subtracting sentence.

8

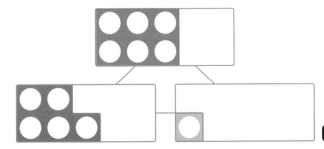

9

Breaking Barriers – Teaching Handbook – Further ideas for developing fluency: adding and subtracting with each number to 10

235

Calculating

12

Activity 9: Subtracting with number rods

Have ready: Numicon 6-Number Rod Tray, number rods

Step 1
Show children the 6-Number Rod Tray filled with pairs of rods showing all the facts for 6 in order.

Step 2
Beginning with the 1- and 5-rod combination, continue the scenario, e.g. 'If six children began an activity and one finished quickly how many would be left to work at the activity?' Remove the 1-rod, leaving the 5-rod in place.

Step 3
Say the number sentence and record as 6 – 1 = 5.

Step 4
Pointing to the 2- and 4-rod combination, continue the scenario, removing the 2-rod. Say the number sentence and record it (see **Fig. 10**). Continue for each combination.

Step 5
Talk with children about the patterns seen in the rods and in the written number sentences.

Step 6
In another session begin with the 6-rod, writing 6 – 6 = 0, then 6 – 5 = 1 and reverse the order. Another variation could be 6 – 0 = 6, 6 – 1 = 5, and so on. Each time use the apparatus to support children in writing the subtracting patterns.

Activity 10: Using the Numicon Post Box to learn subtracting facts

Have ready: Numicon Shapes, Numicon Post Box, Subtracting Covers 1–5 and 6–10 (cut from photocopy master 24)

Step 1
Set up the Post Box (between two children if possible). The first child posts through a 6-shape, covering some holes using a subtracting cover and saying the subtracting sentence.

Step 2
The second child posts back the Shape that shows the answer.

Step 3
Both children then write the subtracting number sentence.

Step 4
Repeat, taking turns to go first.

Activity 11: Using the Numicon Feely Bag to learn subtracting facts

Have ready: Numicon Shapes, Numicon Feely Bag, Numeral Cards 1–10 (cut from photocopy master 11) 'the difference between', 'and', 'is' Words for Calculating (cut from photocopy master 26b)

Step 1
Place Shapes 1–5 in a Feely Bag. Place a 6-shape on the table.

Step 2
Children take one Shape from the Feely Bag and work out what the difference would be between that Shape and the 6-shape.

Step 3
They say the number sentences and use the word cards to show it, e.g. **Fig. 11**.

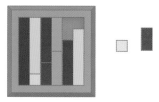

6 – 1 = 5
6 – 2 = 4

the difference between **6** and **5** is I
the difference between **5** and **6** is I

Calculating

12

Activity 12: How many more to make ... using Numicon Shapes?

Have ready: Numicon Shapes

Step 1

Children put Shapes 1–6 in order.

Step 2

Pointing to the 1-shape ask, 'How many more to make 6?' or vary by asking, 'One and what make 6?' Place the 5-shape in position to check.

Step 3

Continue for each Shape.

Step 4

Repeat, but vary by arranging Shapes 1–6 in random order.

Activity 13: How many more to make ... using number rods?

Have ready: Numicon 6-Number Rod Tray, number rods

Step 1

Show children the Number Rod Tray with the 1–6 rods arranged as a staircase. Explain that children are going to pretend the rods were the children doing the activity.

Step 2

Beginning with the 1-rod, ask children, 'If one child had started the activity, how many more would be able to join in if six were allowed altogether?' Fill in the gap with the 5-rod.

Step 3

Point to each of the rods in the Number Rod Tray, in turn, and ask how many more are needed to equal 6 each time. Make connections with adding facts.

Extending the activities

Connecting activities

- Use opportunities during the day to encourage children to know when to use number facts to solve problems and then to use their knowledge of facts to give the answer.

For pupils moving on quickly

- Use a Feely Bag containing two Shapes that equal, e.g. 6. Tell children you have two Shapes in the Feely Bag that, together, equal 6. Show them one of the Shapes and ask them to say the Shape that is still in the Feely Bag.

- Remind children about the parts and wholes with number facts. Say, e.g. 'If four and six are two of the parts what could the other part be?' (It could be 2 or 10.) Simplify by explaining which parts you are showing them until they become more confident.

- Using the parts and wholes sheet put a set of Shapes in position and talk with children about the subtracting facts they can see.

Fractions: part–whole relationships

Educational context

The activities in this group build on children's own experiences of part–whole relationships within familiar everyday situations, e.g. sharing marbles, a fruit bar, or pizza equally with someone else. Because some of the key ideas children meet in relation to fractions are challenging, this group of activities are visual, practical and use everyday familiar items to enable children to develop their understanding of the relationship between wholes and parts. Children are then given opportunities **to develop understanding of 'one half' as being a special share of a whole – one of two equal parts**.

Children will need to have prior understanding of 'greater than', 'less than' and 'equivalence'. The practical work in this activity group lays the foundation for fraction notation, but it is not introduced at this stage.

Aims

- To recognize wholes and parts of wholes in everyday contexts
- To be able to separate parts from wholes in a collection of real items presented as parts and wholes
- To identify wholes and corresponding parts of a whole
- To create shares and equal shares of a whole or an amount
- To identify and create two equal parts, realizing that a whole can be halved in different ways
- To understand that one half means one of two equal parts of a whole thing or amount
- To be able to share using halves
- To be able to represent half an even Numicon Shape
- To recognize the pattern that is visible when halving even Numicon Shapes in size order

Communicating

Imagery
Numicon Display Number Line

Equipment
See the individual 'have ready' for each activity, various items for the activities in the 'Extending the activities' section.

Words and terms for instruction (supported with signs and symbols)
share, cut, look, separate

Mathematical words and terms (supported with signs and symbols)
whole, wholes, share, shares, sharing, half, halves, parts, piece, equal, equal parts, equally, how many?

Assessment

Individual Record of Progress: Fractions 1–12

Putting the activities into context

Talk with children about common situations involving whole things, e.g. ask children when they last did something with their family. Have some real-life scenarios set up, e.g. 'Part of my puzzle is missing. Can you help me find the missing piece to make it whole?', 'Would you like a part of this chocolate bar?' Make the part–whole relationship explicit and concrete in discussion about the scenario.

Talk with children about situations where they might need to share things with someone else. Be sure to include in the conversation situations involving whole sets of discrete objects, e.g. wrapped sweets, beads, marbles, cherries: 'I have a pack of cards. Can you help me share them all equally between the group so that we can play a game?'; and continuous wholes, e.g. cakes, chocolate bars, pizzas: 'How could we share this whole cake fairly between the four of us?'

Link to Number, Pattern and Calculating 1

Calculating 5

Link to Number, Pattern and Calculating 2

Calculating 16; Numbers and the Number System 6

Calculating

The activities

Activity 1: Wholes and part–whole relationships

Have ready: a selection of wholes and parts, e.g. a whole jigsaw and a jigsaw piece, a full orange and a segment, a full chocolate bar and a piece of chocolate, an unsliced loaf or wrapped loaf and a slice of bread, a flower and a petal, two sorting rings or card circles

Step 1
Tell children they are going to be looking at whole things and parts that make up a whole. Place the items randomly on the table and ask children to identify the wholes from the selection of parts and wholes. Continue until each child has had a turn.

Step 2
Mix up the items again. Label one sorting ring or paper disc 'wholes' and the other 'parts'. Demonstrate sorting into wholes and parts by placing the petal in the parts ring or circle and saying, 'This petal is part of the flower, so I am putting it here in the circle labelled "parts".' Children sort the rest of the items into parts and wholes.

Step 3
Ask questions about why particular items have been placed in each group. Check understanding by asking children to explain, label (or sign) to justify their categorization.

Step 4
Mix up the items for a third time. Children identify the wholes and their parts and put the pairs together, e.g. put the slice of bread with the loaf. Again, ask children to explain their grouping to check their understanding.

Smaller steps
- Begin by modelling each step, e.g. pick up the orange and say, 'This is a whole orange. Can you find me another whole thing?'

Further practice
- Practise the activity often, varying the selection of items used for parts and wholes.

Activity 2: Halving continuous wholes

Have ready: Numicon Shapes, discs of modelling clay to represent pizzas, plastic knives, two large pizzas (or pizzas made from modelling clay) and a knife

Step 1
Tell children that a friend is coming over for tea but there is only one pizza. Ask them what they think they should do. Agree that the best thing would be to cut the pizza into two equal parts. Give out the modelling dough discs and the plastic knives and ask children to cut their pizza into two equal pieces. Discuss 'fair shares' and ask children if they think they have cut two equal parts. Listen for children who use the word 'half', or ask children if they know how much of the pizza they will get and explain that one of two equal parts is a called a half.

Step 2
Discuss what 'half' means and then cut one of the large pizzas in two so that one piece is noticeably bigger than the other. Ask children if what you have done is fair and to explain their answers. Listen for and reinforce the use of 'half'. Agree that this is not a fair share because the pizza is not cut in half.

Step 3
Carefully cut the second large pizza in half. Children look at the two pieces and compare them. Agree that the pizza is cut in two equal parts and that they would be able to share this fairly with their friend.

Step 4
Show children an 8-shape and ask if they know what a half of this would be. Ask if they can think of a way to check. Agree that to find half of the 8-shape we need to find two Shapes the same that fit on top of the 8-shape. Children find two Shapes that are the same to fit on top of the 8-shape (see **Fig. 1**).

Step 5
Give children Shapes separated into even and odd numbers. They find a half of each even Shape 2–10 and lay out their findings in order, from smallest to largest (see **Fig. 2**).

1

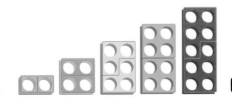

2

13

Step 6

Discuss children's findings about half of each even Shape. Look and listen for those who see a pattern in the relationship of the Shapes and their halves. Discuss the patterns and draw children's attention to them (see 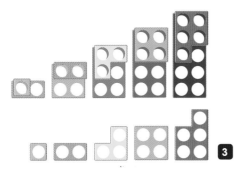Fig. 3).

Step 7

Give children a template for 12 using a 10-shape and a 2-shape. Ask them to find a half of 12. Look and listen for children who refer to the pattern they saw in Steps 4–6 and know that two 6-shapes will fit over the 12 template and that this continues the pattern they saw before.

Step 8

Children continue the pattern with a template for 14. Look for those who see immediately that 7 is half of 14.

Smaller steps

• Give children modelling dough discs cut in two, some with equal parts and some obviously not. Discuss and ask children to identify the fair shares. Explain that these equal pieces are called 'half'.

Further practice

• Provide lots of practical, real-life opportunities for halving a whole, e.g. sharing a small carton of milk equally between two glasses, pouring batter into cake tins, cutting a cake in half.

• Model and reinforce the term 'half' in each scenario.

• Practise Steps 4–6 often and remind children about the patterns seen in this activity.

• Provide paper disks for children to fold in half.

Activity 3: Equal parts of discrete wholes

Have ready: Numicon Feely Bags containing 12 Numicon Coloured Pegs (1 Feely Bag per child), a pack of game cards (used for snap, pre-selected so that they can be shared equally with the group, e.g. 12 cards for a group of 3 or 4 children)

Step 1

Explain to children that they are going to look for 'fair shares': special situations where all of the parts need to be equal when sharing. Show children the pack of cards and ask

how they think the cards can be shared between them, so a game can be played fairly. Discuss ideas and check by sharing out. Agree what a 'fair share' is.

Step 2

Deal the cards and ask children how many cards they each have. When they agree that they all have a 'fair share', play a game of snap. (The distribution of cards at the end of the game should be kept by children for Step 3.)

Step 3

Ask children to look at the cards they each have after the first game of snap. Discuss if these are now fair shares and who might win or who might be 'out' first if another game was played. Ask if this would be a fair game. Children explain their answers and discuss. Agree that, for a fair game, the shares need to be equal.

Step 4

Allow children time to practise dealing the cards and ask them to check that they all get fair shares each time, reinforcing the term 'fair share'.

Step 5

Tell children that you have a Feely Bag with Pegs in to represent apples. Say, 'I have a bag of twelve apples and I need to share them fairly between six children. How many apples will each child get?' Give children a Feely Bag each with 12 Pegs in and ask them to work out how many apples each child will get. Give them time to model their thinking and talk about their ideas.

Step 6

Children agree how many apples each child will get and model the sharing out process with the Pegs to illustrate, saying, 'Yes, there were twelve apples in the Bag and six children. If we share the apples out fairly, they get two each.'

Smaller steps

• Keep the group size small (1-1 or 1-2) for children who are struggling and use fewer cards in the game of snap.

• Make a cake batter and ask children to share the mix between bun cases or cake tins.

• Provide opportunities to share small amounts of familiar items into two or three groups using real-life scenarios.

Further practice

• Show children three bowls of dried snacks with differing numbers of snacks in and ask if they look like 'fair shares'. Ask children to explain their thinking and ask if they know a way to check. Discuss ideas and agree a way to make sure the three bowls have equal shares. Children share the snacks between the bowls equally.

Calculating

13

Activity 4: Equal parts of continuous wholes

Have ready: Numicon 8-, 1- and 2-shapes, Numicon Coloured Pegs, a chocolate bar with 8 pieces

Step 1
Explain to children that they are going to think about 'fair shares' again. Show them the bar of chocolate and say that a boy wants to share it fairly with his 3 friends. Children think about how the chocolate bar could be shared equally between the 4 children. Listen to and discuss their ideas. Agree that the chocolate bar will need to be broken up to be shared.

Step 2
Ask children if they know how many pieces of chocolate the 4 friends will get each. Ask them how they could share out the pieces. Discuss their ideas.

Step 3
Give children the 8-, 1- and 2-shapes and Pegs. They use the 8-shape to represent the chocolate bar and select from the Pegs, 1- and 2-shapes to try out their ideas.

Step 4
Discuss the ways children illustrated their ideas and ask them again how many pieces of chocolate each of the 4 children would get. Ask them to explain (or sign) and model their answers or, if necessary, model their correct ideas and provide a commentary as you do this, e.g. 'Yes, there are eight pieces of chocolate. If we share these out between four children, they will each get two pieces.' (See **Figs 4 & 5**).

Step 5
Agree that each child will get 2 pieces and check by placing 2-shapes over each group of 2 Pegs (see **Fig. 6**). Check by putting four 2-shapes over an 8-shape (see **Fig. 7**).

Smaller steps
- Provide more real-life scenarios for simple sharing, e.g. a packet of 4 hot cross buns shared between 4 people. Ensure that children have the opportunity physically to break apart the continuous wholes, in this case the pack of buns, and share them out.
- When ready, move on to representing this action using Shapes. For example, use a 4-shape and four 1-shapes or Pegs to represent the packet of 4 hot cross buns and share out the Pegs between 4 children.

Further practice
- Practise the activity often, using a variety of real-life problems and different even Shapes.

Activity 5: Halving discrete wholes sets

Have ready: Numicon 10-shapes, Numicon Coloured Pegs (at least 20), Numicon 1-shapes, a bag of 12 wrapped sweets, two card circles or sorting rings

Step 1
Show children the bag of 12 sweets and say, 'A girl has a bag of twelve sweets and wants to share them with her friend.' Remind them of their previous work on fair shares and halves and ask them if they know how many sweets each child will get. Look and listen for children who say they will get half each or those who know that each child will get 6.

Step 2
Children check their answer by separating the sweets into two equal shares of 6, using the two card circles or sorting rings if necessary. For those who do not know it will be half, or 6, ask them to share out the sweets between the circles or rings and discuss their answers.

Step 3
Lay out 20 Pegs on the table. Children order the set of Pegs and tell you how many there are. Remind them to make groups of 10, if necessary. They check by placing 10-shapes on top of the groups of Pegs (see **Fig. 8**).

Step 4
Ask children what half of 20 of anything is. Look and listen for children who see that the 20 is already shared out into two groups of 10 and that half of 20 is 10. For those who are not sure, allow time for them to separate the group of 20 pegs into two groups of 10.

Step 5
Discuss their findings and agree that half of 20 is 10.

Smaller steps
- Use a smaller number of items to halve.
- Continue to use two card circles or sorting rings for halving activities.

Further practice
- Repeat the activity often, varying the number of items to be halved.

 4   5   6   7   8

Extending the activities

13

Connecting activities

- Find wholes and parts in the environment; take children around the school building and outside space looking for wholes and parts.

- Collect pictures of parts and wholes (e.g. a cake and a slice, a pack of cards and a playing card) and play memory games where children take turns to find matching parts, wholes and pairs.

- Children make up, answer and illustrate their own real-life problems where sharing and halving are a focus.

- Make a scrapbook of real-life situations involving sharing parts of a whole. Each child designs a problem and presents it to the rest of the group for them to solve. Include the problems and solutions in the scrapbook.

- Provide lots of practical, real-life opportunities to share continuous and discrete wholes to enable children to experience the equal sharing of wholes in a variety of contexts.

- Provide a selection of regular paper shapes for children to fold in half.

For children moving on quickly

- Take further the work in Activities 2 and 5 by working on halves of even numbers.

Practical multiplying

14

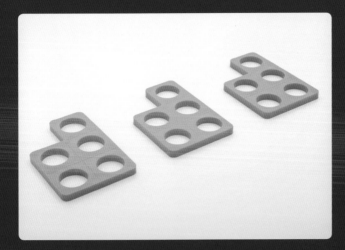

Educational context

Multiplicative situations are ones that require a child to process and work with three elements: groups of equal size, the number of groups and the total amount as they occur, in a range of contexts.

This activity group focuses on practical situations where questions can be asked in order to help children gain a sense of repeated adding, 'how many times?'; it does not focus yet on scaling – 'how many times bigger?' Children will begin to develop an understanding of multiplying through these practical, real-life activities in a range of contexts before moving on to representing multiplying with the Numicon Shapes.

At this stage, children are not asked to record their work formally, nor are they introduced to the multiplying symbol; this will be the focus of the next activity group, once children have experienced practical multiplying, talked about it and are becoming familiar with the language of multiplying in practical situations.

Aims

- To recognize and identify repetition in everyday situations
- To understand that 'times' means how often an object or action is repeated
- To use 'lots of' or 'groups of' to describe repeated sets
- To represent repeated 'lots of' or 'groups of' with Numicon Shapes
- To show repeated 'groups of' or 'lots of' with repeated groups of objects
- To begin to see multiplying as repeated adding

Communicating

Imagery
Numicon Display Number Line

Equipment
See the individual 'have ready' for each activity, various items for the activities in the 'Extending the activities' section.

Words and terms for instruction (supported with signs and symbols)
listen, tap, clap, bang, repeat, spin, count, order, go and get, action, move, put together, group

Mathematical words and terms (supported with signs and symbols)
times, how many times?, lots of, groups of, repeat, equal groups, add, adding, altogether, how many altogether?, pattern, total, amount

Assessment

Individual Record of Progress: Calculating 55–60, 64

Putting the activities into context

Discuss everyday situations where the word 'times' is used to indicate that actions, events or items are repeated. For example, 'How many times did you play outside yesterday?', 'I've noticed that you've said thank you four times today already.' Use opportunities in PE and break times to reinforce this, e.g. 'Run round the hall three times.', 'How many times can you do a star jump?'

Link to Number, Pattern and Calculating 2

Calculating 8

The activities

14

Activity 1: Exploring repetition in everyday situations

Have ready: a quiet space, a clock that ticks loudly or a second hand that 'ticks' visually, stethoscopes

Step 1

Tell children they are going to focus on listening and working together. They close their eyes and listen. Ask what they heard and discuss. Children find out how many times a clock ticks from when you say 'go' to when you say 'stop'. Encourage any children with a hearing impairment to watch the hand ticking visually.

Step 2

Place the clock so children can hear or see the second hand. They close their eyes (or focus on the clock face if you are doing this visually). Remind them that they are going to find out how many times the clock ticks from when you say 'go' to when you say 'stop'. Give them about 10 seconds between saying 'go' and 'stop' and then ask, 'How many times did the clock tick?' Discuss answers, focusing on any responses that were not in the region of 10. Repeat if necessary.

Step 3

Repeat Step 2, but this time focus on using the stethoscope to listen to their heartbeat. Ask children how many times they heard a heartbeat. Reinforce the word 'times' by saying, 'Oh, so you heard a heartbeat … times.'

Smaller steps

- Be mindful of children's strengths and needs, e.g. do not use the listening-based activities for a child with hearing difficulties.
- Model the steps and shorten the length of time for listening, watching and carrying out a repeating action.
- For children who find it difficult to count quickly, substitute counting heart beats or clock ticking with counting objects that are being dropped slowly one by one into a tin.

Further practice

- Provide additional opportunities to practise these steps in a range of real-life situations. Be sure to include different sensory experiences involving sight, touch, listening, gross and fine motor actions.
- Provide additional opportunities to explore repetition in a range of scenarios, e.g.:
  - Pass a ball between two or three children and ask, 'How many times can you pass the ball without dropping it?', 'Can you pass the ball five more times?'
  - Read out a poem, focusing on the rhyme, and say, 'Listen carefully for words that rhyme with … . How many times did you hear a rhyming word?'
  - Ask children to pour cups of liquid into a bowl and ask, 'How many times did we pour a cupful into the bowl?'

Activity 2: Repeating sounds a number of times

Have ready: Numicon Spinner and 0–5 Numeral Overlay (cut from photocopy master 20), a quiet space with room for the group to sit in a circle, a drum and other percussion instruments (e.g. triangle, tambourine) – one instrument per child, a large piece of paper, flip chart or board to write on, coloured pens, device for recording (e.g. tablet, video recorder or audio recorder)

Step 1

Children work together to make repeating sounds a number of times. They will need to concentrate, listen carefully and take turns. Ask them to listen carefully while you clap twice. Ask how many times you clapped. Children take turns to clap two times as you go round the circle. Ask, 'How many times did we clap altogether?' Look and listen for children who suggest counting in twos. Discuss how this could be written using the adding symbol and record this on the board, e.g. 2 + 2 + 2 + 2.

Step 2

Children make up a piece of music with the musical instruments. Each child selects an instrument and agree who will go first. Go round the circle and draw or write the name of each instrument in order on the board. Spin the Spinner to find out how many times each instrument will be played and record this next to the instrument on the board. If '0 times' is spun, agree that this means 'no times' and that the child who plays that instrument will not play it when it is their turn.

Step 3

Tell children you will be the conductor and help them to play the musical piece. Go round the circle, giving each child a turn playing their instrument the agreed number of times. Children talk about and describe their piece of music, making reference to the notes on the board. Look and listen for children who use the words 'times' and 'repeat'.

Step 4

Repeat Steps 2 and 3, allowing children to swap instruments before spinning the Spinner again to make a different piece of music. Record their music in video or sound format.

Step 5

Play the recording, asking children to listen and/or watch. Ask children to describe the music using 'times' and 'repeat(ed)'.

Smaller steps

- Work with a smaller group or split the group so that one group is watching and listening while the other is taking part.

Further practice

- Practise the activity often, varying the activities, resources and repetitions, asking children for suggestions as to what sounds could be repeated.

Calculating

14

Activity 3: Repeating actions in practical situations

Have ready: Numicon 2-, 3-, 5- and 10-shapes, Numicon Spinner and Numicon Shape Overlay (cut from photocopy master 20), plain cupcakes (one per child), sweets or chocolate buttons or similar small edible items, laminated card circles to represent the cupcakes (four per child), a large piece of paper, flip chart or board to write on, coloured pens

Step 1
Remind children about their previous work on 'times' and 'repeat'. Explain that they will all be decorating four cupcakes. The cupcakes will all be decorated in the same way with a 'group of' three sweets.

Step 2
Children take turns to put 3 sweets on 1 cupcake. Model saying 'one times a group of three'. Ask children to decorate their other cupcakes in the same way. Then discuss that groups of 3 have been repeated 4 times. Record on the board or paper as a repeated adding, e.g. 3 + 3 + 3 + 3 (see **Fig. 1**).

Step 3
Give each child four card circles to represent cupcakes and have ready 2-, 3-, 5- and 10-shapes.

Step 4
Spin the Spinner and ask children to put the corresponding Shape on each cupcake. Ask, 'How many times do you need to get a 5-shape?' Record this on the board as a repeated adding (see **Fig. 2**).

Step 5
Ask children if there is an easier way to record this. Discuss and agree that you could write 'four times a 5' or 'four groups of 5', or 'four lots of 5'. Repeat Step 4, saying the number sentence out loud and recording it on the board using 'times' (see **Fig. 3**).

Smaller steps
- Provide additional opportunities to make repeating actions.
- Use a smaller number of laminated card circles.
- Work with a smaller group.
- Discuss the term 'lots of' to ensure children understand that here it means 'groups of'.

Further practice
- Repeat the activities often to give children further experience of practical multiplying.
- Provide lots of opportunities to repeat actions a number of times using the language of multiplying. For example: touching their toes 5 times for a warm up activity in PE (five times 1 or five lots of 1), handing out 6 pencils per table to 4 tables in the classroom, setting up 4 paint pots on each table for a painting activity. Ask children to look out for and suggest ideas for repeated actions and objects.

Activity 4: How many 'times' with repeating Numicon Shapes and number rods

Have ready: Numicon Shapes in a basket or tray, Numicon Baseboard for each child, large sheet of paper, pens

Step 1
Remind children about their work on 'times'. Show them the basket of Shapes, but place it on another table.

Step 2
Ask a child to go to the basket and get a 5-shape. Ask how many times the child went to the basket: ('one time') and what they got ('a five shape'). 'One times a five shape.'

Step 3
Repeat Steps 1 and 2 three more times. Show children the collected 5-shapes and ask 'How many 'times' have you collected a 5-shape?' Model saying, e.g. 'You have collected four times a 5-shape.' Record the sentence in words under the Shapes: 'four times a 5-shape'. Some children may now be able to generalize to say 'four times five'.

3 + 3 + 3 + 3   **1**

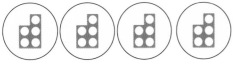

5 + 5 + 5 + 5   **2**

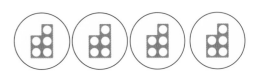

5 + 5 + 5 + 5

four times a 5   **3**

Extending the activities 14

Step 4

Repeat Steps 2 and 3 often, varying the type of Shape that children are collecting, and varying the number of times you ask them to collect.

Step 5

When children can do the above steps and explain what they are doing using the correct language, ask a child to go and collect a given number of Shapes all at once. For example, 'Collect three times a six shape.' Vary the type and the number of Shapes children collect.

Step 6

When children can collect a given number of Shapes all at once, put the basket of Shapes on the table in front of them and repeat Step 5. It is surprisingly difficult for some children to do this without the action of walking to collect Shapes.

Step 7

Show children a repeated adding pattern on a Baseboard using the last Shape a child picked up, e.g. **Fig. 4**. Discuss and agree that you can say, e.g. 'three times a seven'.

Step 8

Children make their own repeated adding pattern on a Baseboard and share it with the group, saying the corresponding sentence. Repeat and scribe each time.

Smaller steps

- Repeat Steps 1–4 often, emphasizing the word 'times'.
- Emphasize the language and get children to practise using it often.

Further practice

- Repeat the activity with number rods instead of Shapes.
- Place five of each of the 2-, 5- and 10-shapes in the Numicon Feely Bag. Children take turns to feel for between 1 and 5 of the same Shape.
- Show children items arranged in groups, e.g. socks, cutlery sets wrapped in napkins (knife, fork and spoon) and ask them to lay them out a given number of times. Discuss and agree the oral sentence to go with the action, e.g. 'three times two socks', or 'three times two.' Record them under the items.
- Practise these activities often, using Numicon Shapes and varying with the use of number rods, until children can confidently say the multiplying sentences to go with their actions.

Connecting activities

- Take children on a learning or environment walk to spot repeating patterns and multiplicative situations, e.g. look specifically for things such as a row of parked cars and ask, 'How many wheels on a car?', 'How many cars are there?' Model, look and listen for those who say, 'three times four wheels', or 'three times four'.
- Collect everyday situations where multiplying is evident through photographs and pictures. Make a display or group book called 'How many times?'
- Provide lots of practical, real-life opportunities for children to practise multiplying in a variety of contexts.

For children moving on quickly

- Explore further the work begun in Activity 4 and ask children to provide opportunities to select and lay out a specified number of Shapes, saying the sentence to go with it.
- Begin to ask if children know how many there are 'altogether'.

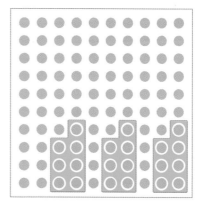

4

Introducing the 'x' symbol

Educational context

This activity group builds on the introduction to multiplying through repeated adding in the previous activity group, in which groups of objects, actions and sounds were repeated a number of 'times'. The children now meet the idea that **multiplying is what we do instead of repeated adding** and the sign (action) for 'times' is introduced. At this stage, children are not looking for the product but are **focusing on action** and use of the word 'times' in multiplying expressions, e.g. '3 times a 5'. When they are secure with this, the 'x' symbol is introduced and they learn to record multiplying expressions using numerals and the 'x' symbol, in response to seeing Numicon Shapes repeated a number of 'times'. All the activities may be repeated with number rods.

Finally, in Activity 5 **the term 'product' is introduced, so children can now write complete multiplying sentences using the equals symbol and record the product.** The examples use the familiar sequences of 2, 5 and 10 that children have worked on in Numbers and the Number System 21, helping them to begin to develop recall of 'times' facts for these that will be needed in the next activity group on dividing.

The activities help to prepare children for important **links between multiplying and standard measures**, e.g. when children are learning to tell the time, we can point out that when the minute hand goes round a whole clock face 3 times, 3 hours will have passed; when we record standard measures, '3 m' or '3 kg' are shorthand for '3 times a metre' or '3 lots of one metre', and '3 times a kilogram' or '3 lots of one kilogram'.

Aims

- To model multiplying practically, by laying out repeated groups
- To begin to use the correct language of multiplying
- To build multiplying expressions with words and cards
- To recognize the sign for multiplying
- To begin to use the sign for multiplying

- To recognize the symbol for multiplying
- To begin to use the symbol for multiplying
- To write the symbol for multiplying

Communicating

Imagery
Numicon Display Number Line, Numicon 10s Number Line

Equipment
See the individual 'have ready' for each activity, various items for the activities in the 'Extending the activities' section.

Words and terms for instruction (supported with signs and symbols)
group, put, get, lay out, build

Mathematical words and terms (supported with signs and symbols)
sign, symbol, lots of, groups of, times, set, repeat, multiply, multiplied by, total, how many?, how many times?, how many altogether?, product

Assessment

Individual Record of Progress: Calculating 61–69

Putting the activities into context

Talk with children about everyday situations where multiplying is needed. Discuss that the word 'times' is used when actions, events or items are repeated, e.g., 'How many times did the team score a goal in last night's match?', 'How many times have you written the date today?' Use opportunities in PE and break times to reinforce this, e.g., 'Bounce your ball four times.', 'How many times can you skip?'

Talk with children about their work so far on 'times' and reread their book or display of collected examples of multiplying in the environment (if they completed this extension work in Activity Group 14). Discuss the language they already know and the activities they have done.

Link to Number, Pattern and Calculating 2

Calculating 8 and 9

Link to Number, Pattern and Calculating 3

Calculating 5 and 6

The activities

15

Activity 1: Introducing the multiplying sign

Have ready: Numicon 2-shapes, a pair of sports socks for each child, simple outlines of children cut out and laminated (at least seven), a board or paper to write on, pens

Step 1

Show the socks to children and say that you need some help getting the kit ready for the school sports team. Explain that each team member needs two socks and you need to know how many socks you will need altogether.

Step 2

Ask children to stand in a line and give them two socks each. Discuss how many socks they each have and how they could work out how many socks altogether. Look and listen for those who suggest counting in twos or who say, e.g. 'four times two'. Write, 'two times a pair of socks' on the board or paper.

Step 3

Explain that your sports team has seven players. Place the seven outlines of children on the table and say that you will use a 2-shape to represent the pair of socks worn by each player.

Step 4

Ask children to put a 2-shape under each player to represent the socks they need. Look and listen for children saying 'seven times two'. Record the multiplying expression '7 times 2' on the paper or board.

Step 5

Repeat Steps 3 and 4 several times with different sized teams.

Step 6

Tell children that you need a sign for the word 'times'. Remind them of the actions and symbols for adding, subtracting and equals and agree that you need a sign for multiplying. Demonstrate and explain that it is called the 'multiplying sign'. Ask children to practise, making sure they form the sign correctly (see **Fig. 1**) and do not confuse it with the adding sign.

Step 7

Repeat Steps 3 and 4 several times more, encouraging children to use the sign for multiplying alongside what they say.

Smaller steps

- Take learning walks and nature walks where children have the opportunity to see repeated additions and groups in the environment. Draw attention to such situations and use the language of multiplying.
- Work slowly through the activities and model the language of multiplying.
- Go back to the activities in Calculating 14 to reinforce and overlearn.

Further practice

- Repeat the activity until all numbers 1–7 have been used for the number of 'times'.
- Revisit the display that was created in the previous activity group and add written representations to their examples of multiplying in the environment.
- Ask children to suggest other pairs that could be repeated, e.g. gloves, shoes, and so on.

Activity 2: Using the multiplying sign and building related expressions using the equals symbol or 'product'

Have ready: Numicon 5-shapes, Numeral Cards 0–10 (cut from photocopy master 11), Words and Symbols for Calculating (cut from photocopy master 26a), plant pot and a packet of bulbs or large seeds, board or paper to write on, pens, six card circles to represent plant pots

Step 1

Show children the plant pot and bulbs and say you need some help planting. You need to plant 6 plant pots with 5 bulbs in each. Tell children that the card circles represent the plant pots and ask which Shape can be used to represent the bulbs.

1

Calculating

15

Step 2
Lay out the six card circles. Ask children to plant five bulbs in each. Ask children to say the multiplying expression, e.g. '6 times 5'.

Step 3
Give children the numeral cards and 'times' card. They build a sentence with the cards. Remind them to make the multiplying sign as they say the multiplying expression (see **Fig. 2**).

Step 4
Repeat Step 3 with a different number of plant pots and bulbs. Make sure children say the expression and make the multiplying sign, then build it with word and numeral cards.

(Some children may say the total, but the focus at this stage is on children understanding the 'x' sign and what a multiplying expression looks like, nor have they yet learnt that when we multiply we use the term 'product' instead of 'total'.)

Smaller steps

- Use real plant pots and bulbs to carry out the activity, then model with the representations of plant pots and bulbs (card circles and 5-shapes).
- Provide lots of additional concrete and practical opportunities to practise in real-life scenarios.
- Provide lots of additional opportunities to practise laying out repeating groups of Shapes in a variety of scenarios, with fewer repeats.
- Provide a consistent model of the language used.
- Provide additional opportunities to practise the multiplying sign.

Further practice

- Give children multiplying expressions for them to say and build with Numicon Shapes or number rods. Encourage them to make the multiplying sign as they read the expression.
- Give children multiplying expressions as prompts for them to make up their own multiplying stories.

Activity 3: Using the multiplying sign and building multiplying expressions

Have ready: Numeral Cards 0–10 (cut from photocopy master 11), Words and Symbols for Calculating (cut from photocopy master 26a), Numicon Spinners and Spinner Overlays 1 (cut from photocopy master 20)

Step 1
Place the Shapes and Spinners on the table. Spin the Spinner with the Shape overlay and then spin the one with the numerals overlay. Ask children to pick the Shape shown on the first Spinner the number of times shown on the second Spinner.

Step 2
Ask children to lay out their Shapes, say the multiplication, making the multiplying sign, and make the multiplication with word and numeral cards.

Step 3
Repeat Steps 1 and 2.

Smaller steps

- Provide real-life activities, e.g. setting the table, planting pots and so on and model the multiplying language clearly using 'times'.
- Give additional time to the initial plant pot activity using a smaller number of plant pots and bulbs.

Further practice

- Work in pairs with Numicon Spinners to build multiplying expressions using the language and sign for multiplying.

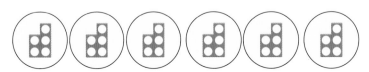

6 times **5**   **2**

Calculating

15

Activity 4: Introducing the 'x' symbol

Have ready: Numicon Shapes, Multiplying Expressions (cut from photocopy master 6), paper, pencils

Step 1
Tell children that a garage needs to put new tyres on 3 jeeps. Agree that each jeep has 5 wheels (four and one spare). Take a handful of 5-shapes and tell children that these can represent the jeeps.

Step 2
Lay out one 5-shape and ask children how many tyres will be on the jeep. Agree this will be 5. Say, sign and write '1 times 5'.

Step 3
Repeat Step 2, adding another 5-shape. Say, sign and write '2 times 5'. Repeat, adding a third 5-shape, writing '3 times 5'.

Step 4
Tell children that it takes a long time to write the word 'times'. Explain that there is a symbol that represents the multiplying sign and 'times' which helps us to write multiplying sentences. Explain that it is called the multiplying symbol and model writing 'x' for 'times' next to the jeep sentences. Reinforce by making the multiplying sign when saying 'times'.

Smaller steps
- Continue to model and talk about multiplying with practical activities and using the 'x' sign, giving children time to assimilate these ideas and remembering to motivate the symbol with the sign for multiplying.

Further practice
- Children work in pairs with Spinners to build multiplications using the language, sign and symbol for multiplying.
- Play a game using Multiplying Expressions (photocopy master 6). Children work with a partner to select a multiplying card, build the multiplication with Shapes and record the multiplying expression underneath. Repeat with number rods. Encourage children to continue to do the multiplying sign with their arms.

Have ready: Numicon Spinners and Spinner Overlay 1 (photocopy master 20)

- Spin for a Numicon Shape and then for a number. Children put out Shapes the given number of times. They say, sign and write the multiplying expression using the 'x' symbol.

Activity 5: Finding products and looking for patterns

Have ready: Numicon Shapes, additional Numicon 2-shapes

Step 1
Remind children of what they did in Activity 4. Say that this time, the garage needs to replace tyres on 4 motorbikes. Agree that each motorbike has 2 tyres. Take a handful of 2-shapes and tell children that these will represent the motorbikes.

Step 2
Lay out a 2-shape and write next to it '1 × 2', saying the multiplying expression, 'one times two tyres.' Children learn to say and write complete multiplying sentences (see **Fig. 3**).

Step 3
Tell children that when multiplying, the total is called the 'product'. Model completing the first sentence and ask children to complete their own, e.g. 1 × 2 = 2.

Step 4
Ask children to say what the number sentence would be for two motorbikes. Discuss and write 2 × 2 = 4.

Step 5
Continue the pattern for three and four motor bikes.

Smaller steps
- Take time over each step until children are secure, before moving on to the next one.

Further practice
- Practise with 5- and 10-shapes, making links with step counting.
- Find products by placing repeated Shapes on the Numicon 10s Number Line.
- Find products by placing repeated number rods in the Numicon Number Rod Track.
- Show children written multiplying sentences, e.g '3 × 10 =' for them to read, build with Numicon Shapes or number rods and find the product.
- Use children's completed multiplying sentences for them to make up their own multiplying stories.
- Tell children multiplying stories for them to say and write multiplying sentences, e.g. 'Wendy had saved five 10p coins. How much money had she saved altogether?' Child writes 5 × 10p = 50p.

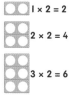
1 × 2 = 2
2 × 2 = 4
3 × 2 = 6

Calculating

Extending the activities

Connecting activities

Explore simple multiplying problems involving measures.
Children model the problem with Shapes and record the
multiplying sentence, e.g:

- Length: Three children each need 10 cm of string for their
  model. How many centimetres of string are needed
  altogether?
- Length: The school benches are 2 metres long. There are
  6 benches. How long will they be if they are fitted end
  to end?
- Weight: Mum, Dad and Joey and Pat were picking apples.
  They all picked 2 kilograms. How many kilograms did they
  pick altogether?
- Time: There are five groups of children in the class. Each
  group spends 10 minutes on the computers. How many
  minutes will be spent on computers altogether?
- Money: Thomas saves up 5p of his pocket money each
  week. How much will he have saved in seven weeks?

For children moving on quickly

- Introduce the times tables for 2, 5 and 10 following
  Numicon *Number, Pattern and Calculating 2 Teaching
  Resource Handbook*, Calculating Activity Group 9, Activities
  2–6.
- Repeat Activity 5, giving children opportunities to find
  products with other multipliers. Use 4-shapes to represent
  cars that have 4 wheels, and 6-shapes to represent
  minibuses that have 6 wheels. Ask children to lay out the
  Shapes on the Numicon 10s Number Line to help them see
  the product (see **Fig. 4**). Repeat with number rods (see **Fig. 5**).

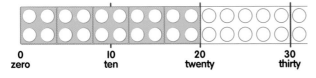

Practical dividing

Communicating

Imagery
Numicon Display Number Line, Numicon 10s Number Line, Numicon 1–100 cm Number Rod Track

Equipment
See the individual 'have ready' for each activity, various items for the activities in the 'Extending the activities' section.

Words and terms for instruction (supported with signs and symbols)
look, make, group, lay out

Mathematical words and terms (supported with signs and symbols)
groups, 'how many groups of … in … ?', 'how many in?', parts, equal, equal parts, equal groups, product, dividing

Assessment

Individual Record of Progress: Calculating 70-74, 75, 78

Putting the activities into context

Talk with children about everyday situations where 'How many groups of … in … ?' and 'How many in … ?' questions are asked, e.g. 'I have twenty sweets and each child wants four, how many children can have a share of the sweets?' Provide concrete opportunities for children to physically group items to answer these types of question. Use opportunities in the classroom to make grouping and dividing explicit, e.g. when handing out resources and grouping children for activities, e.g. 'There are six children here and we need to work in twos. How many groups will there be?'

Link to Number, Pattern and Calculating 2

Calculating 7 and 15

Educational context

The activities in this group introduce **dividing as the 'undoing' of multiplying** and build on previous work on pattern, sequence and multiplying. The activities use similar contexts to the multiplying activity groups in order to draw attention to the **inverse nature of multiplying and dividing**.

This activity group focuses on practical situations where **'how many … in … ?'** questions can be asked in order to help children gain a sense of the grouping structure of dividing. Children will begin to develop an understanding of dividing through these practical activities, in a range of contexts, before moving on to representing dividing using Numicon Shapes and number rods.

At this stage, children are not asked to record their work formally, nor are they introduced to the dividing sign; this will be the focus for the following activity group, once children have experienced practical dividing, talked about it and are becoming familiar with the language of dividing in practical situations.

Children need to be able to count in steps of 2, 5 and 10, and have secure understanding of the multiplying in the previous two activity groups before starting this work on dividing.

Aims

- To recognize grouping in everyday situations
- To understand dividing as 'how many groups in?'
- To begin to learn the language of dividing
- To model dividing practically by laying out repeated groups of structured apparatus and real objects
- To notice that there is an inverse relation between multiplying and dividing

Calculating

The activities

Activity 1: Grouping items

Have ready: small items such as wrapped sweets, 1p coins, marbles

Step 1

Put 12 sweets on the table and ask, 'How many groups of two can we make?' Discuss and group into twos.

Step 2

Say, 'How many groups of two have we got'?

Step 3

Repeat Steps 1 and 2 asking, 'How many groups of three … four …, one …, twelve …?' Discuss children's findings and model saying the dividing sentence each time, e.g. 'There are six groups of two in twelve', 'There are three groups of four in twelve' and so on.

Smaller steps

- Practise counting in twos, fives and tens.
- Provide additional opportunities to group a small number of items into twos.

Further practice

- Repeat this activity with different items, making different sized groups.
- Make the action and language clear.
- Encourage children to use the language of dividing: 'How many groups of … in … ?' and 'There are … groups of … in …'.

Activity 2: Exploring grouping and making links with multiplying

Have ready: Numicon 2-shapes, enough pairs of sports socks to give each child a pair, eight simple outlines of children cut out and laminated, a board or paper to write on, pens

Step 1

Tell children that you need some help sorting out the kit for the school sports team. Say, 'I have … socks and each player needs two. How many pairs of socks can I make?'

Step 2

Ask children to stand in a line and give them 2 socks each. Ask the question again. Agree how many pairs of socks can be made.

Step 3

Tell children that you now have 16 socks and need to check that there are enough pairs of socks for each player in the team. Remind children that each team member needs 2 socks. Tell children that you will use 2-shapes to represent the pairs of socks and that, to help, you have a pile of cut-out children.

Step 4

Put eight 2-shapes in a pile on the table, and put the laminated child outlines next to them. Model the problem with the 2-shapes and cut-out children.

Step 5

Ask, 'How many pairs of socks can I make?' then, 'So, how many twos in sixteen?'

Step 6

Help children to make the link with multiplying. Ask questions, e.g. 'How many times is the 2-shape repeated?', 'How many lots of two are there?' and 'How many groups of two are there?' Agree that this helps us to know how many twos there are in 16.

Smaller steps

- Model simple grouping with real items and physically model the grouping action, e.g. group 10 sweets into twos and place them in paper bags. Then represent this with other items, e.g. provide paper squares and 2-shapes and ask children to place the 2-shapes on the paper to represent sweets in the bags.

Further practice

- Repeat the activity using 5-shapes, and again with 10-shapes. Use the context of 5p coins and 10p coins, packs of five and ten stickers, multipacks of snacks, and so on.

Activity 3: Introducing the Numicon 10s Number Line for grouping

Have ready: Numicon 3-, 8- and 10-shapes, Numicon 10s Number Line for each child, Numicon Coloured Pegs, six pre-made cupcakes, 18 sweets, chocolate buttons or similar small edible items, six card circles for each child to represent cupcakes, board or paper, pens

Step 1

Remind children about their previous work on grouping. Explain that today they will be helping to decorate some cupcakes and that the toppings need to be put on in groups of 3.

Step 2

Show children the cupcakes and sweets or chocolate buttons. Remind them that they are working in groups of 3. Ask, 'How many cupcakes can we decorate if we have eighteen chocolate buttons?'

Step 3

Children put 3 chocolate buttons on each cupcake. Say, 'There were eighteen chocolate buttons, each cake needed three. How many cupcakes did you decorate?'

16

Step 4

Give each child 6 card circles to represent cupcakes and have ready the 3-Shapes. Repeat Steps 1–3 using the card circles and 3-shapes. Again ask, 'How many cakes did you decorate?' Agree 6 and ask, 'So, how many threes in eighteen?'

Step 5

Give each child a 10s Number Line and ask them to put their finger on 18. Children can build 18 with a 10- and an 8-shape or mark it with a Peg. Give them the 3-shapes and repeat the cupcake question. Ask, 'So, how many threes are there in eighteen?' Ask children to model and discuss. Agree there are 6 threes in 18.

Step 6

Tell children that finding 'how many groups in' is called 'dividing' and encourage them to use the term when modelling dividing situations, explaining that instead of saying 'I am finding how many … in …' , I can say 'I am dividing … by …'

Step 7

Repeat Steps 4–6, encouraging children to say the dividing sentences out loud and use the term 'divided by'.

Smaller steps

- Use a smaller number of cupcakes in the practical steps and group in twos.
- Repeat simple, practical grouping activities using real items. Keep instructional language simple and model the dividing language to go with grouping.
- Use the Numicon Pan Balance to investigate 'How many … in …?', e.g. 'How many twos in twelve?'

Further practice

- Repeat the activity often, finding out 'how many … in …' using different numbers, and using the term 'divided by'.
- Repeat the activity from Step 4 onwards, with number rods and the Numicon 1–100 cm Number Rod Track.
- Use everyday situations as they arise or set up some grouping scenarios when working with the group, e.g. 'Today we are working in groups of two. There are six of you, so how many groups will I have?'

Activity 4: Exploring dividing on the Numicon 10s Number Line

Have ready: Numicon Shapes, Numicon 10s Number Line for each child, Numicon Coloured Pegs, Numicon 1–100 cm Number Rod Track, 'How many … in …?' Questions (cut from photocopy master 5) in a pile face down on the table, number rods

Step 1

Tell children that they are going to be working out the answers to some dividing questions. Remind children how to mark the number being divided on the Numicon 10s Number Line. Select a card from the pile, read it out and remind children or model how to lay out the division on the 10s Number Line. For example: 'How many threes in twelve?' Mark 12 on the 10s Number Line and lay 4 3-shapes along the line from 1 to 12. Look carefully at the Shapes and discuss with children that this shows multiplying and dividing. They can see that when we multiply we repeat groups and when we divide we see how many groups are in the number (see **Fig. 1**).

Step 2

Repeat Step 1 with different 'How Many … in …?' Questions (cut from photocopy master 5).

Smaller steps

- Select and use only the question cards that children can answer successfully.
- Continue to support the modelling of the division question on the 10s Number Line.
- Model the language clearly for children as they lay the Shapes along the line.

Further practice

- Allow time for children to practise further, selecting the 10s Number Line and Shapes or the 1–100 cm Number Rod Track and rods to model their division.
- Give each child a 10s Number Line. Ask children to take turns to pick a card and read it to the group. Then they mark the total on their own 10s Number Line and lay out the Shapes along it. Ask the child who picked up the card to answer the question.
- Ask a child to pick a card and read it aloud to the group. Model how this is done using the Number Rod Track and rods, e.g. 'How many twos in ten?' Find 10 on the Number Rod Track and mark it with a Peg, then lay 2-rods along the track to find how many fit from 1 to 10 (see **Fig. 2**). Ask the child who picked up the card to answer the question.

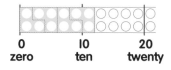

Extending the activities

Connecting activities

- Ask questions about contrived or real-life situations to show the grouping structure of dividing, e.g. 'Eight legs, how many chickens?' 'Ten arms, how many starfish?' 'Twelve gloves, how many pairs?'.

For children moving on quickly

- Children choose a number of identical Numicon Shapes and set them out to show the multiplying sentence. They write it and then say the inverse dividing sentence, e.g. for five 10-shapes, they write $5 \times 10 = 50$, then say 'there are five tens in fifty' and 'fifty divided by ten equals five'.

Introducing the '÷' symbol

Educational context

This group of activities builds on the practical dividing opportunities in the previous activity group where children have experienced grouping in different, real-life contexts. Here, children consolidate their knowledge of 'divide' and 'dividing' to build on their previous work on grouping which focused on 'How many groups of … in … ?' and introduced the term 'divided by'.

Now the sign for dividing (see Fig. 1), and the symbol '÷' are introduced with the term 'divided by' that children met in the previous activity group. It is essential that children are confident with the multiplying activities in Activity Groups 14 and 15 and also with the practical dividing in the previous activity group before they begin this work. The action of setting out Numicon Shapes or number rods along the Numicon 10s Number Line or Numicon 1–100 cm Number Rod Track and the resulting images support children in **making the link between multiplying and dividing**. These images also help children to assimilate the complicated language that surrounds dividing. However, to avoid confusion, it is also important to use words and terms consistently.

The activities continue to use the familiar sequences of 10, 5 and 2, so that children can assimilate the new ideas about dividing using numbers with which they are already familiar and confident.

Aims

- To begin to use the inverse relation between multiplying and dividing
- To use the term 'divided by' in grouping dividing situations
- To recognize the sign for dividing
- To use the sign for dividing
- To recognize the symbol for dividing
- To write the symbol for dividing

Communicating

Imagery
Numicon 10s Number Line, Numicon 1–100 cm Number Rod Track

Equipment
See the individual 'have ready' for each activity, various items for the activities in the 'Extending the activities' section.

Words and terms for instruction (supported with signs and symbols)
look, group, lay out, fill, stop, start, sign, say

Mathematical words and terms (supported with signs and symbols)
sign, symbol, groups, groups of, set, repeat, dividing, divide, total, how many?, how many groups?, how many … in…?, equals

Assessment

Individual Record of Progress: Calculating 76–83

Putting the activities into context

Remind children of their previous work on multiplying and dividing. Explain that they will be answering dividing questions again today but will be learning the sign and the symbol for dividing.

Talk about everyday grouping scenarios with a familiar context such as, 'There are twelve fish fingers, each person wants three for their tea. How many people can be served?'

Link to Number, Pattern and Calculating 2

Calculating 15

Link to Number, Pattern and Calculating 3

Calculating 7

Calculating

The activities

Activity 1: Introducing the dividing sign

Have ready: Numicon Shapes, Numicon 10s Number Line, Numicon 1–100 cm Number Rod Track, Numicon Coloured Pegs, number rods, enough pairs of sports socks to give each child a pair, board or paper to write on, pens

Step 1

Tell children that you need some help sorting out the kit for the school sports team again. Say, 'I have … socks and each player needs two. How many pairs of socks can I make?'

Step 2

Ask children to stand in a line and give them 2 socks each. Ask the question again. Agree how many pairs can be made. Remind children of 'divided by' and 'dividing' and ask them to say the dividing sentence that goes with the answer: '… divided by two equals … ?'

Step 3

Tell children that there is a sign to learn for 'divided by' or 'dividing' and show them the action. Ask children to practise (see **Fig. 1**).

Step 4

Tell children you now have 20 socks. Agree that each team member needs 2 socks. Tell children they can use 2-shapes to represent a pairs of socks and work on the 10s Number Line, or they can use 2-rods and the Number Rod Track to work out their answer.

Step 5

Allow time for children to investigate and discuss. Ask, 'How many pairs of socks can I make?' then, 'So, how many twos in twenty?' Discuss.

Step 6

Say, 'So, twenty divided by (make the dividing sign) two equals ten.' Ask children to use the dividing sign and say the sentence with you.

Step 7

Repeat Steps 4–6 using different even numbers of socks (no remainders). Encourage children to use 'divided by' and the dividing sign when giving their answers.

Smaller steps

- Work slowly and model the language of and sign for dividing often.
- Spend more time working on the practical and oral activities in Calculating 16.

Further practice

- Introduce other dividing questions involving groups of 5 and 10.
- Provide additional opportunities to practise these actions using different scenarios and model the language used.

Activity 2: Using the dividing sign and saying dividing sentences

Have ready: Numicon Shapes, Numicon 10s Number Line, Numicon 1–100 cm Number Rod Track, Numicon Coloured Pegs, number rods, board or paper to write on, pens

Step 1

Show children a plant pot and some bulbs and say you need some help planting. Remind them of the similar activity they did when multiplying (Calculating 15, Activity 2). Tell children that you have 25 bulbs and each plant pot will have 5 bulbs in, but you don't know how many pots you need to buy.

Step 2

Ask which Shape or rod can be used to represent the bulbs. Agree on the 5-shape or 5-rod, and that we need to find out how many 5s are in 25.

Step 3

Allow children to use the 10s Number Line and 5-shapes, or the Number Rod Track and 5-rods, to work out their answer.

Step 4

Explain that when we work out 'how many in', we can also say 'twenty-five divided by five equals … ?' Ask children to repeat and fill in the answer, making the dividing sign as they say it.

Step 5

Repeat Steps 1–4 with different numbers of bulbs and group sizes. Make sure that children say the sentence orally and make the dividing sign.

1

Calculating

17

Smaller steps

- Provide lots of additional opportunities to practise laying out repeating groups of Shapes in a variety of scenarios to find out 'how many ... in ... ?'
- Provide a consistent model of the language used.
- Provide additional opportunities to practise the dividing sign when carrying out practical grouping activities.

Further practice

- Work through dividing questions such as '18 divided by 6', '10 divided by 5' with rods and the Number Rod Track to work out the answer. Children make the dividing sign as they explain what they have done.

Activity 3: Introducing the '÷' symbol

Have ready: Numicon Shapes, Numicon 10s Number Line, Numicon 1–100 cm Number Rod Track, Numicon Coloured Pegs, number rods, a board or paper to write on, pens

Step 1

Remind children about the garage that was putting 5 tyres on jeeps. Tell children that the garage has 20 new tyres to put on some jeeps. Take a handful of 5-shapes or 5-rods and tell children that these will represent the jeeps, each needing 5 tyres.

Step 2

Ask children to use Shapes and the 10s Number Line or rods and the Number Rod Track to find out how many cars the garage can fit new tyres to. Agree that to find out how many jeeps, we need to solve the dividing problem 'twenty divided by five equals ... '.

Step 3

Write '20 divided by 5 equals' on the board. Tell children that it takes a long time to write 'divided by'. Explain that there is a symbol that represents the dividing sign and 'divided by' which gives us a quicker way to write 'divided by'.

Step 4

Model writing '÷' for 'divided by'. Explain that it is called the dividing symbol and write it next to '20 divided by 5 equals.' Writing '20 ÷ 5 = 4', reinforce it by making the dividing sign when saying 'divided by'.

Step 5

Repeat Steps 1–4 with different numbers of tyres. Record each dividing sentence in words and then write it in numerals and symbols next to this.

Step 6

Get children to practise writing the dividing symbol.

Smaller steps

- Spend more time modelling and talking about dividing.
- Continue the practical activities and use the sign for dividing until children are confidently using the sign for dividing, then work through Activity 3 at an appropriate pace for the children.

Further practice

- Give children written dividing questions and ask them to use Shapes and the 10s Number Line or rods and the Number Rod Track to work out the answer.
- Children solve dividing problems using Shapes or rods and write the dividing number sentences.

Activity 4: Using the inverse relationship between multiplying and dividing with the tens sequence

Have ready: Numicon Shapes, Numicon 10s Number Line

Step 1

Remind children about the garage in Activity 3. Tell children that the garage also hires out minibuses that have ten wheels that need new tyres. The garage has 40 tyres. Ask children, 'If there are forty tyres, how many minibuses can have new tyres?' Model the problem with apparatus (**Fig. 2**).

Step 2

Ask children whether they could say the dividing sentence for this. Agree 'forty divided by ten equals four' and that this shows there are enough tyres for 4 minibuses.

Step 3

Ask children whether they could also say a multiplying sentence. Agree 'four times ten equals forty'. Children say both sentences, making the appropriate signs.

Step 4

Ask them to write both number sentences: '4 × 10 = 40', '40 ÷ 10 = 4'. Discuss that knowing multiplying facts like '4 × 10 = 40' helps when working out dividing questions.

Step 5

Repeat with other multiples of ten.

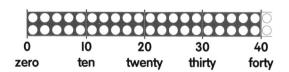

0	10	20	30	40
zero	ten	twenty	thirty	forty

2

Calculating

17

Smaller steps

- Write pairs of inverse multiplying and dividing facts on separate slips of paper for children to look for pairs that match together. They read the matching number sentences aloud.

Further practice

- Children build a multiplying fact on the Numicon 10s Number Line or Numicon Number Rod Track. They say the multiplying and dividing number sentences shown and write them.
- Give children multiplying sentences for them to write the inverse dividing sentence. Vary by giving them dividing sentences for them to write the inverse multiplying sentence. Encourage children to use Numicon Shapes or number rods to check their answers.

For children moving on quickly

- Repeat these activities for twos and fives.

Extending the activities

Connecting activities

- Work with the Numicon Pan Balance to investigate empty box dividing and multiplying questions. Ask children to record all of the facts they can find.
- Explore simple dividing problems involving measures. Children model the problem with Shapes or rods and record the dividing sentence, e.g.:
  - Length: 'There is 30 cm of string and children need 10 cm for their model. How many children can have a piece of string?'
  - Length: 'The school hall is 12 metres long. How many benches that are 2 metres long can fit along it?'
  - Weight: 'The family of four picked 8 kilograms of apples. They all picked an equal amount. How many kilograms did they each pick?'
  - Time: 'The class had 50 minutes in the computer suite. They were 5 groups of children. How long did each group have?'
  - Money: 'Thomas has saved up 35p by saving 5p a week. How many weeks did he save for?'

For children moving on quickly

- Introduce times tables for 2, 5 and 10, following Numicon *Number Pattern and Calculating 2 Teaching Resource Handbook*, Calculating Activity Group 9, Activities 2–6.
- Repeat Activity 3, giving children opportunities to find products with other multipliers. Use 4-shapes to represent cars that have 4 wheels (see **Fig. 3**).
- Repeat Activity 3 with number rods (see **Fig. 4**).
- Repeat Activity 4 again, using 6-shapes to represent minibuses that have 6 wheels. Ask children to lay out the Shapes on the Numicon 10s Number Line to help them see the product.
- Spin a Numicon Spinner with Numicon Shape Overlay (cut from photocopy master 20) and select that number of Shapes or rods. Lay on the 10s Number Line or Number Rod Track and say the related multiplying and dividing facts.

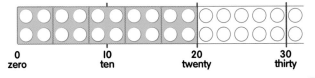

Key Mathematical Ideas: Equivalence, Part-whole relationships, Fractions, Division, Mathematical thinking and reasoning

Calculating

Fractions – Exploring halves and quarters of wholes

18

Educational context

This activity group builds on earlier work in Calculating 13 on halving, using everyday experiences of partitioning wholes into halves and other equal parts. At this stage, children have not met the sharing structure of division, so the focus is on **practical experience of finding halves and quarters**. Links are not therefore explored between fraction notation and division (though fraction notation is introduced. For children who are ready to make these connections, it is recommended that teachers refer to *Number, Pattern and Calculating 2 Teaching Resource Handbook*, Numbers and the Number System 6 and Calculating 16.

Children who are exposed to this group of activities will need to have an understanding of greater than, less than, and equivalence. Familiarity with number rods would be advantageous as the part–whole relationships are more easily seen when using this equipment.

Aims

- To recognise wholes and parts of wholes in everyday contexts
- To create equal shares of a whole or an amount, working with halves, quarters and thirds
- To identify and create two, three and four equal parts, realizing that a whole can be split into parts in different ways
- To be able to share using halves and other equal parts
- To connect dividing into two parts with finding a half
- To connect finding a third with dividing into three equal parts

Communicating

Imagery
Numicon number lines

Equipment
See the individual 'have ready' for each activity, various items for the activities in the 'Extending the activities' section.

Words and terms for instruction (supported with signs and symbols)
cut, share, look, fold, separate

Mathematical words and terms (supported with signs and symbols)
part, whole, equal, equal size, 'fair share', half, halve, is one half of, one half of… is…, quarter, quarters, is a quarter of, one quarter of… is…, third, thirds, is a third of, one third of … is… divide into

Assessment

Individual Record of Progress: Fractions 10–14

Putting the activities into context

Remind the group about common situations that involve 'whole things', e.g. ask when they last ate a whole chocolate bar. Have some real life scenarios prepared e.g. 'Part of my puzzle is missing, can you help me to find the missing piece to make it whole?' Make the part-whole relationship explicit and concrete in discussion about the scenario.

Talk about situations where children might need to share something equally with one or more people. Be sure to include in the conversation situations where whole items such as cakes, apples and pizzas need to be shared e.g. 'How could we share this whole cake fairly between the four of us?' or groups of items such as sweets, raisins and marbles need sharing out e.g. 'I have a bag of sweets, can you help me to share them all equally between three people?'

Talk specifically about thirds and quarters, e.g. ask children if they have heard the word 'third' used before. Some children may link this to the ordinal number, e.g. third in line, third turn, third birthday. Make the link between these situations and the number 3 clear.

Link to Number, Pattern and Calculating 2

Calculating 15 and 16

Calculating

The activities

Activity 1: Halving wholes

Have ready: pre-made discs of modelling clay to represent cakes and some plastic knives, a selection of modelling dough discs of different sizes, comparable items, e.g. a large fruit bar and a small fruit bar, a large and small orange, a large and small piece of paper and so on

Step 1
Tell the children that they have a friend coming over for tea and they need to share the cake fairly with their friend. Ask them what they think they should do. Agree that the best thing would be to cut the cake into two equal parts.

Step 2
Give out the modelling dough discs and the plastic knives and ask the pupils to cut their cake into two equal pieces. Remind them of 'fair shares' and ask if they think they have cut two equal parts. Listen for pupils who use the word 'half', or ask the pupils if they know how much of the cake they will get. Remind the pupils that one of two equal parts is a called a half.

Step 3
Cut one of the cakes in two so that one piece is noticeably bigger than the other. Ask 'is this fair?' Ask the children to explain their answers. Listen for and reinforce the use of 'half'. Agree that this is not a fair share because the cake is not cut in half.

Step 4
Cut the second cake carefully in half. Ask the children to compare them. Agree that the cake is cut in two equal parts and that they would be able to share this fairly with their friend.

Step 5
Show the children the large fruit bar and ask 'If we have to share this between two people, what will we need to do?' Look and listen for those who suggest halving it.

Step 6
Show the children the second, smaller bar and ask 'Which fruit bar would you rather have half of?'

Step 7
Break the two bars in half and compare. Discuss that half of the larger bar will give them more fruit.

Step 8
Show the children other items that can be halved and compared. Discuss which half of the smaller or the larger will give them more.

Smaller steps
- Present the pupils with modelling dough discs and cut in two, some with equal parts and some obviously not. Discuss with the pupils and ask them to identify the fair shares. Explain that these equal pieces are called half.
- Provide additional opportunities to work through Steps 5–7 practically with different items.

Further practice
- Provide lots of practical, real life opportunities for halving a whole, e.g. sharing a small carton of milk equally between two cups, pouring batter into cake tins and so on. Model and reinforce the term 'half' in each scenario.
- Practise Steps 4–6 often, encouraging children to notice that half of a smaller whole is less than half of a larger whole.
- Provide paper discs for the group to fold in half.

Activity 2: Sharing wholes into equal parts

Have ready: lots of Numicon 1-shapes, a picture of an animal with a litter of young, two card squares or circles to represent baskets for each child

Step 1
Tell the children that the animal in the picture has had a litter of 12 young and they need to be split equally into 2 baskets ready for bed. Ask the pupils how the young can be split equally between the baskets. Discuss their ideas.

Step 2
Put out 12 Numicon 1-shapes in the 12-shape pattern and two card squares (see **Fig. 1**) and tell the children that they represents the 12 young. Ask how they can share the young between the baskets – split the litter in half so they have room to sleep. Look and listen for children who recall appropriate addition, multiplication or division facts.

Step 3
Give time for the children to model their suggestions. Discuss and agree that they all show 12 young shared between 2 baskets or half of the 12 young are lying in one basket (and the other half are in the second basket). 'Ask what is a half of twelve young?' Agree that this is 6.

Step 4
Repeat Steps 1–3 with different sized litters of young, keeping to two baskets.

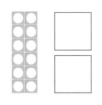

18

Smaller steps

- For any children who are struggling, go back to halving real objects such as a cake, pizza or fruit bar.
- Move on to halving, sharing out, and an even numbered collection of sweets between two children.
- Provide lots of opportunities to repeat the steps in this activity using small, even numbered litters of young.

Further practice

- Provide different problems and scenarios that require a collection of items to be halved.
- Begin to use different equipment, such as number rods or Numicon Coloured Counters, to model the action of halving.

Activity 3: Practical exploration of halves and quarters

Have ready: lots of Numicon 1-shapes, a picture of a dog or cat with a litter of young, four card squares or circles to represent baskets for each child

Step 1

Remind the children of the animal in the picture and its litter of 12 young. Tell them that the young are growing and need more space, so they need to be split equally into four baskets to be able to sleep comfortably. Ask the children how the young can be split equally between the four baskets. Discuss their ideas.

Step 2

Put out 12 Numicon 1-shapes in the pattern for 12 and four card squares and tell the children that they represent the 12 young and the baskets. Ask how they can share the young equally between the baskets so that they have room to sleep.

Step 3

Give time for the children to model their suggestions. Discuss and agree that they all show 12 young shared between four baskets. Say that one quarter of the young are sleeping in each basket. Ask 'What is one quarter of twelve young?' Discuss and agree that one quarter of 12 young is 3.

Smaller steps

- Reinforce Activity 2 until the child is confident with halving the litter.
- Provide lots of opportunities to repeat the steps in this activity.

Further practice

- Provide different problems and scenarios that require collections of items to be shared into halves and quarters.
- Begin to use different equipment, such as number rods or Numicon Coloured Counters, to model the action of halving and sharing into quarters.

Activity 4: Halves and quarters using Numicon equipment

Have ready: Numicon shapes, Numicon Coloured Counters, number rods

Step 1

Remind the children of the term 'quarter' and ask where they might have heard them before. Tell the children that they are going to be thinking about quarters in today's activity.

Step 2

Remind the children of the animal and its litter of 12 young. Tell them that they have grown big enough to be homed with families and the owner wants them to be homed in groups. Say 'The litter of young will need to be split into quarters, so how many young will be homed together?' Agree that this is four groups and ask the children to investigate how many young will be in each group.

Step 3

Allow the children to work through the problem using their choice of equipment.

Step 4

Show the children 12 built with Numicon Shapes and number rods (see **Fig. 2**). Agree that four 3-shapes fit exactly.

Ask 'what is a quarter of the twelve young?' Discuss and agree that a quarter of twelve young is three.

Smaller steps

- Begin by doing the activity practically using card circles to represent houses.
- Repeat Activity 4 using halves.
- Provide lots of opportunities to repeat the steps in this activity.

Further practice

- Carry out the steps again and leave the apparatus out. Discuss the link between the division facts.
- Allow time for the children to use the correct language in context.
- Make a book of stories involving division and fractions starring the litter of young.

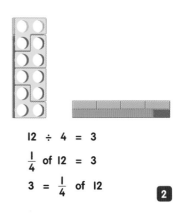

$$12 \div 4 = 3$$

$$\tfrac{1}{4} \text{ of } 12 = 3$$

$$3 = \tfrac{1}{4} \text{ of } 12$$

2

Calculating

18

Activity 5: Introducing and explaining fraction notation

Have ready: a picture of an animal with a litter of young, card squares or circles to represent baskets for each child. Numicon Shapes, number rods, Numicon Coloured Counters, pencil and paper, boards and wipe pens

Step 1
Remind the children of the animal in the picture and its litter of 12 young and the activities they have done to find a half, third and quarter of the litter. Say 'When we found a half of the litter, what did we do?'

Step 2
Ask the children to model the twelve young being split into two equal parts from the equipment you have on the table. Discuss and reinforce the language of half, equal shares, two equal parts.

Step 3
Write $\frac{1}{2}$ on the board or paper and ask the children if they have seen or used this before. Ask the children what they think it means. Discuss and agree that this means 'half' or 'a half'.

Step 4
Show the children 12 built with Numicon Shapes and number rods. Ask them to show the two equal parts using the equipment (see **Fig. 3**).

Step 5
Discuss and agree that the children have shown the 12 young split into two groups and that each group is a half. Say 'A half of twelve puppies or kittens is 6.' Write on the board $\frac{1}{2}$ of 12 is 6 (see **Fig. 3**).

Smaller steps
- Provide lots of opportunities to repeat the steps in this activity.

Further practice
- Carry out the steps again and leave the apparatus out. Discuss the link between the division facts and fractions.
- Allow time for the children to use the correct language in context.
- Make or go back to the book of stories involving division and fractions featuring the litter of young and add the corresponding fraction stories to the pages.

Extending the activities

Connecting activities
- Work with the Pan Balance to investigate sharing even Numicon Shapes or number rods into two halves. Children may also discover that some even Shapes or rods can be shared into quarters, whereas others may not. Children can record their findings as, e.g. 'half of 8 equals 4'.

For pupils moving on quickly
- Some children may be ready to repeat Steps 1–6 of Activity 5 with a focus on thirds and quarters.
- Use Numicon Spinners with $\frac{1}{2}$, $\frac{1}{3}$ and $\frac{1}{4}$ Fraction Overlay (cut from photocopy master 22) and Shapes to play a game. The children spin the Spinner and then select a Numicon Shape to illustrate the fraction.
- Using 2–20 numeral cards (cut from photocopy masters 11 and 12), play a game where each child takes a card, builds the number with shapes or rods and then find a half.
- Move on to thinking about $\frac{2}{4}$, $\frac{2}{3}$, $\frac{1}{6}$ and $\frac{3}{4}$ using the activities above.
- Using 2–20 numeral cards (cut from photocopy masters 11 and 12), play a game where each child takes a card, builds the number with Shapes or rods and then finds a quarter. Adjust the numeral cards used for challenge and support, e.g. work up to numbers to 100 when children are ready.
- Begin to support the children in writing and recording their own division and fraction notation.

$12 \div 2 = 6$
$\frac{1}{2}$ of 12 = 6
$6 = \frac{1}{2}$ of 12 **3**